THE COP WHO WOULD BE KING

THE COP WHO WOULD BE KING

Mayor Frank Rizzo

Joseph R. Daughen
and Peter Binzen

Little, Brown and Company
Boston, Toronto

FIRST EDITION

T 11/77

Unless otherwise noted, all photographs are courtesy of
the Philadelphia *Evening and Sunday Bulletin.*

Library of Congress Cataloging in Publication Data

Daughen, Joseph R
  The cop who would be king.

  Includes bibliographical references and index.
  1. Rizzo, Frank. 2. Philadelphia — Mayors — Biography.
  I. Binzen, Peter, joint author. II. Title.
F158.52.R58D38   352′.0083′0924 [B]   77–24242
ISBN 0–316–09521–4

Designed by Chris Benders

*Published simultaneously in Canada
by Little, Brown & Company (Canada) Limited*

PRINTED IN THE UNITED STATES OF AMERICA

For Harry Sions

Authors' Note

Harry Sions was a senior editor at Little, Brown and Company. Although his work kept him shuttling between his own office in Manhattan and the home office in Boston, Harry chose to live in Philadelphia, a city he truly loved.

He and Frank Rizzo met just once, in the winter of 1973, when one of us introduced the men to each other. A few months earlier, Harry, who had watched Rizzo's rise to power with interest and suspicion, had become convinced that the former policeman was an urban phenomenon worthy of examination. The meeting in Rizzo's City Hall offices strengthened that conviction. That is how this book came to be written.

Harry Sions died on March 26, 1974, before the manuscript was completed. He was an enormously talented editor and a good friend, and there is a lot of Harry Sions in these pges.

We informed Rizzo in December 1972 that we planned to write a book about him. We did not seek, nor did we receive, authorization from him. The statements attributed to Rizzo were made, almost without exception, in the presence of one of us or in a public forum, such as a news conference or campaign rally. Statements made in our presence that Rizzo specifically said were off the record — and there were many — have been excluded. Rizzo did not ask for, nor did we offer, blanket off-the-record treatment of his remarks.

The events described in Chapter Two did not all occur on the same day. The chapter is a composite picture of a day in the official life of Frank Rizzo.

We want to thank our wives, Virginia Binzen and Joan Daughen, for their encouragement and help. And we appreciate the interest shown by Roger Donald, Little, Brown's editor-in-chief, and his assistant, Mary Tondorf-Dick. A special word of thanks to Charles Martyn, librarian of the Philadelphia *Evening and Sunday Bulletin*, whose comprehensive files were an invaluable source, and to B. Dale Davis, the newspaper's executive editor, for his support and assistance.

Joseph R. Daughen
Peter Binzen
Philadelphia
April 4, 1977

THE COP WHO WOULD BE KING

Chapter One

AT 6:30 P.M. on November 4, 1975, the Bellevue Stratford Hotel looked as if it had been taken over by the Philadelphia Police Department.

Blue and white police vehicles — jeeps, wagons, patrol cars — were jammed against the curbs at all four corners of the intersection of Broad and Walnut Streets, two blocks from City Hall. Uniformed officers patrolled the sidewalks, pacing back and forth in seeming aimlessness, looking at pedestrians on their way to the subway station beneath the hotel or to the Horn and Hardart restaurant across the street. Visitors seeking to enter the hotel to go to their rooms or perhaps to eat in the Stratford Garden had to pick their way through groups of blue coats congregating on the steps at both the Broad Street and Walnut Street entrances.

Inside, teams of detectives, walkie-talkie umbilicals dangling from their ears, roamed the lobby, silently inspecting the faces of those who entered. Dozens of others were scattered throughout the hotel, prowling hallways and guarding the freight elevators that passed the rear of the second-floor ballroom. Fifty more detectives sat on gold-colored straight-backed chairs inside the ballroom, waiting.

The balcony overlooking the ballroom was closed off. Twelve plainclothesmen were positioned there, and all twelve stared down at the stage, which was empty save for a bulky speaker's stand bolted to the floor and a large sign hanging overhead and running the width of the stage. The sign, in police-car blue and white, said "RIZZO CARES — VOTE DEMOCRAT NOVEMBER 4."

Shortly after 7 P.M., a ripple of tension flowed through the crowd of policemen outside the hotel. "He's on the way," one of them announced. A few minutes later, a small blue van pulled up to the curb at the Walnut Street entrance and the blue coats surged protectively around it, walling it off from passersby and onlookers. The van's doors were opened and the policemen could see Francis Lazzaro Rizzo, the mayor of Philadelphia, the man they called the General, looming out of his wheelchair like a darkly brooding mountain. Standing around Rizzo, ready to lift his two-hundred-fifty-pound body from the van, were Police Commissioner Joseph F. O'Neill, Policemen James Turner and Anthony Fulwood, the mayor's bodyguards, and Joseph Rizzo, who four years earlier had been promoted to the rank of fire commissioner by his brother, thus leapfrogging over the heads of twenty-one higher-ranking officers and fifty-one men of equal rank.

"Here comes Chief Ironside," said a young policeman to the officer beside him.

Rizzo was in a wheelchair because of an injury he had suffered on October 12 during a huge, nine-alarm fire at the ARCO refinery in Southwest Philadelphia. At the time, the city was preoccupied with refinery fires. Less than two months earlier, on August 17, Commissioner Rizzo had declared a fire at the Gulf Oil Company refinery in the same neighborhood under control. Hours later the blaze flashed out of control, killing eight city firemen, causing injury to fifteen others and turning the refinery into a sea of fire.

The disastrous outcome of the Gulf fire shocked the fire department and the city. Philadelphia's three daily newspapers printed hundreds of column inches about the fire and its tragic consequences. Local television stations broadcast lengthy special programs showing grieving family members and carrying viewers inside the Cathedral of SS. Peter and Paul for the mass funeral service. And questions were raised about the competence of the mayor's brother. One publication, after investigating the firefighting effort, said this:

"All along, the men who were in a position to know questioned Joe Rizzo's technical know-how. As a battalion chief he had commanded a few engine companies — hardly the administrative background necessary to run a whole department. And as a fire-ground commander Rizzo had been a decent line officer — nothing more. Now, at the Gulf refinery disaster, he had been faced with the most difficult, most challenging kind of firefighting situation. Did he really have the necessary depth of command experience and technical training to handle it? Did Joe Rizzo and the refinery experts he was counting on know what they were doing at the Gulf Oil holocaust? Did those eight firemen have to die?"*

It was with the Gulf tragedy fresh in mind that the mayor, early in the evening on Columbus Day, received the news that a fire was raging at the ARCO refinery. He was campaigning for reelection at a political dinner when he heard about it and he left abruptly to drive to the fire scene.

Rizzo and a group of his aides were standing near the fire when an explosion occurred. In the confusion that followed, he collided with bodyguard Fulwood, a young black giant, and fell to the ground, breaking his right hip. One of Rizzo's spokesmen said later that night that the mayor had gone to the fire to warn against any unnecessary risk-taking by firemen.

The accident effectively ended Rizzo's campaign three weeks before Election Day. But as he was lifted from the van and channeled through a corridor of blue coats to the Bellevue Stratford's freight elevators, which would carry him to the fourth floor suite where he would receive the election returns, Rizzo was confident of victory.

"The election was over the day I announced," Rizzo had said earlier in the day when he voted at the Seventh Day Adventist Church, not far from the mansion he owned in the exclusive Chestnut Hill section of the city, a mansion his critics charged he could not possibly afford, a charge fueled by Rizzo's refusal to explain how he did pay for it. "I think it will be a quick one tonight."

Fulwood pushed the wheelchair down a hallway swarming with plainclothes and uniformed police to the Rizzo suite. Within minutes the two rooms were overrun with well-wishers, reaching to shake Rizzo's hand or pat him on the back.

His family was there: wife Carmella, a petite redhead, a policeman's wife uncomfortable in a public role, jealous of her privacy;

* *Philadelphia* magazine, November 1975.

5

son Franny, several inches shorter and many pounds lighter than his father, an employee of the Philadelphia Electric Company working on safety programs; daughter Joanna, tiny and reserved like her mother, a schoolteacher.

Standing near Rizzo were a nurse and two physicians, Dr. James Giuffre, who ministered to his general medical needs, and Dr. Arnold T. Berman, who had operated on him in Hahnemann Hospital on October 13 and inserted a metal pin in his damaged hip.

Also in the room were three newspaper columnists, one each from the *Bulletin*, the *Daily News* and the *Inquirer*. The three shared certain distinctions: they never wrote anything critical of Rizzo, they defended him against all attacks, and they were given ready access to him and the opportunity to visit in his suite on election night along with the union leaders, politicians, jobholders, financial contributors and other admirers come to pay homage to him.

Whatever lack of journalistic merit attached to their Rizzo-can-do-no-wrong attitude, there was no doubt they accurately reflected the feelings of many who lived on the often dangerous urban frontier where the city's combative, vital juices flowed.

Americans for Democratic Action could label him a fascist bully. Some black leaders could call Rizzo a racist. And former U.S. Senator Joseph S. Clark, who was mayor of Philadelphia from 1952 to 1956, could describe him this way: "He's certainly a Hitler. He's a typical dictator demagogue. He makes George Wallace look like an amateur. He's created a terrible atmosphere of fear in this city. He's a stupid, arrogant son-of-a-bitch — and that's on the record."*

But to the people who began filling up the ballroom in the Bellevue Stratford on the night of November 4, Rizzo was the next thing to a Saviour.† They did not frown on him because he was a high school dropout who had spent twenty-seven years in the police department, battling his way up from patrolman to commissioner.

And to those in the suite on the fourth floor Rizzo was a hero with a compelling, almost mystical, magnetism. Martin Weinberg, for example, was a bright young attorney who served for two years as chief legal officer for the city and had taught law at Drexel University. Weinberg, who quit his city job to work in Rizzo's

---

* Philadelphia *Evening Bulletin*, October 29, 1975.
† The Bellevue Stratford Hotel, a Philadelphia landmark since 1904, went out of business on November 18, 1976, as a result of a mysterious illness that swept an American Legion convention there the previous August, killing twenty-nine persons. The grand old hotel never recovered from the publicity surrounding the so-called "Legionnaires' Disease."

campaign, could look at Rizzo and in dead seriousness say, "Mr. Mayor, you're a man of destiny. You can't lose."

As people continued to file into the suite Rizzo, leaning on an aluminum walker, heaved himself out of the wheelchair and onto a gold-cushioned carved wooden chair. The throng pressing in on him grew so great that his brother Joe took up a position in front of him, acting as a traffic cop and guarding against the possibility of someone stumbling or being pushed onto the injured leg.

A week earlier, Rizzo had left Hahnemann Hospital for the first time since his operation. Riding in the blue van, he was taken to the city's Convention Center to make a very brief appearance at a fund-raising dinner. His voice was weak and shaky and he was noticeably pale, drained of the fierce vitality that those who knew him were accustomed to.

But on this election night, it seemed that a spark of that old vitality had been rekindled, that the awesome physical strength was returning to this Gulliver who was temporarily bound to a chair.

Frank Rizzo was fifty-five years old but he was easily one of the most physically imposing men in political life in the United States. He was six feet two inches tall and some of his two hundred fifty pounds had settled into a paunch. But his hand-tailored, size fifty-long suits could not conceal the bulging arms that seemed always about to burst through the expensive fabric, just as the collars on the white shirts he wore seemed to be straining against his nineteen-and-a-half-inch neck.

His hair was black, with just a whisper of gray at the temples, and sleek as a seal's coat. Before any kind of public appearance he invariably ran a comb through his hair, smoothing it down with fingers the size of large, meaty sausages.

Rizzo's dark brown eyes, set in a beefy face with a full nose, provided a window onto his emotions. When he had to listen to mundane details of city government a glaze would settle on the eyes, an opacity of boredom. During what he referred to as "bull-shit sessions" with friends, the eyes would soften and take on a roguish twinkle of delight. And when he was angry his nostrils would flare equinely and his eyes would smolder, then erupt into twin lances of liquid fire.

In his appearance and in his speech there seemed always to be bubbling dangerously close to the surface a barely repressed violence, an intimidating hint of menace.

Surrounding all this was the legend he had built for himself as a fearless, head-busting, hell-for-leather cop who could stuff a night-stick into the waistband of his tuxedo, leave a formal dinner and break up a potentially riotous situation where hundreds of angry blacks and whites appeared ready to launch a racial war.

"I'm gonna make Attila the Hun look like a faggot after this election's over," Rizzo often said during the campaign, jovially indicating how he was going to deal with his enemies. White liberals and many blacks were horrified at the remark because they saw themselves, and such things as civil liberties and the right to dissent, as Rizzo enemies. The people in the ballroom were not horrified. Rizzo's enemies — "lenient" judges, integrationists who disrupt neighborhoods, criminals, do-gooders — were their enemies, too.

Rizzo was a heavy smoker normally but he hadn't had a cigarette since his accident. Now, with the polls closed and the vote count under way, he turned to Hillel S. Levinson, a prematurely bald forty-year-old lawyer, and asked for a cigarette. Levinson supplied the cigarette and whipped out his own lighter to light it. When Levinson was around, Rizzo never had to worry about a light for his cigarette.

Levinson, tall and slender, was a former track star at Temple University. Whenever Rizzo needled him by calling him "the fastest Jew in the East," Levinson just smiled. He also smiled when Rizzo would say, "Hilly makes out great with the broads. They just love that bald head, don't they, Hilly?" Levinson was then separated from his first wife and had not yet remarried.

Levinson had worked in an auto leasing agency and had practiced some law when he went to work in Rizzo's 1971 campaign. Although he had no government experience, Levinson was named Philadelphia's managing director by Rizzo after that election.

The managing director is responsible for the city's delivery of services to the public through the ten operating departments. Under his control are the commissioners of police, fire, public health, welfare, streets and sanitation, water, public property, licenses and inspections, recreation and public records. Levinson, who continued long after the election to wear the gold campaign watch bearing a likeness of Rizzo, was paid $42,000 a year. He was also under indictment for allegedly extorting political contributions from contractors who did business with the city.*

After Levinson provided the light for Rizzo's cigarette, the

---

* The indictment was later quashed for technical reasons.

Mayor Rizzo, aided by a cane, returns to his office two months after being injured at a refinery fire.

mayor assured him he would have "four more years" as managing director.

The first returns were encouraging to Rizzo and set off cheers among the supporters in the suite. He was winning more votes than his two chief opponents were getting between them.

Charles W. Bowser, a short, chunky forty-five-year-old black man, was running a distant second as the candidate of the maverick Philadelphia Party. Bowser was a lawyer with an impressive record as an administrator. He had been deputy mayor to James H. J. Tate, Rizzo's predecessor, the first black to hold that post. Before that he had been head of the Philadelphia Anti-Poverty Action Committee, a quasigovernmental organization. Most recently he had been executive director of the Philadelphia Urban Coalition, a group funded mostly by white businessmen to deal with a variety of urban problems.

Bowser was a Democrat and he had sought the endorsement of the Democratic Party leaders to run against Rizzo in the spring primary election. The party bosses, who wanted to depose Rizzo, told Bowser that while he was probably the best-qualified candidate, they didn't think a black man could beat Rizzo. So Bowser formed his own third party and won the support of the ADA and people like former Senator Clark and John R. Bunting, chairman of the First Pennsylvania Bank, the city's largest. These people, and the blacks who identified with Bowser, would not have voted for Rizzo under any circumstances, and the mayor recognized the value of having someone in the race to siphon off anti-Rizzo votes, to divide the opposition to him.

"All I want is for Charlie Bowser to please stay in the race," Rizzo told us early in the campaign.

Thomas M. Foglietta was a dark, handsome bachelor, forty-six years old, who had dreamed for most of his life of being mayor of Philadelphia. Foglietta, like Rizzo, had been born in South Philadelphia. Unlike Rizzo, he had not moved away from the old neighborhood. He stayed in school, became a lawyer and developed a taste for opera and an appreciation of the cultural contributions made by Italians and Italian-Americans.

Foglietta was a Republican and in 1955, at the age of twenty-six, became the youngest person ever elected to the city council. He was reelected to three additional four-year terms before he resigned in March 1975 to become the Republican nominee for mayor. It was a nomination declined by many other prominent

Republicans who were well aware that, four years earlier, Rizzo had won more Republican votes than the GOP candidate.

But Foglietta believed he could beat Rizzo. He felt that, as a South Philadelphia Italian-American, he ought to be able to cut into Rizzo's strength there. And if he could get the votes of the liberal white Democrats and the blacks who distrusted Rizzo, he could win the election.

By the time Foglietta got to his headquarters at Sixteenth and Ranstead streets, a couple of blocks from the Bellevue Stratford, he was running third and he realized what Bowser had done to his chances.

Back in his suite, Rizzo accepted a telephone call from Walter H. Annenberg, the millionaire publisher of *TV Guide*, who had been ambassador to England during Richard M. Nixon's presidency. When he received the appointment, Annenberg owned two of the three daily newspapers in Philadelphia: the *Daily News* and the *Inquirer*.

Annenberg, who lived in suburban Wynnewood and had a $5,000,000 estate in Palm Springs, had been quite taken with up-from-the-streets Rizzo. He was given nighttime tours of the city in Car One, with police radio crackling, when Rizzo was police commissioner. He had dinner regularly with Rizzo. When Joe Rizzo was looking to pick up some extra money moonlighting, the *Inquirer* hired him to work on its loading platform.

Best of all, from Rizzo's point of view, was the way Annenberg used the news columns of the *Inquirer* to further the Rizzo myth. He would tolerate no criticism of his friend. When Joe McGinnis, who went on to write *The Selling of the President 1968*, wrote a column berating Rizzo, Annenberg ordered into the next day's newspaper a lead editorial defending Rizzo and condemning the *Inquirer* columnist. McGinnis subsequently resigned.

Annenberg was a Republican, but he lent Rizzo $50,000 to help him finance his 1975 Democratic primary election campaign. For the general election, he came up with another loan, this one for $100,000.

By the time Annenberg sold the two newspapers to the Knight Newspapers, Inc., chain in October 1969, the Rizzo legend, the Supercop image, had already been established. The *Daily News* and the *Bulletin* had contributed to this image. But Rizzo was well aware of what Annenberg and the *Inquirer* had done for him. When Annenberg arrived at Philadelphia's International Airport at 7:30 on a brisk morning in April 1969, six months before the newspapers were sold, to fly to his new post in London, Police Commissioner Rizzo was there to greet him. Annenberg did not have to worry about finding a parking place for his chauffeured car. Rizzo directed it out onto the field, next to the jetliner.

Picking up the telephone, and calling Annenberg "Mister," Rizzo read off the vote totals that had been compiled up to that point: Rizzo, 182,687; Bowser, 72,713; Foglietta, 53,251. He exchanged some small talk with Mrs. Annenberg, promised to call her when he returned later that night to the hospital, then hung up.

"What that man did for me nobody'll ever know," Rizzo said, to no one in particular.

Downstairs in the ballroom the same figures were being posted on a blackboard set up on the stage. A fife and drum band paraded around the floor and four young girls, dubbed "Rizzoettes," dressed in red shorts and blue tops, danced enthusiastically.

The crowd responded heartily, clapping, cheering and whistling. There was a certain defiance in the eyes of some as they looked at the reporters seated along one side of the room. The reporters all had seats and a good view of the stage. The only other seats were those that had been occupied earlier by the detectives, and these were far from enough to accommodate the Rizzo partisans. Besides, some of those chairs had been appropriated by the news media, too.

If they had to stand, they would stand. They would not suffer, though. On this night the reporters would suffer, even though they had seats. It was the reporters who had consigned their hero, Rizzo, to an early retirement twenty-six months ago when he had, incredibly, agreed to submit to a lie detector test about a sordid political deal and then flunked the test.

"For the first time in the history of the world a mayor publicly failed a lie detector test," Bowser had gloated, during the campaign.

But if the lie detector incident meant anything to those in the ballroom, it was as a piece of the legend, part of the folklore surrounding Rizzo. So a machine had certified him a liar. So what? He was still their man, their leader, their hope. They would vote for him and they would help him any way they could.

They would help him even if it meant voting for a dead man. Rizzo had asked them to vote for the reelection of City Councilman Francis D. O'Donnell. O'Donnell, who lived in the Northeast, was known as a Rizzo sycophant, never voting in opposition to the mayor on matters before council, and the mayor wanted him reelected. Five days before the election, O'Donnell dropped dead, a fact noted on the front pages and the newscasts. But when the

Mayor Rizzo in the process of flunking a lie detector test.
Warren Holmes, the polygraph operator, is at left.

votes were counted, O'Donnell had 276,000, 128,000 more than his nearest Republican rival, and the city had elected a dead man.

John Chiara, a dapper thirty-eight-year-old advertising executive whose firm handled Rizzo's campaign advertising, held up ten fingers to reporters, indicating Rizzo would be in the ballroom in ten minutes. Someone mentioned to him that neither Bowser nor Foglietta had conceded.

"Well, when we get to two hundred thousand or two hundred fifty thousand we're gonna take it anyway," Chiara replied.

The sudden appearance of a small army of policemen in the wide doorway at the left side of the stage tipped off the crowd of about 500 that Rizzo would make his entrance soon. And just then, new vote totals pushed Rizzo up to 200,138. The people, most of them white, all of them wearing Rizzo straw hats and/or Rizzo buttons, roared their approval. These were the faithful, the true Rizzo believers.

One of them was Mrs. Theresa O'Donnell, a friendly woman, a grandmother, a retired employee of the Philadelphia Common Pleas Court system. She was well groomed, with short dark hair, and she was wearing a stylish blue suit. Pinned to the suit in various places were six Rizzo buttons. She was asked why she wanted Rizzo to be mayor.

"I'm not a Philadelphian," she said. "I'm a Times Square girl. I moved here thirty-five years ago and it was a wonderful city. But I've seen it go downhill. We need a man like Rizzo. We can't have a cultured, educated, *gentle* man. He couldn't handle it. He has to deal with . . . well, you know what he has to deal with.

"We need a tough man. Rizzo is a tough man. I used to live in North Philadelphia, but I had to move. There were some nice ones but then the others started moving in and I was scared. They'll shoot you in a minute. I had to move to Roxborough and pay three times the rent.

"I'm Italian, you know. I married an Irishman. Rizzo's like an Italian father. He's protective. He uplifts women. We need that. We need somebody stern, who will look out for us. I'm a grandmother. I don't want anything to happen to my grandchildren."

Mrs. O'Donnell was asked if she felt safer walking the streets because Rizzo was in the mayor's office.

"Look, one man can't do it all," she replied. "He can't put them in jail. I'll tell you what I like about Rizzo. He goes after the ones I blame. The judges. The judges are the ones. He does as much as anyone can."

Did the fact that Rizzo held himself out as a representative of the working man while living in a mansion some said was worth $400,000, a sum far beyond his means, bother her at all, Mrs. O'Donnell was asked.

"No, no, I don't believe all that," she said. "Don't you think Tate's got more money? They all have more money than Rizzo. If Bowser got in don't you think he'd get it? Don't you think Foglietta'd get it? That's politics. Look, I worked in the courts and I got choked, pushed and threatened by the people I worked with. You take Earl Vann [a black politician who supported Rizzo]. Because he supports Rizzo they all call him an Uncle Tom. Where do they get off? They want to better themselves? Let them go right ahead. But not at my expense. That Bowser. He's not capable of it. They won't be ready to be mayor for a hundred years."

As she finished, the people around her started chanting, "We want Rizzo." One man, still wearing his service station uniform, which was covered with Rizzo buttons and stickers, started clapping as he chanted. By this time, all the votes were counted, and Rizzo was a decisive winner. The totals at that time were: Rizzo, 311,879; Bowser, 134,334; Foglietta, 101,001.

It was a phenomenally expensive victory, more expensive than Rizzo's 1971 campaign, which set a record for spending. To get his 311,879 votes Rizzo spent $1,216,598, according to records he filed with the County Board of Elections. That works out to about $3.90 a vote. Bowser spent $160,909, or about $1.20 a vote, and Foglietta spent $108,000, or slightly more than $1 a vote. Including the primary election, where records show Rizzo spent $948,758, Rizzo admitted to spending $2,165,356 in 1975 to be returned to office, an unheard-of amount for a Philadelphia election.

Much of the money came from contractors doing business with the city and from people Rizzo had appointed to jobs. But some of it also came from people like those in the ballroom, people without a lot of money who believed they were in a fight for survival and when the curtains opened and they saw their champion wheeled out onto the stage they cheered mightily.

Theresa O'Donnell may or may not have been typical of them. But there could be no denying that virtually everyone in the ballroom shared common concerns and were drawn to Rizzo for much the same reasons. For the most part they were the "white ethnics" from the neat row houses — the Poles from Richmond, the Ukrainians from East Poplar, the Irish from Schuylkill, the Italians from South Philly, the Germans from Feltonville, the Russian Jews from

Mayfair and other parts of the overwhelmingly white Northeast. These whites, like their black counterparts, either could not or did not want to retreat to the suburbs. They had to live with the hazards of the city.

Outside its central business district, Philadelphia is a city of neighborhoods much like villages, each with its own defined area and personality. These often-neglected residential sections hold the key to the city's future. They provide stability, continuity, identity. So long as they are able to retain their character and desirability, so long as they continue to "work" as residential sections, the city itself will "work." But if the neighborhoods — the Kensingtons, Frankfords, and Roxboroughs — deteriorate and their people flee, the larger city will find itself saddled with a disproportionate share of poor people needing more municipal services, an eroded tax base and grim prospects for survival.

In the 1960s and early 1970s, it was hard to believe in Philadelphia or most other major American cities. With few exceptions, the great metropolises were seething with violent crime, racial strife, school tensions, narcotics peddling and homicidal street gangs.

What the white ethnics in Philadelphia feared most of all was the growing presence of blacks, which many believed was the direct cause of the increase in crime. The fear could be measured. In the rush to get out of center city after work. In the drop-off of white shoppers in downtown department stores on Wednesday nights. In the continuing exodus of whites to the suburbs.

Philadelphia's black population was 26 percent of the total of 2,002,512 in 1960. By 1970, blacks made up 34 percent of the 1,950,098 who lived in the city. As a group, the blacks were younger, poorer, more given to crime. Most of the holdups, muggings, rapes and murders were — and are now — committed by blacks against blacks. Between 75 and 80 percent of the inmates in Philadelphia's four adult prisons are black.

But crime rates are largely a function of socioeconomics. People living at the lowest rung of society have always accounted disproportionately for lawlessness. The Irish filled Boston's jails in the mid-nineteenth century just as blacks filled Philadelphia's in the late twentieth century. In the Philadelphia neighborhoods where crime was relentlessly advancing in the 1960s, however, frightened families were not much interested in sociology. What they were concerned about was the fact that their neighborhoods, their schools, their way of life, were imperiled and nobody was doing anything to help them.

While the outlook for the blacks in North and West Philadelphia may have been bleaker still, they at least had their champions during this period. Martin Luther King was only the most visible symbol of a coalescence of forces working to improve the lot of the blacks. Congress, spurred by its liberal white members, produced massive amounts of legislation designed to aid blacks. Business and industry moved toward equal hiring and promotion policies. Schools, often prodded by the courts, became laboratories to test methods whereby black children could be better prepared to meet the future. And every day, on the front pages of the newspapers and on the television news programs, the spotlight was trained on these developments.

In the white ethnic neighborhoods, though, things only seemed to get worse. It was their children who were shaken down for their lunch money. It was their taxes that were raised to pay increased welfare benefits. They were leaderless. When they did organize to protest, nobody listened. Worse yet, they came off looking like a bunch of red-necked bigots.

And so they turned to Frank Rizzo. In an era of rising crime, other cities had elected policemen to run their government. But they were not like Frank Rizzo. They were college-educated, with degrees in sociology or law. Rizzo was an eleventh-grade dropout, a lusty, brawling, profane street cop who let "the experts" worry about the causes of crime while he busied himself with busting heads.

Yet Rizzo professed his belief in Philadelphia. And his belief in the neighborhoods. Fishtown and Juniata and Bridesburg had a right to guard their sections against change, especially racial change. Rizzo would defend that right. With Rizzo in charge Philadelphia would be a better, and safer, place. The women in the row house neighborhoods would continue to scrub their front steps in the morning. On summer evenings, the men would continue to sit on folding chairs on the sidewalk. The kids would continue to play on Lighthouse Field. Frank Rizzo would be their protector, their father figure, their *padrone*.

"Frank Rizzo for governor," someone in the ballroom shouted.

But then a strange thing happened. Rizzo's bodyguards pushed his wheelchair smack up against the oversized speaker's stand, totally screening him off from the view of those on the ballroom floor. Someone looking toward the stage could see the line of policemen in front, could see the bodyguards, could see Joe Rizzo and the other sixty persons gathered onstage, but couldn't see the mayor. The crowd started protesting.

"Maybe we can get it out of the way, this podium, so I can see them all," Rizzo said, his words picked up by the lavaliere microphone around his neck.

Told the stand was bolted to the floor, Rizzo had his wheelchair moved to his left. His right side remained screened by the stand and only those on his left had a reasonably good chance to see him.

"I have my doctor with me who tells me I should go home to my hospital bed," Rizzo said.

He thanked his wife, his children, his aides and the audience for their help. Then he singled out some of those onstage for attention.

"Hillel Levinson," he said. "You all know what they did to Levinson to get to me, but I don't think they'll be successful."

Referring vaguely to the criticism leveled at his brother, Rizzo said: "He is the greatest fireman in the world. Joe, you're safe for four more years."

Rizzo was onstage less than ten minutes. Before he left to return to Hahnemann Hospital, he mentioned Tommy Foglietta.

"If there's anything I can do to help him, I'll be around," said the *padrone*.

He did not mention Charles Bowser.

Chapter Two

THE HUGE PILE of gargoyled stone that has been the seat of Philadelphia's government since 1887 sprawls over four and a half acres in the heart of the downtown business district, interrupting the flow of traffic because it bestrides the crossing of Broad Street and Market Street, two of the city's principal thoroughfares.

The years, and the pigeons, have dropped a curtain of grime over City Hall. But neither the corrosion outside nor the long periods of corruption within have been able to destroy the natural majesty of the building. Schoolchildren and other visitors still find themselves drawn irresistibly to the familiar statue of William Penn, twenty-six tons of cast bronze atop a tower rising almost 548 feet from the ground. Alexander Milne Calder sculpted the statue and designed the tower that supports it. Together, the two loom like a giant sentry over the main building, which was modeled after the Louvre by architect John McArthur, Jr. Calder spent twenty-one years of his life working on this building, creating hundreds of statues, busts and symbols to decorate the inside and outside walls, overhangs, window wells and niches.

The man who steps out of the black Lincoln Continental each morning shortly before 8:30 notices none of this although, in his own way, he loves City Hall. With his bodyguards beside him, he heads for the door, already held open, at the northeast entrance to City Hall. The elevator is waiting for him, and he greets the operator with a genuinely friendly "Good morning." As long as elevator operators can vote there is little chance that automation will come to City Hall.

The car stops at the second floor and the men aboard get off and turn to the right. The long hallway is faintly depressing because it is nearly deserted and because it should have been modernized years ago. But it is clean. During the night workmen have scraped up the cigarette butts, swept up the scraps of paper and polished the floors.

The man walks briskly to the first doorway on the right. The collision at the ARCO refinery fire is still more than two years away and there is no hesitation in his step now. He says hello to the policeman on duty in the hall and one of his bodyguards pushes the door open. He greets the two plainclothesmen at the reception desk and one of them releases the electronically controlled lock which bars access to the offices beyond. He strides past the desk of his two secretaries and the offices of two of his assistants, coming at last to a large rectangular room. He enters the room and walks over to the far wall and touches one of the teak panels. The panel swings open noiselessly, providing entry to the cleverly concealed private quarters. He slips out of his suit coat, which he carefully hangs up, closes the teak panel behind him and sits down at his desk. The metal name plate on the desk reads "Frank L. Rizzo, Mayor."

Rizzo picks up one of the forty or fifty filter-tipped cigarettes he will smoke this day and fires it with a gold-colored lighter. He is sensitive about how his smoking will affect his image and he asks photographers not to photograph him holding a cigarette. They usually oblige him. With a cigar-sized index finger he punches a button on his telephone console, buzzing for his coffee. It is the start of another day and Rizzo, just as he has done most of his adult life, is looking forward to it eagerly, zestfully, his juices already in full flow.

Sitting at his desk in shirtsleeves — always white, usually French-cuffed — Rizzo dominates the room. A half-dozen chairs, separated by smoking stands, are ranged in an arc about six feet from the desk. Behind him is a credenza crammed with electronic equipment that enables him to control the lighting in the twenty-four-by-thirty-two-foot chamber, raise and lower the temperature by means of a self-contained air conditioning system, operate a large color television set with doors that slide back automatically, and monitor the burglarproof locks on the three doors into his quarters. If the lights on the monitor are red, the doors are locked; if green, the doors are open.

Although the office is unusually well furnished, the walls are bare. There are no paintings, no prints of Independence Hall, no sketches, nothing. Frank Rizzo doesn't like such things, and he doesn't care who knows it.

The City Hall pressroom, which most of Philadelphia's newspapers, radio and television stations work out of, is diagonally across from the mayor's office. The pressroom is city property and, over the years, reporters have been moved from room to room depending upon the whim of the current administration. Throughout these travels four or five paintings on loan from the Philadelphia Museum of Art have accompanied them. Until Rizzo.

"This place is a shithouse," Rizzo declared one day, walking through the pressroom. He ordered the city's department of public property to remove the paintings and ship them back to the museum, to remove anything else that might be hanging from the walls, and to paint the walls an institutional white.

In May 1972, five months after he assumed office, Rizzo had made clear his stand on art. His predecessor, Jim Tate, had commissioned the Lithuanian-born Jacques Lipchitz, one of the world's foremost sculptors, to create a statue called "Government for the People," to be placed on the plaza of the Municipal Services Building, just north of City Hall.

Lipchitz went to work and produced a plaster cast of the statue at a cost of $122,500. His concept was so exciting that a model of the statue was prominently displayed by New York City's Metropolitan Museum of Art during the showing of a Lipchitz collection in 1972. But to finish the job $178,000 more was needed to cast the statue in bronze in an Italian foundry and mount it on the plaza. Rizzo refused to put up any more city money.

"It looks like a plasterer dropped a load of plaster," the mayor said.

R. Sturgis Ingersoll, a wealthy Philadelphia art collector, over the years had given the city more than a hundred works of art worth more than a million dollars, including Lipchitz's "The Prayer," Picasso's "Man with a Lamb," and Matisse's "Serpentine Woman." Ingersoll was enraged at Rizzo.

"Mayor Rizzo's statement about the Lipchitz monument is sickening," Ingersoll said. "Four years ago I gave Philadelphia a collection of sculptures, including an important Lipchitz, values far in excess of the total cost of the proposed monument. If the mayor expresses the attitude of his administration, I somewhat wish that my gift to the people of Philadelphia had been given to the Metropolitan or the National Gallery in Washington or even to Keokuk or Kalamazoo. What kind of mayor have we?"

Rizzo did not take Ingersoll's criticism quietly. Using the technique he found so successful throughout his career, he attacked. It was no longer a difference of opinion over art. It was a battle between good and evil. Later, he would begin to call some of those who disagreed with him crooks and use the police department to try to put them in prison. But, at this point, he did not dare go that far with Ingersoll, a widely respected Establishment figure. Only the hint was there, warning of the demagoguery beneath.

"I'm concerned with the art people who are out to rape this city," Rizzo told reporters. "Not rob — I say rape. We're not going to permit people to take advantage of us. I might not be an art expert, but I want to see something that I can understand, not just those art experts."*

What he would like to see, said Rizzo, was a statue depicting a benevolent policeman with his hand on a boy's shoulder, while the boy looks up trustingly at the symbol of law and order.

So there were no paintings in the mayor's office. And there would be none in the pressroom. The closest concession to art Rizzo would make could be found in his den, hidden behind the teak panel. There, on a shelf near his desk, was a large limed-oak colored frame. Pressed beneath the glass, on pseudo-parchment, were the words to Joyce Kilmer's "Trees."

"That's a beautiful poem," he would tell his visitors.

The door to the office opens and Abie Kanefsky enters, carrying a steaming cup of coffee in a large brown cup with a pedestal base. Abie is a short man, not more than five feet tall, with a battered nose and a combative look in his eyes — except when he looks at Rizzo. Then the eyes become warm, almost adoring, the eyes of a fifty-year-old puppy.

Abie is wearing a dark gray work shirt and black trousers.

---

* Late in 1975, after a delay of more than three years, a group of citizens announced it had secured private financing to complete work on the Lipchitz and have it placed on the plaza. Rizzo did not object.

Underneath the shirt is a sweatshirt bearing the name and likeness of Rizzo. Abie is indebted to Rizzo, perhaps owes his life to him, and he is properly grateful. He will be Rizzo's go-fer until the day he dies, if that is what the mayor wants.

The two men met early in 1971 when Abie wandered into Rizzo's campaign headquarters at Seventeenth and Chestnut streets and stood silently until someone noticed him. Rizzo took Abie in hand, paid him a small salary, bought him some new clothes, made sure he ate three meals every day and permitted him to sleep in the office. Abie became Rizzo's man, responsible for keeping the candidate's office clean and for seeing to it that a fresh pot of coffee was on hand at all times.

After Rizzo was in office, he fixed Abie up with a city job. He set him up in an office across the hall from his own and there Abie tended his coffeepots and came running when Rizzo called. Within a year Abie looked healthy and had saved enough money to put a small payment down on a little house. And he was on the city payroll permanently because Rizzo had gotten him Civil Service status.

"They can get rid of me but they'll never be able to get rid of Abie," Rizzo often said.

On occasion, Abie is permitted to defy Rizzo and get away with it, but only under very special circumstances. Defiance normally makes Rizzo angry, and he makes no effort to conceal his anger. His dark eyes snap and their usual gleam of humor vanishes. His voice becomes louder, with a menacing edge. He rises out of his chair, his hands closing into massive fists. But on this day Abie defies him and gets away with it.

"Abie, get me some more coffee," Rizzo says.

Abie looks at Dr. Giuffre, a physician not much larger than himself, who is there to treat Rizzo for an eye infection. He looks next at Rizzo, then back to Giuffre. "No," he says.

"What do you mean, no?" Rizzo barks.

"He says no," Abie replies, nodding at Giuffre.

"Come on, Abie. Gimme half a cup."

Abie stands silently, nervously, looking at Giuffre.

"A quarter of a cup," the physician says. Abie pours a quarter of a cup.

"Jesus Christ," says Rizzo.

Abie is able to defy Rizzo because his motives are pure — he is looking out for the health of his patron. His defiance is in fact a tribute and, like most patrons, Rizzo needs tribute. In one way,

Abie's very existence, his survival, is a tribute to the patron's power and generosity. Throughout his career, and especially as mayor, Rizzo would play the role of *padrone* with great skill. And he would be greatly satisfied by that role.

Rizzo finishes his coffee and Giuffre and Abie leave. He gets up, goes to a door connecting another office with his own, opens it and says, "Philip, come in here." Deputy Mayor Philip R. T. Carroll, a lean blond-haired man, moves quickly into the mayor's office carrying a yellow legal-size notepad. Carroll, seven years younger than Rizzo, has been a city employee since 1952, serving in a variety of bureaucratic roles. In 1964 he was named administrative officer of the police department, a civilian job, and when Rizzo became commissioner three years later he kept Carroll on.

Carroll, who graduated from the University of Pennsylvania's Wharton School in 1948, seemed destined to serve out his career as a middle-level Civil Service employee for the city. When Rizzo left the police department to run for mayor, Carroll had nineteen years of government work behind him and he chose not to quit to go to work in Rizzo's campaign.

After Rizzo was elected, he turned to the man closest to him, Albert V. Gaudiosi, a Pulitzer Prize reporter who was his campaign manager, and offered him the job of deputy mayor. Gaudiosi accepted. At that time, Carroll was ticketed for a second-echelon post paying $25,000 a year. At the last minute, Gaudiosi backed out. He lived in suburban Montgomery County, his wife was happy there, and he did not want to move into the city, as he would have to do if he were to accept Rizzo's offer.

With the nonchalance that has marked many of his appointments, Rizzo asked Carroll if he wouldn't rather be deputy mayor than deputy managing director, where he would have supervisory authority only over a few city departments. Carroll accepted and, instead of being across the street at the Municipal Services Building earning $25,000 a year, he found himself in City Hall, right next door to the mayor, earning $42,000 a year. Within a year, Carroll, once a faceless bureaucrat with a limited future, would become the second most powerful man in the government.

"What have we got, Philip?" Rizzo asks.

The city is in a financial bind, struggling to make do with limited resources because Rizzo, unlike most big city mayors, refuses to consider raising taxes. It is a popular position. After years of spending huge sums of money, Philadelphia is still plagued by urban ills.

White residents continue to leave the city, shrinking its real estate tax base. Rizzo reasons that increased taxes would only drive white residents out faster, and he is convinced that whites must remain if Philadelphia is to survive.

But there are problems that demand attention — and money. Together, the city and public schools will spend more than a billion dollars during this fiscal year 1973–74, but is it enough? The board of education complains that it is being starved, that it will not have sufficient funds to finish the school year. Philadelphia, with 105 juvenile gangs, virtually all of them black, is becoming the gang capital of the nation. Gangs are murdering three or four persons every month, in addition to the hundreds of other homicides that occur in the city. But responsibility for gang control programs has been given to a middle-aged woman whose prime qualification seems to be that she was one of the few black persons who supported Rizzo for mayor. In the midst of the financial crunch, the gang control staff is down by 14 percent and prospects for further reductions are good. The health department is being whipsawed by budget restrictions. Home visits by nurses have been cut back. There are ten district health offices, but there are not enough physicians to supervise them, forcing individual doctors to be responsible for the operation of two and three districts. The department has been without a commissioner since Rizzo took office, the top-level staff has been depleted by resignations and the planning division has been abolished.

The material on Carroll's notepad, however, does not concern these problems. It deals instead with the continuing preoccupation — or obsession — of the Rizzo government: the war against Rizzo's enemies. The list of enemies is long, and it grows regularly. Those on the list have found that it is not hard to qualify. All that is necessary is to publicly disagree with Frank Rizzo. Then your city tax records may be examined, policemen may ask questions about you, you may even be followed. And the mayor may vilify you.

On the enemies list this day were Rizzo's three Democratic predecessors as mayor, Joe Clark, Richardson Dilworth and Jim Tate. Clark, who was mayor from 1952 to 1956 and served in the U.S. Senate from 1957 to 1968, had opposed Rizzo's attempt to remove from the Philadelphia Home Rule Charter the prohibition against any mayor serving more than two consecutive terms. For that, Rizzo denounced Clark as "a senile, dirty old man."

Dilworth, mayor from 1957 to 1962, resigned as president of the board of education so that he could fight Rizzo's bid to be elected mayor. When Rizzo took office, he accused Dilworth of being a drunk and began investigating him. Without offering proof, he charged that Dilworth's law firm had improperly received hundreds of thousands of dollars in legal fees from the city while Dilworth was mayor. He promised to produce a detailed list of these legal fees, and this is one of the projects on which Carroll is working.

Tate, mayor from 1962 to 1971, appointed Rizzo police commissioner and used his decisive influence with the Democratic Party to win party endorsement for him as the candidate for mayor. After his election, Rizzo said Tate was "crazy," accused his administration of being "corrupt," and began investigating him. This investigation, too, was Carroll's responsibility. And, like virtually all of the investigations into Rizzo's enemies, it would produce nothing.

But the list of enemies would continue to grow everytime someone disagreed with Rizzo. Eventually, midway through Rizzo's first four-year term, the Southeastern Pennsylvania Chapter of Americans for Democratic Action would hold a party and the guests would be composed exclusively of Rizzo enemies. The enemies included persons like Sam Evans, a hulking, elderly black man who had made some money promoting concerts, had become involved in Democratic politics and had landed a job as vice president of the city-controlled nonprofit corporation planning the Philadelphia Bicentennial celebration.

When Rizzo took office, he eyed Evans's $65,000-a-year salary and decided he would get rid of him. First Pennsylvania Bank Chairman John Bunting was head of the Bicentennial group. Rizzo ordered Bunting to fire Evans. Bunting refused, so Rizzo simply dissolved the corporation. When a new corporation, Philadelphia '76, was formed, Bunting was not invited back. Nor was Evans. The man who took over Evans's number two spot in the new corporation was Albert V. Gaudiosi, Rizzo's campaign manager. Although the pay scale was reduced because plans for the celebration were cut back, Gaudiosi was still given an annual salary of $50,000 — $10,000 more than the mayor's. And Gaudiosi was in a position to help Rizzo with his political plans. He didn't even have to move from Montgomery County into Philadelphia.

More than 400 persons attended the ADA's party. Those who couldn't make it sent regrets and said they wished they could be there.

Carroll's briefing ends with a report on the progress of the campaign to get George X. Schwartz, the president of city council, and

Philadelphia '76 Vice President Al Gaudiosi (left), Deputy to the Mayor Tony Zecca (center) and Rizzo have a curbside conference.

Peter J. Camiel, the chairman of the Democratic Party, two men who supported Rizzo in his first race for mayor. A special police squad, Carroll says, is digging into their backgrounds, their business dealings, their personal affairs. "Good, good," Rizzo says.

"It's unbelievable," Rizzo would later tell us. "When I was a cop, I used to think that a guy with a pipe who hits you over the head and takes your money was bad. But these public officials, especially the lawyers, they're robbing from everybody. If you or me tried to take a buck, they'd have us in jail. These guys do it, it's a legal fee.

"I'm convinced we would have better public officials if we took them right out of Leavenworth. Politicians. They're crooks. All they're interested in is lining their own pockets. They don't care about the public, the little guy. They only want to take care of themselves.

"Look at old Sam [a former Democratic politician]. He loses the election and what do they do? They make him a watchdog. *Watchdog. Twenty thousand a year.* Sam would take wet matches. He'd take a patched condom."

Heartened by Carroll's forecast that Schwartz and Camiel face certain doom, Rizzo turns to the newspapers. He ignores the sports pages and all but ignores national and international news. On that night in October 1973 when President Nixon announced that he had selected House Minority Leader Gerald R. Ford to succeed Spiro T. Agnew as vice president, Rizzo was in his favorite hangout, the Vesper Club on Sydenham Street, with his cronies. He watched Nixon on television.

"When he said Ford, I said, 'Who?'" Rizzo later told us. "I never even heard of this guy."

Rizzo does not always like what he reads about himself in the newspapers, although after an initial flash of annoyance he is generally able to respond to criticism with humor. His sense of humor has served him well over the years, enabling him to leave his enemies floundering. He has the sense of timing of a stand-up comedian and an ability to manufacture wisecracks that very often will reduce nosy reporters to laughter and divert them from their targets.

On this day in 1973, however, he is furious about a story in the *Daily News*. The story says that the plumbing in the mayor's private bathroom broke down, forcing him to use the public facilities at the end of the hall. Because of the breakdown, the story says, the public property department fixed up one of the stalls in the public washroom for Rizzo. Not only was the stall supplied with a lock, but a wire mesh roof was placed atop it so that no one could bomb the mayor with paper missiles or cigarette packs or candy wrappers while he was inside attending to his business. Rizzo is still boiling when Filippo Anfuso, the new Italian consul in Philadelphia, comes to pay his first call on the mayor. Anfuso is accompanied by a reporter.

Anfuso is a tall, shy man with a quiet, aristocratic bearing. He immediately is overwhelmed by Rizzo, who clasps his hand, drapes a heavy arm over his shoulders and begins peppering him with good-natured bantering. How are you, Filippo? How do you like Philadelphia? How about our girls, Filippo? They're pretty, huh? You've noticed them, huh? A good-looking guy like you, you ought to make out okay. A photographer's flash goes off a half-dozen times. Then Rizzo shows Anfuso through his quarters.

When he pushes the teak panel, opening the way to the private rooms, Rizzo's face darkens and he remembers the *Daily News* story. He glares at the reporter, who works for the *Bulletin*, and says:

"What has your profession sunk to, writing about shithouses?" Anfuso's dark eyebrows jump. Rizzo's hand shoots out, grabs the reporter's arm and pulls him into the Italian marble-clad bath-room.

"I want to show you something," Rizzo says. He flushes the toilet. It works perfectly. "See, it works." He opens up the shower door to reveal a luxurious marble chamber. "See that." He turns the water on in the marble sink. "See this? What the fuck are you guys talking about? Shithouses." Anfuso is staring, wide-eyed.

The tour over, Rizzo leads the way back into his office. He unwraps a package and lifts out a lovely blue and white Philadelphia Bowl, which he gives as a present to Anfuso.

"There," Rizzo says. "That'll hold four pounds of rigatoni."

Rizzo, unlike many of the persons who work for him, does not usually stay in his office at lunch time. Escorted by his bodyguards, he and whoever may be his guest at the time leave City Hall, usually on foot, and head either for the Stouffer's restaurant in Penn Center, just west of City Hall, or the private Urban Club, on the top floor of the Penn Central's Penn Center Station. Walking along Kennedy Boulevard, Rizzo and his party resemble a small fleet, drawing stares and exclamations from passersby, who will often break in to shake the mayor's hand.

On taking office, Rizzo had four bodyguards, veteran policemen, three of them black. It is the black bodyguards that Rizzo points to when accusations of racism against him arise, as they frequently do. If he were a racist, runs the argument he uses in defense, would he place his life in the hands of black men? When one of the bodyguards died of a stroke, Rizzo replaced him with a white policeman.

Returning from the substantial lunch he enjoys — a small steak, or fish when he is watching his weight — Rizzo is still raging over an incident that occurred earlier in city council.

It is the fifth week of a schoolteachers' strike and the end is not in sight. Rizzo will not budge from his pledge not to increase taxes. A tax increase would be needed to meet all the demands of the teachers.

When it is pointed out to him that his no-tax increase pledge now appears to be in conflict with his pledge to keep the schools open, Rizzo replies with disarming frankness. "I guess I gotta choose between promises," he says. He chooses to hold the line on taxes and take a teachers' strike.

The coalition of groups opposed to Rizzo have been demonstrating regularly at City Hall demanding a tax increase to pay for a contract settlement with the teachers. Today, the groups descended on council chambers to pressure the seventeen councilmen to vote for a tax rise on their own, in defiance of Rizzo.

The group is raucous, growing louder as it becomes clear that council has no intention of raising taxes. In the crowd are some students from the largely black Benjamin Franklin High School, renamed Malcolm X High School by its student body and faculty. An uproar develops in the middle of the council session when a leader of the group, Dr. Donald Cox, hurls a live chicken on to the floor to show what he thinks of council's courage. The chicken flutters around in fright, then defecates. The councilmen are outraged. An attendant grabs the chicken.

"That Goddamn bum," Rizzo storms, back in his office. "That chicken was alive. He scared the hell out of it. That's inhumane." He punches the button on his speaker telephone and orders his secretary to get Police Commissioner O'Neill on the line.

"Joe, what can we do about locking that bastard that threw the chicken into city council up? How did he get it in there, under his coat or what? Where's the chicken now? What happened to it? He gave it to a kid from Ben Franklin High? Oh, oh. That's the end of that chicken. It's in the oven. They ate the evidence. Okay, Joe."

Next, the mayor talks to Mrs. Eloise Danenhower, of the Society for the Prevention of Cruelty to Animals. He appears to be truly upset.

"I was going to retire that chicken to the police academy, Mrs. Danenhower. I felt sorry for it. It could have just walked around up there and we could feed it, you know, two hands of corn a day. I got more mascots up at the K-9 kennels. You know, you see them running loose and you feel sorry for them, so I send them up to the kennels."

Rizzo is still annoyed that council refused to go along with his plan to air-condition the kennels where the city's police dogs are kept. He is a man with very definite ideas about the worth of policemen and police dogs, and the worthlessness of criminals. When discussing crime generally, his voice hardens, his nostrils flare and his dark eyes seem frozen. But this changes when he is confronted with a specific atrocity. Then, he becomes agitated, the eyes burn with emotion, and his speech is peppered with references to "dirty bastards," the electric chair, nooses and ten-thousand-year prison terms.

"Did you read about that sonofabitch in New Orleans?" Rizzo says, referring to Mark Essex, a deranged black Navy veteran who had holed up atop a downtown motor lodge in New Orleans a few days before, sniping at policemen and civilians alike. Before he was slain on the roof of the motor lodge by sharpshooters in a police helicopter, Essex had murdered six persons, three of them policemen.

"I'd have taken care of that bum, and nobody would have gotten hurt," Rizzo blurts out. He rises quickly from his chair and slips out from behind his desk. He clasps his huge hands together in front of him and begins swinging his massive arms from side to side, an awesome flesh and blood pendulum.

"I'd have gotten a crane with a big iron ball," he says, arms still swinging. "Then, I'd have smashed the shit out of the top of that building. I wouldn't fuck around with him. I'd have gotten the dirty bastard."

A group of reporters troops in to Rizzo's office to listen to the mayor on a radio talk show. He does the show periodically, and, through a moderator, accepts calls from the public. He is eager to go on the air to further his campaign against George X. Schwartz. Just the day before, he and Schwartz denounced each other in talks with reporters.

"He says we're following him. We got spies. Wonder what he's upset about. Is the net beginning to close in? I think it is," said Rizzo. "I'm responsible for the net and I'm going to throw it and I'm going to catch him. What is happening, we're investigating many areas, like redevelopment, housing, zoning and a lot of other things. We're not investigating any particular guy but everything we investigate we find a bit of George Schwartz and his law firm.

"If he's going to make the net, well, shame on him. He should have behaved himself. I publicly state that I give anyone permission to tap my phones, to put eavesdropping equipment in my office and investigate me from the day I was born. When you're doing your job and doing it honestly, you don't have to worry about who's following you."

"The city is approaching a Gestapo state," Schwartz had replied. "I hope he reveals to us the full extent of the investigation. It's coming right out of his office. His office is the focal point of it all. Mr. Carroll is supposed to be the deputy mayor. But all he's doing is fishing. Carroll is the *Gauleiter*. I welcome it, but let's make it public, not private. Midnight conferences, evening conferences, calling all kinds of people into the mayor's office. It's a hell of a way to run a city."

Now Rizzo is ready to attack Schwartz again, this time over the radio. Schwartz, he believes, left after the council meeting for a long weekend in Florida. He launches into a monologue about Schwartz's activities. It would turn out, incredibly enough, that he had never bothered to examine in detail for himself the material that Carroll and the special police squad were compiling. He simply relied on their assertion that they were getting the goods on Schwartz.

"We have so much information that it would take us sixteen terms [in office] to complete it," Rizzo tells the radio audience. The moderator, Joel Spivak, asks if Schwartz shouldn't have an opportunity to respond. Rizzo says, "You won't be able to find him. He leaves town on Thursday afternoons and doesn't return until Tuesdays."

But Schwartz is in his City Hall office, holding a telephone, waiting for Spivak to tell him he is on the air.

"You have a police state here," Schwartz says. "That's what I've been complaining about."

"No, Mr. President, that's police work," Rizzo replies, clearly startled to learn that his enemy is in his office, two floors above his own. "We're just trying to catch people, we're just trying to catch crooks."

"What I want to talk about is the McCarthy tactics, the Hitler tactics," says Schwartz.

"This isn't McCarthyism, Mr. President. McCarthyism is when you accuse people of things that aren't true. You haven't been accused of anything."

"McCarthyism, again."

"Well, that's an old line that I've heard many times, Mr. President. It's not a police state when you come up with officials who violated their public trust."

Before the show is over, Rizzo and Schwartz are shouting at each other, denouncing each other. When it is over, Rizzo is more determined than ever to see Schwartz and his ally, Party Chairman Camiel, behind bars. (But he will be unable to come up with the evidence to back up his charges.)

For the remainder of the afternoon, Rizzo is on the telephone, as he is a good part of each day. There is a call to Arlen Specter, the Republican district attorney, urging him to investigate, prosecute and jail Schwartz and Camiel. There are calls made to and received from reporters. For the first twenty-two months of his administration, until November 1973, Rizzo is probably the most accessible major elected figure in America. Although he has two or three persons on his personal staff whose job is ostensibly to deal with the press, Rizzo functions as his own press secretary. When a reporter calls, he usually picks up the telephone within seconds. And, when he has an idle moment, he will call reporters, sometimes to plant a story, most often to "bullshit."

"Did you hear Schwartzie today?" he asks one reporter, after the radio show. He admits to being taken aback on learning that Schwartz was in his office. "The sonofabitch surprised me. I thought he was in Florida." There is a chuckle, an appreciation of the humor in his being surprised. But the combativeness rushes back. "Did you listen to it? I really knocked his cock off, didn't I?"

It is the tail end of the normal working day when Rizzo remembers a situation that was brought to his attention the night before, when he attended a funeral in Kensington, an all-white Philadelphia neighborhood that voted heavily for him. He tells his secretary to get Captain Barnes, the black policeman who is in charge of towing away abandoned automobiles.

"Barnesy, I had occasion to go to Kensington last night. They're my people there, Barnesy. You know, Lehigh Avenue, Allegheny Avenue. I must have seen thirty fucking abandoned cars, Barnesy. They were all over the place. At least thirty of them.

"These are my people, Barnesy. You must be a racist, Barnesy. I go in the black areas and they're clean as a whistle. Not a Goddam abandoned car in the black areas, Barnesy. Now you got to take care of my people. Don't forget, I'm your angel, Barnesy. Get on it, okay, Barnesy?" The black policeman says something that makes Rizzo laugh and he hangs up the telephone, smiling.

Most of the offices in City Hall are beginning to empty. It is after five o'clock and the workday is over. Except on the second floor, where there is no letup in activity in the mayor's office. And the lights stay on in the pressroom across the corridor, because reporters are waiting for Rizzo to go home so they can end their day.

This is the hour when Rizzo prefers to hold his political strategy sessions — "scheming," he calls it — which very often turn into bull sessions. At times, Al Gaudiosi will walk over from the Philadelphia '76 offices in the Philadelphia Saving Fund Society building two blocks away.

Although the city charter prohibits appointed officials or employees from engaging in partisan political activity, that does not discourage those who work for Rizzo from participating in discussions about methods of furthering the mayor's political career. Two deputies to the mayor — Mike Wallace, a tall, thin, tight-lipped young lawyer, and Joe Braig, a short, tough-talking lawyer who served a term in the state House of Representatives — have known political skills, and it is considered doubtful that they placed these skills on the shelf when they went to work in City Hall. Wallace and Braig will sit in on the meeting, and so will Phil Carroll. Bobby Jacobs will sometimes be invited. Jacobs was a City Hall reporter for the *Bulletin* until he decided to take Rizzo's offer of a job. Now he works under Carroll, coordinating the many investigations into the mayor's enemies. It is not unusual for Marty Weinberg, first as city solicitor and later as a campaign worker, or Hillel Levinson to attend. Some of these are usually there on Friday evenings to accompany Rizzo to dinner at the Vesper Club.

The discussion is wide-ranging, yet always revolving around Rizzo and his future, his goals. For most of those present, their futures and Rizzo's are inextricably entwined. They talk about the Democratic ward leaders they can count on in the fight with the leaders of the organization, and about the councilmen and state legislators who are loyal. Rizzo is like many other politicians when it comes to loyalty: it is a quality to be prized above all else, more important than brains or money. The possibilities of a Rizzo race for the governorship against incumbent Democrat Milton J. Shapp are explored. At this point, the chances look good. Inevitably, the talk reverts to Rizzo's favorite subject, his days as a cop.

"I come from a tough arena," Rizzo says. "Taking on guys like Schwartz and Camiel is nothing. I've been out there with my life on the line. I saw things you wouldn't believe. I remember one time when I was working a wagon and we got a call out at the PTC car barn. A bus driver collapsed, and these guys he worked with were all standing around when we got there. We started to work on the guy, getting him in the wagon, you know? And these other guys, one or two of them, said, 'Hey, let him go, it's a move up.' A *move up*, for Christ's sake. They wanted the guy to die so they could move up, get a better run or shift.

"Talk about tough. A lot of guys cried at different things, you know? Big, tough cops. I never cried. The toughest thing was the kids. One time we were working a wagon and we got a call over by the Pennsylvania Railroad tracks near Tastykake. The kids would go back there and try to steal cakes. This time a train got a kid. We got there and there was this little kid, he was laying outside the tracks, his legs were inside, cut off above the knees.

34

"What do you do? I picked the kid up and put him on the stretcher and I put the legs on the stretcher. I was holding him on the way to the hospital. He said to me, 'Please don't tell my mother.' That's when you cry. You look at a kid, his legs are gone and he says don't tell my mother."

John Devine is waiting when the meeting breaks up. Devine is six feet two, strong and silent. He was a police sergeant who served as Rizzo's chauffeur when Rizzo was police commissioner. Now that Rizzo is mayor, Devine's hours are even longer. He drives Rizzo in the big black car, sees to it that his personal needs are taken care of, runs interference for him, greets him in the morning and is still around hours later when the day is done.

Rizzo climbs into the car, which is waiting for him on City Hall's sidewalk. The old building is bathed in floodlights, a Rizzo idea to discourage muggers, and Calder's tower soars dramatically away from the main building, up into the dark. Rizzo notices the lighting with approval.

The car pulls away and Devine heads for Rizzo's home. Devine is a bachelor, about seven years younger than his boss. It is a standing joke that he has no social life because Rizzo ties him up fourteen to sixteen hours a day. And, when Rizzo arrives home, he senses that Devine has something to tell him.

As he gets out of the car, Rizzo says goodnight to Devine. Devine asks Rizzo if he can have some time off. Why? Rizzo wants to know.

"I'm getting married tomorrow," Devine answers. Rizzo is shocked. Devine never told him. He asks about the girl, wishes them well, learns they are going to Puerto Rico for a ten-day honeymoon.

"Unbelievable," Rizzo would say later. "When the hell did he find the time?"

Chapter Three

THE CONVENTIONAL portrait of Philadelphia is that of a staid, stodgy Quaker city where the sidewalks roll up early. Philadelphians are supposed to be conservative, corrupt and contented. While this description may still fit some of the upper crust, it clearly does not fit Frank Rizzo's white ethnic constituency — the Irish, Italians, Poles and Ukrainians, the working-class Catholics and Jews who have given such Philadelphia neighborhoods as Bridesburg, Feltonville, Fishtown, Manayunk, Moyamensing, Southwark, Schuylkill and South Philly their extraordinary vitality and flavor.

For many of these immigrant groups, the vaunted City of Brotherly Love has through much of its history been "a city of poverty, crime, and violence, of racial and ethnic tensions which often flared into riots."* The opportunities Philadelphia offered poor European whites (and poor Southern blacks) were often illusory. And "for many the urban experience was shattering and devastating."†

Because Philadelphia lacked multistory tenement buildings, liv-

---

* *The Peoples of Philadelphia*, edited by Allen F. Davis and Mark H. Haller, Temple University Press, 1973, p. 11.
† Ibid.

ing conditions in its slums at the floodtide of immigration were perhaps not as shocking as were those in New York and other cities. (In fact, social reformer Jane Addams referred in 1902 to the "happy condition of Philadelphia.") Philadelphia also attracted proportionately fewer immigrants than did New York, Chicago and Boston, leading Lincoln Steffens to characterize it in 1903 as "the most American of our greater cities." At the same time, though, the Philadelphia white ethnics waited longer for political power. Not for 280 years was a Roman Catholic elected mayor. And Frank Rizzo was the first Italian-American to reach the top at police headquarters and City Hall.

The exploitation of Italian immigrants was widespread. Until Congress passed legislation in 1864 opening the way for importation of cheap foreign labor, the few Philadelphia Italians were, for the most part, artists, musicians, priests or professional men.* The 1870 Census counted only 516 native Italians in the citywide population of 674,022. But then industry recruiters, seeking workers to mine coal, lay railroad tracks, make steel, run sewing machines and help build cities, began signing up landless, often illiterate, peasants in Campagna, Calabria, Basilicato, and other impoverished parts of southern Italy and Sicily. Each month thousands of poor Europeans sailed for the New World in the stinking holds of overcrowded transports. Between 1890 and 1910 Philadelphia's population soared by half a million, most of them immigrants and many, like Frank Rizzo's father and mother, from Italy.

The system of recruiting Italian workers was run by *padrones*, or bosses, who hired the peasants abroad, arranged their passage, found them places to live on arrival and helped them settle in. Without Welcome Wagon, the United Way or other social services to assist newcomers, the *padrones* could serve a useful purpose and some did. A great many, however, were completely unscrupulous, taking excessive commissions, cheating the immigrants at every turn and making them over-dependent on the bosses.

"The Italian laborer submits to these extortions," the U.S. De-

---

* A pre-Revolutionary immigrant from Italy, John di Palma, played for George Washington. Washington, Jefferson, Hamilton and John Adams sat for a Philadelphia sculptor, Giuseppe Ceracchi. Lorenzo da Ponte, who had been Mozart's lyricist, lived much of his life in Philadelphia. Nicholas Monachesi painted the fresco at the city's Merchants' Exchange. John Casani cast the great City Hall statues, including the one of William Penn that tops the building. In 1818, the Reverend Carlo Mariano landed with thirteen other immigrant priests from Italy, each with his own books, bed, bedding, clerical vestments and "mechanical tools." In 1856, Father Mariano became the first pastor of St. Mary Magdalen de Pazzi Church in South Philadelphia. It is the oldest Roman Catholic church in the nation serving only Italian immigrants and their descendants.

partment of Labor reported in 1897, "because he has no other alternative; he must work for his bosses or starve. Complaints are useless, for to whom would he complain? He knows that the boss (*padrone*) may welcome a pretext to discharge him and then have the opportunity of exacting a new *bossatura* (commission) from his successor who is so easily found."

Like those in other cities, the Italian peasants who immigrated to Philadelphia took unskilled jobs in construction, street grading and cleaning, snow shoveling, garbage and trash collection. The Pennsylvania Railroad was, according to Caroline Golab, "the single instrument most responsible for initiating the Italian influx to Philadelphia."* In 1920, the railroad reported 13,500 Italians on its rolls. Italian labor built City Hall, the tallest building in Philadelphia, as well as the Reading Railroad Terminal and the Broad Street and Market Street subways. The *padrone* system channeled Italians to jobs in the city streets department, Miss Golab found. In 1897 that growing immigrant group acquired "an exclusive claim on the work of keeping the streets of Philadelphia clean."† Another early agreement gave Italians a virtual monopoly on street grading and on the construction and maintenance of the city's trolley lines.

Italian immigrants in Philadelphia also worked as hucksters, peddlers, vendors, rag-pickers, shopkeepers, barbers, shoemakers, confectioners, waiters, stonecutters, masons, plasterers. They helped build blue-stocking Chestnut Hill, where Rizzo now lives. In the early years of this century they were second only to Jews in the number working as tailors and in the needle trades. Rizzo's father was a tailor before he became a cop.

Well into the 1900s, older Americans tended to dismiss Italian-Americans — all of them — as inferior. "The Italians are rural dwellers dropped into the unaccustomed, brutal parts of great cities, wrote Robert F. Foerster.‡ "Like a low-grade ore, they have value in the large. Work that demands training, responsibility, discretion is not for the great majority. But work that is simple and monotonous, that exhausts through duration rather than from concentrated application, that can be performed by men disposed in a

---

* *The Peoples of Philadelphia*, edited by Allen F. Davis and Mark H. Haller, Temple University Press, 1973.
† The streets department, though headed by Italian-Americans, is no longer an exclusive Italian preserve. Many blacks work there now, and a black leader of the sanitation men opposed Rizzo's mayoralty bid in 1971.
‡ Robert F. Foerster, *The Italian Emigration Of Our Times*, Harvard University Press, 1924.

gang, under the more or less military supervision of a foreman, so that the worker becomes himself like a part of a machine, such work the Italians, helot-like, have performed satisfactorily."

Employers seemed to regard Italians as a race apart. Some did not even consider them Caucasians. "One white man is as good as two or three Italians," a New York shipper responded when Foerster asked his opinion of Italian labor. A southern businessman put it this way: "It makes no difference whom I employ, negro, Italian or white man."

"I am unable to say very much in favor of Italian labor," noted a third employer. "We would prefer to employ Huns [Hungarians], Slavs or Poles if we could get them. The dearth of other foreign labor has compelled us to introduce Italian labor." Another anonymous employer said of the Italians: "They have no special qualifications; in fact, they are usually paid somewhat less than so-called white labor." "Our opinion," still another employer told Foerster, "is that generally the amount of work done per Italian laborer per day is not equal to the amount of work done per laborer per day by our other white laborers or by negroes."

A U.S. Labor Department study in 1897 found Italians at the bottom of Philadelphia's economic pyramid. The average weekly pay of workers in the city's slums was then $8.68. For Italian workers, the average was $5.93, nearly one-third less. "The difference is doubtless due to the fact that the persons embraced in these exclusively Italian families . . . were employed as a rule at occupations of the lowest grade, requiring no skill and but little manual dexterity or strength," the department reported. It also noted that joblessness among Philadelphia Italians was twice as severe as in the work force generally.

Press coverage of Philadelphia's Italian-American community in this period was often mindlessly demeaning. Most of the news gathered in what the papers termed "the Italian quarter" was crime news. The Black Hand Society and the Mafia made frequent headlines. Just as major crime in American cities today consists largely of blacks robbing, beating, raping and murdering blacks, so much of the earlier crime consisted of Italian criminals preying on Italian citizens. The *North American Review* blamed "laxity of the immigration laws" and "inefficiency of the police" for permitting "thousands of ex-convicts from Naples, Sicily and Calabria" to take advantage of their "honest and industrious" fellow countrymen. The Philadelphia *Evening Bulletin* disagreed. It blamed the victims themselves.

"The truth, apparently, is that the reason why so many brutal blackmailers are able to escape justice," the newspaper said in an editorial, "is to be found in the pronounced unwillingness of those they have victimized to report all the facts to the police, or to give their best aid to the task of running down and punishing the scoundrels who prey upon them."

The *Bulletin* called on "Italians who have attained positions of influence" to persuade their less successful brethren to "regard the law and its officers as the most efficient guardian of their peace and property."

"When the great bulk of Italians living in American cities learn to trust American courts and laws for their own protection," said the newspaper, "the partial immunity of the thugs among them will speedily disappear."

(Much later, when crime was mounting in Philadelphia in the 1960s, Police Commissioner Frank Rizzo made virtually the same appeal to blacks. But liberals, taking the *North American Review*'s earlier position, responded that the police were corrupt and that the criminal justice system was both racist and inhumane.)

In education, too, the "other Philadelphians" were shortchanged. When the immigration wave rolled in, the city school board took the view that children of newcomers were fit for little but vocational training. In 1920, Board of Education President Simon Gratz complained that too many boys were selecting academic instruction rather than manual training or trade courses. He urged more emphasis on mechanical trades since that was "the work they were to follow in active life." Superintendent Edwin C. Broome reminded Philadelphians in 1923 that the object of education was "to prevent children from becoming misfits in the world of industry." Clearly, both Gratz and Broome were addressing not the wellborn — their right to academic instruction was never questioned — but the working class. (History repeated itself here also when Mayor Rizzo's school board in 1972 set up "skills centers" for working-class children, most of whom are now black.)

Public education was supposed to be a great leveler, the "balance wheel of the social machinery," in Horace Mann's phrase. In fact, however, Philadelphia's schools tended to perpetuate class differences. Historian Richard Verbero found that they "helped maintain the class barriers that land ownership or family status" had given to some of the immigrants before they left Italy.* Not surprisingly, he found that "most of those Italo-American youths who completed

* *The Peoples of Philadelphia*, edited by Allen F. Davis and Mark H. Haller, Temple University Press, 1973.

high school and, especially, those who went on to college, were the children of the Italian middle and professional classes." Verbero also discovered, by studying Philadelphia school board journals from 1918 to 1941, that the high school dropout rate was higher for Italian students than it was for other immigrant groups. The number of Italian boys graduating from South Philadelphia High School over the twenty-three-year period was disproportionately small, he found. (Rizzo was one of the dropouts.)

"Clearly, this data is consistent with the Italian peasant tradition of youth economic exploitation and rejection of extended education," wrote Verbero.

After World War I, fear of bolshevism and anarchism led to extensive Americanization programs in public schools throughout the United States. The idea was to make good citizens of the immigrants' children by stressing love of God, country and capitalism. In Philadelphia, the job was made difficult by a cash shortage. Throughout the 1920s, Philadelphia ranked next to last among American cities in per capita spending on public education. Only Baltimore spent less. As late as 1930, the city continued to operate numerous South Philadelphia public schools that had no indoor toilets.

Yet the Americanization program seems to have worked very well. For immigrants in big cities like Philadelphia, life was often brutish and short, to be sure. But conditions back home had been far more harsh. There they had been "politically, economically and socially abused by an endless series of invaders and devastators, and subjected to what is widely regarded as the most stupid and corrupt ruling class of all European peoples."* Centuries of such misery had left the luckless peasants "demoralized and prostrate before their avaricious barons, their deceitful lawyers, their usurers, the Church."

That is why so many of them jumped at the chance to emigrate. And that is why they came to love their "sweet land of liberty." They supplied the manpower to fight its wars and they rarely questioned its policies. In Philadelphia and elsewhere it was the Italian-Americans and the other white ethnic groups that continued to believe in the nation's institutions and its value system long after others had given up on them. And while many questions were raised about Frank Rizzo's capabilities as police chief and as mayor, nobody ever questioned his patriotism.

* Joseph Lopreato, American Italian Historical Association, *Proceedings of The Fourth Annual Conference*, October 23, 1971.

Chapter Four

FRANK RIZZO'S FATHER grew up in Calabria, in the extreme south of Italy. Arid, hilly, with few minerals and only marginal farming, Calabria is one of the poorest sections of Europe and also one of the most sparsely populated. Northern Italians of all classes tend to dismiss Calabrians as ignorant, uncultured, mean-spirited peasants.

Rafael Rizzo's hometown, Chiaravalle Centrale, is tucked back in the Apennine hills near the sole of Italy's well-worn boot. About 7,500 persons live there today in tiny stone houses with faded red tile roofs. Many of the houses are centuries old. In their struggle for survival, the poor farmers cultivate every foot of arable land. Mainly they grow olives and grapes. Many keep a cow or two, a few chickens, maybe a couple of pigs and goats.

In the fall of 1972, the year after Frank Rizzo's election, Tom Fox, then a Philadelphia *Daily News* columnist, visited Chiaravalle Centrale. Before Fox headed south by train, Romans warned him to expect the worst. But Fox, who has never made any secret of his admiration for Frank Rizzo, got a hero's welcome. Everybody in Chiaravalle Centrale seemed to know that after twenty-seven years in *l'uniforme blu*, Rafael Rizzo's policeman son had run for *sindaco di Filadelfia* on a platform of *legge e ordine* and had defeated *il repubblicano* W. Thacher Longstreth, whom one Italian newspaper had described as "bianco, protestante, *snob*, educato a Princeton."

In the small house where Rafael Rizzo was born on April 7, 1894, Fox dined with Rizzo relatives. As wine flowed, family photographs were passed around the table. Some went back sixty years and more. One of Rafael appeared to have been taken when he was about fourteen years old. He was a handsome youth, with his face well scrubbed, his dark hair neatly cut and parted in the middle. He wore a stiff white collar. His jaw was firm and his expression serious as he peered directly at the camera. It was a fragment of the past, a proud family's treasured photo of a devoted son.

After three days in Chiaravalle Centrale, Fox concluded that even now family ties remain firm there. He found poverty but no dirt. "The people of the village cannot control the politicians," he wrote, "but they do control the children. It was these Old World values that shaped the character of Frank Rizzo." Fox viewed Rafael Rizzo's son as "an extension of the ancient culture." (But the Big Bambino's critics disagreed. They saw him as an extension of an abomination in the Italian culture: Benito Mussolini's fascism.)

Rafael Rizzo emigrated about 1909. He may have come with his older brother, Giuseppe, or with one or two schoolmates. The details of his passage and the exact date are obscure. He was probably about fifteen when he settled in South Philly's Little Italy.

The boy from Calabria must have wondered at the swarms of newcomers and the babble of tongues. In one respect, though, Philadelphia may have seemed like just a big small town: it was a city of walkers. Life was lived in the streets. Electric trolleys had been running since 1892, but natives and immigrants alike were just getting used to the Market Street subway-elevated line, which had opened in 1907. There were horse-drawn wagons and carriages, of course, but very few automobiles, hardly any trucks and no honking taxicabs. So men and women strolled in the streets and children played in them. Foot patrolmen walked their beats and lamplighters walked their rounds. Philadelphia was dotted with farms. The entire northeastern section of the city, now chockablock with row houses, shopping malls, light industry and heavy traffic, was wide open countryside.

Many of his fellow *Calabrese* took unskilled laboring jobs, but Ralph — his Christian name was quickly Americanized — hired himself out as an apprentice tailor. He toiled as a tailor for about seven years, learning English and retaining his boyhood interest in music and the clarinet. On May 5, 1917, just one month after the United States declared war against Germany and the Central Powers, twenty-three-year-old Ralph Rizzo joined the Philadelphia police department. It was an unusual move for such an immigrant. Philadelphia Common Pleas Court Judge Armand Della Porta, who much later helped organize a Sons of Italy unit within the police department, thinks there were no more than five or six Italian-Americans on the force when Ralph Rizzo signed up.

Soon after putting on his police uniform, Officer Rizzo married Teresa Erminio, a tall, handsome woman who had emigrated from the Naples area. Within a year or two after their marriage, the couple moved into a neat two-story row house at 2322 South Rosewood Street in South Philly. That is where they reared their four strapping sons.

South Philly is a twelve-square-mile, saucer-shaped alluvial plain between the Delaware River on the east and south and the Schuylkill River on the west. About 250,000 people live there now. More than two-thirds of them are white and most of the whites are Italian-Americans.

There's a saying, "You can take a man out of South Philly but you can't take South Philly out of a man." The same aphorism has been applied to Brooklyn, the Bronx, South Boston, East Baltimore and any number of ethnic enclaves. These proud old neighborhoods are states of mind rather than geographic entities. In their best days, which in some cases are now over, they had their own tribal rites and traditions, their own sights, sounds, smells and often pugnacious ways of life. Each developed a distinctive character which marked its people as a breed apart.

Certainly, South Philly, with its bocce players, its cacophonous open-air market and its strutting, caparisoned Mummers marchers, has a flavor all its own. Beyond that, it has always been home for astonishingly diverse and talented men and women. Marian Anderson was born in South Philly in 1902 and began her world-acclaimed career as a contralto by singing in neighborhood churches at the age of eight. A boy named Alfred Cocozza went to school with Frank Rizzo. Later he would become Mario Lanza. From South Philly's working-class row houses have come Eddie Fisher, Chubby Checker, Joey Bishop and Fabian Forte. Tommy Loughran, onetime world light-heavyweight boxing champion, grew up in South Philly. So did Willie Mosconi, the billiard master, and restaurateur Toots Shor and William Z. Foster, the former U.S. Communist Party leader. Pius Lanzetti, one of South Philly's most notorious criminals, was slain by rival mobsters there on New Year's Eve in 1936. Angelo Bruno, currently the city's ailing boss of organized crime, still lives in a modest-looking house on Snyder Avenue less than a dozen "squares" from South Rosewood Street, where Ralph and Teresa Rizzo reared Frank and his three brothers.

When the Rizzos moved in, South Rosewood was a narrow, pleasant residential street west of Broad, Philadelphia's major north-south artery. It's still pleasant today. Houses there now sell for about $15,000 and up. The Rizzos probably paid a fraction of that. The neighborhood had been largely German and Irish. They joined a westward movement of Italian-Americans across Broad Street. Little Italy was expanding.

Edwin H. Vare, then Philadelphia's political boss, lived in South Philly and the section that the Rizzos moved into was called "Vareville." A onetime ashcart driver, Republican Vare had built a contracting fortune from municipal construction work. To fill out his unskilled work force, he imported Italian laborers and found places for them to live. He gave them coal in the winter, toys for the children at Christmas and food at election time. In some cases he paid their poll taxes. In return for these favors, Vare gained the immigrants' political loyalty — and the Philadelphia GOP got enough votes to hold power for a record sixty-seven years.

For many immigrants, big, bald Ed Vare, the brusque, overbearing political boss, was an all-powerful *padrone*. They depended on him for a livelihood and they feared him. Frank Rizzo told us that as a boy he recalled seeing the Italian laborers lining up at Vare's house to be paid by a paymaster. He said Vare cheated them.

"They couldn't read or write," Rizzo said of the immigrants. "He [Vare] took them over. He would turn the clock back on them. You know, they're working and it's four o'clock. All of a sudden, it's three o'clock. Most of them were too scared to say anything.

"You could see them on payday, right there. A big drunk or two would pay them and make their deductions — for their fares from Italy which Vare had paid. He charged interest, too. It got so all they were doing was working to pay off the interest.

"I was just a kid," recounted Rizzo, "but I knew what was going on. Every once in a while you'd see a guy who knew he was being shortchanged, and he'd complain. And they'd push him, shove him, you know, scare him."

Rizzo said that his own father regarded Vare, who had been a Pennsylvania state senator, with awe. The elder Rizzo was deferential in the contractor politician's presence even though he never worked for him. "When he [Vare] went by with all of his flunkies around him," Rizzo related, "my father would always go like this" — Rizzo stood and bowed from the waist — "and take off his hat and say, 'Hello, Senator.'

"I said to my father," Rizzo continued, " 'Why do you do that? Why do you bow and say hello to a man like that?' And my father said, 'I could lose my job. He's a powerful man.' "

"I made up my mind then," Rizzo said, "nobody's going to push me around. Frank Rizzo doesn't bow to anybody."

The trouble with this story is that when Edwin H. Vare died at the age of sixty on October 16, 1922, Frank L. Rizzo was one year, eleven months and three weeks old. But even though it's apocryphal, the tale may be worth repeating for what it reveals about the Rizzos, father and son. It's hard to imagine two men more different.

Pounding a beat and playing a clarinet in the police and firemen's band, Ralph Rizzo was an unobtrusive cop. In forty-one years on the Philadelphia police force, he was never to rise above the rank of patrolman. He may have lacked the education to pass the exams for promotion or he may have lacked the political influence. Alternatively, he may have lacked the ambition. The late Ernest L. Biagi, South Philadelphia author and historian who knew Ralph Rizzo, said he was "a musician, not a policeman," and he referred to the mayor's father as "an artisan."

James Reaves, a retired twenty-five-year police veteran, worked out of the same South Philly station house with Ralph Rizzo in the 1940s when Reaves was a rookie. He remembers the older man as being quiet, conscientious and cautious, a true peace officer.

"As far as I know," Reaves said of Ralph Rizzo, "he never made a pinch. His way was more to mediate disputes. You know, if two fellows were fighting, he'd tell them to get off the street and go home."

Ralph Rizzo was more devoted to his family than to his job. It was a growing family. Frank, born October 23, 1920, was followed four years later by Joseph, two years after that by Ralph, Jr., and finally, in another two years, by "the baby," Anthony.

In close-knit immigrant homes of that era, fathers often ruled their family roosts autocratically. "I mean they thought they were big czars," said a South Philadelphian named John Fosco, who grew up not far from the Rizzos. "And when they came home that was Christ that walked in the door. Everybody had to bow down and wait on them."

Ralph Rizzo was one such autocrat. The soft-spoken, clarinet-playing cop who gave few orders on his beat was always giving orders at home. (In this reversal of roles, he was the mirror opposite of his oldest son. Frank Rizzo has always enjoyed being super-cop in public but at home he's a quiet family man who rarely throws his weight around.)

"My Dad set tough rules," Rizzo once told a national television audience, "and you played the game by his rules or you didn't play. . . . There were no democratic formulas . . . boom, you got knocked down."

A former friend of Ralph's in Chiaravalle Centrale told Tom Fox of visiting the Rizzos on South Rosewood Street when Frank was a tiny baby. "All the time, Ralph spank Frank with the belt," he said. "All the time. But that's why Frank turn out good." Frank Rizzo would say amen to that. In an autobiographical fragment written for the Philadelphia *Inquirer* after his mayoralty triumph in 1971, Rizzo recalled his father catching him smoking. "[He] caught me flat out, and he let me have it. He didn't know anything about slappin', he just waffled me. He didn't smoke and he didn't expect his kids to smoke." Yet Frank grew up to become a very heavy smoker.

Former boyhood pals of the Rizzo brothers during their years on South Rosewood Street still remember Officer Ralph Rizzo. "He was mean and tough and he didn't like us kids," Louis Potere, who went to grade school with Frank and later moved to suburban Delaware County, said of the boys' father. "He was a miserable guy but he was pretty straight."

Thomas Oteri's parents ran a butcher shop on the corner where Frank Rizzo worked as a delivery boy. Oteri himself operated the shop in 1976. He had been a lifelong friend of the Mayor. "In our day," Oteri said, "all our parents had to do was look a little bit crosseyed and we'd jump. His [Frank Rizzo's] father was very strict. They didn't get away with nothing. My parents were the same way."

Danny Troisi, another boyhood chum of Frank Rizzo, recalled that the father was both "very strict" and hot-tempered. He required his sons to be home at nine o'clock at night, even on summer Saturdays when the other kids were down at Marconi Plaza playing their guitars and talking to girls. If the family curfew was broken, said Troisi, Ralph Rizzo would become enraged and he would punish the offenders.

Troisi said he will never forget one impulsive and destructive act of Ralph Rizzo. It occurred, said Troisi, when he and Frank Rizzo were about fifteen years old. With savings from odd jobs, Frank and his brothers had chipped in and purchased a bicycle. They did it without consulting their father. He was furious.

"One day he came home from work unexpectedly," Troisi said of Officer Rizzo. "He saw the bicycle in the yard. He got violent about it. He got a hatchet and chopped it up. He took it into the yard in front of the house and, you know, threw the pieces outside. Fortunately, the mother was devoted to the kids. She knew he was out to beat the kids up so she warned them. They all had to stay out until the father went back to work."

Because of Ralph Rizzo's fierce temper, said Troisi, the neighborhood boys rarely entered the Rizzos' house when he was there. On the other hand, they all liked Mrs. Rizzo. She was friendly with her neighbors and, according to Troisi, often had coffee with one woman who was an inveterate numbers player. Mrs. Rizzo also enjoyed the illegal lottery, said Troisi, but he said she "wouldn't dare have a [numbers] slip in her house."

To hear the Rizzos and some of their friends tell it, growing up in South Philly in the 1920s and thirties was one great big bowl of rigatoni. Joseph F. Rizzo, who owed his appointment as Philadelphia's fire commissioner in 1972 to his older brother, the mayor, nostalgically recalled an old brass bed with big spindles in the South Rosewood Street house.

"Frank and I slept together in it," he told the Philadelphia *Bulletin*'s Sandy Grady. They were bedmates, he said, for thirteen years. "You know, kids pair off in families. Tony and Ralph, who were the youngest, paired off. And Frank and I — he was four years older than me — were inseparable as kids. We went to the Baldwin [public elementary] School together and St. Monica's parish. I always looked up to Frank. We all did."

"We had many good days," said Tommy Oteri. "We had little but enjoyed it more. We weren't afraid of anything. Now you have to have bars on the windows and you can't leave a car in the street very long or it might be stolen. They're letting these kids get away with everything."

Frank Rizzo, in the *Inquirer* piece that appeared under his by-line, recalled buying "George Washington" cake from a German bakery for a penny a slab and then sitting on the curb and eating it.

The cake, he said, was made of leftover raisins and dough, and was a favorite of his. He remembered hanging out at Grazioni's candy store and getting $10 a week as a delivery boy for Oteri's father.

"I always brought my pay home to my mother," Rizzo said. "It was the greatest thrill of my life to hand that pay to my mother and watch her eyes. I used to run home and give it to her, just to see her smile. She gave me fifty cents for myself."

In contrast to Rizzo's recollections are those of another South Philadelphian whom we'll call Philip Russo. Russo grew up near the Rizzo family but never knew the brothers and never got into politics or the public spotlight. He became a carpenter-contractor and, when we interviewed him, he and his wife and two sons were living in a comfortable house on a tree-lined street half a mile from South Rosewood. We picked him as a more or less typical South Philadelphian who, while faring well economically, has chosen to remain in the old neighborhood. The Russos, in fact, had twice moved to South Jersey and twice they had moved back. South Philly was in Russo's blood. Yet he had no illusions about the past.

"Years ago," he said, "you couldn't walk around here. "They used to have policemen walking around here. And if you looked like you were from out of this neighborhood, they chased you outa here. It was the same way with the library on Shunk Street. No way. You walked in that library, they'd throw you out. If they knew you were from outa this neighborhood, they'd kick you right outa the library.

"You know the Broad Street Subway? If you ever got caught on the subway, whether you paid or not, they'd throw you out. If you were a kid they knew you didn't have no money to ride the subway. So they'd just throw you out. I don't care if you were at Spring Garden [in North Philadelphia] or wherever you were, you walked home. You walked five, six, ten miles, whatever it was. You walked home."

The block where Philip Russo lives now was formerly German-American turf. Kids like Russo wouldn't dare walk on it. It was his recollection that many sections of the city were closed to Italian-Americans.

"If you were Italian, you couldn't walk past Broad and Pollock [deep in South Philly] unless you were with a gang. They'd beat you up. The Irish and Polacks. I'm not talking about colored people; I'm talking about white people. The same way with Fairmount Park. We used to walk [five miles] to Fairmount Park from here. There's the Girard Avenue Bridge [over the Schuylkill]. You couldn't walk over the top of the bridge because you'd get jumped and they'd beat you up. We used to walk underneath, hand over hand. Through all the steel and all. It was either that or you got beat up, you got killed. The colored we didn't worry about. They never bothered us. Never. If you were Italian, you fought your way around. The colored people never came out at night.

"Today they [the Italians] intermarry. Years ago, no way. Don't tell me. I come from thirteen kids. And if somebody came into my house with blond hair and blue eyes they got thrown right out the door. I mean the guy might have just came in and asked for a cuppa coffee or something, they beat him up.

"My brother Joe always kidded about that. You ever want a free meal, just put on a black wig. 'Cause everybody in my family all had dark hair. But yet my sister Jean had Irish friends. My brother Joe had Irish friends. All thirteen in my family married Italians. Except Joe, he married a Syrian. But she's more Italian than any of them.

"You talk about [water] pollution. The Delaware River years ago was dirtier than it is today. The Delaware. 'Cause I swam in there, and I know it was dirtier than it is today. The streets were filthier than they are today. There was no cars in them days but there was dirty streets. I mean people were dirty. In fact, I don't know how schoolteachers put up with some in them classes because I know the kids in there were filthy. I mean dirty. I mean nobody got washed. Did you ever hear people say, 'Well, Saturday night is rolled around, I think I'll take a bath'? Well, that was the truth. It was so bad that my father used to have to wash our head with vinegar. I mean soap and water wasn't enough, he actually had to wash up with vinegar to clean us off."

One of Philip Russo's comments on *la dolce vita* in South Philly forty years ago bears indirectly on Frank Rizzo, boy and man. Russo said: *"If you were Italian, you fought your way around."* Rizzo's adult record as a fighter will be documented later. What we discovered by talking to people who knew him as a boy was that Frank Rizzo fought then, too. He fought all the time, in the schoolyard and out, at recess and after school. Fighting became a way of life for him in first grade. Other boys may have been good students or good athletes, well liked by girls or standouts socially. Frank Rizzo did not excel in any of these ways, but as a fighter he was exceptional. Mrs. E. B. Powell remembers that very well. She used to teach first grade in the old Baldwin Elementary School in South Philly and Frank Rizzo was one of her pupils.

"He was well cared for by his mother," Mrs. Powell, retired and living in South Philadelphia, said of the future mayor. "He had snappy black eyes and black hair and he was well behaved in class. His mother and father were very strict with him. They put up with no nonsense. Frank was very fond of play-acting. He was a ham at heart, I think, and he loved to imitate actors. He wasn't any genius, just a run-of-the-mill student, but he brought in nice homework.

"The thing about him was that outside of class he was always fighting. At recess. After school. He wouldn't even know the boy. He'd go up to him and, Bang. I think he was a bully at heart. Once Miss Engel, the principal, caught him. She took him into her office. You could hear him hollering six blocks away."

Mrs. Powell said that since all of young Frank's battling took place outside of her classroom she might not have remembered him except for his "wonderful parents." She was especially fond of his mother. "Mrs. Rizzo would invite four or five Baldwin teachers to her home for a spaghetti lunch every month or so," she said. "And she made the best spaghetti I ever ate."

Rizzo entered the Baldwin School in September, 1926, a month before his sixth birthday. He made satisfactory progress at Baldwin, which has since been torn down, and went on to Edwin H. Vare Junior High. It was named for the political boss before whom such immigrants as Ralph Rizzo bowed and scraped. Frank got through Vare in the regulation three years. The June 1936 issue of the school paper listed him as a member of the ninth grade that was being promoted to senior high. It said his nickname was "Riz" and his hobby was "fishing." It disclosed that Frank received an orchestra pin for playing the clarinet like his father. His name did not appear on the honor roll.

For each ninth grader, Vare's school paper, *The Pilot*, printed a line or a phrase that the student himself often repeated or that was associated with him. These were called "slips of the tongue." In one boy's case, it was "Cut it out, Mugs." In another's, "Jumpin' Catfish." In the case of roughhouser Riz, the tag line, in retrospect, is full of meaning: "I didn't do it!"

From Vare, Rizzo went on to the big South Philadelphia High School, now coed but then for boys only. One of the school's top students, Anthony P. Zecca, would later serve as a top deputy to Mayor Rizzo. "We didn't know each other in school," Zecca told us. "I was a goody-goody."

Rizzo's academic records have mysteriously disappeared from

South Philadelphia High School, where they should be stored. A board of education official said the records were either stolen or misfiled. The scanty information available indicates that Rizzo dropped out — "voluntarily withdrew" in educational jargon — in November 1938, when he was eighteen and in eleventh grade. He should have completed eleventh grade the previous June.

Rizzo says he quit school in 1939 following the sudden death of his mother after gallbladder surgery. He was nineteen and in twelfth grade, according to Rizzo. It's Danny Troisi's recollection that both he and Rizzo dropped out midway in their senior year at Southern after their books were stolen from the locker they shared. School officials wouldn't let them attend classes until they turned in the books, said Troisi, and so they withdrew.

"It's a vague thing but I remember positively that the reason we left was because of the books," he said. "We were close to graduation."

Although Franny Rizzo's academic achievements in junior and senior high schools are lost to history, his legendary exploits as a playground rassler and tough street scrapper live on. Over and over, the stories are told of his leadership qualities, his courage and resolution in defending the weak against the strong, in fighting for the underdogs and routing the cowards and bullies. He's the first to tell such stories.

"Downtown," Frank Rizzo wrote in the *Inquirer*, "it always seemed I was the big brother. I seemed to dominate the groups. I was always the guy they came to when they wanted to get things done. There was about 30 or 40 kids and they always called Franny. 'Let's go see Franny and get him to help us,' they'd say."

"Frank was always the leader," his brother, Ralph, a Blue Cross employee, told reporter Greg Walter. "He'd always take on the bully — and every neighborhood has a bully. But in those days we fought fair. Nobody ever kicked anybody when he was down — that was a cardinal sin. Frank was never afraid of anybody especially if he thought they were bad."

"If there was a bully in the neighborhood," Joe Rizzo said of his older brother in an interview with the *Bulletin*'s Sandy Grady, "Frank took care of him. I remember one day a kid was skating on our block and a big dog knocked him down and was mauling him. Frank ran over and picked up the kid and whirled him around in the air, using the kid's skates to knock the dog flat."

Louis Potere, another of the old gang but not a sycophantic admirer of Mayor Frank Rizzo, remembered him as a tough, self-appointed enforcer, who kept his brothers in line. Ralph Rizzo, Jr., was the family cutup, said Potere, and when Ralph got into minor scrapes Franny would "bang the shit" out of him.

"If he caught us stealing hubcaps, he'd give us hell," Potere said of the oldest of the four Rizzo boys. "And when he had you down he didn't quit, neither. He didn't quit until he drew blood, that guy."

Frank Rizzo's best friend in junior and senior high school, the boy he waited for on the corner on cold winter mornings to walk to classes with, was Danny Troisi. Troisi became an insurance agent and moved across the Delaware River to New Jersey. He grew a beard and in 1972 he stuck a McGovern-for-President decal on his automobile. In a tape-recorded interview with us, Danny Troisi, whose parents emigrated from Abruzzi, in the mountains east of Rome, noted first that not all Italians are alike.

"You talk to an old Italian," Troisi said, "he'll tell you that different *paeses*, different areas of Italy, are known for different characteristics. You say, 'What are the characteristics of a Sicilian?' He'll say, 'They carry knives.' The *Abruzzese* are known to have receding chins, high hairlines, light skins; they're scholars, more or less. The *Calabrese* are known, typically, to be hard heads. In other words, if you remember the expression, you'll find that it fits.

"Tommy Oteri, he's a Sicilian. He's a butcher and he always has a knife in his hand. We [*Abruzzese*] regard the southerners as being pretty crude or low-lifes. Whether it's right or not, I don't know but in Rizzo's case he's a *Calabresi* and he fits perfectly the description of the people of that group. They've got hard heads and they're very strict with their women, very stern in everything they do. Everything by the book."

Troisi began to talk more directly about his boyhood friend and their experiences growing up together in South Philly.

"I knew Franny best. He was a born policeman. He truly liked to fight. He was doing that job for the government before they paid him. Sometimes too efficiently, because he would get carried away. When he began fighting he didn't know when to stop. When he found Ralphie and Louis and me stealing hubcaps, he started a fight with his brother which turned into a violent one. We tried to break it up because he was going to hurt Ralphie.

"Franny was always fighting. After school, like in the hallways, he would say, 'Danny, hold my clarinet because I've got to meet so-and-so.' And I would have the clarinet. He was taking clarinet lessons from a Mr. Dingler. There was also another teacher named D'Adorio. So whenever there was a fight, D'Adorio or Dingler would come running out. And because Franny didn't have to carry a clarinet, we could get away without them catching him. But Dingler was always on top of Franny. You know, he used to grab him by the sideburns and lift him up.

"That seemed to be his biggest mark, that he was always involved in fights. He always felt that he had to protect somebody. He was aggressive. He was a street fighter, not fast but bullish. He always had a sort of Robin Hood attitude. He really did act in that manner. Like I was playing half-ball with a man who used to play with the A's. We were playing in the street and the ball hit him in the face. He came right over to me. He was angry and he hit me. And I crouched down. Franny was 'way across the street and I heard him yell, 'You touch him and I'm gonna break your arm,' or something. And he ran over. They faced each other. That was a threatening thing because this guy was good. Franny protected me, and he was always doing that.

"He had no fear at all for his personal safety. I've seen him walk into a group of four or five guys. I've never seen him fight four or five guys but he would walk into a group and single one out and start a fight with him. It was a status thing with Fanny. He resented anybody being tougher than him. If he didn't like a guy in the group you could tell it. Because he would be hovering over that guy looking for an excuse to belt him. But he would never hit from behind. Never on any conditions would he sneak up on a guy and jump him.

"As a matter of fact, he deliberately went out of his way to pick up audiences. Like before he would fight somebody, we used to make dates — 'I'll meet you at four o'clock in front of Vare.' You know. And everybody in the school knew who Rizzo was going to fight today. They would all be waiting because sometimes the fight would be more promising than other times. The teachers couldn't get to you. Because when the teachers came out they had to go around the fence.

"Fighting was all that Franny had going for him. He wasn't eloquent. He didn't have any girls. He didn't drive an automobile. I think each of us has certain things that we try to make the most out of. In this case, he was big and strong and he liked being boss."

Troisi sat in the kitchen of his small frame, single house in South Jersey drinking coffee as he spoke these clipped sentences into a tape recorder. Now he turned to a crucial question. As mayor of Philadelphia, Frank L. Rizzo would take and flunk a lie-detector test, thus becoming the first big-city mayor in American history to suffer such an indignity. What was his youthful reputation for veracity?

"He wasn't dishonest. You could never say that he stole. But as a boy he always stretched the truth. Him and X (another boy named by Troisi) were regarded as the two bullshitters. You didn't say it to his face unless you were joking when you said it — otherwise you'd get a mouthful of teeth. X was a great exaggerator. Rizzo, too.

"In Franny's case, when you would catch him in lie, he knew how to walk away from it — because it was a comical thing. Whereas X would stick to it even though he knew he was lying. In Franny's case it was a magnification more than anything else. Franny wouldn't make an outright lie but he would exaggerate the truth. As a boy. So you really don't know what traits he would carry now."

Troisi paused to consider the next question. Aside from his penchant for fighting, what kind of boy was Franny Rizzo? What was he really like?

"Franny was quiet but he wasn't profound. He was sort of bullish. You would have to say that. Looking back, Ralphie had a personality. Franny didn't. Some guys want to go to the racetrack or play poker. Rizzo was never motivated by anything like that. He'd walk by a game, say 'What'cha playin'?' and walk away. He would never say, 'Deal me in.'

"Franny was never any good at sports. He was too heavy. But we would rollerskate. I remember once when we were skating, Franny and Angelina N... had an argument. She was a very pretty girl who flitted from one boy to another. Not a bad girl but she had a lot of boy friends. When Franny and her had an argument, she took off her skate and she was trying to hit him with it. Franny was running and she kept running after him. I'll never forget it.

"At night we'd go down to Marconi Plaza. Most of us played the guitar. We used to go down there with the girls and play the guitar. But at eight-thirty Franny would run. He had to be in early at night. And he went in early. That was it. The other brother, Ralphie, used to sneak out at night. Franny stayed in the house.

"We had a standard joke: 'You better go home, Franny, it's almost nine o'clock.' He would laugh and say, 'Who in hell are you kidding?' The next thing you'd know he'd disappear. I think he was in deathly fear of his father hitting him. Because I think he would have hit his father back. And he was smart enough to know it. If he had, there would have had to be a dead Rizzo because they were both hardheaded.

"The Rizzos' house was well furnished. I remember going into the house if we knew the father was out. In those days tomato pie — pizza — was pretty standard. I remember going in the basement of their house and eating it periodically. On the walls they had cloth tapestry. That impressed me.

"The father drove around in a 1932 Chevy for about ten years. It was a coupe. He was always chasing us in it. It wouldn't be unusual for him to drive down from the police station in the thirty-two Chevy to make sure the boys were sleeping, and then go back to the beat."

What about race relations in South Philly in the 1930s? As a boy did Frank Rizzo, who would later be denounced as a bigot and a racist, mistreat black youths?

"There weren't any Negroes down there," Troisi answered. "There wasn't any discrimination because we were never exposed to black people. In our graduating class at Vare we elected a fellow named Lee to be our president. He was part Negro and part Chinese, I think. There were hardly any Negroes at Southern then." (The school is now predominantly black.)

"If Rizzo is anti-Negro, I think it would be based on the shortsightedness of a policeman. He never fought a Negro as a kid. Conceivably, being on the police department, it's easy to misplace poverty with a tendency toward breaking the law. Rich people don't have to steal.

"In my case, as an insurance man, my debit is in that area that's mostly black. There are many black people that bug the hell out of me because they lie and make me come back and they don't pay their bills. But then the ones that I like, the nice ones, I've adjusted to accepting them."

Reflecting on his friend of long ago, Danny Troisi had a final thought. It concerned Frank Rizzo's spirituality. "Rizzo was never religious," he said. "He talks about St. Monica's a lot, but if he went to church that was the limit of his religion.

"Franny and Joseph were close," Troisi concluded. "Joseph done whatever Franny told him. He idolizes his older brother. And the Oteris look up to Rizzo like a god. Personally, [I think] he's a very *mortal* person."

After Franny and Danny dropped out of Southern High the old gang broke up. Everything changed. The year 1939 was traumatic for the Rizzos. Frank enlisted in the U.S. Navy. His father decided to move the family out of Little Italy. And then, very suddenly, his mother died.

Teresa Rizzo was just thirty-nine. Her death shocked the neighborhood. Unlike her brooding husband, Mrs. Rizzo had been one of its mainstays. She was known and liked by everybody on South Rosewood Street.

"She had a heart as big as her body," Mrs. Edward F. Lawson, a longtime friend, told reporter Fred Hamilton.* "She's the kind of woman who would shake hands with one hand and put the coffee pot on with the other. Her house was always open to visitors and the table was usually set for dinner guests. Mrs. Rizzo was a little warmer than the father. But she never let the boys get away with anything."

Mrs. Lawson also told Hamilton that "Francis is the picture of his mother."

Despite the tragedy, the family went ahead with the move ten miles north to a larger, two-story single house at 1021 East Mt. Pleasant Street in Philadelphia's middle-class West Oak Lane Section. Frank Rizzo, telling his life story in the *Inquirer*, said his father decided on the move one day when the police band was playing a concert in Temple University Stadium.

"He saw all that beautiful ground up there and he decided that was where he wanted to live," Rizzo said of his father. "It was pretty tough. . . . He had just bought the house and then my mother died. . . . He never married again. A lot of nights my father wouldn't even get into bed, just sat up in the big overstuffed chair in the front room."

Ralph Rizzo, Sr., lived in the house until his own death at seventy-four in 1968. By that time, his youngest son, Anthony, was dead, the victim of a cerebral hemorrhage at the age of thirty-two. He'd followed Frank into the police department.

During most of 1939, though, Frank was an ordinary seaman in the U.S. Navy. After completing basic training at Great Lakes, he was assigned to the U.S.S. *Houston*, a cruiser. But then in November, 1939, he was given a medical discharge after reportedly developing *diabetes insipidus*, a rare ailment resulting from a defect in the pituitary gland.

His Navy stint is one part of his life that Rizzo would just as soon forget. His official city biography makes no mention of it and he has never discussed it publicly. The armed forces will not permit

* *Rizzo: From Cop to Mayor of Philadelphia*, by Fred Hamilton, The Viking Press, 1973, pp. 27–28.

public inspection of service records without consent of the veterans themselves. In Rizzo's case such consent has not been given. So far as is known, however, he made a full recovery from the illness and has never suffered a recurrence.

Back in Philadelphia, Rizzo took a construction job and then worked as a rigger on a crane in the heat treatment plant of the Midvale Steel Co., now Midvale-Heppenstall Co. While visiting relatives in Germantown, he met a pretty young woman who was working in a chocolate factory. She was four years older than he was and only about half his size. She was living at home with her parents who were Italian immigrants. Her name was Carmella Silvestri.

Frank Rizzo and Carmella Silvestri were married at her parish church, Our Lady of the Holy Rosary, on April 18, 1942. The bride was twenty-five and the groom twenty-one. It was wartime and the newlyweds had very little money and few resources. They lived first with his widowed father and then with her father, a shoemaker who was also a widower.

Rizzo was making $75 every two weeks at the steel plant. His father-in-law gave him $1,200 for a down payment on a house at Washington Lane and Morton Street in Germantown. The couple moved in and lived there for eleven years before buying a red brick house on Provident Street in Mt. Airy for $16,250 in 1956. They lived there until moving into their controversial and costly place in Chestnut Hill in 1975.

In 1943, while Rizzo was still working as a rigger, his son, Francis, was born. A daughter, Joanna, followed five years later. Perhaps it was fatherhood that caused him to make a drastic career change, one that would have profound effect not only on Frank Rizzo but on the entire city. On October 6, 1943, seventeen days before his twenty-third birthday, Francis Lazzaro Rizzo followed his own father into the Philadelphia police department. Growing up in South Philly, he'd fought every kid on the block. Now the citizens and taxpayers would pay him to fight for them.

Chapter Five

WHEN Frank Rizzo decided to become a cop, the Republican machine that had run Philadelphia since 1884 was crumbling. Ahead loomed a series of political scandals and suicides that would end its rule in disgrace and usher in a decade of liberal reform.

But this was 1943. The Republicans, while growing steadily weaker, still controlled City Hall. They controlled spending and patronage. And they continued to operate the "Police Bureau" as if it were a GOP club.

To be sure, their iron grip had loosened a little. Back in Ed Vare's heyday, cops had been forced to kick back part of their pay to the Republican organization as a condition of employment.* They had hustled Republican votes on election day. And they had been held responsible for results in their districts. If a GOP precinct turned Democratic the police were blamed and the captain transferred.

---

* Extracting such political "contributions" from public employes still goes on in parts of Pennsylvania although it is illegal. Pennsylvanians refer to the practice as "macing," an appropriate term derived from the heavy medieval war club with spiked metal head, or mace, that became a symbol for authority.

By the 1940s, such overt politicizing of police was rare. But party loyalty remained important. It wasn't easy for a registered Democrat to get a position on the force. What this meant for Applicant Rizzo was that he needed an endorsement from his Republican ward leader.

The GOP leader of Philadelphia's 38th Ward, where Rizzo lived, was a beefy, hot-tempered Dutchman and middle-level city official named Carl W. Myers. Rizzo didn't know Myers but he persuaded a couple of Republican committeemen, Ernest Lanzetta and Rocco DiGiacomo, to put in a good word for him.

"Some of the boys from the Thirty-eighth came in and said they were interested in him [Rizzo]," Myers told us before his death in 1975. "I okayed his appointment. In those days it helped to have [political] support because there were a lot more names on the eligibility list than there were vacancies in the police department."

Thanks in part to Carl Myers, Rizzo got his badge. Later, though, the ward leader would have reason to regret his routine sponsorship of the new cop.

Patrolman Rizzo's starting salary was $2,225 a year, or $42.71 a week. The top pay for patrolmen then was just $7 a week more than that, or $2,590 a year. The public safety director, James H. (Shooey) Malone, received $10,000 a year, a princely sum. He headed both police and fire departments.

The city's top policeman, Superintendent of Police Howard P. Sutton, earned $7,500. An assistant superintendent got $4,700. Malone's assistant, Herbert E. Millen, received $4,250. Millen, later to become the city's first Negro judge, was the ward leaders' contact for police appointments.

Police inspectors were paid just $3,380 a year and police sergeants, $2,875. The force included ten "fingerprint operators" at $2,200 each and ten "hostlers" who were paid $1,600 a year to look after the police horses.

Most of the 4,150 patrolmen were, like Rizzo, high school dropouts — although that derogatory term was not used. Many were, like Rizzo, the sons of immigrants. Some were, like him, policemen's sons. But comparatively few shared his ethnic background. In a city long run by white Protestants, the Irish were at last ascendant. Superintendent Sutton was a Protestant, as all of his predecessors had been, but most of the police inspectors and captains were not. The forty-three police captains included two Italian-Americans and one Polish-American. The others bore such names as Finn, Hallman, Callahan, Connor, Driscoll, Gorman, McDermott, Harrity, Harkins, Gibbons. Among the nine inspectors were McCoy, Hardiman, McFarland, Burns, Hubbs.

The rookie's first assignment was to a blue-collar district of small row houses and heavy industry in the Tioga-Nicetown section of North Philadelphia and lower Germantown. Now virtually all black, it was then predominantly white. Rizzo claims to have been the first Italian-American cop ever assigned there. He told us that he was quickly tested — not by residents but by a house sergeant in the 39th District police station, at Twenty-second Street and Hunting Park Avenue.

As Rizzo recounts the story, the sergeant kept riding him mercilessly and finally taunted him as "you dago bastard." Though outranked, the newcomer turned on his tormentor, threatening to "beat the shit" out of him. The sergeant backed down. The ethnic slurs stopped.

"He never called me that again," said Rizzo, "and I think he respected me more for what I done."

Shiny shoes. People who knew Frank Rizzo as a beginning cop on his way up have varied recollections. But they agree on this: Rizzo always looked as though he had just stepped from a police recruiting poster. He was meticulous about his appearance. And his shoes were always shined. "I used to go home at night and shine my shoes and press my own pants, polish my badge, shine my leather and generally work at keeping neat," Rizzo recalled.

"He was always so nice looking," said Mrs. Henry Katzmann, wife of Rizzo's first patrol-car partner. "Henry would come home and tell me about this rookie whose shoes shined like looking glass."

Another citizen impressed by Officer Rizzo's spit-and-polish was a Democratic state legislator named James H. J. Tate. Tate would later become mayor, make Rizzo police commissioner and then break with him amidst savage name-calling. Writing his memoirs in 1973, former Mayor Tate observed that although he had had only a "nodding acquaintance" with the young policeman he quickly recognized that Rizzo was "very popular" in his district. And Tate respected his "neat appearance and formidable attitude."

Six months after he joined the force, Patrolman Rizzo got his first press notice. It was modest enough, a one-paragraph item in the *Bulletin* on April 21, 1944:

Frank Rizzo, 1021 E. Mt. Pleasant av., a patrolman attached to the 22d st. and Hunting Park av. station, was burned on the hands last night when he tried to extinguish a fire in an awning on the drug store of I. M. Ostrum, at Tulpehocken and Baynton sts. He was treated at Germantown Hospital.

In 1974, we contacted I. M. Ostrum. He was sixty-nine years old and living in retirement in suburban Wyncote, Pennsylvania. He told us that he'd sold his drugstore in 1962 after operating it for twenty-three years. He remembered the 1944 awning fire. And he remembered Rizzo.

"We had those roll-up awnings with a fringe on the bottom," he said. "Somebody would flip a cigarette and the awning would catch fire. It happened more than once. In this case, Frank came and put out the fire. We tried to give him first aid and then sent him to the hospital.

"Frank lived in the district and his family were neighbors of ours. His father-in-law was a shoemaker there. His brother-in-law was a barber. Joe Silvestri. Joe's Barbershop, at 80th and Ogontz. I still frequent that barbershop. I understand Rizzo goes there every week. A fine, outstanding family. The highest caliber."

Ostrum couldn't say enough about Frank Rizzo.

"As far as I was concerned he was a terrific guy. He didn't look for trouble but didn't shy away from it. He was what I would call a real good policeman. Just don't get into a fight with him. He could certainly handle himself."

> "A (police)man who is unwilling to use force is viewed as a danger to everyone who works with him, and he cannot be allowed to persist in his ways . . . A policeman . . . does not condemn men for being afraid, but he does not want them around him when he is working. They are only a danger and a burden."
> — Jonathan Rubinstein, *City Police*

Retired Patrolman Henry Katzmann was seventy-three years old and working as a church sexton in Philadelphia in 1974 when Nancy Greenberg, a *Bulletin* reporter, interviewed him. He contrasted his own attitude toward police work with that of his young patrol partner in the 1940s.

"I never went past patrolman — never took the tests — but that's not the real difference. It all has to do with fear. I felt fear, I'd been picturing my wife and kids without a husband and father, and all Frank was thinking of was getting the crooks. . . .

"I liked the [patrol] car, it made the time pass fast — but that young fellow, he was more your action type. He had to be out with the people. You knew he'd be something. It was in the cards. . . .

"They print stories about him beating people up, there's a story about him blinding a guy with his fist. Well, he'd give anybody a break unless he was jumped. He hated intoxicated types and you knew the drunk was headed for Temple Hospital if he laid a finger on Frank.

"You know he didn't really mind coloreds, just drunks. I can say one thing in his favor — he *never* used a blackjack. Then he rarely used his fists, either. Always the club, and you had to jump him from behind to get it — or resist arrest . . .

"You want to know about Frank. Well, I'll tell you one thing he always told me — this will be a surprise. He said he'd never go anywhere if he listened to his father. His father . . . always told Frank to be careful about sticking his neck out, to take it easy. He stuck his neck out whenever he could but it would bother him that he wasn't listening to his father, you could tell."

The 39th Police District, to which Rizzo was first assigned, included a tough Irish neighborhood that was known as Swampoodle because a creek ran through it. Swampoodle was filled with cop-haters. One of its best-known citizens was said to have beaten a policeman to death with a wagon spoke.

One winter night Rizzo collared two armed men running from a store in Swampoodle after a holdup. He was taking them to a police call box when a Republican committeeman identified the suspects as constituents of his and demanded that Rizzo release them or risk finding himself pounding a beat in Siberia. With that, Rizzo threw the GOP functionary into the wagon with the two crooks. Next to show up was the Republican ward leader, who happened to be Rizzo's political sponsor, Carl Myers. Myers had no more luck than the committeeman, though, in getting the cop to relent. For protesting too loudly, he also went into the van.

When word of what Rizzo had done filtered downtown, all hell broke loose. The police brass was furious. The old-pol cops, products of the Republican machine, expected the rookie to get his comeuppance. At a hearing the next day, the holdup men were held for court and the committeeman was fined. Rizzo's superiors arranged for the ward boss's release. And they transferred Rizzo to the desolate west end of the district, where his chief job was to patrol three cemeteries.

Not for long, however. Businessmen in the other end of the district "began to wonder where he was, and when they found out, they demanded and got his return."

Rizzo told this story to Joseph P. Barrett, a reporter who grew up in Swampoodle, and Barrett published it.* He omitted Carl Myers's name but the reference was clear. However, Myers, before he died, told us that the colorful anecdote was a piece of fiction and a "damn lie." He said that he rarely went down to Swampoodle, never interfered with Officer Rizzo's arresting anyone and never was put in a police wagon. But Rizzo sticks to Barrett's account and says that for defying Myers and Republican committeeman Maurice (Dippy) Devlin, he was briefly banished to the graveyards.

At a Democratic fund-raising dinner in 1972, Mayor Frank Rizzo was overheard drinking and joking with a convicted gambler named Gilbert Croce. The eavesdropper was an undercover agent for the Pennsylvania Crime Commission. Reporting on "widespread, systematic" police corruption in Philadelphia, the crime commission later cited the incident as evidence that Rizzo wouldn't get rid of the bad apples.

Thinking that Croce might be a Mafioso soldier, reporters dug into the story which had gotten national press coverage and made page one of the New York *Times*. They discovered that Croce was a fifty-four-year-old Negro with heart disease, who was better known as Mike Todd. He'd gotten to know Rizzo in the 1940s, Todd said, when the future mayor was walking a beat in the 39th District and Todd was a grocer at Seventeenth Street and Pulaski Avenue in the Nicetown section. They became friends and Todd sometimes accompanied Rizzo on his four-to-midnight patrol. Rizzo, he said, was "something special."

"You could tell it by the way he shined his shoes, his belt, by the way he walked."†

At Christmastime during Rizzo's first year in the district, a North Philadelphia numbers banker routinely distributed "envelopes" to police, Todd said. He said the money was passed in a Laundromat down the street from his grocery. The numbers banker tried to give

* In *Philadelphia* magazine, March 1970.
† Adrian Lee, Philadelphia *Bulletin* columnist, interviewed Todd at his bedside in Temple University Hospital.

an envelope to Rizzo but the big rookie cop rebuffed him, saying, as Todd recalled the scene· "Not for me, you ain't! I don't want your money. And if I catch you or any of your people writing numbers, I'll lock you up."

Ever since then, said Todd, he had respected Frank Rizzo "like no other man I know." After his grocery went sour, though, Mike Todd himself began writing numbers. He took "a couple of pinches" but remained friendly with Rizzo. Whenever they met the policeman would say, "Stay straight, Mike, you're my friend."

Frank Rizzo, the honest cop. The scourge of Swampoodle and the sworn foe of crooks. Rizzo rejecting graft. "I don't want your money. And if I catch you . . . I'll lock you up." A star is born and a legend grows. There was a later legend — one built on rumor and innuendo — that Rizzo was always quietly on the take. That he, too, accepted "steady notes" — regular graft. Rumors but no proof. Whispers but no charges. In Rizzo's case, you're either a true believer or a nonbeliever. No middle ground. And Mike Todd's a true believer.

Late at night on February 27, 1948, Lou Yollin, a Yellow Cab driver, stopped for a fare at Broad Street and Erie Avenue, where Patrolman Frank Rizzo was on duty. Five men shouldered Yollin's fare aside and pushed their way into his cab. When Yollin shouted a protest the five began beating him. Yollin yelled for help. According to a brief newspaper account, "Rizzo saw the fight and pitched in."

In a bloody seven-man battle, Rizzo subdued two suspects. He and his prisoners were treated for cuts at Temple University Hospital. In the accident ward, one of the two reportedly threatened to kill Rizzo.

We got in touch with Lou Yollin. He remembered the incident. "I was driving the night shift, seven to three," he said. "I was waiting for a fare when these five jumped in. One of them put a gun to my back. I jumped out of the cab and yelled, 'Frank!' He was across the street. Everybody knew Frank then. He came running and we both fought 'em."

By 1950, Rizzo had won a name for himself as a big, tough, well-groomed patrolman who seemed to know what he was doing on the street at Broad and Erie. Down at City Hall, Samuel H. Rosenberg, the new public safety director, had an eye out for promising talent. He needed reliable men because his force was in disarray. The U.S.

Senate rackets investigating committee, headed by Senator Estes Kefauver, had concluded earlier that year that Philadelphia police were taking $152,000 a year in graft.

Seeking to end the crime wave within the police force, Rosenberg transferred his second-in-command to the "pawn shop division," relieved three police inspectors as untrustworthy, sidelined two vice squad officers and assigned another high-ranking officer to the motor harbor patrol.

On October 17, 1950, Police Inspector Craig D. Ellis, head of the vice squad, drove to a lonely country road outside the city, scrambled up an embankment and fired a fatal shot into his head with a service revolver just a few hours before his scheduled appearance before a federal grand jury probing police corruption. Two other police officers committed suicide. Three city officials did. Reports of Republican high crimes and misdemeanors made sensational campaign material for Philadelphia Democrats who were preparing to dislodge the long-entrenched GOP in 1951.

But that was a year away. In the meantime, honest, earnest Sammy Rosenberg had a job to do as public safety director. None of the scandals had touched him personally but he would be rated on his ability to clean up the police bureau. What he needed most were competent subordinates.

"I was looking for talent that I could have confidence in," recalled Rosenberg. He lived in Mt. Airy and was driven to work each day past Broad and Erie — Rizzo's corner. Rosenberg didn't know the patrolman but was struck by his "spick-and-span" appearance and his bearing. Rosenberg asked his driver, David Carr, who the officer was. Carr told him. Rosenberg had met Ralph Rizzo casually. "A mild man, not nearly Rizzo's size," he remembered.

Rosenberg checked Frank Rizzo's record at the 39th District and found it was exemplary. Not wanting to wait for Rizzo to take an examination, he promoted the patrolman to acting sergeant, gave him a raise to $3,800 a year and assigned him to a trouble spot in South Philadelphia. Rizzo had waited seven years for his sergeant's stripes but that was a short time by police standards. And, anyway, he was just starting.

Philadelphia's police department, like most large urban crime-fighting forces, divides itself into paramilitary units covering the city twenty-four hours a day. Each of nine police divisions has its own radio band. Each of twenty-two police districts has its own patrol cars and a complement of about two hundred armed men who enforce the law within its boundaries.

In each police district, the basic operating unit is the squad. Every day three squads work different eight-hour shifts while the fourth is off. They rotate shifts every week. Squad members work six consecutive days, then get two days off.

Philadelphia police squads now are headed by lieutenants. In 1950, sergeants ran them. Acting Sergeant Rizzo was given command of a squad at the 33d District, Seventh and Carpenter streets, a mile from the house on South Rosewood Street where he'd grown up. His father worked out of the same station house.

Rosenberg, who was a lawyer and had been secretary to two mayors, warned Rizzo of a sticky political situation in the 33d. Its Republican ward bosses were linked to rackets men, who were linked to the district cops.

Rizzo said Rosenberg told him: "I want you to clean it up. You won't get any interference and you'll get a free hand. Nobody will bother you. I just want it cleaned up."

"Well, brother, I went down there to the Thirty-third and I wrecked them," Rizzo relates with characteristic braggadocio. "The Republican ward leaders came running to my father and told him, 'We'll deal with your son when we get reelected. We'll take care of him.' But that didn't bother me.

"The next thing I knew I was told to take the examination for sergeant, and I came out number one on the list. I think maybe Judge Rosenberg marked my paper. Later, I got a call to come to Rosenberg's office and he swore me in as sergeant. Then he threw away the list. I was the only one appointed. I didn't have any politicians going for me, just Sam Rosenberg. I was sent back to the Thirty-third and wound up having my father in my squad."

Most of the time, Patrolman Ralph Rizzo put up silently with his sergeant son's bulldozer tactics. At rollcall one night, though, he spoke up. It was a scene that those who observed it will never forget. Right there in the rollroom before all the other cops the father admonished his son for being so aggressive, so forceful. His advice was: "Go easy."

What Frank Rizzo thought at that moment will never be known. What is known is that he paid his father no heed. And his patron praised him.

"Rizzo went down [to the 33d District] and did a bang-up job," Rosenberg told us recently. He was then secretary to Philadelphia's common pleas court board of judges. Some of the ward leaders in South Philadelphia thought Sergeant Rizzo was being "too tough," recalled Rosenberg, and there were "repercussions."

"That didn't change my position," he said. "I found Rizzo an aggressive person and if given a job he'd do it."

George Kronbar, police inspector in the South division at the time of Sergeant Rizzo's assignment there, was a soft-spoken honest cop widely respected both inside and outside the department. Rosenberg, in closed-door testimony before the Kefauver anti-rackets committee, had named Kronbar as one of two inspectors in whom he had "complete confidence."

As Rizzo advanced up the police ladder, Kronbar would come to detest his loud mouth and his habit of turning against those officers who had helped him get ahead. At this early point in Rizzo's career, however, Kronbar thought highly of him.

"I had a helluva job in South Philadelphia," Kronbar told us before his death in May 1974. "There was damn little law enforcement down there. But I got a free hand from Rosenberg and I appreciated any support I received from subordinates. I was impressed with Rizzo as a sergeant and later as a captain. He was doing a good job."

There is evidence, too, that despite their personality differences, Ralph Rizzo was proud of his son and grateful to Rosenberg for recognizing his potential.

"Not long after I'd sworn in Frank as a sergeant," Rosenberg told us, "the doorbell rang one day at my home in Mt. Airy. It was Ralph Rizzo. He lived not far from me and he kept a small vegetable garden. As I opened the door, I could see that he'd brought some vegetables in a shopping cart, the kind you get in a grocery. There were tomatoes, string beans, lettuce, you know, what you find in a backyard garden. He said he wanted to show his appreciation for what I had done for his son, and he asked if I wouldn't accept the vegetables that he had grown.

"I did accept them," Sam Rosenberg said, "and I can tell you I was deeply touched."

In the fall of 1951, the Democrats did it. They ended sixty-seven unbroken years of Republican rule by electing liberals Joseph S. Clark as mayor and Richardson Dilworth as district attorney. As part of the shakeup, police and fire commissioners were appointed to run the two departments, which had been administered by the public safety director. Sam Rosenberg's post was abolished.

The first police commissioner, an honest career man named Thomas J. Gibbons, made George Kronbar chief inspector of all uniformed forces. Gibbons consulted with Kronbar in finding temporary replacements for seven incompetent or crooked police captains who enjoyed Civil Service protection and hence couldn't be fired without prolonged departmental hearings.

Kronbar recommended Sergeant Frank Rizzo for one of the temporary appointments. On January 16, 1952, Rizzo got his acting captaincy. It was a big break. And it came in the administration of two reformers, Joe Clark and Dick Dilworth, who would later denounce Rizzo in the strongest possible terms as a Hitler, a demagogue and, in Clark's words, "a stupid, arrogant son-of-a-bitch."

Commissioner Gibbons assigned Acting Captain Rizzo to West Philadelphia. The assignment gave Rizzo exposure to people he didn't know very well: black people. He'd grown up in a white section, and during his first nine years as a policeman he'd enforced the law in predominantly white neighborhoods. As head of the 16th Police District, at Thirty-ninth Street and Lancaster Avenue, he began dealing with Negroes on a daily basis.

Seeking to stop gambling, whoring and bootlegging, he led raids against black after-hours clubs, stores and even private homes, where he hunted untaxed booze. These forays soon attracted press attention. On March 26, 1952, the late Frank Brookhouser, then an *Inquirer* columnist, reported a flood of civil-rights protests against Rizzo's raiders. Rizzo himself was said to have traded insults with Negroes in language they understood. The complaints by West Philadelphians, Brookhouser wrote, had "reached the point where the DA's office just doesn't know what to do with them." The DA was Dilworth and at that point he did nothing.

Living in Rizzo's West Philadelphia police district then were a number of black lawyers and professional men with political ambitions. They had formed a group called YIPAC (Young Independent Political Action Committee), and it was this organization that filed many of the complaints against Rizzo. Harvey N. Schmidt, who later became a common pleas court judge, lived just a block and a half from Rizzo's police station. He belonged to YIPAC along with Cecil B. Moore, a lawyer who later became a city councilman (and a sworn foe of Rizzo); Lynwood F. Blount, who later became a judge; beer distributor Earl Vann, who later became a city councilman (and a Rizzo partisan), and newspaper editor John A. Saunders, among others.

"The reports we kept getting," said Schmidt, recalling the events of 1952, "was that Rizzo was using strong-arm tactics, that he was breaking doors down and being extra tough because ours was a black neighborhood."

A delegation from YIPAC took the complaints to Police Commissioner Gibbons. He suggested they talk directly to Rizzo. "When we went to Rizzo," said Schmidt, "he was responsive. We could talk to him. He agreeably talked to us. We let him know we'd be watching."

By the time Rizzo left West Philadelphia early in May, 1952, most of YIPAC's members had changed their minds about him. "Overall, we believed he did a good job," said Schmidt. "When he left we felt we were living in a better policed district. We sent a letter to Gibbons praising Rizzo's work."

Saunders's recollections are similar. Former city editor of the Pittsburgh *Courier*, he later became managing editor of the semi-weekly, black-owned Philadelphia *Tribune*. "Complaints seemed to follow Rizzo," Saunders said, "but not many of them could be substantiated. He always treated us graciously and then knocked us down with evidence. We'd make a complaint and he'd take us to the back of the station house and show us the gallon jugs of bad whiskey confiscated from Negro homes. I can tell you, if I needed a policeman, he's the one I'd want coming to save me."

Late in April 1952, Commissioner Gibbons conferred with Inspector Kronbar over command of a key police district: center city. The captain of this district was being transferred out. Gibbons needed a replacement. Kronbar suggested Acting Captain Rizzo and Gibbons just as promptly made the appointment.

The first week in May Rizzo moved his gear into the captain's office of the old 19th District station house, now gone, at Twelfth and Pine streets, in the heart of Philadelphia's entertainment section. This was to be his base of operations for the next six years and ten months. His West Philly raids had won him a nickname as the "Cisco Kid." Now he proceeded to build on that notoriety.

Less than a week after his transfer, Rizzo raided the Top Hat Cafe in the Locust Street strip of girlie shows and clip joints, arresting the owner, two bartenders, a waitress and nine patrons for disorderly conduct.

At a hearing, David Kanner, attorney for the defendants, told the magistrate: "I'm concerned if there is any violation of constitutional rights here. This man led a reign of terror in West Philadelphia."

"Don't you get involved with me," Rizzo shot back, "or you'll be worrying about your own rights."

Rizzo accused one of the Top Hat's customers of ripping his suit. It was a seventy-dollar suit, he said, and he'd only worn it once before. When the customer offered to pay $10 to have the coat fixed, Rizzo agreed to his discharge. The other defendants also were released.

Kanner, recently recalling the case, said of Rizzo: "I didn't take any stuff from him. He wasn't going to 'Cisco Kid' me. He was a tough cop. When they saw him walk by they really moved. I was a tough kid then myself. If I was right I wasn't afraid of anybody. The only thing I ever gave a cop was a hard time.

"Rizzo was so eager to enforce the law that he overstepped the bounds somewhat. But he was a good cop. He looked after his men."

In June, 1952, Frank Brookhouser reported that Rizzo's continuing raids on nightspots had "the town in an uproar." In one swoop on a small hotel, wrote Brookhouser, half a dozen couples were hauled into Twelfth and Pine but were later released without being accused of anything. It appeared to be a case of shoddy police work or a deliberate attempt to frighten people.

Rizzo then announced a drive to rid central Philadelphia of racketeers. He began with the arrest of two men as common gamblers. He threatened to lock up Frank (Blinky) Palermo, a boxing rackets figure, if Palermo didn't quit loitering downtown. Palermo and his lawyer, Joseph Sharfsin, complained to Gibbons. The commissioner backed up his captain.

But while Rizzo was keeping an eye on racketeers District Attorney Dilworth was keeping an eye on Rizzo. Like a lot of other Philadelphians, Dilworth never trusted Rizzo. Before his death in 1974, Dilworth, who succeeded Clark as mayor and later headed the Philadelphia Board of Education, discussed his years as DA in a long tape-recorded interview. He gave us this evaluation of Captain Rizzo:

"He was a very well-organized man. He knew every area of the city. He knew who was in every area. He knew the racketeers and all that. But we were also firmly convinced that he followed what the old-time inspectors had done. He would say to one group, 'You people can operate but you've got to turn everybody else in to me. And if you get out of line, if you start any violence, I'll chop your balls off.'

"As a result, it was always fairly orderly in his districts, but there was also quite a lot of corruption. And we were certain that he was involved in the corruption. We knew that he had meetings, on Wednesday mornings I think it was, over [ex-boxer] Lew Tendler's restaurant (on South Broad Street), and the worst-looking gangsters, numbers bankers and all would come in and then go out.

"Now he claimed that he had to have those meetings to keep them in order. We were convinced that these were corrupt meetings. But we were never able to prove it. We tried to bug the place but he was too smart for us there. He uncovered the bugs."

At 2:30 A.M. on January 14, 1953, Acting Captain Rizzo was driving home from work after a long shift at Twelfth and Pine. A citywide transit strike had begun at midnight. Rizzo, though off duty, was on the lookout for strike-related violence. Passing Germantown and Chelten avenues in the Germantown business district, he saw a "highway disturbance."

"I saw a group of men kicking at a man who was on the ground," Rizzo later testified.

The man on the ground was Thomas V. Cassidy, twenty-five, a striking streetcar motorman. Although Rizzo didn't know it, Cassidy was near death, the victim of a random street brawl.

The fight had boiled up without warning just a few minutes earlier. Cassidy, after voting at a tumultuous meeting of the Transport Workers Union, AFL-CIO, to shut down the Philadelphia Transportation Company, had caught the last trolley home to Germantown.

With a fellow motorman named James Loftus, he had had "a few beers" and was standing on the corner when two cars carrying half a dozen young men stopped for a red light. The six had just left a party for an Army-bound friend. They had been drinking, too.

Germantown, now predominantly black, was then heavily Irish and Italian, and fights were not uncommon. In this instance, the Irish-Americans on the sidewalk and the Italian-Americans in the automobiles exchanged insults. As the cursing continued, the motorists piled out of their cars. Both sides started throwing punches. In a flurry of blows, Cassidy, a rugged hundred-ninety-five-pounder who had driven a tank in Germany in World War II, fell. Then Rizzo drove up.

Another cop might have continued on his way. Jesus Christ, 2:30 in the goddamn morning in the goddamn middle of January. The car was snug and warm but it was cold as hell out there. He was off duty. Outnumbered, too. And out of his district. Why worry about a bunch of blipping punks? Why get involved? If they felt like fighting, let 'em fight. He was late getting home already.

Rizzo never hesitated. He was never one to mediate delicate situations when his fists or a club would do. He relished direct action. In certain circumstances, such instinctive, almost mindless, intervention could be disastrous. On January 14, 1953, it almost certainly saved a man's life.

"I left my car with my police club and went toward the crowd," Rizzo testified at the subsequent trial of Cassidy's attackers. "It was a general melee. Everybody was throwing punches."

With club in hand, Rizzo managed to protect the fallen man from further blows. He grabbed two suspects, but a third snatched his club. With that, the policeman drew his service revolver, retrieved his club and "ordered the three of them to stand against a wall."

When help arrived, Cassidy was rushed unconscious to a hospital for emergency brain surgery. His skull was fractured and he had a three-inch cut over his right eye. The right side of his body was in a "state of contraction." The examining physician reported having difficulty moving Cassidy's stiffened right arm and leg.

Rizzo took his prisoners to the station house. According to later testimony, he struck one of the men eight or ten times across the face "for nothing."

As Cassidy's wife, Eileen, rushed to the hospital, his older brother, John, went to the police station. He told us that when he walked in Captain Rizzo was discussing the incident with a Democratic committeeman, who had been summoned by the family of one of those under arrest. From snatches of conversation that he overheard, John Cassidy concluded that the committeeman, an Italian-American, known as "Black Mike," asked Rizzo to go easy on the suspects. He cited their common Italian ancestry.

According to eavesdropper John Cassidy, Rizzo flatly refused. Cassidy said he will never forget the words that the cop spoke to the committeeman: "I know they're our kind. I'm ashamed they're our kind. They're going to jail or I'll turn in my badge."

Tom Cassidy remained in a coma for thirteen weeks and he was hospitalized for seven months. In June 1953, he was released from a veterans' hospital long enough to testify at the trial of the three men accused of nearly killing him. His right arm was in a brace. He dragged his left leg as he walked slowly to the witness stand in Philadelphia's quarter sessions court. His testimony proved to be of little value because he could barely remember anything that happened that night. The beating had robbed him of his memory.

John Patrick Walsh, one of the city's top criminal lawyers, represented the defendants. When Rizzo took the stand, Walsh sought vainly to shake his story. "Rizzo was a good witness," Stanley L. Kubacki, the prosecutor, told us. Kubacki, now a judge, said that Walsh, in trying to discredit Rizzo's testimony, made "scathing derogatory references" to him as the "Cisco Kid."

After a five-day trial, the defendants were convicted of what Kubacki, in his final plea, termed a "savage, cruel and utterly depraved" beating. The sentences were imposed later by Judge Peter A. Hagan. Two defendants got six-to-twenty-four-months each in county prison. The third, a youth of nineteen, was sent to an industrial school for juveniles for an indefinite term not to exceed three years.

The case was soon forgotten and Thomas V. Cassidy dropped out of sight. Recently, we looked him up. He was a maintenance man in a Pennsylvania Bell Telephone Company branch office in Germantown, no more than fifty yards from the fight scene. He still walked with a limp and his right arm had remained partially paralyzed. He was still bothered by faulty vision.

Life had been hard. The savings that Cassidy and his wife had put aside as down payment on a house paid for his long hospitalization. The "trolley company" refused to rehire him. He could qualify only for marginal work as a "glorified janitor" with the telephone company. His pretty wife later divorced him to marry a man who could earn more money, Cassidy said, and he didn't blame her. He found another wife but his second marriage failed, too. When we met he was living in a trailer camp about twenty-five miles outside Philadelphia.

Cassidy had adjusted to his bad luck, however. He had plenty to complain about but wasn't complaining. "I can't write or climb a ladder or do much of anything," he said, "but I'm content. I have to be. I wasn't supposed to ever walk or talk again. I was supposed to be a vegetable."

Five minutes more on the ground that winter night in 1953 and Cassidy would have died, his doctors told him. That's why he's still such an admirer of the burly, controversial cop who rescued him.

"If anybody ever says anything bad about Rizzo," Tom Cassidy said, "I always stick up for him. He saved my life."

On March 8, 1954, Frank Rizzo, having finished in the top twenty among eighty-six officers who took the required Civil Service exam, was sworn in as a police captain. He was thirty-three years old and he had been on the force for ten and a half years. Philadelphia police captains then started at $5,652 a year and reached a maximum of $6,480. Rizzo and his wife had paid off the $5,000 mortgage on their house at Morton Street and Washington Lane, Germantown, and had moved up to a larger house at 8224 Provident Road in middle-class West Oak Lane. Rizzo continued to work out of Twelfth and Pine.

While the General in the White House spoke softly in the lackluster 1950s, the street cop from South Philly swung a big stick. Little by little, Police Captain Frank Rizzo became the enforcer of public morals in one of the nation's cultural centers. He waged war on those whose standards of behavior, even appearance, differed from his own.

Late in April 1954, Rizzo raided three nightclubs in a crackdown on girlie shows. His men arrested seven entertainers, two taproom owners and a bar manager on morals charges. Magistrate Amos Harris freed them all. He said Rizzo had not proved that the shows were obscene.

"I've seen worse on television, in magazines and on the newsstands," the magistrate said. He and Rizzo got into a hot argument. Harris emphasized that he was "the law in the court." Rizzo bellowed a warning to the defendants: "Keep your lawyers!" He promised to repeat the raids.

After a raid at Lou's Moravian Bar, at 1507 Moravian Street, the following month, Sidney Mass, son of the owner, pointed a quivering finger at Rizzo and screamed: "This man is the Nero of the Nightclub Belt!" Rizzo: "You're running a dive — the worst I've ever seen in the center city area." Asked why two dancers had been arrested for public indecency and "obscene exhibit," the self-appointed censor replied: "It wasn't their lack of clothing we minded so much; it was their gyrations."

One night Rizzo, in civilian clothes, drew $20 from the police department expense account and went alone to a bar where he suspected girls were hustling drinkers. He put a ten-dollar bill and two fives on the bar and ordered a whiskey and chaser. Two young things took barstools on either side of him. Each was served by the bartender, who collected from Rizzo. When one girl left, another immediately took her place. More drinks were served and paid for from public tax money. In twenty minutes, according to Rizzo, his $20 was gone and he still hadn't finished his drink. He called the cops but the case was dismissed. The bar girls had made a monkey out of the Cisco Kid.

Early in 1954 a new stripper came to town. Her name was Blaze Starr but on the burlesque circuit she was also known as "Miss Spontaneous Combustion." She was a twenty-one-year-old West Virginia farm girl whose grandpa in Twelve Pole Creek had six toes on each foot, she said, and made the "best goddamn moonshine" in Mingo County. With raven dark hair, flashing eyes and generous physical endowments — she wore a size 38 bra at the age of sixteen — Blaze Starr soon began packing customers into night-clubs in Rizzo's district.

Her show-stopping act featured a big cat that removed the strip-per's clothes by finding small pieces of meat hidden in them. She first used a young male leopard. After it died in an off-stage mishap she sent away for a mail-order Asiatic black panther, "a mean little devil, constantly clawing, growling and screaming." The panther wandered off after a burglary at Blaze Starr's apartment, but she got it back in a couple of days, and her show went on.

In May, 1954, she was arrested for staging what detectives termed an "obscene exhibition" at Steve Brodie's Show-Bar. Next day the charges were dropped and Blaze Starr danced for forty more weeks without police interference. Then on February 8, 1955, she was seized with two others at the Black Cat Cafe, 254 South Fifteenth Street. Police described their dancing as "lewd and ob-scene" while Blaze Starr termed it "interpretive." Magistrate Sam-uel Clark, Jr., released the dancers to give himself time to decide "what constitutes morality in the case." He later threw out the charges.

Blaze Starr left town soon after that and wasn't heard from again until publication of her autobiography in 1974. In it, she alleged that Rizzo had had her arrested at the Black Cat for putting on a "filthy, dirty, obscene and rude" performance. Three weeks later, though, he took her into custody while she was on stage, drove her around town and urged her to quit stripping, the dancer said of the policeman. Her account continued:

He pulled the car over to the curb. I sat there quietly while he checked in with the police station. When he hung up the microphone, he glanced over and smiled. I sensed what he was after.

"You want to come up to my room?" I made it a question.

"Yeah. Where are you staying?"

"The Rio Hotel on Locust Street."

The author said Rizzo replied: "I can't come there. That's where all the strippers stay and I might be recognized. But I do have a friend who has an apartment nearby. I'll meet you."

She said she agreed. In her book, Miss Starr does not tell what happened next. However, her publisher, Praeger Publishers, hired a professional polygraph examiner to check out her story. The polygrapher, Rudolph Caputo, Jr., of New York, told a *Bulletin* reporter, Lou Antosh, that in administering the lie detector test, he asked the stripper: "Did you have sexual relations with Frank Rizzo in that apartment?" She said yes, and the test results indicated that she was telling the truth, Caputo told Antosh. Praeger said Miss Starr passed the test "with flying colors." When Philadelphia newspapers picked up the story in 1974, Mayor Rizzo issued a one-sentence reply through his deputy: "I will not dignify these outrageous charges by a response."

There are two ironies here. One is that while Rizzo appeared to be insulted by Blaze Starr's "outrageous charges," her account merely tended to confirm what he has been saying privately about himself all these years: namely, that he is quite a Don Juan. With chums who share his male talk and barracks humor, Rizzo brags frequently of his bedroom conquests.

The other irony goes to Rizzo's credibility. After Blaze Starr's story came out Philadelphia's mayor was hardly in a position to call the erstwhile "Panther Girl" a liar. After all, she passed her lie detector test. He flunked his.

On leaving Philadelphia's police training academy, each rookie is issued a .32-caliber revolver with twelve lead bullets. He must carry his gun when on duty but has the option of lugging it or leaving it home when not working. The lead bullets flatten and fall when they hit a solid object, thus reducing the risk of ricochet. In an average year more than thirty persons are killed by Philadelphia police bullets. Sometimes the cops themselves are victims of accidental police shootings.

All rookies are also issued nightsticks. These clubs are among the oldest of police weapons. The twenty-inch-long Philadelphia model is made of hardwood. It is held by a leather thong. If applied to the head, heart, throat or groin, the nightstick can be lethal. Few high-ranking police officers carry clubs. Rizzo was an exception. Never was his combat readiness better illustrated than by the widely published photo of the commissioner at a fancy-dress civic function with his nightstick protruding from his tuxedo trousers. The picture shocked his critics, but no matter. His club was Rizzo's security blanket.

Philadelphia does not issue blackjacks to its policemen but they are permitted to purchase them, and many do. The blackjack, or jack, is a round or flat piece of lead encased in leather. A flat-headed jack fits easily into a policeman's back pocket.

Even now, one hears stories that Captain Frank Rizzo chased around town with two pearl-handled revolvers in the 1950s, terrorizing outlaws like a frontier marshal in Dodge City. As far as we can determine, Rizzo never owned a pearl-handled gun and never fired the service revolver that he did carry. What he did use, often with fearsome effect, was his nightstick. And, occasionally, his jack. Henry Katzmann said that Patrolman Rizzo never used a jack. Maybe not. But Captain Rizzo did. The jack and the club.

Late one night in August 1955, Captain Rizzo spotted a car speeding through the nightclub district. He said later that its occupants were shouting insults at women pedestrians and their escorts. Rizzo and Patrolman Herman Levin hailed a taxi and caught up to the car. Inside were six Navy enlisted men serving as medical orderlies at the Philadelphia Naval Hospital.

Rizzo got out of the cab, identified himself and told the Navy corpsmen they were under arrest. He later testified that one replied: "You can't touch us. We're government property." A fight ensued. Rizzo alleged that the sailors began pushing him around. He admitted resorting to "some force" to subdue them. He took them back to Twelfth and Pine, where a magistrate fined the six $10 each and court costs on charges of intoxication, disorderly conduct and resisting arrest. As far as Rizzo was concerned, that ended the matter.

But the Navy personnel wouldn't let it go at that. They obtained warrants accusing Rizzo and a turnkey named Robert O'Brien of police brutality. The result was a full-dress magistrate's hearing that lasted three hours and forty-five minutes. In their testimony, five corpsmen denied Rizzo's account. They said they had left a tap-room at Thirteenth and Locust streets and had driven just one block to Twelfth when Rizzo overtook them in a taxicab. One conceded that the sailors had been singing a song but he denied they were loud or abusive.

The driver, Corpsman George R. Bodin, Jr., then twenty-one, of Ferndale, Michigan, charged that without provocation Rizzo dragged him from the car and beat him viciously with a nightstick. He said the attacks continued in the station house. The other four sailors also testified that Rizzo punched and clubbed them and repeated the beatings at Twelfth and Pine. Corpsman Harry J. Nuel, then twenty-five, of Philadelphia, said that after being lined up with the others he was struck by Rizzo and then was "worked over with a rubber hose" by O'Brien in the cell block.

The Navy men all came from working-class white backgrounds. To counter their testimony, Rizzo and his lawyer, Pennsylvania State Representative Benjamin R. Donolow, produced nearly forty pro-police witnesses. Also representing Rizzo was a lawyer from the police union, the Fraternal Order of Police. After hearing conflicting testimony, the late Magistrate E. David Keiser dismissed the atrocious-assault charges against Rizzo and O'Brien. "Nothing can be gained by going into court with all this hysteria," he said. He urged Navy authorities to meet with city officials to iron out the problem, but no such meeting was ever held.

In 1974, we reached one of the former Navy corpsmen to get his view of the cop who later became mayor. He lived in nearby New Jersey. "I have no comment," he said and refused to discuss the incident. We contacted the father of another former corpsman in the Bronx. The father said his son had never told him of the case.

Former Philadelphia Police Commissioner Thomas J. Gibbons, who accepted service of the warrants naming Rizzo and O'Brien, remembers the incident vividly. In nine years as commissioner, from 1952 to 1961, Gibbons never spoke out publicly against Rizzo. But now, as a dog track security officer in Florida, he is well out of the reach of Frank Rizzo and he doesn't hesitate to say exactly what he thinks of Rizzo's police work.

"He beat those sailors for no reason," Gibbons told us. "He caused me nothing but trouble. His father was a better police officer than he'll ever be."

"He inspired fear. When he walked the street a whole wave of fear preceded him. All these little guys, small-time hoods, were scurrying up alleys when they saw him coming. He was a real fist-in-the-belly guy. A cold rage would come over him; he'd go almost blank and then, *bang*, in the gut . . . he had this whimsical way of just clobbering you."
— Anonymous citizen's description of Captain Frank Rizzo, as reported in *Philadelphia* magazine, July 1967

At 1:15 A.M. on May 27, 1956, a twenty-two-year-old South Philadelphian named Alexander J. Castelli parked his car at Thirteenth and Sansom streets. The space he chose was reserved for buses to pick up and discharge passengers. A Philadelphia Transportation Company tow truck had just removed one auto from the zone. A passerby who had seen what happened cautioned Castelli that if he didn't find another parking space his car might be taken away, too. Angry words were being tossed back and forth when Captain Frank Rizzo happened by in plain clothes.

He quickly intervened and, as a result, the shouting match escalated into a bloody fight. Both Castelli and Rizzo blamed the other for starting it. Castelli claimed that Rizzo failed to identify himself and appeared to be drawing a gun when he was in fact reaching for his badge. Rizzo said he identified himself promptly but that Castelli cursed him, struck him in the face, got out of the car and hit him again, ripping his topcoat. He said he had to use his blackjack to subdue the motorist.

Regardless of how the fight began, there is no denying that it was extraordinarily one-sided. Rizzo suffered only minor cuts and bruises. Castelli was blinded in the right eye by blows from Rizzo's blackjack. His jaw was broken. He was hospitalized for weeks.

When a policeman beats up a civilian, the victim is often charged with assaulting the cop. That is what happened in Castelli's case. A jury cleared him of assaulting Rizzo but found him guilty of resisting arrest and driving while drunk. Castelli's lawyer said he would file for a new trial but he never did. A year earlier, Castelli had been convicted of plotting to hijack a truckload of whiskey. His jail sentence was suspended. No charges were ever placed against Rizzo.

We reached an uncle of Castelli in 1975. He said his nephew had died several years earlier. He thought his death was from natural causes unrelated to the blinding by blackjack. One fact was clear, however: unlike Tom Cassidy, of Germantown, South Philly's Alexander J. Castelli had no reason to be grateful for Rizzo's swift intervention in a random sidewalk dispute.

> "The constant demand for vice arrests and the violations of the law that men must practice to get good arrests makes it nearly impossible for a [police officer] to prevent some of his men from indulging in practices that are blatantly criminal. . . . 'Farming,' the planting of evidence, is practiced throughout the department."
> — Jonathan Rubinstein, *City Police*

In April 1958, Rizzo's police arrested two men at a parking lot. The charge was "illegal lottery." The evidence consisted of three torn slips of paper with what the police said were nineteen numbers plays written on them. The incriminating papers had been found in a pile of wood. The case against the accused gamblers was so flimsy that the magistrate, the late M. Philip Freed, would normally have thrown it out. At the hearing in Rizzo's station house, however, Freed held both men in $300 bail for common pleas court. He announced loudly that he wanted a higher-level judge to "see what kind of a numbers arrest the police are making in a district which is in the heart of the gambling area."

At this, Rizzo came charging out of his office and confronted Freed on the bench.

"Your honor, I understand you've made some remarks about my men," he roared.

"If you have any complaint," Freed shot back, "take it up with the commissioner of police."

Rizzo (shouting): "You're a faker!"

Freed (shouting): "You're a faker!"

Rizzo: "You're a phony!"

Freed: "You're a phony!"

Rizzo, getting the last word: "You're a misfit!" Turning to the court stenographer, he ordered: "Put that in the records!"

Next day Rizzo conceded that his men sometimes made arrests without ample evidence just to keep numbers writers "on the move."

"It's done all over the city," he said of this illegal procedure. He described the previous day's defendants as the "kind we like to harass." The evidence was feeble, Rizzo conceded, and Freed knew it. "He did it [held the defendants] just to make us look bad," moaned the policeman.

Freed, one of the few magistrates with a law degree, did not just hold Rizzo up to ridicule. He also made an important point about law enforcement. The fact was that in all of Rizzo's years in the city's gambling and nightclub center he never made an important rackets arrest. Not one.

The nearest thing to a French-style salon in Philadelphia is Emlen Etting's pad on Panama Street. Etting is a wealthy artist. His wife, the former Gloria Braggiotti, is a writer and lecturer. They travel widely and entertain often. Andy Warhol has dined at the Ettings', as have Jacques Tati, Tennessee Williams, Maureen O'Hara, Peter Brooks. E. E. Cummings was there. So was Noel Coward. So, once, was King Umberto of Italy, while in exile in Portugal.

On a Friday night in October 1958, Etting gave a post-theater party for Josh Logan, the director, whose play, *The World of Suzie Wong*, had just opened in Philadelphia. Logan couldn't make it but the show's star, nineteen-year-old France Nuyen, was among twenty-five guests. Also there were members of the cast of another play, *A Handful of Fire*. An absentee was Mrs. Etting, then traveling in Europe.

Panama Street is only about a dozen feet wide. Many of its houses were reclaimed from deterioration in the 1920s and fixed up in fancy French, English and Italian decor. They're expensively furnished but small. Noise carries. A late-night party on Panama Street never goes unnoticed — especially by uninvited neighbors.

At 12:10 A.M. on the October night in question, two of Rizzo's cops rapped on Etting's door. They'd gotten a complaint about a noisy party. The two, whom Etting later described as "quite polite," asked him to "cut it down." They left. About ninety minutes later, following a second complaint, three police cars showed up.

"I answered the door to find the street full of police vehicles and the doorway full of police," Etting later reported. "Right there in front of my guests they told me I was under arrest." When he asked what the charges were, said Etting, the policeman replied: " 'You're running a disorderly house, and if you don't tell these people to go home, we're going to arrest all of you.' There was considerable yelling by then and the police were doing most of it. The whole thing was incredible."

Etting's noisy party moved to the nearby house of a friend. There were no arrests. Panama Street quieted down and the neighbors got some sleep. But Etting, who was then president of the Alliance Française in Philadelphia, had been humiliated before his guests by Rizzo's loutish underlings. The beastly policemen had not only ruined his party but they had threatened him with a ride in, as Etting put it, "a Black Maria, I think you call it." (Wrong: Philadelphia police emergency wagons were then red.)

Next day he protested to Mayor Dilworth, who had succeeded Joe Clark in 1956. Etting said the police were "loud, crude and behaved like Cossacks." He referred to the "Gestapo tactics of center-city police." Dilworth ordered an investigation by Police Commissioner Gibbons. Gibbons cleared the cops. "The officers behaved in gentlemanly fashion," he said, "and I can find no evidence to bear out the remarks attributed to them. Some people like parties; some people like to go to bed early. When you have both in the same neighborhood, you have complaints."

Although it fizzled out, Etting's beef got wide press coverage. The Associated Press sent the story of Rizzo's alleged "Cossacks" all over the nation. As time passed, word got around that it was Rizzo himself who pounded on Etting's door. Somebody even remembered the exact words he used. According to a "reliable report" published in *Philadelphia* magazine in 1967, the Cisco Kid had warned the artist-host: "Unless you and your goddamn pansy friends get back in the house, quiet down and shut up, I will put you all in the paddy wagon and throw you in with the drunks for the rest of the night."

Etting himself would now rather "forget the whole damn thing." And his wife, Gloria Braggiotti Etting, who missed all the excitement, says of Rizzo: "I admire him. I like his honesty. I think he's a strong person and whether there's a small matter or a big one he'll be in the middle of it."

In 1959, Philadelphia shook to the tramp of police boots in coffeehouses. That's right, coffeehouses. Captain Frank Rizzo led the raids. Frank Rizzo, the city's (nation's?) toughest cop, locking up kids for playing chess. Or listening to hi-fi music. Or drinking Italian coffee. Or talking. As far as we can determine, that's all the kids were doing in Philadelphia's coffeehouses in those days. No evidence of hard drugs. No booze. No swearing. Certainly no guns or knives. No secret conspiracy to undermine the republic or bomb Twelfth and Pine.

Just kids sitting around quite late at night in company of their own choosing. White kids mostly but some black kids, too. Bearded youths. Long-haired fellows. And quite late at night. That's an important point. Just as Emlen Etting's neighbors objected to his late-night parties, some of the coffeehouses' neighbors opposed their carryings-on. The raids were defended by the liberal administration of Mayor Richardson Dilworth (who personally detested Rizzo). And the police captain won a promotion to inspector.

America was obviously not the same place in 1959 that it became in the 1970s. Back in those days judges still thought they could define obscenity. Books were banned. Movies were censored. Occasionally, a publisher was jailed. And in April 1964, more than five years after Rizzo's coffeehouse raids, Lenny Bruce, the entertainer, was arrested in New York's Greenwich Village for a performance that the prosecutor labeled "obscene, indecent, immoral." Lenny Bruce seized in Manhattan. Convicted. Given a four-month jail sentence. And his prosecutor, Richard H. Kuh, later became New York's district attorney.

Even so, Rizzo's raids on the coffeehouses were something special. Philadelphia had never before been treated — if that is the word — to such a spectacle. Few, if any, other cities had. Coffeehouses are, after all, among the most civilized of human institutions. There were coffeehouses in Europe in the sixteenth century. London coffeehouses attracted literary lions of the eighteenth century. Viennese coffeehouses have long been known for the quality of their conversation and their coffee. New York's long list of coffeehouses included one opened by the children of its quondam police commissioner, Theodore Roosevelt.

Philadelphia's coffeehouses perked up in the mid-1950s. They differed from the great and storied European coffeehouses in that their proprietors were, for the most part, young people with other jobs. Their customers were mostly students. College students. Art students. Some older high school students. This was a time between two wars — Korea and Vietnam. There was a draft but nobody worried much about it. Students were said to be apathetic. They weren't really. They just didn't have as many obvious things to hate as did the later Kent State–My Lai–Watergate generation. They weren't hooked on hard drugs. Marijuana was coming into widespread use. What turned on many students then was the espresso machine. That and the chessboard and the hi-fi.

Early in 1958, Melvin Haifetz, an army veteran just returned from Europe, began frequenting Philadelphia's coffeehouses while

84

attending classes at Temple University. He didn't drink coffee but liked the places' atmosphere and thought he might want to try running one. When the Humoresque Coffee Shop at 2036 Sansom Street went up for sale that May, Haifetz, who was young (twenty-two years old), impressionable and, as he now says, "somewhat naive," borrowed from his mother and bought the business for $1,500.

The Humoresque, with capacity for about forty persons on one floor, had been grossing only $10 or $12 a night. Haifetz set about fixing it up to his taste. To dim the lights he placed sheets of tin over the fluorescent fixtures. On a bulletin board he posted poems written by patrons on notepaper and napkins. He began exhibiting art work of the coffee drinkers. Light classical and semiclassical music came from a hi-fi in a closet. On the closet door were painted wisecracks about the scratchiest records in town.

A one-lung espresso machine that Haifetz picked up somewhere for $200 made the coffee. It was no match for the triple-barreled jobs costing $1,200 in other shops, but Haifetz got by. He ran his place all by himself. He bought pastry at a nearby shop for a quarter a piece and sold it to his customers at a dime markup. If he ran out of coffee or tea he could always borrow from Ed Halpern's Gilded Cage, at 261 South Twenty-first Street, or at Jack Spiller's Artist's Hut, 2006 Walnut Street. Their competition was friendly.

To newly arrived customers, Haifetz would recite his list of coffees, teas, snacks and soft drinks, take orders and ask: "Chess or checkers? Can I get you something to read?" He was open from seven or eight at night until two or three in the morning. When everybody finally cleared out it was Haifetz who swept the floor and washed the dishes.

Business, slow at first, improved. Soon he was doing maybe $20 a night. But some of his neighbors were unhappy about the Humoresque. "We had good relations with most of them," Haifetz recalled, "but the people who owned a nearby laundry were very unfriendly. This was a time when 'beatniks' were suspect, beards were ostracized. My goatee drew criticism. There were complaints about white girls drinking coffee with black kids. About drugs — although there was never a drug arrest and I never saw anybody light up a marijuana cigarette. There were complaints about the noise and about cars parked on the sidewalk late at night. Nothing very serious."

In the fall of 1958, police stopped by to talk to Haifetz about the complaints they had been getting. Rizzo testified later that Haifetz conceded that homosexuals patronized the Humoresque. Haifetz recalls only that a police sergeant spoke of some "characters" frequenting the place. "He told me he was overlooking the complaints," Haifetz says now, "and he asked me to *cooperate*. I think he probably wanted some money but I didn't pick it up at the time. And nothing happened for quite a while after that."

On the night of February 12, 1959, the Humoresque was filled. Young people were talking, doodling, listening to hi-fi music, sipping espresso coffee and eating Haifetz's buns. "It was as orderly as the Academy [of Music] on concert night." Haifetz remembered. "All of a sudden in the front door came about five cops led by Rizzo shouting, 'This is a raid!'"

Besides Rizzo, the raiding party consisted of two plainclothesmen and four uniformed officers. They made the trip from Twelfth and Pine in three patrol cars and an emergency wagon. They were armed and carried an arrest warrant.

"There were about thirty people in my place," Haifetz told reporters who covered the raid. "Rizzo and his men checked every one of them, demanding to know their ages and asking for proof. There were some married couples present. They also were subjected to the check. There were four boys and four girls. Captain Rizzo told the eight: 'You have no business being here. I'm going to take you into the police station and bring your parents to let them know that kind of people you are associating with.'

"That remark," said Haifetz, "was an insult to everyone else in the place. Rizzo was speaking very loudly and rudely. He behaved in the manner of one of Hitler's storm troopers. He saw me standing in the doorway. He called me 'a creep' and referred to my place as a 'den of iniquity.'"

At a subsequent federal court trial, Rizzo admitted calling Haifetz names. "That was during a private conversation with several of my plainclothesmen and I was referring to Mr. Haifetz as a creep," Rizzo said. He also told of drawing a weapon.

"Yes, that was me and it was a blackjack," he informed the court. "When I was inside talking to some of the minors, several of the others walked up to me and one put his hands on my chest. I told him, 'Never put your hands on a policeman.' I wasn't sure what was going to happen. I took my blackjack out of my back pocket and put it in an overcoat pocket, just in case I would have to use it."

Rizzo's raiders put Haifetz and about twenty patrons into the police vehicles and transported them to the station house at Twelfth and Pine. "They put us in cells overnight and wouldn't let us make any phone calls," said Haifetz. "My attitude was: 'What's happening here?'"

Police were mortified to discover that one of their prisoners was the brother of a fellow officer under Rizzo's command. A second young man under arrest also had a brother on the Philadelphia police force. These two suspects were quickly slipped out of the police station with no charges being placed against them. At a magistrate's hearing the next morning, Haifetz was charged with operating a disorderly house. Seventeen juveniles were fined $12.50 each for breach of the peace.

In a second raid at the Humoresque the following night five girls between the ages of fifteen and seventeen were picked up, taken to Twelfth and Pine, lectured by police and released to their parents. Rizzo made that raid without a warrant. "I did not have one," he said later, "and I did not need one."

Five nights after the first foray, Rizzo, accompanied by another noted police raider, Detective Captain Clarence Ferguson, again went coffeehouse-crawling. This time, besides hitting the Humoresque, they toured such places as the Gilded Cage, the Artist's Hut and the Proscenium, at 2202 Chestnut Street. There were no arrests but the raids attracted a lot of attention. By this time Rizzo was the center of controversy. Residents of the central business district met to discuss his crackdown on the coffeehouses.

When a speaker at the open meeting criticized the raids, Rizzo stepped forward to reply, but Commissioner Gibbons grabbed him by the arm. "No, no," he said as he restrained Rizzo. The police captain turned to his boss. "One word, commissioner," he pleaded uncharacteristically. "Please." But Gibbons waved a finger in his face and shook his head.

After another speaker called for an injunction against further raids, however, Gibbons sprang to Rizzo's defense. He told the crowd that a fourteen-year-old-girl had given police a statement that she had visited the Humoresque to "make acquaintance with Lesbians."

"That is my case," said Gibbons. "It's the case of all decent citizens in the city." Gibbons asked Rizzo to take a bow but warned him not to speak. Rizzo got in a few words, anyway. "I have a lot to say," he said, "but I've been ordered not to by my boss. The coffeehouses have been made to look like the offended and we have been branded the offenders."

Although the meeting tabled a vote of confidence for Rizzo, most of the middle-class downtown apartment dwellers appeared to prefer his raiders to Mel Haifetz's turtle-necked, bearded, stay-up-late coffee drinkers and music lovers. There was a generation gap. Most of the residents were older than most of the coffeehouse attenders. And there was a politicoeconomic gap. The conservative middle-class residents feared a decline in real estate values if their sturdy neighborhood of brownstone town houses and luxury apartments were to become a kind of Greenwich Village. "I feel," said a Roman Catholic priest, "that we have to keep center city respectable. . . . I'm on Captain Rizzo's side in that respect."

Without naming Rizzo, a resident asked whether "anti-egghead, anti-nonconformist, anti-intellectual" elements within the police department provoked the raids. No, said Gibbons. And he added: "We have quite a few intellects in the department, ourselves."

A week later, Haifetz filed a $25,000 federal-court suit accusing Rizzo of "damaging" his business. The suit described the Humoresque as a place where customers were encouraged to "engage in games of pure skill called chess with equipment provided by him [Haifetz]; to engage in the reading of literature with books and magazines provided by him, and to listen to classical music played on a high-fidelity recorder." The Humoresque's clientele, the suit alleged, took part in "literary discussions" and composed "original prose and poetry, some of which is displayed on a bulletin board."

In December 1959, U.S. District Judge Thomas J. Clary threw out the suit. He found that the coffeehouse had "become a gathering place for homosexuals and narcotics addicts." Meanwhile, a quarter sessions court jury convicted Haifetz of running a disorderly house. The presiding judge, Leo Weinrott, a longtime Rizzo admirer, told Haifetz to close the shop or go to jail. He set March 1, 1960, as deadline for shutting down. Before then, Haifetz sold the business and went into another line of work — real estate.

Haifetz, who still lives and works in Philadelphia, remains convinced that Rizzo's harassment put him out of business. "The black and white issue may have been the basis of the complaints against us," Haifetz said when we interviewed him in 1975. "I never picked it up. If black and white grooved together that was their scene. You stayed out of it. In court, the police produced a string of witnesses who claimed to have been in the shop often and to have seen drug users, perverts, homosexuals, undesirables. With all that testimony, they weren't able to cite one drug transaction, one homosexual act, or anything. The police would have done anything to prove I ran a

Captain Frank Rizzo and Police Commissioner Thomas J. Gibbons
(in light jacket) defend Rizzo's coffeehouse raids.

disorderly house. Well, they shut me down but they never proved it."

Another former coffeehouse operator, Edward Halpern, claims that Haifetz's place gave "everybody a bad name." Halpern, whose brother, Alan, is editor of *Philadelphia* magazine, ran the Gilded Cage from 1956 to 1969. He then went to work for the federal government. He said he thought the police had some justification for shutting down the Humoresque because "there was much going on there."

Halpern recalled Rizzo calling him into his office at Twelfth and Pine in 1956 or 1957. "He said he'd had complaints — necking in cars, blacks and whites. I said, 'Captain, anything you want to do, that is legal, tell me how to clean house.' Homosexuals. Blacks and whites. I wanted to cooperate. I never had a bit of trouble with him [Rizzo]. The only trouble I had was with my neighbors who called police sometimes."

While Ed Halpern described Rizzo as a "straight shooter" and a "gentleman," his wife, Esther, had a totally different opinion. "He frightened me when he walked into the Gilded Cage with his gold braid," she said of Rizzo. "We did get business after that but he did a great deal to smear our names. He's a gorilla. I feel Philadelphia deserves something better than him. It's a shame we got a third-rate nothing."

The coffeehouse raids now can be seen to have greatly increased Frank Rizzo's power inside the police department and out. Just as the Halperns disagreed about him, so did the city. Intellectuals were appalled. The American Civil Liberties Union was shocked. Nora Sayre, the social critic, was thinking of Rizzo's coffeehouse raids when she wrote much later: "Creeps, kooks, liberals, phonies, fags, ultraliberals, lefties, hoodlums and bums — Rizzo's morality dictates that he must save his city from the shaggy perverts whose politics or culture spread like dandruff."*

What was most significant about Rizzo's invasion of the poetry-reading dens, however, was that it caused no great outcry. He was criticized by a few but commended by many. His superiors backed him. Mayor Dilworth, a certified liberal Democrat, kept silent. He later told Nora Sayre that many center-city residents were offended less by the police captain's brutish tactics than by the coffeehouses' curious clientele.

Philadelphia's late managing director, a respected Establishment figure named Donald C. Wagner, backed Rizzo. He said he thought the police had sufficient grounds for the crackdown. One exception, he said, was Rizzo's threat of nightly visits by fire and health inspectors to one coffeehouse, the Artist's Hut. "Rizzo was 'way out of line on this," Wagner said.

But Rizzo got no real reprimand. Had he been sharply rebuked for the coffeehouse raids and Mel Haifetz vindicated, his career as a cop may have taken a different turn. He might have gained a fresh awareness of the importance of civil liberties in the American political system.

Instead of a putdown, however, Rizzo got a promotion. In March 1959, he was named a police inspector and shifted to Northeast Philadelphia. Although the promotion drew little comment at the time Rizzo himself surprisingly raised questions about it in 1973 when he was mayor. He accused Dilworth of giving him the promotion solely to gain the support of Italian-American voters in South Philly.

Rizzo recalled that Dilworth had angered South Philadelphians by proposing a parking fee on their narrow streets. "He was trying to figure out how he could recoup," Rizzo said of Dilworth, "and

---

* In *Sixties Going on Seventies*, Arbor House, 1973.

decided, 'We'll make Rizzo an inspector.' I flunked the oral tests [for inspector] but then on the third try I got real intelligent."

Dilworth immediately denied the allegation, insisting that as mayor he didn't "monkey around with police promotions." And, anyway, the protest over his parking fee proposal erupted in the summer of 1961 — two full years after Rizzo got his promotion.

Even after this was pointed out to Rizzo, he kept insisting that Dilworth's attempted wooing of South Philly voters was behind the promotion. "That is guaranteed," he said. It was unusual for a man in public life to insist that he received preferential treatment solely on the basis of reverse discrimination. But Frank Rizzo is nothing if not unpredictable.

Chapter Six

In December 1963, Rizzo was named one of four deputy police commissioners at $9,400 a year. The National Association for the Advancement of Colored People protested. Its Philadelphia chapter said Rizzo was "completely incompetent," lacked the "necessary education" for top police command and had a long record of "persecuting Negroes" with "storm trooper tactics."

Both the promotion and the NAACP's reaction to it marked turning points in Rizzo's career. During his first twenty years in uniform he had been a relatively minor cog in the police bureaucracy, getting an unusual amount of publicity because of his colorful and combative actions, but not making police policy or commanding very large numbers of cops. Now that would change. Increasingly, he would take responsibility for selecting laws to enforce, deciding on tactics, deploying police, conducting entire operations.

Similarly, during his first two decades as a cop, Rizzo had rarely gotten involved in racial disputes. Most of his time had been spent in white sections of the city or in the downtown entertainment district. He was widely known as a foe of unconventional dress, demeanor and behavior but, the NAACP to the contrary notwithstanding, less so as a persecutor of Negroes. In fact, Police Commissioner Howard R. Leary, in defending his deputy, said he had never heard him accused of being anti-Negro.

Now that, too, would change. Deputy Commissioner Rizzo and later Commissioner Rizzo would become embroiled in one heated controversy after another with Philadelphia blacks. In the process, critics would label him a racist who persistently and relentlessly brutalized blacks. On the other hand, his people would see Rizzo as a hero in blue saving the city from anarchy.

It was a tempestuous time in urban America. The civil rights movement was in full cry. Ghetto blacks were demanding better schools, housing and jobs. Despite Lyndon B. Johnson's remarkable Great Society programs, progress seemed slow. Frustrations mounted. "The streets are going to run with blood," Malcolm X warned in January 1964. "Whole sections of cities will be bright with flame. Black people are going to explode. It'll be like a war."*

The rioting began in Harlem that summer and quickly spread to Jersey City and Rochester. Later there would be far bloodier and more destructive uprisings in black sections of Detroit, Cleveland, Newark and Los Angeles. In North Philadelphia the explosion occurred on a Friday night late in August, just as the Democratic National Convention ended in Atlantic City, New Jersey, with LBJ's renomination. Deputy Commissioner Rizzo spent a long tense weekend at the riot scene without once swinging his nightstick. Leary forbade his men from clubbing or shooting rioters even though the looting of stores went on openly. Leary was later commended for his forbearance but Rizzo never forgave his superior.

The spark was a routine traffic complaint on a hot summer night. A motorist got into a spat with her male companion. As they quarreled their car blocked an intersection on Columbia Avenue, the busiest commercial street in the heart of the city's largest Negro section. When two policemen showed up there was an argument, a harmless scuffle and two arrests. A crowd that had been drawn to the scene hooted the white policemen as they drove off and then gradually dispersed. That seemed to be it. But false stories about

---

* Malcolm X was only partly right. There were many riots but no race wars. "Hate Whitey" was the byword in many ghettos but the rioters rarely strayed from their own segregated neighborhoods. Ghetto merchants, often Jews, saw their small stores looted and burned, but the white-controlled strongholds of wealth and influence in the downtown business and financial districts were largely untouched. Thus, although rioting spread from city to city like a raging epidemic the virus was actually confined to sections where most of the rioters lived.

Inspector Frank Rizzo stands by disapprovingly as members of the American Nazi Party picket a downtown hotel where Communist Party leader Gus Hall was scheduled to speak in October 1962.

what had happened quickly issued from North Philly's tireless rumor mill.

According to one account, the traffic squabble had ended with the white cops killing the black woman motorist. According to a second, they had slain her and she was pregnant. According to a third, the victim of police bullets had been a young Negro boy. These baseless rumors flashed through the 410-block area where 240,000 North Philadelphians, many of them poor and virtually all of them black, lived in often congested and ramshackle housing.

The mood turned ugly. Somebody threw the first stone. Soon rocks were flying up and down Columbia Avenue. Crowds turned into mobs and the principal shopping district became a battleground. The rioting began about 10:30 on that Friday night, August 28, 1964, and continued for the rest of the weekend. Commissioner Leary took personal command. He was a short man, barely tall enough to get past the height requirement of five feet, eight inches, for city policemen. Quiet, bookish, some thought introverted, he'd studied law at night while walking a beat and gotten his degree from Temple University Law School in 1947. His ideas often ran counter to those of most cops. He favored, for ex-

94

ample, a civilian board to review the conduct of police, a concept that Rizzo hated.

When the rioting began, Leary ordered his men to arrest law-breakers where possible but not at the risk of a direct and dangerous confrontation between the predominantly white police force and the aroused black community. He didn't want his men wading in with guns drawn to break up the looting. As a result, the badly outnumbered police failed to halt looters from smashing hundreds of store windows and walking off with television sets, radios, bicycles, furniture, clothing, groceries and other merchandise worth hundreds of thousands of dollars.

Before order was finally restored losses from vandalism, fire and theft at more than six hundred stores exceeded $2,000,000. Six hundred persons were arrested and a twenty-one-year-old black man was killed by a policeman after allegedly threatening the officer with a long knife. But the anarchic pillaging ended with just that one fatality. Leary's cool handling of the situation led directly to his appointment as New York City's police commissioner by Mayor John V. Lindsay in 1966.

As commander of uniformed forces, Deputy Commissioner Rizzo spent the entire weekend in North Philadelphia. He followed orders but disapproved of Leary's way of dealing with the lawlessness.

"On the first night of the riot," recalled William P. Naulty, a Philadelphia *Bulletin* police reporter, "I saw Leary and Rizzo quarreling on a corner up there. They kept their voices down but I was close enough to overhear them. Rizzo told Leary the riot could never be contained if the police holstered their guns. He absolutely disagreed with the order. He didn't disobey it, though."

Leary's style was clearly not Rizzo's. On the civilian review board question and many other issues the two were poles apart. Rizzo never challenged his boss publicly, but after Leary left for New York Rizzo denounced him in the strongest terms. He called Leary a "gutless bastard."

The summer of 1965 found Rizzo again spending long days and nights in North Philadelphia. This time he was stationed at the wall of Girard College during marathon demonstrations by the NAACP. The school was an all-white island in a black sea. It was also one of the most unusual schools in America. Stephen Girard founded it. A flinty, one-eyed French immigrant, Girard became, in the first decades of the nineteenth century, Philadelphia's richest man, with a huge shipping fortune, and one of its most public-spirited citizens. On his death in 1831, he left the bulk of his $6,500,000 estate to found a free boarding school for "poor male white orphan children" between the ages of six and eighteen. His aim was to instill in generations of indigent orphans "a pure attachment to our republican institutions and to the sacred rights of conscience."

Girard College opened its forty-three-acre campus in 1848. For nearly a century it was operated by public trustees appointed by Philadelphia mayors without challenge to its racially discriminatory admissions rule. Thousands of fatherless white boys, drawn from many states, were taught "facts and things rather than words and signs," in accordance with its no-nonsense founder's wishes. Rarely did they step outside the ten-foot-high wall that Girard ordered built and "capped with marble and guarded with irons on top."

After World War II, with North Philadelphia having long since been transformed from leafy countryside into a crumbling slum, attempts to break Girard's will began. In 1957, the U.S. Supreme Court ruled that public trustees could not carry out a deliberate policy of racial discrimination and exclusion of Negro children. A Philadelphia court got around that ruling by replacing the school's public trustees with private ones. Girard College thus retained its color bar.

That was the situation on May 1, 1965, when NAACP pickets began marching at the wall for admission of Negro boys to Girard College. The picketing was organized and led by the NAACP's Philadelphia chapter head, Cecil Moore. A black criminal lawyer and ex-Marine from "West-by-God-Virginia," Moore was then and remains today one of the city's most colorful characters. For years he has combined effective civil-rights work with a well-publicized penchant for silk suits, long cigars, bourbon whiskey and the company of women. His arrogance and his rude rejection of middle-class living style eventually led the national office of the NAACP to oust him from his Philadelphia post. In 1965, though, he was riding high and the Girard College picketing was his finest hour.

It pitted him against a cop he'd known and disliked since 1951 when Acting Captain Rizzo briefly commanded the 16th Police District in West Philadelphia. As we noted earlier, a group of Negroes at first protested Rizzo's raids there but later praised his performance. Moore was among the original protesters. Unlike the others, he never changed his mind. He had watched Rizzo's subsequent rise with mounting disgust.

Starting on May Day and continuing through the summer and fall of 1965, black demonstrators, often joined by white liberals, marched every day at the Girard College wall. Moore's aim was to force the city and state to act. It was a shrewd move on his part because by this time the school's policy of racial segregation had become a public embarrassment. And its high stone wall stood as a clear and unmistakable symbol of white racism.* So the modern Joshua marched around his Jericho hoping that the wall would "fall down flat." It did, finally, but only after many tense days and nights, fights with police, sleep-ins, attempts to scale the barrier and a spate of national news stories. Rizzo was in the thick of the action.

On the night of June 24, one hundred pickets broke ranks outside Girard College's main gate and ran into heavily traveled Girard Avenue, blocking traffic, clashing with police and attracting a crowd of fifteen hundred North Philadelphians. Store windows were smashed and two policemen were slightly injured in arresting nineteen demonstrators. Fifty police cars piled into the street, and there was a lot of shouting and hollering but no major outbreak of violence.

Next day, Moore, who had helped disperse the pickets, commended Commissioner Leary for acting "with coolness and fairness" to avert "what would have become a bloody mess." Moore said nothing about Leary's deputy, who was also at the scene. He now asserts, however, that Rizzo acted "viciously" that night, ordering his men to run their police motorcycles up on sidewalks to terrify the crowd. Moore also claims that when Leary protected a black demonstrator named George Brower from a police beating Rizzo deliberately struck his superior on the head. Rizzo denies this charge. Leary, when asked by us to comment, declined to do so.

Three weeks later, city, state and federal officials met to discuss the Girard College crisis. Governor William W. Scranton had become convinced that the only sensible solution was to open the school to Negro boys. How to do it was the question. The meeting was held in the Pennsylvania State Office Building on North Broad

---

* Actually, Stephen Girard apparently wanted the wall erected to protect the "tender minds" of his scholars from the "clashing doctrines and sectarian controversy" that raged among Philadelphia's Protestants and Catholics at that time. In his will, he prohibited ordained clergymen from ever passing through the gates of his school — and to this day they are kept out.

Street, less than a mile from Girard College. Demonstrators picketed the meeting place. Rizzo was there, too, with a large complement of police. As the governor entered the building by a rear door, pickets spotted him and his protective police cordon. They reportedly shouted obscenities at the police and got in their way.

A fight broke out. Rizzo claimed the pickets struck the first blow. When a policeman tried to move a picket back from the entrance, Rizzo said, the officer was punched. Moore, however, said that the police attacked the pickets without provocation. Two policemen were slightly hurt and Rizzo himself was hit on the arm. Three pickets took much more of a beating. One was knocked unconscious and two others received head injuries. All three were arrested on charges of assaulting the police.

At a court hearing for the trio their lawyers blamed Rizzo for the arrests and demanded that he be required to testify. Although one hundred fifty off-duty policemen showed up for the hearing, Rizzo was not among them, and he didn't testify. Not for eight months did the three defendants go on trial, and it was four months after that, in July 1966, when a verdict was entered.

The presiding judge, Stanley Greenberg, convicted them of assault and battery.* At the same time, he praised Rizzo and his men for "remarkably restraining under the most trying circumstances from taking actions that might have resulted in serious injury." Moore was outraged. Without naming Rizzo, he said that the convictions would give "a license to that deputy commissioner to continue his activities. He is a brutal hoodlum." Instead of showing restraint, said Moore, Rizzo had been "sitting there lighting a tinderbox."

Although Moore lost this battle, he won the war over Girard College. His pickets, sometimes joined by such concerned whites as the Right Reverend Robert L. DeWitt, then the Episcopal bishop of Pennsylvania, continued their daily demonstrations until December 17, 1965. Then the City of Philadelphia and the Commonwealth of Pennsylvania joined the mothers of seven Negro boys who had been denied admission to Girard College in filing a federal court suit to end its all-white admissions policy.

U.S. District Court Judge Joseph Lord found the color bar unconstitutional. He ruled that it violated the Fourteenth Amend-

---

* Through court bungling, the three defendants never served their prison sentences, which ranged up to one year. When this oversight was discovered in 1971, the district attorney, Arlen Specter, decided it was too late to correct the mistake. He withdrew a request for execution of the sentences.

ment's guarantee of equal protection of the laws. The U.S. Court of Appeals for the Third Circuit, in Philadelphia, upheld Judge Lord. Girard College's trustees appealed to the U.S. Supreme Court, which, on May 20, 1968, rejected their plea. That fall Girard College admitted the first nonwhite students in its hundred-twenty-year history. It is now better integrated than most of Philadelphia's public schools.

In August 1966, Rizzo got his first crack at the top police job. He was named acting commissioner while Commissioner Edward Bell, who had succeeded Leary, went on vacation. Mayor Tate was away, too, at his place at the Jersey Shore. In their absence, things began to happen. According to Rizzo's later account, informants told police that the Student Nonviolent Coordinating Committee, a militant civil-rights group, was stockpiling arms in Philadelphia. Rizzo said he was skeptical at first. But then, he later reported, an informer turned in three sticks of dynamite with detonating caps, and other sources confirmed that SNCC was hoarding explosives.

Acting Commissioner Rizzo decided to move against the militants. From a friendly judge, he obtained warrants to raid four SNCC offices in North and South Philadelphia. By pulling detectives from every police division in the city, he organized four twenty-man raiding parties armed with rifles and shotguns. Walkie-talkie radio teams supplemented regular police communications. All cops completing tours of duty at midnight on August 12 were mobilized into a thousand-man "backup" force.

At 12:10 A.M. on August 13, the raiders left in fifteen police cars. Rizzo remained at police headquarters. In Ocean City, New Jersey, Mayor Tate got on an open phone awaiting word of the mission's outcome. The word, when it came, was anticlimactic. Rizzo's small army encountered no resistance. It encountered very little of anything. At three of the four SNCC meeting places, the raiders found nothing more dangerous than antiwar posters and unflattering caricatures of President Lyndon B. Johnson. At the fourth, they confiscated two and a half sticks of dynamite and arrested four persons. It turned out that the TNT lacked detonators. Also, there was no city ordinance at that time which prohibited the storing of explosives.

Even so, Judge Leo Weinrott held each of the four defendants in $50,000 bail "in view of the fact that dynamite was involved." They were charged with conspiracy. A police investigation disclosed that three of the four had played no part in the storing of the dynamite. They were discharged. The fourth, a nineteen-year-old boy, was found guilty of conspiracy and placed on probation. That was it. The raids by Rizzo's heavily armed policemen had garnered big front-page headlines in the newspapers, but not much else.

In the aftermath, black civil-rights leaders jumped on Rizzo. James Forman called him a "racist" and said he had ordered the raids to "promote his personal ambitions." SNCC charged that Rizzo "planted" the dynamite. Stokely Carmichael said: "The next time Racist Rizzo brings his troops into our neighborhood he's going to have to answer to all of us." Cecil Moore, interviewed in 1975, termed the dynamite raids "the same goddamn bunch of racist hysteria — Rizzo shit."

But Rizzo's generalship impressed vacationing Mayor Tate. Less than a year later, he would name Rizzo to succeed Commissioner Bell. And this choice, Tate would say, was a "ten-strike" in his own reelection campaign in the fall of 1967.

Chapter Seven

THE 1967 PRIMARY election campaign had been a grueling one for Jim Tate but by May 16, the day the ballots would be counted, he knew he had survived the attempt by the Democratic organization to dump him in favor of City Controller Alexander Hemphill, a pipe-smoking white Protestant lawyer. Even before the votes were tabulated, Tate was planning ahead, looking toward November and a far tougher contest against Arlen Specter, the articulate young district attorney who was to be the Republican candidate for mayor.

At 7:45 P.M., fifteen minutes before the polls closed, Tate opened his campaign for the votes of those he knew he would need if he were to win in November — the increasingly conservative ethnic whites who were disturbed by racial problems in the schools and fearful of crime in the streets. He started that campaign by announcing the appointment of Frank Rizzo as police commissioner to replace Edward J. Bell, who was resigning for reasons of "health."

"Rizzo is in complete command and will have a free hand in running the department," said Fred T. Corleto, the city's managing director and technically Rizzo's boss.

Within hours, Tate's confidence in his ability to defeat the organization was vindicated. He piled up 152,949 votes to 81,238 for Alex Hemphill.

The outlook for November was not nearly so bright. Tate had been a ward politician all his adult life, and he knew where the votes were. Since Franklin Roosevelt had put the coalition together back in the 1930s, the votes for the Democrats had come out of the black neighborhoods and out of the white working-class neighborhoods in places like South Philadelphia and Fishtown and Port Richmond.

But Tate, along with politicians in big cities all across the country, had detected an alarming trend. The blue-collar white voter was no longer automatically pulling the Democratic lever. That was made clear in 1965 when Specter, the man Tate would have to beat in November, was elected district attorney over Democrat James C. Crumlish. Specter won even though the Democrats had about 250,000 more registered voters than the Republicans, and he won by pitching his campaign directly at the problem that was troubling the white voters that Tate needed — violence in the streets. Perhaps his most effective weapon was a television commercial showing a white woman walking down a dark and lonely street, her heels click-clacking on the sidewalk. The noise of heel striking cement was, for a moment, the only sound in the commercial. Then, more ominous footsteps were introduced, the footsteps of a faceless street-prowling monster bent on rape. The click-clacking speeded up, the woman was terrified, running for her virtue, running for her life. Fade-out. Arlen Specter would handle the rapists. It worked. Whites who had voted for Tate in 1963 crossed over by the thousands to vote for Specter.

The Democrats still had a substantial 190,000 more registered voters than the Republicans in 1967, but Tate knew that thousands of white Democrats would defect to Specter. He had no hope of winning a majority of the white vote. He would have to receive a large majority of the black vote, which was then approaching 30 percent of the 955,000 total, and hang on to enough of the disenchanted white vote to eke out a victory.

The first part of this strategy did not appear to be too difficult. While the black community was not overly fond of Tate, it had no reason to love Specter. And, as a bloc, the blacks in recent years had proved themselves to be more loyal to the Democrats than any other group. During the campaign, Tate would woo them by launching a patchwork program aimed at finding young blacks employment, would appoint some blacks to prominent positions and he would trot out the endorsements of the faithful black leaders.

The second part of the strategy depended largely on Frank Rizzo. Rizzo was Tate's signal to the white voters that the blacks would be kept in line, that City Hall was interested in them.

As the campaign developed, Tate performed like an experienced sleight-of-hand artist working the crowds at a carnival. He appointed Charles Bowser, who would run against Rizzo eight years later, deputy to the mayor, the first black ever named to that high post. He appointed another black, printing executive Clarence Farmer, to head the Commission on Human Relations. He sent a "Jobmobile" into the ghettos to recruit young black persons for five hundred city jobs, jobs that would vanish after the election.

In the evenings, Tate toured the white areas, and his message never varied: he had appointed Rizzo police commissioner and when he was reelected, he would reappoint Rizzo. Would Arlen Specter make a similar commitment? He was in favor of legislation that would require the state to give financial aid to nonpublic schools, a not-unpopular position in a city where 148,000 children attended Catholic schools. What was Arlen Specter's position?

Day after day, Tate hammered at Specter with these twin themes. And day after day the name of Frank Rizzo, which was already well known, grew in importance. In effect, Tate was trying to turn the election into a referendum on Rizzo, trying to win back the votes of the whites he had lost by throwing his arms around the tough cop.

To show that he meant business, Tate issued in July 1967 an emergency proclamation banning citizens from gathering in the streets in groups of twelve or more. A little-known ordinance passed in the 1850s gave the mayor the power to take such action. The first time it had been used was in 1964, after blacks began rioting in North Philadelphia. Although there were no similar disturbances in 1967, Tate issued his proclamation anyway. And Rizzo enforced it, in a manner which was to become typical for him.

On July 30, twenty-two persons went to the Cathedral of SS. Peter and Paul on the Benjamin Franklin Parkway, a short distance from City Hall, to demonstrate against the proclamation. Rizzo had them arrested, and the demonstrators, among whom was Spencer Coxe, executive director of the Philadelphia chapter of the American Civil Liberties Union, filed suit in U.S. District Court attacking the constitutionality of the mayor's proclamation. The city's lawyers recognized the shaky legal basis for granting the mayor the power to limit the right of the people to gather together and, rather than expose that power to a court test, dropped the prosecution of the twenty-two who had been arrested.

Rizzo was furious, not at the questionable, nineteenth-century law, but at the demonstrators who had escaped from him. His reaction was predictable. Eight of the twenty-two, he said, were "card-carrying Communists." He had that "documented." But he refused to identify the eight, or to make public his documentation.

"The trouble with Frank Rizzo is that he keeps having these delusions that he is really J. Edgar Hoover," Joe McGinniss wrote in a column in the August 18, 1967, Philadelphia *Inquirer.* "And, operating in that great tradition, he has decided that the best thing to do with his enemies, since he is unable to keep them all in jail, is to stand up and scream that they are Communists. . . . He put way in the back of people's minds the thought that anyone who makes a fuss about what Frank Rizzo does as police commissioner might somehow be connected with the Communists. If you are a man with power, that can be a very convenient thing to have people think about your critics."

"No, I'm not going to name them and I'm not going to show my documentation to anyone else. These people are card-carrying Communists and that's all I'm going to say about it," Rizzo said.

Tate supported Rizzo, as he did every time his police commissioner found himself criticized. "If Rizzo is against Communists, I'm for Rizzo," was Tate's inane and irrelevant reply when he was asked if he approved of Rizzo's tactic of making charges and then refusing to back them up.

In an election fight in which he had bet his own future on the appeal of Frank Rizzo, Tate could hardly have done anything but support his police commissioner. But while he was using Rizzo for political purposes, Tate also genuinely believed he had given Philadelphia the best police chief in the nation. "Rizzo has been my best appointment, without question," Tate said, in an interview in the Philadelphia *Bulletin* as he was preparing to leave office at the end of 1971.

Even though he was a Republican, Specter was favored to beat Tate. Several scandals had spun through City Hall under the Democrats, the party was torn apart by the bitter primary fight, and Tate, colorless at best, had not been a particularly distinguished leader.

As Tate traveled through the white wards, demanding to know if

Specter would reappoint Rizzo, the Republican remained cool. Early in the campaign, Specter let it be known that he would not respond to that question. If he named his police commissioner before the election, Specter said, would he then be asked to name his water commissioner, his fire commissioner? He would not play that game, and thus he played into Tate's hands. Knowing that Specter would not respond, he raised the question again and again.

Toward the end, Specter knew the issue was hurting him. But he had taken a position on the matter and he would not change. He had been under pressure before, when he ran for district attorney as a Republican without changing his Democratic registration first. And he had served as assistant counsel to the Warren Commission investigating the assassination of John F. Kennedy. It was Specter who developed the controversial "single-bullet" theory that held that Kennedy and Texas Governor John Connally, who was in Kennedy's car in Dallas on November 22, 1963, had been wounded by the same bullet.

Just as he refused to say whether he would reappoint Rizzo, Specter also would not be drawn into debate on the merits of the state legislation providing aid to nonpublic schools. It was not a local issue, he said, and had no place in the campaign for mayor. He was right, of course, but Tate unashamedly used the question of aid to parochial schools to play to the large, mostly white, Catholic population in the city.

Tate's strategy was not a huge success, but it did succeed. On November 7, despite his championing of Rizzo and his demand for state aid to parochial schools at a time when the public schools, the schools for which he had official responsibility, the schools which were then 58 percent black, were starving, the blacks stayed loyal to the Democratic Party. Tate did not come close to winning a majority of the white voters. But he did hold on to enough of them to squeeze back into office by 11,000 votes, the narrowest margin of victory in a mayoralty election since 1911.

The real winner, however, was Frank Rizzo. Earlier in the year, he had been overjoyed when Tate named him police commissioner, the first Italian-American to ever hold the post. It was a position of power, with a budget of close to $60,000,000 and an army of more than seven thousand policemen, that he had lusted after.

By the time the election was over, Rizzo saw the police commissionership in a new light. It was a vehicle that could carry him to even greater power. He was convinced, as were large numbers of politicians, commentators and analysts, that he was responsible for

Tate's victory and Specter's defeat. All Specter had to do to win the election, Rizzo said afterward, was to promise to name Frank Rizzo police commissioner.

The irony of the situation lay in the fact that Specter *had* promised to appoint Rizzo. But he had made the promise privately to Rizzo. Indeed, he was far closer to Rizzo than Tate was. As the city's prosecutor, he was in close, daily contact with the police department. Although they were not social friends, the two men liked and respected each other. Their relationship would continue throughout Tate's second term, and after he was gone from City Hall for good.

Rizzo, confident that Specter would keep his word, knew that he would be police commissioner no matter who won the election. And, while he never said it publicly during the campaign, he vastly preferred Specter.

Publicly, Rizzo described Tate as the best friend a cop ever had. Privately, he despised Tate, though he would disguise his feelings until after Tate had named him police commissioner, fought to make him the Democratic nominee for mayor and worked for him in the general election. It was a characteristic that would emerge time and again during Rizzo's career. Those who offered him a helping hand would inevitably feel the weight of his heel on their heads as he climbed higher, after they could no longer do anything for him.

Howard R. Leary was the first to be touched by Rizzo's scorn, once Rizzo had reached a position of some prominence. Leary was the police commissioner in 1963 when Rizzo was named a deputy commissioner.

Leary neither liked nor trusted Rizzo, but he recognized the political considerations that led Tate to insist on his promotion. Although Rizzo obeyed Leary's orders, and publicly gave no hint of the opinions he harbored, after Leary left to become police commissioner of New York City Rizzo would denounce him in the strongest terms. Leary was not a typical Philadelphia Irish cop. His advocacy of a civilian board to review police conduct was hated by Rizzo.

Leary read books, books that didn't have anything to do with police science. On occasion, he could be found at the Academy of Music. Once, driving past an excavation site near Fairmount Park, he saw a rock that had been unearthed. It was a huge rock, a magnificent rock, with the sun glancing off its sharp planes as it rose in cold, hard majesty. Leary, for once, acted on impulse and arranged to have the rock transported to a spot outside "the Round-house," the three-story police headquarters shaped like a curved dumbbell, with two cylindrical wings joined by a narrower, concave corridor, at Eighth and Race streets, near the western end of the Benjamin Franklin Bridge. The rock drew snickers from the blue-coated men who entered and left headquarters, but Leary liked to look at it.

"Leary was a gutless bastard," Rizzo would say, after Leary had moved on to New York. "If it wasn't for me, they'd have burned the town down in 1964. That sonofabitch would've let them get away with it. You couldn't reach him after five o'clock. *Sensitive*. He pretended he liked the opera."

Leary left Philadelphia in February 1966, but his successor, Eddie Bell, did nothing about the rock. When Rizzo took over in May 1967, the rock was still there.

"The first thing I did, I picked up the phone and said, 'Get rid of that fuckin' rock Leary put outside,'" Rizzo said. "That simple bastard found this rock somewhere, big as a house, and he thought it was artistic. He had them drag it from Fairmount Park and put outside police headquarters. *A fuckin' rock*. No way I was gonna keep that."

When Leary turned in his resignation on February 15, 1966, Tate announced that he had decided to reject the traditional method of selecting a new police commissioner, the method whereby the mayor simply named his choice. Instead, Tate appointed a panel of twelve citizens, headed by Jefferson Fordham, dean of the University of Pennsylvania Law School, to interview candidates from all over the country in order to come up with the best man.

One of those who presented his credentials to the panel was Deputy Commissioner Edward J. Bell. Bell was forty-three, a career cop and a friend of Tate's. As a captain, he had been in charge of the district in the Tioga neighborhood where Tate lived, and he saw to it that the mayor's row house on North Seventh Street was always well protected by police. Bell had done nothing to distinguish himself but, with one exception, he had a clean record. Shortly before the 1963 primary election, the election in which Tate was first nominated for mayor, it was discovered that the polling place for a Northeast Philadelphia precinct was in the basement of 730 Marchman Road. Eddie Bell and his wife, Marie, lived at 730 Marchman Road. They had moved there late in 1959 and in July 1960, Bell had registered as a Democrat from that address. The following year, the Democratic-controlled Board of Elections decided to move the polling place in that precinct from a site that had been used for ten years to Bell's basement. The owner of the new site was listed in city records as Marie Bell, and she received thirty-five dollars for the use of her basement.

The Philadelphia election code did not forbid the placing of polling machines in policemen's basements. But it did prohibit any policeman, in uniform or out, from being within a hundred feet of a polling place on Election Day unless he was there to quell a disturbance. Bell refused to talk about the voting machine, but it is safe to assume one of two things took place during the four elections it was in the captain's basement. Either Bell did not go home on election day, except to vote, or there were disturbances inside 730 Marchman Road.

Frank Rizzo did not ask to be interviewed by the panel even though he, like Bell, was a deputy commissioner at the time. "The goddamn thing was stacked," he said later. "I wasn't going to make an ass out of myself and waste my time."

The panel worked for six weeks before it came up with a candidate. When it did, the recommendation was not pleasing to Tate. The panel's choice was Bernard L. Garmire, then the police chief in Tucson. Tate was annoyed by the choice. He had nothing in particular against Garmire except for the fact that Garmire was not Eddie Bell. So he accused the panel of doing "a superficial job," dismissed it, and appointed Bell anyway.

The circumstances of his appointment crippled Bell from the start. He was a tense man, ill-equipped to deal with the bruising politics of the police department and the Tate administration. Before a year had passed, he was complaining about his health and taking more and more time off. He began telling his friends that he would prefer to be at the New Jersey shore running a boatyard which he and his brothers had purchased. Rizzo, the deputy in charge of the uniformed forces, moved into the vacuum and started running the department.

The pressure became too much for Bell early in 1967, when Tate realized he would have to fight the Democratic organization in the primary election if he were to be renominated. At a meeting attended by his top people, Tate said he planned to use every resource at his command to defeat the party. And, he said, everybody in the room had an obligation to cooperate because, if the party won, their heads would roll, too. One of those in the room was Eddie Bell.

Tate had learned about the muscle available to the mayor when he was president of the city council. Richardson Dilworth was mayor then, and Tate often disagreed with him. When the disagreement was over something Dilworth considered important, Dilworth would pick up the telephone and call Dave Malone, a thin-lipped, grandfatherly-looking man who served as the mayor's enforcer. Malone had been chief of county detectives when Dilworth was district attorney. After he became mayor, Dilworth appointed Malone to a new post, executive assistant to the police commissioner. The commissioners whom Malone served, Thomas J. Gibbons and Albert N. Brown, were known to have never turned down a suggestion made by the executive assistant.

After Dilworth had made his telephone call, things would start happening in Tate's Forty-third Ward. Bookies would be squeezed by the police. Cars would be ticketed for illegal parking. Bars and private clubs would be raided. Tate's office would be mobbed with constituents come to complain about police harassment.

In an interview with the *Bulletin,* Tate had this to say about the Dilworth-Malone operations:

I came into office as mayor on Feb. 12, 1962, Lincoln's Birthday. A lot of people feel this was a day of freedom for city employees. It freed a lot of people from the yoke Dilworth had cast on them. His was a government of fear. Dave Malone was his gestapo. He tapped wires for the mayor. Malone was always trying to get things on people for Dilworth. He and his man would even check city employees' trash and their waste baskets at home to see what mail they were getting. Then Malone would run to Dilworth with information about people, particularly about people in the police department.

In an interview with us before his death early in 1974, Dilworth made no mention of checking wastebaskets. But he did admit he used Malone to arrange police raids in the Forty-third Ward whenever Tate tried to frustrate him on an important program he had introduced into the city council.

Tate did not have a Dave Malone to run political errands when he was mayor. But, as he geared up to fight the party in the 1967 primary, he did have Eddie Bell, or at least he thought he had him. Storing a voting machine in his home was one thing, but arresting people just because they lived in a ward that was unfriendly to the mayor was another, and Bell would not go along with it. His health suddenly worsened, and on April 10, Tate named Rizzo acting commissioner.

After he became mayor, Rizzo recalled Tate's desire to harass ward leaders who were opposed to him, a desire that Rizzo said was never fulfilled through his actions. He also recalled the man he frequently referred to as "my dear friend" when he was deputy police commissioner, Eddie Bell.

"He [Tate] called me in and on his desk he had a long list of bars," Rizzo said. "It was like a computer printout, page after page of 'em. He handed it to me and he says, 'Raid them.' I said, 'Raid them? What for?' I know what for, but I wanted to hear him say it. He says, 'These wards been giving me trouble. I want you to lock them up.' I threw the list down on his desk. 'No way I'm gonna do that,' I said.

"Bell was a weak sonofabitch. Tate had him crazy. He was afraid to answer the telephone. I wasn't going to let him use the police for politics. I told him I wouldn't do it. He said, 'You're being insubordinate.' I said, 'Insubordinate, my ass. You can stick the fuckin' job up your ass.' I told him to go fuck himself. He was pounding on the desk."

Defiance of the type Rizzo claimed to have hurled at Tate usually resulted in one thing: the defiant one was fired. According to Rizzo, he not only got away with his defiance; within a couple of months he was appointed police commissioner.

Despite the internal uproar over Tate's use of the police for political ends, despite Bell's poor health, despite the refusal Rizzo said he gave Tate, the raids nevertheless came off on schedule by the Philadelphia police. Raiders swooped down on taprooms in those wards where the ward leaders were opposed to Tate, and more than three hundred persons were arrested. Tate was subsequently able to oust eight hostile ward leaders, and the others eventually caved in.

Chapter Eight

PHILADELPHIA NOT ONLY GOT a new police commissioner in 1967; it also got a new superintendent of schools. Mark R. Shedd, a cool, young New Englander with a Harvard doctorate, was appointed to run the city's 270,000-pupil school system at $36,000 a year just as Frank Rizzo took over the 7,500-man police force at $29,000.

Shedd's mandate was to shake up the school system. He proceeded to do just that. Under Richardson Dilworth, a reform board of education named two years earlier had already launched a successful drive to wipe out the teacher shortage, reduce class size, build new libraries and kindergartens, add auxiliary personnel for classroom teachers, buy more textbooks and vastly increase financial support through higher local taxes and bigger state and federal subsidies.

Bricks and mortar were thus not the new superintendent's major concern. His job was to convert the hidebound school bureaucracy — an "arthritic turtle," someone had called it — into a vital organization truly serving the needs of young people. Shedd had come from a small school district in Englewood, New Jersey, and he'd had no previous experience in urban education. But he was convinced that kids were kids wherever you found them. Too many of them were bored by school. So the system, said Shedd, had to become more open, more receptive to change, less cautious, austere and autocratic.

He encouraged all kinds of innovation and experimentation. He encouraged risk taking because, in his view, there were "no safe bets and we must all be gamblers." The result, in a very short time, was an astonishing outpouring of new ideas, new approaches — alternative schools, magnet schools, learning centers, a "school without walls," an "advancement school," weekend student retreats, a bill of rights for students, and so on. Some of these efforts worked better than others and some didn't work at all. Together they gave Philadelphia — and Mark Shedd — a national reputation for educational trend setting.

But if Philadelphia's new superintendent of schools believed in taking chances, Philadelphia's new police commissioner didn't. Not in law enforcement and not in education or child rearing, either.

It would be hard to imagine two more different personalities than the street cop from South Philly with his unwavering faith in hickory-stick school discipline and the pedagogical boat-rocker from Maine with his commitment to change and his conviction that in dealing with young people "we cannot meet discontent with dogmatism."

While Rizzo urged respect for law and properly constituted authority, Shedd advocated a "social revolution — a revolution in human values and human relationships."

"If this [revolution] does not occur," he said soon after taking office, "I see no reason for bothering to educate our children. And if it is to occur, the schools must be the cauldron, whether we like it or consider it our traditional role or not."

In a very short time, Rizzo and Shedd, bearing separate but equally awesome responsibilities in the nation's fourth largest city, came to distrust and despise one another. They were on a collision course. And the collision came with shocking suddenness on November 17, 1967.

It was another Rizzo enemy, Cecil B. Moore, who helped set the stage. As an independent candidate for mayor that fall, Moore asked Superintendent Shedd for permission to hold some of his campaign rallies at black high schools. Up to then, politicking had not been allowed at city schools. But Shedd granted Moore's request on grounds, as he explained later, that black power was a "rapidly growing issue" in Philadelphia and "any attempt to restrain Mr. Moore would have boomeranged."

As a result, Moore took his rough-and-tumble campaign to a number of high schools, where he drew large crowds. Though nearly all of his listeners were too young to vote, Moore stirred them with slashing attacks on his old foe. Rizzo's name wasn't on the ballot, but he was a key issue in the election, and Moore spent much of his time talking about him.

He ridiculed Rizzo as a numskull who never completed high school. "You kids stay in school," he counseled his student audience one day, "or you may wind up as police commissioner." He joked about the positive effects of student disorders, observing that they at least gave "cops a chance to see what the inside of a school is like." "And who knows," he added, "one of them might even read a book while he's in there."

Near the close of the mayoralty race, Moore visited predominantly black Germantown High School with Dick Gregory, the entertainer and social critic. While Moore attacked Rizzo, Gregory urged the students to become politically active. "When rights are destroyed over a long period of time," he said, "it is your duty to destroy or abolish that government. Nonviolence is not a duty, it's a favor."

In the election itself on November 7, Moore ran very poorly, getting less than 2 percent of the citywide vote. Elsewhere times were changing. Cleveland, Ohio, and Gary, Indiana, elected their first black mayors that same month. In Philadelphia, a black mayor seemed many years away. Despite Cecil Moore's miserable showing, however, his unorthodox campaign achieved something significant: it helped politicize black students.

Just a few days after the ballots were counted, student leaders at half a dozen black high schools announced plans to protest the "white policy of the Board of Education." The students demanded Swahili as an elective foreign language. They demanded black studies courses. They demanded permission to wear dashikis, tiger-teeth necklaces and other symbols of their growing racial pride.

Citing wretched schools that cheated minorities of their right to quality education, the students called for volunteers to help give the "white-dominated system an eviction from the black community." As name-calling increased, tensions grew. On November 14, Shedd spoke publicly of the "high degree of alienation" among young blacks. He considered the situation "explosive." "I'd like to feel that the people in our schools know how to cope with it," he said, "but they don't."

To dramatize their demands, the black students scheduled a demonstration for the morning of Friday, November 17, outside board of education headquarters. Shedd met with the student leaders beforehand to discuss the rally. It was his impression that about three hundred and fifty demonstrators would show up. He advised his high school principals not to encourage students to attend but not to prevent them from doing so. He and his staff thought that the police department's small civil disobedience squad assisted by the school board's own security officers could handle the crowd. No uniformed police officers were assigned.

Philadelphia's massive, ten-story school administration building stands just south of the Benjamin Franklin Parkway, a broad, tree-lined boulevard running from City Hall to the Art Museum. The parkway is Philadelphia's Champs Elysées. Nearby are the Franklin Institute, the Fels Planetarium, the Academy of Natural Sciences, and the main branch of the Philadelphia Free Library, as well as the school board's "Palace on the Parkway."

The administration building is the school system's nerve center. The superintendent's office is there. The board meets there. More than a thousand school administrators and clerical employees work there. For all of these workers, it was business as usual on November 17, a cloudy, chilly day. Youthful demonstrators started assembling in front of the building about 9 A.M. Their numbers gradually increased.

At a discreet distance, Police Lieutenant George Fencl, head of the civil disobedience squad, watched the gathering throng. Fencl, a quiet-spoken, thoroughly professional cop, had had long experience dealing with dissenters. Over the years his small unit had kept the peace at rallies of Birchers, Nazis, Ku Kluxers, draft-card burners, welfare mothers, consumer advocates and such zany gripers as the Joe Must Go Committee, which helped force the ouster of former Philadelphia Eagles football coach Joe Kuharich. Everybody trusted Fencl.

As it became apparent that far more than three hundred and fifty students were coming, Fencl radioed for reinforcements. A small detachment of uniformed policemen took up positions in the area. Still, there was no trouble. For many the demonstration was a lark, a day off from school. The *Bulletin* reported: "Most demonstrators treated the affair as a picnic. They laughed, asked news cameramen to take their pictures and danced before television cameras. Some boys held girls over their heads to have their pictures taken."

Inside, Shedd and a few aides conferred with student leaders in the school board's ornate first-floor meeting room. With him were the two blacks on the nine-member school board, Vice President Henry H. Nichols and George Hutt; Executive Deputy Superintendent Robert Poindexter, and a group of staffers including Bernard Watson, Marcus Foster* and Frederick Holliday. With the students were a number of civil rights leaders, all of them black. Shedd was the only white man in the room. The negotiations continued for an hour.

Outside, the big crowd was growing restive and picketing began. As more and more students arrived, some spilled into a landscaped courtyard in front of the school administration building. From upper-story windows secretaries watched the weaving movement of young people. Some of the older women clerks felt besieged.

Then hundreds of students streamed into the area from the all-male and nearly all-black Franklin High School on North Broad Street. They'd left their school chanting "Black Power! Black Power! Black Power!" and had double-timed to the demonstration site. With them were hundreds of students from their neighboring high school, all-girls' William Penn. Fencl put the number of new arrivals at over nine hundred and the total of demonstrators at close to three thousand — nearly ten times as many as had been expected.

A couple of students climbed onto the roof of a parked car owned by Poindexter, the highest-ranked black school administrator. The radio antenna was snapped off. Other youths grabbed a flag from the Boy Scouts of America headquarters just west of the school building. The increase in noise and movement alarmed Fencl. "It was at this time," he reported later, "that I assessed the situation to be no more a demonstration but now a riotous situation." He put in a call to police headquarters for more help.†

When the call came in, Rizzo was at City Hall attending

---

* Foster, one of Philadelphia's most respected educators, left the city to become superintendent of schools in Oakland, California. On November 6, 1973, gunmen using cyanide-tipped bullets shot him to death as he was leaving a school board meeting. Two self-described members of the Symbionese Liberation Army were convicted of Foster's murder.
† The call later became a subject of controversy. Some civil-rights leaders suspected that Commissioner Rizzo made the decision to bring in reinforcements without hearing from Fencl. When we asked him many years later, however, then Inspector Fencl insisted that he had placed the call and he said that in another similar situation he would do so again.

swearing-in ceremonies for one hundred and eleven new police sergeants and corporals. He immediately bundled the newly promoted officers into buses, which sped them to the scene, less than a mile away. Rizzo went along and took personal command on his arrival just before noon. He then faced the tensest situation in his still brief tenure as chief. The big crowd of young blacks had done nothing yet to provoke police action. There had been no arrests, no injuries and only a few dollars' worth of damage to parked autos and trampled shrubbery in the courtyard. But the next few minutes would be critical. The arrival of busloads of helmeted, club-wielding cops was certain to agitate the already excited crowd. Riot-control skills — of the kind that Fencl had often displayed in the past — would be required to forestall an ugly confrontation.

In this dicey situation, Rizzo moved his men into a military formation across Twenty-first Street from the demonstrators. The police, most of them white, were positioned just a few yards from the nearest of the black students, whom Rizzo later termed "howling, undisciplined and disorganized." But to some inside the school administration building it was the police who seemed menacing. "I went to the window to see what was happening," recalled Richard H. de Lone, Shedd's young white administrative assistant. "Lined up along Twenty-first Street were these guys in real storm trooper outfits — boots, leather jackets, helmets and clubs."

Shedd, still negotiating with the black student leaders, sent Fred Holliday to ask police to move back. Holliday, slightly built, mild-mannered, with a Harvard doctorate, was among a small group of black administrators whom Shedd, in shaking up the system, had promoted. A student accompanied him outside. As Holliday crossed Twenty-first Street, a nervous policeman, not recognizing him and apparently believing he was provoking an incident, grabbed him and threw him to the ground. Holliday's topcoat was torn and the educator himself was bruised. (Later that day, when he showed Rizzo the damage to his coat, Holliday said the police commissioner, in true *padrone* fashion, told him: "I have a tailor in South Philadelphia. I'll give you his name.")

As tensions rose, School Board Vice President Nichols, a Methodist clergyman, also left the building to remonstrate with Rizzo. He found the commissioner in civilian clothes and felt hat and carrying a "long nightstick." Nichols said he persuaded Rizzo to surrender his club to an aide and he thought he talked the chief into keeping his men back. However, Rizzo made clear to newsmen that he would not retreat. "Nobody is going to make a patsy out of the police department," he said as his men contained the milling crowd. "Frank Rizzo and the police department are not going to back away from lawlessness or insurrection. I am the commissioner and I will make the decisions. I am serving notice right here and now that the Philadelphia police will not permit mob rule."

A few minutes after Rizzo said this, police seized a youth who had been climbing on cars. When two officers sought to lead him away the demonstrators surged forward. "They weren't running or charging the police," said de Lone. "They were gravitating towards the action, which was pretty natural." To the police, though, it appeared that a full-scale riot was imminent. In such a fix, the Federal Bureau of Investigation's manual on prevention and control of mobs and riots recommends issuance of an order "directing the people to disperse and leave within a prescribed time and insuring an avenue of escape for them." The order should be issued before the police move on a mob, according to the FBI.

Whether this was the time and place for such an order remains in dispute. There was later court testimony that the arresting officers were being "attacked by the mob" and Rizzo set out to rescue them. His critics reject this version of events. What both sides agree on is that Rizzo acted decisively. He bypassed FBI riot control procedures. "I took complete command," Rizzo testified later. "I gave the orders and I gave only one order." His order to his men, said the chief, was to "move in and disperse." Henry Nichols said he heard the order differently. What he heard Rizzo command was: "Get their asses!" Other witnesses later claimed to have heard the commissioner shout: "Get their *black* asses!"

Whatever the exact words, at 12:34 P.M. about two hundred policemen armed with clubs charged the black students. Swinging their sticks, they met virtually no resistance. Rizzo later alleged that bricks and bottles were thrown at his men but this was denied by Nichols who challenged the commissioner to produce evidence. It also was testified that demonstrators hurled a wooden traffic barricade at police. But there was no battle in the street. Everybody agrees about that. When Rizzo gave his order the unarmed students fled in panic and disorder. Their morning of hooky and horseplay had suddenly turned into a one-sided clash with the cops. Seeking sanctuary, some students ran into the administration building courtyard and climbed through first-floor windows. Hundreds of others, boys and girls, raced south on Twenty-first and Twenty-second streets, hotly pursued by police.

It was a wild scene that lasted only a few minutes yet remains etched in the memory of those who saw it. Each witness has his own recollections. Lois G. Forer, a civil-rights lawyer who later became a city judge, said that "girls were dragged along the street by their hair"* and "a club was broken over a boy's back." Dilworth said the police chased "the children" out of the area, "beating and striking them on the back." He said school clerical workers wept at the sight of the police charge. The Reverend E. Marshall Bevins, an Episcopalian priest, was slugged by police, it was later testified, while trying to help a black girl who had been knocked down. Nichols said that when he pleaded with police not to hit his fellow clergyman a lieutenant shouted: "Shut the hell up or we'll beat the hell out of you." Rizzo himself conceded that his officers "swung their nightsticks occasionally" and he acknowledged seeing "force used on girls." But he denied brutality. "There comes a time," he said, "that a policeman must defend himself even against a woman." De Lone was convinced that what he saw that day was a police riot. He said of Rizzo's men:

They just beat the shit out of those kids who offered no resistance. It was a real stampede. I had seen police brutality before but never at this level. I saw two cops holding a kid while the third hit him over the head. I saw a cop break his billy stick over a kid's shoulder. They were really pounding the shit out of them. It was totally unnecessary and really bloody. Rizzo just couldn't keep his finger off the trigger. He started a police riot. There's absolutely no doubt about it.

After running from the police, most of the fleeing demonstrators calmed down and scattered for their homes. A noisy minority ran pell-mell through center-city streets, bowling over pedestrians and raising hell. They upset lunch stands, disrupted subway operations and, in one case, ripped seats and smashed windows of a bus. Many marched on police headquarters, where they demonstrated angrily.

In the police melee and subsequent petty crime spree, eighteen persons were hurt, none seriously, and fifty-seven were arrested, most of them for disorderly conduct. Fearing possible reprisals, Rizzo put his entire seventy-five-hundred-member force on overtime and the Pennsylvania state police were alerted. But within an hour things were back to normal at the school administration building. Damage there proved less costly than that which was to be caused many months later by a group of white mothers protesting a school busing scheme.

* In her book, *No One Will Lissen*, John Day Co., 1970, p. 269.

In midafternoon, Rizzo returned to the building to call on Shedd, whom he blamed for the violence. The two met alone in Shedd's second-floor office. The day's dramatic events had made unmistakably clear their differing views on how to deal with the frustrations of young blacks. Shedd believed in sitting down and talking with them — although he later agreed that on November 17 the talk probably went on too long while the crowd outside was growing in size and emotional intensity. It was Shedd's recollection that at their meeting in his office Rizzo blew up. "He was livid," said Shedd. "His face and neck were red. He said directly to me, 'Get those fucking black kids back to school. This is my town. No softie from the outside is going to come in and screw it up. If you don't keep those kids in school, I'm going to run your ass out of Philadelphia if it's the last thing I do.'"

In the aftermath of the November 17 disturbances public opinion divided sharply and predictably. The Communist Party of Eastern Pennsylvania called for Rizzo's removal; the Knights of Columbus backed him. The NAACP insisted that Rizzo's charge was "a major case of police brutality;" the Catholic War Veterans called for the ouster of Shedd, Dilworth and Nichols, "who apparently advocate anarchy and disrespect for law and order." Nichols and George Hutt, the other black board member, filed a formal complaint against the police. Hutt said Rizzo ought to be fired "unless he can get better control of his men." Nichols said there were "no serious problems until police began to beat our boys and girls." Dilworth insisted that the demonstrating "children" were blameless and that the police set off the violence.* However, board member William Ross, who would later become its president with Rizzo's support, defended the police commissioner and declared there was "no pattern of violence on the police force." Mayor Tate, vacationing in Florida, hailed Rizzo and told Dilworth to quit "meddling in the activities of the police department over which he has no jurisdiction."

Superintendent Shedd, choosing his words carefully, said: "I personally didn't view anything that would have prompted the kind of action the police took." The police switchboard lit up with three hundred telephone calls within an hour of the incident, all praising Rizzo's role.

---

* At the same time, Dilworth, a man of exceptional candor, admitted that his wife, Anne, favored the use of more force by police. "But that doesn't mean she's for Rizzo," he said. "She's always been against him. She's for hitting Rizzo over the head with a meat ax."

Rizzo followed up with a tough speech to a Jewish group that honored him on November 22. He said the Black Power movement was organized and dangerous and had to be crushed. "No matter what demands of theirs you meet," he told a Brith Sholom dinner, "you can never appease them. The only thing they understand is force and they have to be crushed before they destroy the community."

Despite his strong talk, Rizzo found himself uncharacteristically on the defensive after November 17. In reviewing events, some observers criticized the police charge as crude, amateurish, ill-conceived, a tactical disaster. Instead of containing the mob, Rizzo had simply let it loose on the entire city. Whether provoked or not, some of his men had swung their clubs needlessly against unarmed, nonviolent teenagers. The Black Power threat had been exaggerated. Militant rhetoric aside, there was no coherent plan to take over anything. And while some of those who organized the demonstration may have been "militant racists," as the Philadelphia Crime Commission alleged, most were there just for fun or to petition for redress of grievances.

Civil-rights groups went into federal court seeking Rizzo's ouster. But their suit was as ill-conceived in its way as was the police action they complained of. It was a matter of overkill. Not only did they ask that the Philadelphia police department be placed in receivership and a special master be appointed to run it; they sought to invalidate much of the juvenile justice system on grounds that it discriminated against young people.

A three-judge panel was convened to hear both complaints. In thirteen days of hearings the panel listened to testimony that filled two thousand pages of transcript. But the case against Rizzo was never directly presented. The plaintiffs, after being denied the time they thought was necessary to prove police brutality, concentrated instead on the other complaint.

In dismissing that suit on January 30, 1968, the three U.S. District Court judges — Francis L. Van Dusen, John W. Lord, Jr., and E. Mac Troutman — noted that the court had been prevented "from considering the allegations of brutal police action and other police state methods." They added:

Although the subject of excessive police force on November 17 is not before us, all citizens must be concerned at the extensive testimony on this subject. . . . It is most unfortunate, both for plaintiffs and for the

Philadelphia community, that their civil rights' claims were not stated in a separate court.

In his testimony, Rizzo described the demonstrators as an "undisciplined mob." He denied cracking down on them because they were black.

Q: Well, would you consider it an undisciplined mob of Black Power demonstrators or of children?

Rizzo: It don't make no difference to me what color they were.

In throwing out the challenge to state laws, the judges dealt with Rizzo's performance on November 17 even though it was not directly at issue in the complaint. They said that plaintiffs had "raised a doubt in the Court's mind as to what occurred" but had not "negatived" Rizzo's testimony. They recalled that Rizzo had said he was "required to make a decision during a riotous situation where his officers were being attacked during an effort of others to rescue a prisoner from police custody.

"We do not find on this record," the court held, "that the Police Commissioner acted in bad faith in directing the police to move into the mob." It went on to say, however, that in making arrests the police "may have applied the Pennsylvania criminal statutes . . . overbroadly and indiscriminately in a situation where citizens were exercising their First Amendment rights."

In other words, Rizzo's order to disperse was okay but its execution may not have been. At another point in their opinion, the judges termed the command "justified under the emergency circumstances existing at the time." The demonstration had gone on for several hours, the opinion said, and Rizzo's "forebearance" as the crowd increased indicated that "the police action was not taken in bad faith to 'chill' the exercise of First Amendment rights."

So Rizzo escaped court censure and his critics were left in disarray. But the long-range significance of November 17 in Philadelphia went far beyond the immediate court litigation. The events of that day came to symbolize dramatic divisions in American society: young *vs.* old, black *vs.* white, liberal *vs.* conservative, police power *vs.* civil-rights activism. In Shedd's opinion, November 17 marked the first time that "a major youth-serving institution (the Philadelphia school system) came down on the side of kids, black kids." Rizzo was seen as coming down on the other side. And while it won him instant popularity in a city whose politics is dominated by lower-middle-class whites, it lost him his admittedly slim claim to the trust and confidence of white liberals and the city's growing black population. Rizzo was aware of this. Never again, as police commissioner, did he get into a similar fix. After November 17, when school troubles flared up, he made a point of criticizing white as well as black agitators.

Racial frictions forced the closing of a South Philadelphia technical high school in November 1968. Rizzo again massed a strong police presence — but this time it was to protect black pupils in the predominantly Italian-American neighborhood. In September 1970, testifying before the city council's finance committee, Rizzo expressed impatience with racists regardless of pigmentation. "I'd like to get a helicopter," he said, "and dump all white or black paint over the city and make all the people the same color so we won't have any racial problems."

While Rizzo sought to mend fences with some of his liberal critics after November 17 he did not make peace with either Shedd or Dilworth. His relations with these two only worsened. In some respects, Dilworth and Shedd were an odd couple. Patrician Dilworth, a graduate of St. Mark's and Yale and a fighting Marine in two world wars, performed brilliantly in a long public career as Philadelphia's city treasurer, district attorney, mayor and then school board president. Shedd, by contrast, was a newcomer to Philadelphia and twenty-eight years younger. Where Dilworth was often explosively hot-tempered, Shedd always kept his poise in public. Dilworth, the slam-bang campaigner, spoke his mind on every conceivable issue and relished controversy. Shedd was more careful of his ground when picking fights or accepting challenges. Dilworth's finest moments came in off-the-cuff comments; Shedd was not an effective ad-libber but his carefully prepared speeches were often superb. Despite their differences in age, temperament and style, the men were united in their determination to improve the schools. And they shared the conviction that Rizzo was a menace to the school system and to the city itself. Both Shedd and Dilworth told us that after November 17 Rizzo had them shadowed.

"There is no doubt that I was tailed," Shedd declared in an interview after Mayor-elect Rizzo forced his resignation late in 1971. "Two plainclothesmen in an unmarked car parked outside the administration building and followed me wherever I went. After work, they parked in front of my house. I'd go out and say goodnight to them."

Ten days after the school board brouhaha, Shedd scheduled a meeting with student leaders of the demonstration in Philadelphia's

Mt. Airy, a racially mixed middle-class section. Police were still shadowing him, Shedd said. "To shake the cops," he said, "I started in a school board car from my house, made a couple of stops and then went to Fred Holliday's house. I ducked out the back door of Holliday's place, got in his car and scrunched down in the front seat while he drove to the meeting. For six or eight hours the police had no idea where I was. But that was unusual."

The surveillance became more "discreet" but it continued for many months, according to the superintendent. Then, while he was vacationing in Maine in the summer of 1968, his house was burglarized. "On returning home," Shedd said, "I was surprised to discover that while drawers had been opened and clothes were spilled all over the house, nothing of value had been taken. I especially noted that the files and records in my office at home appeared to have been carefully examined." Shedd is now convinced that Rizzo "ordered the breakin as part of his campaign against [him]."

"There was never any doubt," Shedd told us, "that Rizzo was out to get me from the time I first arrived in Philadelphia." Rizzo concedes that he wanted to oust Shedd and did so. However, he denies ever having ordered police to shadow Shedd or break into his house. Shedd made the charges in a *Bulletin* interview in August 1973, and repeated them in stronger language in a subsequent interview with us. "Not true," Rizzo told the *Bulletin* when the allegations were published. "It didn't happen. We don't do things like that. These guys are seeing cops and robbers in their sleep. What's his proof? We don't break the law, we obey it."

Dilworth, in a tape-recorded interview with us, had this to say about the policeman he had known and disliked so intensely for so long:

Tate was a vindictive man. But Tate seems kindly compared to Rizzo who is one of the most extraordinarily vindictive men I've ever known. And utterly unscrupulous with it. I don't think Rizzo would hesitate to frame anybody.

It was immediately after November 17 that, apparently to impress both Shedd and myself with his power that what he could do to anybody who opposed him, we both had shadows put on us without any motive or warning.

These were what the police have always described as rough shadows. In other words, it wasn't a shadow you weren't supposed to know about. This was a shadow to impress you with the commissioner's power. He wanted you to know that you were having a shadow put on you and that they were there all the time.

*Mark Shedd, whom Rizzo succeeded in ousting
as superintendent of schools.*

*The late Richardson Dilworth, former mayor of Philadelphia,
who resigned as school board president to oppose
Rizzo's takeover of City Hall.*

One nice thing: we did have protection. They would park right outside at night. They would pick me up in the morning when I'd leave and
follow me all day. When I would come down in the lobby of our office
building there would always be two of them there. If I went over to buy
a newspaper they would get ahead of me and give me a bit of a jostling.
And they would buy a paper, and then I would be permitted to buy a
paper. When I went through the swinging doors, one of them would
push me aside and go out ahead of me. And the other would jostle me
from the rear. This went on for a 10-day period.

Dilworth recalled that with relations between Rizzo and himself
steadily getting worse, an intermediary, former City Solicitor Edward Bauer, finally arranged for them to sit down together at
lunch. But that didn't help. According to Dilworth, Rizzo spent
much of the lunch talking about Dilworth's alleged sex life and
drinking habits. Dilworth told us:

At that lunch Rizzo said: "I've got the goods on you. I know that
you're sleeping with at least two women." And I said, "Well, that's news.
I'm getting a little old for that kind of thing." (Dilworth was then 71).
And Rizzo said: "Well, one of them was Mrs. (Rizzo named a woman
prominent in Philadelphia civic and school affairs)": And meant it, don't
you know. He kidded himself into believing this absolutely ridiculous
thing.
And he also said: "I also know what a drunk you are." And I said:
"Well, I have enjoyed at times getting drunk." And he said — this was the
one that really floored me — he said: "I can testify from personal experience because I carried you home at least four times." I said: "I'm sorry,
commissioner, that's an absolute lie. You never carried me home, helped
me home or ever had anything to do with my getting home. I'm not saying there weren't times in the old days when I didn't have to have some
help getting home, but it didn't come from you." But he's now made up
his mind that it did.

Several weeks after the November 17 incident, Mayor Tate met
with Dilworth and the other school board members to discuss
Rizzo's request that police be permitted to enter troubled schools
without first getting permission from school authorities. Rizzo was
there, too. It was a heated meeting. Discussion apparently wandered off the principal subject. According to Dilworth, Rizzo at one
point warned the nine school directors that his men had collected
dossiers on each of them with enough damaging secret information
"to run you out of the city."
Dilworth said he and his fellow board members looked at Rizzo

"in absolute silence and some astonishment." "Our reaction," he said, "was not to say a single word."

Shedd's recollection of the meeting was similar. "Rizzo made it clear he was keeping a close and careful surveillance on board and administration members, and that he had sufficient information on each one of us," Shedd said. "I saw a veiled threat toward me. He made it perfectly clear that he had enough information on every one of the board and members of the administration, on our personal lives, that could be incriminating."

Henry Nichols also corroborated Dilworth's story but Rizzo denied it and threatened to sue.* He never did. But for the balance of his term as police commissioner he kept the heat on Dilworth and Shedd with steady criticism of their operations. The years between 1967 and 1971 were tense ones for the school system. Racial flare-ups often broke out, and Rizzo personally visited every school that needed police to control trouble. To reporters who followed him around in those days, he spoke his mind.

"It's disgraceful to think that students — children — can get away with sit-downs in school," said Rizzo in October 1968, outside Olney High School, where five hundred black students were sitting in. "This is the fault of the Board of Education and the school system. Until the day that Dilworth and Shedd give control of the schools back to the teachers and children back to' their parents we will continue to have this. There's too much outside influence in the school system today. The schools should be run, governed and controlled by the teachers and the Board of Education, not a bunch of teenagers."

Rizzo's comments were welcomed by many Philadelphians, especially working-class whites who shared his contempt for the educational reformers. In this way, Rizzo, while still police commissioner, steadily widened his political power base. Dilworth and Shedd lacked such a base. It was true that a federally funded report had found Philadelphia's public schools undergoing in 1967 "the most dramatic reform in urban education since World War II." A Philadelphia citizens' group, reporting on that year's achievements, had claimed that "probably no large school system has ever moved so far, so fast, and in so many ways as has Philadelphia's during the past 12 months." Despite such reported gains, Dilworth and Shedd were not able to show instant improvement in the teaching of basic skills. Philadelphia pupils continued to lag far

---

* Dilworth aired his charge on the TV program "CBS Reports" in December 1971.

behind national norms in reading and arithmetic. "Functional illiterates" continued to graduate from city high schools. The same problems existed in virtually all large American cities. The differences were primarily ones of degree. But the reformers' failure to solve these problems in Philadelphia cost them whatever chance they may have had of picking up blue-collar backing.

Some of the school innovations in this period were clearly ill-advised. A series of "sensitivity retreats" at which high school students were encouraged to say exactly what they thought of their teachers and principals served mainly to exacerbate tensions across the generation gap. "Never before have professional persons anywhere been subjected to such intimidation, vilification and character assassination without the slightest chance for rebuttal," complained a group of protesting principals.

The controversial retreats, the school board's adoption of a "Student Bill of Rights and Responsibilities" and its elimination of a long-standing dress code for students no doubt convinced many citizens that Rizzo was on target in charging a youth takeover of the schools. Actually, during Shedd's tenure, Philadelphia lost fewer school days because of pupil disruptions than did some smaller suburban districts. And the number of teacher assaults leveled off, too. There were more such assaults in the years immediately before Shedd arrived than after.

In a sense, Shedd and Dilworth were victimized by their own candor. It would have been easier to run a closed school system as the old board had done — a system in which great issues were decided in secret, where achievement tests were homemade and scores were not released. In opening up the system for inspection, Shedd and Dilworth invited parents and taxpayers to examine all the problems that had been swept under the rug for so long. Rizzo then succeeded in blaming the housecleaners for the mess they had inherited.

There was a curious form of doublethink at work in Philadelphia then. Shedd and Dilworth were held responsible for low test scores and all the other problems bedeviling the school system but Police Commissioner Rizzo escaped responsibility for the city's shocking increase in street gang killings, drug abuse and rapes.

Shedd brought some problems on himself, however. His staff neglected Rizzo's white ethnic constituency both inside the school system and out. Typical of his staff's insensitivity was a research paper written by one of the superintendent's assistants. It placed many of Philadelphia's school problems at the door of "second- and third-generation immigrants" who started as teachers and worked their way into administrative jobs. All of these lackluster supervisors seemed to "look, think and act alike," the report suggested, and it implied that no school system could "long survive the rigor of urban life" with such people. Shedd belatedly retracted the paper but the damage had been done.

In other ways, the educational reformers seemed elitist. "We were Kennedy-style liberals who ignored the white ethnics," said Richard de Lone. "This was a real flaw." He believed that the reformers' "basic thrust" — striving to make the schools more open and responsive to the needs of the majority black school population — was desperately needed. Needed or not, Rizzo's "people" didn't like it. And the thrust came from a policymaking school board that did not accurately reflect Philadelphia's social class structure. Five of the nine board members were millionaires. They were decent, well-intended, public-spirited millionaires, but millionaires nonetheless. The board that Mayor Rizzo appointed once he took iron control of the schools was far less distinguished but much more representative of ordinary Philadelphia working stiffs in the row houses of Tioga, Bridesburg and Southwark.

For all of their valiant efforts to make public education work in Philadelphia, Dilworth and Shedd searched in vain for a true constituency. When the Philadelphia Federation of Teachers, AFL-CIO, turned against them their fate was sealed. Celia Pincus, the federation's perky, pint-sized president, had grown up in the liberal, trade-union movement. She had been among those civic leaders who pleaded with Dilworth to accept the school board presidency. She had always admired Dilworth's courage and candor. Gradually, though, she and her fellow unionists concluded that Dilworth and Shedd, in seeking to make the schools more "relevant" for kids, especially black kids, were undermining the authority of teachers and damaging the system. Under the reformers, Philadelphia's traditionally underpaid schoolteachers saw their salaries rise dramatically. But they still turned in for Rizzo in the 1971 mayoralty. Even Shedd conceded that Rizzo picked up votes by promising to fire him "eight seconds" after the election.

With her man in the mayor's office, Celia Pincus took a post, at $18,000 a year, as "educational adviser" to Rizzo. But Rizzo didn't really want an educational adviser and in a few months she was gone. Long before then, however, Shedd was gone and Dilworth was gone and a remarkable educational era had ended in Philadelphia.

Chapter Nine

Jim Tate fulfilled the pledge he had made to the voters during the campaign. He announced that Rizzo would not only be sworn in as police commissioner when the new administration was reinstalled in City Hall, he guaranteed that Rizzo would have a free hand and was assured of the job for a full four years.

"I'm very pleased with the commissioner's record since he took over," said Tate, who made what was for him an unusual trip to police headquarters to personally deliver the message on December 22, 1967, to Rizzo and the officers above the grade of lieutenant who worked for him in the Roundhouse. "He's gratifying. His reappointment is important not only locally, but nationally."

There were some reservations about Rizzo in the black community and among liberals, but most of the citizens agreed with Tate. Rizzo was a tough cop, good at his job, and that is what they wanted. A poll commissioned by the Philadelphia *Bulletin* in September 1967 found that an incredible 84 percent of the public approved of Rizzo's handling of the police department. Only 3 percent disapproved, and 13 percent had no opinion. The survey disclosed that Rizzo, despite a vaguely general reputation of being antiblack, was accepted as a good commissioner by a large number of blacks. But the poll samplings were taken at the end of a summer that was free of the disorder that marked many cities that year, and Philadelphia was grateful. The few racial incidents that developed were handled quickly and with restraint by Rizzo, who seemed to be at the scene of every trouble spot, personally taking charge. Television viewers became used to seeing Rizzo, wearing a helmet, accompanied by hundreds of his men, wherever trouble threatened. If flooding an area in which a minor fracas had occurred between a white shopkeeper and some black youths was overkill, it was overkill that worked in the summer of 1967.

The city did not erupt, as Detroit, with more than forty dead, and Newark, with twenty-five dead, did. And for that, as the *Bulletin* poll showed, Philadelphians, black and white, were grateful. But the blacks would not remain so grateful after Rizzo's style as commissioner became better known to them, after they had seen him in action on other occasions.

These occasions would reinforce an uneasy suspicion that Rizzo was at heart a racist, a northern Bull Connor whose concept of justice consisted of the speedy and expert truncheoning of the skulls of blacks. Rizzo would protest against this description of himself, but his unrestrained, implicitly violent public comments only served to strengthen that impression. Indeed, an examination of his record tended to support Rizzo. His truncheon was used with the same abandon on whites that it was on blacks.

But far more blacks than whites had contact with the police. Four out of five persons arrested for major crimes in Philadelphia were black. Blacks were responsible for most of the street crime, most of the murders, most of the rapes, most of the robberies. It was random violence by blacks against whites — a college student stabbed to death as he waited for a subway train, a seventeen-year-old youth murdered (because he refused a black gang's demand for money) as he entered a downtown bank three blocks from City Hall at high noon — that terrorized many whites and made them afraid to walk the streets.

And when acts of violence occurred, Rizzo responded in characteristic fashion, either with inflammatory rhetoric, which blacks believed was directed at them as a racial minority, or with strong, personal action, which was considered incontrovertible evidence of a sadistic hatred of blacks.

Rizzo's incendiary reaction to crimes of violence led to similar, if less intense, perceptions of him by the frightened whites. When he denounced a particularly atrocious crime committed by a black, these whites saw him as a sympathetic ally who was determined to keep the blacks in line. But when he condemned an act by a white criminal — as he did whenever one took place — both blacks and whites were able to accept that condemnation for what it was: an attack on a specific individual for a specific offense.

The perception of Rizzo as a racist, while related to his own words and actions, undoubtedly was partially rooted in the way people thought about themselves. Blacks historically had been discriminated against as a group, because they were part of a group that was locked out. A door slammed shut in the face of one black was a door slammed on all blacks. When Rizzo ranted about a specific black criminal, there was a tendency to interpret this as a general assault on the entire race, an assigning of guilt to blacks as a group.

Whites, who were used to being treated as individuals, did not feel threatened when Rizzo attacked a white criminal. But a good number of these same whites still saw blacks as group, rather than as a collection of individuals. And, when Rizzo reacted against a black criminal, they perceived it as a rebuke to the group, as well as to the individual. The vocal support Rizzo received from whites who lumped all blacks together, the whites who lived in the neighborhoods where resentment against the blacks was highest, heightened black suspicion of him. In the end, this interplay of emotion did as much as anything else to polarize the city into pro- and anti-Rizzo blocs.

As police commissioner, Rizzo did nothing to help his cause among blacks. In his public statements, he seemed unable to distinguish between black criminals and black activists who challenged authority on the basis of real grievances. In this, he was not unlike those whites who watched with mounting fury the television accounts of blacks marching in protest, occupying public buildings. Demonstrators were seen as thugs. There were "good" blacks, who obeyed the law and sat behind locked doors in their crime-ridden neighborhoods, and there were "bad" blacks, who stabbed and pillaged and defied authority, or encouraged others to do so.

"Hoodlums have no license to burn and sack Philadelphia in the name of civil liberties and civil rights activities," Rizzo said, shortly after Tate reappointed him. "I have no objection to Black Power or White Power or any power — political, economic, educational — as long as it operates within the framework of the law.

"Certainly, people have the right to seek redress for wrongs committed against them and I am in full sympathy with this philosophy. But, while we seek the answers to a better Philadelphia, let not the militant extremists under the cloak of civil rights riot, destroy, loot or attempt to burn down the city."

Rizzo's statement, which was made in response to a report of the Southeastern Pennsylvania chapter of Americans for Democratic Action, was clearly a demagogic attempt to brand unidentified civil rights activists as "hoodlums" who would "attempt to burn down the city." Who were the hoodlums? Was it some of the black, and white, activists? All of them? Those opposed to Rizzo? The truth was that no one had tried to riot, destroy, loot or burn down the city.

Instead of replying to the criticism, Rizzo sought to capitalize on the antagonism that his supporters harbored for black demonstrators. It was a tactic he would use again and again. Ignore the criticism. Attack the critics and their friends. Turn it into an us-against-them situation.

"The deterioration of police-community relations in Philadelphia is reaching a critical state," the ADA report said, without mentioning Rizzo by name. "We are concerned over the arrogance, lack of neutrality and violence exhibited by the police in a tense situation such as that of Nov. 17 [1967] at the School Administration Building, and the increasing 'hardline' on civil liberties and civil rights activities."

Rizzo's answer was to shout that "they" were going to burn the town down.

"I consider it a compliment, coming from them, and I hope they continue to attack and criticize me," Rizzo said, after the ADA accused him on another occasion of politicizing the police.

"What they say doesn't bother me, because from what I've learned in the past, no one takes them seriously because they're so ridiculous. They're a group of self-styled, self-centered intellectuals, and they don't speak for the average citizen but only for themselves. Ninety percent of these ADAers live outside the city and come into Philadelphia for only one reason — to take money out. The majority of the people in the city don't agree with the ADA philosophy."

A major reason for ADA's dissatisfaction with Rizzo was the common perception of him as a racist by the group's overwhelmingly white membership. It was a perception shared by many in the black community.

The racist charge was one that infuriated Rizzo. He *knew* he wasn't a racist. He lived in an integrated neighborhood. He had worked in black areas, and with black policemen, during much of his career. He numbered scores of blacks among his acquaintances — Rizzo called them "friends," although he never had dinner with them or socialized with them, sought their advice or confided in them. For the most part, his black acquaintances were cops, and he maintained an easy and relaxed relationship with them. And he continued his association with them after he became mayor, an association that was marked by an old station-house camaraderie, where the issue of race was dealt with by gruff and brittle back-room humor.

Most of the blacks who worked for Rizzo liked him and would not dream of describing him as a racist. Some of the more thoughtful of them felt he had all the compassion and more for the black man that the ADA-type liberals proclaimed in their reports and at their dinners. But they noticed that while he was a whiz with cops, he just didn't seem to understand blacks who were not cops or criminals. He stiffened when asked to face blacks in situations other than one-on-one. He would help, they said, as long as you asked for his help. And he wouldn't help only cops. He would help anybody who was down, even a guy with a record. The *padrone* would find you a job, get you an apartment, put you in touch with the right politician in City Hall. Just don't *demand* things of him. Frank Rizzo bowed to no one. Ask him to fix up a black family with a decent house to live in and he would try. Ask him to tackle the housing problem and he would be baffled.

Tony Fulwood didn't think Frank Rizzo was a racist. Fulwood was the young, giant black policeman whom Rizzo brought with him to City Hall as a bodyguard after he became mayor. Rizzo spoke to Fulwood the way a tough but genial sergeant would speak to a rookie cop, and he was delighted when Fulwood returned his gibes. And the exchanges were frankly racial and ethnic.

"Wait for me in the car, Fulwood," Rizzo said one day. "And no eatin'. I don't want chitlin's and greens all over the inside."

"What about rigatoni?" Fulwood retorted.

On another occasion, Rizzo, Fulwood and several others were striding along Kennedy Boulevard toward Stouffer's Restaurant for lunch — where Fulwood and the other bodyguards, black and white, would eat at a separate table — when the mayor announced that he had a joke to tell.

"Come on, Fulwood, I want you to hear this," he said. He assumed the character of a man walking splayfooted backward and forward on the sidewalk, snapping his fingers and chanting, "Seventy-two, seventy-two, seventy-two," while curious passersby gaped at their mayor.

"Hey, man, whutchuall doin' that for, walkin' and countin' like that?" Rizzo said next, slipping into the role of a black man questioning the walker.

"It brings you good luck," Rizzo had the walker respond. "Come on, you do it. Walk forward, then backward, and say, 'Seventy-two, seventy-two.'"

With a great flourish, Rizzo strutted up the sidewalk in an exaggerated imitation of the manner in which he believed a black Saturday night cowboy might walk. Then he reversed himself and began strutting backward, repeating, "Seventy-two, seventy-two," with an inflection he thought was straight out of the ghetto.

Suddenly, he stopped dead and described with his hands and voice the image of a body plummeting from sight. "Whooooosh." The walker had removed a manhole cover and tricked the black man into walking backward until he plunged into the hole.

"Seventy-three, seventy-three, seventy-three," the mayor said, as he once again walked splayfooted up the sidewalk, snapping his fingers and pretending to be looking for another black, after having replaced the imaginary manhole cover.

Tony Fulwood grinned.

Although some might have found the point of the joke in questionable taste, it was of a piece with the rough, hard banter that Rizzo enjoyed, whether with blacks or whites. There appeared to be no malice in it. Instead, there was a recognition of the fact that there were differences between the races. And it was a way for Rizzo to needle Tony Fulwood, a young man he genuinely liked.

This was a side of Rizzo that was largely unknown in the black community. Along Columbia Avenue in North Philadelphia and the Fifty-second Street "strip" in West Philadelphia, the man the blacks saw was the General. That was the name Rizzo's men had pinned on him when he was the commissioner, and he was proud of it. He often described the police department as a paramilitary organization. What more suitable nickname could there be for the head of that organization than the General, which carried with it the connotations of forcefulness, power and command?

He carried himself like a general. Hair always neatly trimmed and combed. Faultlessly dressed and groomed. The shiniest shoes. Gleaming car. Spotless office.

"When I was a cop, I used to shine my leather every night," he told us. "The holster, the belt, the boots. Until you could see your face in the sonofabitch. That's why it gets me when you see these guys walking around in baggy pants."

Rizzo said he continued to shine his own shoes even after he became mayor. No one else could do it as well. He outlined a complicated procedure, starting first with a liquid polish, then wax polish, topped off with Simoniz and rubbed with a Turkish towel.

"You could walk through water in them and just wipe them off," he said.

If the General was an imposing and fearsome figure in the ghetto, he was a genuine hero in the Roundhouse. No police commissioner in memory had been able to win the complete loyalty of so many members of the department as Rizzo did, and in a very short time.

He had enemies, of course. Police station politics is as rough as politics anywhere. Policemen are chronic gripers, and very often their target is the man at the top. A cop's job, while it has its perquisites, is not a pleasant one, particularly in large cities. Like cops in most big cities, Philadelphia's policemen traditionally have believed they were underpaid, unloved, misunderstood, unappreciated and at the mercy of politicians.

They were especially suspicious of the quality and quantity of the support they could expect from the police commissioner as they went about their tension-filled duties. Before Rizzo, there was a good deal of doubt about the loyalty they could expect from whoever was the occupant of Suite 318 in the Roundhouse.

Eddie Bell was a nice guy, but he had lost favor when he spoke out in favor of retaining the hated police advisory board. Howard Leary was even worse, in the minds of many cops. He had more friends in the ADA than he did in the police department. He was a stronger advocate of the police advisory board than Bell. And he was remote, a scholarly type, not one of the boys. It was suspected that, at heart, Leary was really a liberal. Al Brown was another nice guy, but he had served too long as Tom Gibbons's deputy for any cop to trust him.

Gibbons had been the commissioner from 1952 until 1960, and the PAB was established during his tenure. He fired cops he thought were brutal or crooked. He started using officers designated as staff inspectors to investigate allegations against cops. It was said that he arranged to listen in on telephone conversations of cops he mistrusted.

One of the station houses Gibbons was known to have an avid interest in was the one at Twelfth and Pine streets, and he had this interest in it when Frank Rizzo was the captain in that district. It is known that this interest led Gibbons to listen in on a conversation in which Frank Rizzo was said to have described him in extremely unflattering terms, questioning his ancestry, his manhood, his courage and various other attributes in explicit, police station language.

This conversation occurred in the late 1950s, and it is known that Rizzo found himself in deep trouble with Gibbons around that time. It is also known that if Rizzo had not gone to a city councilman from South Philadelphia named Paul D'Ortona and asked for his help, and if D'Ortona hadn't interceded for him, Rizzo would not have remained a captain for long, and might never have been named inspector, deputy commissioner, commissioner or, finally, elected mayor.

Rizzo was not like Gibbons or Leary or any of his predecessors. He would admit only grudgingly that, in theory, it was possible to encounter a crooked or brutal cop. In practice, he almost never conceded that such a cop existed. He saw cops as the white hats fighting the real enemy, criminals, and he was determined to deal with them in his own way.

To fight this enemy, Rizzo started out with a Police Department numbering about seven thousand employees. The size of the General's army, however, increased quickly, climbing to eight thousand and then to more than nine thousand. And the budget climbed even faster, from less than $60,000,000 to $81,000,000 to more than $100,000,000. Nothing was too good for the department ruled by the man who had gotten Jim Tate reelected. Not even if it cost more than the combined budgets of the streets and fire departments, or the public health and public welfare departments.

Rizzo saw to it that his men — and it was always "my men" or "my guys" — got pay raises, with starting officers being increased from $6,900 a year to almost $10,000, and time and a half for overtime, instead of compensatory time off, which the cops called "counterfeit money."

Despite the infusion of more money and manpower, and despite the presence of a tough-talking police commissioner who had been given a free hand, crime continued to increase in Philadelphia, just as it did around the nation. Homicides climbed from 234 in 1967, Rizzo's first year as commissioner, to 352 in 1970, his last year. Robberies jumped from 2,919 to 6,377.

Yet Rizzo was able to boast that Philadelphia was the safest big city in America and he could point to FBI statistics which he said proved his claim. What he did not say, however, was that the FBI reports merely reflected what the agency had been told by the nation's various police departments. When Rizzo bragged that FBI statistics showed for 1969 that Philadelphia had an incidence of only 18.2 major crimes per 1,000 population, he failed to point out that the FBI was simply reporting what Rizzo had told the agency the incidence of crime was.*

The FBI made no attempt to check the figures it received from the police departments. It accepted the figures supplied by the departments, matched them against population figures, and published the reported crime rates. On that basis, Philadelphia has claimed to be the safest of the ten largest cities every year since the 1950s. In 1969, Rizzo's figures portrayed Philadelphia as having the lowest crime of the fifty-eight largest cities.

But the figures provided by Rizzo, and his predecessors, have long been suspect. In 1968, for example, Baltimore Police Chief Donald D. Pomerleau noted to reporters that his city, with half the population of Philadelphia's, had reported 67,157 major crimes while Philadelphia reported only 33,439. Pomerleau then pointed out that Philadelphia reported more murders than Baltimore, adding the comment:

"Ha, I guess ole Frank can't hide bodies."†

Even though Rizzo consistently claimed, on the basis of his questionable statistics, that Philadelphia was the safest big city, he never tried to claim that crime wasn't a major problem. Indeed, he

---

* The seven crimes included in the "major crimes" category are homicide, robbery, rape, burglary, aggravated assault and battery, larceny over $50 and auto theft.
† The suspicions of Pomerleau and others were confirmed when the Law Enforcement Assistance Agency published a crime victimization study in 1974 of thirteen selected cities. The study was based on interviews with approximately 22,000 persons in each of the cities. The interviews, conducted by the U.S. Census Bureau, sought to determine the rate of victimization in each city in order to compare that rate with the reports prepared by the police departments.

The study found that for every major crime reported by the Philadelphia Police Department in 1972, 5.1 crimes were actually committed. The gap between police-reported crime and actual crime, according to the study, was far greater in Philadelphia than in any of the other cities tested.

The LEAA found that in every city the actual rate of crime was higher than the rate reported by the police department to the FBI. Donald Santarelli, who was then head of LEAA, said the difference between the actual and the reported crime rates could be explained in part by the fact that half of those interviewed "did not feel it was worth it to report a crime."

Where citizens do not report crimes, the local police department cannot, of course, include those crimes in the statistics they turn over to the FBI. The much greater difference between Philadelphia's ratio of unreported to reported crime, however, lends support to accusations by such experts as former New York City Police Com-

never missed an opportunity to warn of the dangers of crime and lenient judges, and he did so with such bombast and flamboyance that he attracted more and more television and newspaper coverage.

The news out of City Hall was generally dull and colorless. Mayor Tate probably knew more about the nuts and bolts of the city's government than any of his predecessors, but he knew it the way a mechanic knew how to fix a machine invented by someone else. He was a technician with no grand concepts or bright visions. And he disliked the news media to the point where he would go for months without speaking to reporters. Much of the big news made by Tate came when he issued his "emergency proclamations" banning groups of twelve or more from the streets. Invariably, these proclamations would be issued at Rizzo's request, with Rizzo providing the reasons why they were needed, and with Rizzo being quoted at length in the newspapers and on television.

Unlike reporters in City Hall, reporters in search of a story in the Roundhouse were rarely disappointed. Rizzo was always willing to oblige. And the stories he gave out indicated that something was happening in the Roundhouse even if it wasn't in City Hall.

Where police sergeants only occasionally and lieutenants only rarely patrolled the streets in radio cars, Rizzo saw to it that two sergeants and one lieutenant from each of the city's twenty-two districts were put on regular daily patrol. He issued orders that all patrol cars in black neighborhoods be integrated. He computerized the department's record-keeping, then tracked the areas of crime incidence through the computers and revised the boundaries of the patrol sectors to conform to the findings of the computers.

Rizzo established the nation's first "Granny Squad," in which policemen disguised themselves as vulnerable citizens — like grandmothers — to attract muggers. He built the K-9 Corps up from a few handlers and dogs to a major unit of some six dozen German shepherds and policemen trained to handle them, with many of the teams being assigned to the subway entrances that people feared to enter. Foot patrolmen were issued walkie-talkies, enabling them for the first time to be in constant touch with headquarters. Patrol cars were equipped with flashing red lights and

---

missioner Patrick V. Murphy that Philadelphia has deliberately underreported crime to the FBI.

Where Philadelphia had 5.1 major crimes for every one reported, the LEAA found this ratio in other cities: Newark, New Jersey, 1.4 to one; St. Louis, 1.5; New York, 2.1; Baltimore, 2.2; Atlanta, 2.3; Cleveland, 2.4; Portland, Oregon, and Dallas, 2.6; Detroit, 2.7; Chicago, 2.8, and Los Angeles and Denver, 2.9.

sirens, heretofore used only on emergency wagons. And Rizzo ended the inefficient and expensive practice of buying regular panel trucks and converting them for use as emergency wagons by requiring suppliers to produce specially built wagons.

Rizzo failed in his attempt to have the city purchase two armored personnel vehicles because a huge cry of protest was launched by blacks and civil-liberties groups, accusing the police commissioner of wanting to introduce "tanks" onto the streets of Philadelphia. Tate, who originally supported Rizzo's request, backed down in the face of the opposition and did not press the city council to fund the purchase.

But Rizzo did succeed in purchasing three air-conditioned, radio-equipped buses. With these buses, he could move 150 policemen to a scene of trouble quickly. Moving policemen by the busload was in keeping with Rizzo's theory that superior force must be used, or at least displayed, to quell disturbances. This theory was proved out in the days following the assassination of The Reverend Dr. Martin Luther King, Jr., on April 4, 1968. While many other American cities were being put to the torch, Rizzo and his roving army of policemen helped keep Philadelphia peaceful. Throughout Rizzo's four summers as police commissioner, Philadelphia was spared the riotous conditions that visited other cities.

Rizzo's performance was being noted outside of Philadelphia, too. On July 16, 1968, Richard M. Nixon, campaigning for President, was met at the city's International Airport by Rizzo and Rizzo was invited into the Republican's car for a ten-minute conference.

"Before coming here I asked to see Rizzo," Nixon told reporters after the conference. "Because he was unable to meet with me later in the day, I talked with him at the airport. Rizzo's record has met with the approval of all law enforcement officers across the United States. He has an effective record. I wanted to get his views. As I see it, other cities could use Rizzo's ideas. His program has much support among all elements of the Philadelphia community."

On September 20, 1968, just a month after he received the Republican presidential nomination, Nixon returned to Philadelphia and once again was greeted by Rizzo.

"I think you guys are setting the right standard of justice and law," Nixon said to Rizzo, who called him "Dick." Nixon would express similar sentiments about Rizzo on three subsequent visits to the city while he was President.

With the support of a Democratic mayor, and the high praise of a law-and-order Republican President, Rizzo was emerging as the dominant figure in Philadelphia's government. And he knew how to further that emergence. Each morning, reporters from the three daily newspapers were invited into the commissioner's office for coffee and conversation. For the most part the men who covered police headquarters had spent years trying to pry tidbits of information from closemouthed detectives who feared the wrath of their superiors if they talked. They could perhaps get a "Good morning" from the past three commissioners, but very little else.

Rizzo, however, chose to bestow favors rather than withhold them. He provided the reporters with coffee and a delightful half hour or hour each morning, during which he regaled them with hilarious inside stories, like the one about the aging Mafia don who had been arrested in a national park in Arkansas while "cornholing" a hotel bellhop. Most importantly, he was the source of news, often news that ended up on page one.

During the period of his commissionership Rizzo was portrayed as the swashbuckling protector of the city, determined to save the citizens from the criminals who stalked the streets. He took no vacations, appeared at the scene of virtually every newsworthy crime and seemed to be available to comment on every event bearing on the criminal justice system whether it occurred within his jurisdiction or not.

"I say it is cruel and unusual punishment to keep these criminals sitting there on Death Row year after year," Rizzo said, in response to Milton J. Shapp's announcement after his election as governor of Pennsylvania in 1970 that the electric chair would not be used during his administration.

"It would be more merciful to carry out the verdict of the jury as provided by law — put them to death quickly."

When a suburban housewife was found murdered, outside of Philadelphia's jurisdiction, Rizzo was asked to comment and obliged by saying, "When they come up with the people who did that, I could throw the switch myself."

"We need two thousand more policemen to stop this," Rizzo said, after two of his men were wounded in a shootout in the summer of 1970. "The only other thing we can do now is buy tanks and start mounting machine guns."

Ironically, as major crime in Philadelphia increased by 10.8 percent in 1969 and a whopping 23.4 percent in 1970 (especially considering the fact that Rizzo was widely believed to be underreporting crime in those years), the popularity of the police commissioner seemed to grow. Each time a heinous crime was committed, Rizzo was given the opportunity to appear on television and be quoted in the newspapers denouncing criminals in language designed to appeal to a frightened citizenry.

"If the prisons are crowded, if we need more prisons, let's build them," he told the Pennsylvania Crime Commission in 1968. "We must isolate the hardened criminals. Most of these hardened criminals are beyond rehabilitation.... They are being pampered."

In August 1969, in an unprecedented breach of the separation of powers, Rizzo arranged for a highly publicized meeting, attended by Mayor Tate and District Attorney Specter, with sixteen Philadelphia judges. During the hour and a half meeting Rizzo lectured the judges on the need for them to impose longer sentences on those convicted of crimes. Earlier, he had accused "a certain few judges of playing a deadly game of Russian roulette with the citizens of Philadelphia as the potential victims."

Pennsylvania judges are elected on their own for ten-year terms, and once elected are free to act as independently as they wish. It was a measure of Rizzo's growing power that these judges permitted Rizzo to criticize them in harsh terms publicly, then agreed to sit still for a private tongue-lashing from him. After that meeting, Austin Norris, a black attorney who had been a force in city politics for fifty years, wrote a letter of protest to the president judge, Vincent A. Carroll.

"These are dangerous times and the rights of the individual may be in jeopardy, the independence of the judiciary threatened and judges scared into unjudicial and senseless sentences, mainly on Negroes," Norris wrote. "More than 80 percent of persons arrested for crimes of violence are Negroes, and more than 90 percent of their crimes are committed against Negroes."

Norris's letter appeared in the Philadelphia newspapers one day and was thereafter forgotten, to be replaced by the news of Henry Stevenson, a sixty-nine-year-old merchant who was stabbed to death in his North Philadelphia grocery store. In a city where murders were occurring at a rate of better than one every day, there were many gruesome stories to be told, and the ones usually given the most prominence involved white persons being killed by young blacks.

Francis George, twenty-one, a University of Pennsylvania student, son of the chairman of Penn's history department, murdered in an unprovoked attack as he walked through Powelton Village, a residential community near the campus. "One of them held me, the other stabbed me," George told passersby who found him on the sidewalk just before he died.

Rachela Steinberg, twenty-three, a Temple University graduate and assistant public relations director for a Jewish organization, stabbed twenty-five times and murdered in her center-city apartment. She was the only daughter by a second marriage of Abraham Steinberg, seventy, whose first wife and three children were murdered in a Nazi concentration camp. "Our daughter was our life," Steinberg said. "An animal killed our daughter."

David H. Fineman, twenty-one, a junior-high-school teacher, shot to death as he walked to his car parked on the Temple campus after an evening postgraduate course. "We just wanted to shoot somebody, anybody," one of the two black youths arrested was quoted by police as saying. Police said he told them that before the shooting his friend had said, "Let's go out and get us a whitey."

David Bodenstein, sixty-one, shot in the head and killed instantly. His wife Mae, fifty-eight, the right side of her head crushed, dead on the operating table at Temple University Hospital. Both of them found on the floor of their North Philadelphia shop, the D & M Variety Store, by customers. The heavy steel gate used to protect the premises when the store was closed had eight locks attached to it.

Isadore Selez, sixty, a South Philadelphia junk dealer, set upon in his shop by four boys, the oldest eighteen, the youngest fifteen, who beat him and slashed his throat with a hacksaw. All the money he had with him — $31 — was stolen.

Austin Norris's plea, in the face of a steady stream of bloodshed, did nothing to stem the growth of Rizzo's power.

After Nixon's law-and-order-oriented "silent majority" had voted him into office in 1968, the idea that Rizzo's police power might be transformed into another kind of power began to take hold on the police commissioner and his friends. Almost three full years before Philadelphia's 1971 mayoralty election, Al Gaudiosi, then a *Bulletin* rewrite man and reporter, began openly to discuss in the newsroom his friend Rizzo's candidacy for mayor. And he made it clear he intended to work for a Rizzo candidacy.

As rumors of Rizzo's political ambitions became widespread, Mayor Tate did nothing to discourage them. As the leader of a generally mediocre administration, he turned more and more to Rizzo, the one superstar he had. And Rizzo exploited his boss's

143

weaknesses to shape city government the way he thought it ought to be shaped. On December 22, 1969, at Rizzo's insistence, Tate abolished the police advisory board. As its title indicated, the PAB was advisory in nature and sought to bring a civilian viewpoint to cases where police conduct was questioned. It could hold hearings and make recommendations, but it could not on its own discipline any officer. Punishment remained the exclusive prerogative of the police commissioner.

In the eleven years of its existence, the PAB had handled about a thousand cases brought against policemen, mostly for alleged police brutality. As a result of those cases, one policeman was dismissed and about twenty others received suspensions. No other policeman missed a day's pay. But the mere concept of civilians — outsiders — reviewing the conduct of police had long been offensive to Rizzo and the Fraternal Order of Police. And so Tate, despite the protests from the black voters who elected him, acceded to Rizzo's wishes and did what the FOP had gone to court to do and failed — he abolished the PAB.

Tate's obeisance to Rizzo, however, boomeranged less than two months later. The streets department, a three-thousand-man operation with a $40,000,000 budget, was without a commissioner. It was and is a sensitive department, responsible at that time for collecting 1,100,000 tons of refuse and garbage yearly, and for designing, constructing, maintaining and lighting the city's streets.

When the commissioner's job became vacant, Tate did not turn to any of the department's deputies. He did not consult any traffic engineers. He went instead to Rizzo and Rizzo told the mayor he had the ideal man for the job: Chief Inspector Joseph F. Halferty, a likable Irishman who was in charge of the police department's uniformed forces. Halferty at one time had been in charge of the foot traffic division — that is, the city's traffic cops — and that was his strongest qualification for the job.

Nevertheless, on February 2, 1970, Tate named Halferty acting streets commissioner, touching off perhaps the biggest crisis in his ten years as mayor. The sanitation workers, most of whom were black, objected to a policeman being put in charge of their department. They responded with a slowdown, and trash began piling up on the streets. Ten days later the city obtained from common pleas court an injunction prohibiting the slowdown from continuing, but the streets remained littered with sacks of rubbish. On February 16, with thousands of tons of trash uncollected, Halferty was sworn in as commissioner. The sanitation workers moved at their own pace and refused to work overtime, even though Tate had declared that a state of emergency existed. Tate, Rizzo and Halferty caved in on February 25. Halferty resigned as streets commissioner and returned to the police department, and trash collections resumed.

Despite the streets department fiasco, Tate — who was ineligible to run for a third term as mayor under the city charter — and other politicians began to look at Rizzo as a potential candidate for political office. And the reason Tate was inclined toward Rizzo was that he was aware of the fact that white Democrats in the row houses of Fishtown and South Philly were walking away from the Democratic Party to which the blacks had given such loyalty.

"Early in 1970, [Congressman] Bill Barrett mentioned to me several times that Rizzo would make a good candidate for governor," Tate wrote in his memoirs. "I countered by saying that he was not sufficiently known throughout the state, although he would get a huge vote in Philadelphia because of the 'safe streets' issue, for which most people thought he was responsible. . . . *One thing that was becoming obvious was that the old Democratic coalition of the City Committee, organized labor, the workng class whites, liberals and blacks and other minorities was breaking down. The working class whites, for example, who were not able, or did not choose to leave the city, were developing increasingly Republican tendencies. I felt that Rizzo could bring the white working class vote back into the Democratic Party.*"*

It was among these whites — many of whom had refused to vote for Tate — that Rizzo was strongest. He stood with them against those who threatened their way of life, the (black) muggers and killers, the bleeding-heart judges, the neighborhood-changers, the hoodlums in the schools. And as events unfolded in the year before the mayoralty election, the tough cop strengthened his hold on the frightened, and angry, ethnic whites in the urban outposts.

School Board President Dilworth, who had no love for Rizzo, appeared to confirm what the police commissioner had been saying about the dangers in the schools when he announced on April 19, 1970, that pupil absenteeism systemwide was an incredible 20 percent — almost three times the rate of most surrounding districts — and in some individual schools was chronically 30 percent.

"But this isn't just what people call 'playing hookey,' " Dilworth

* *In Praise of Politicians*, by James H. J. Tate, with Joseph P. McLaughlin, Philadelphia *Bulletin*, January 23, 1974. Emphasis added.

Police Commissioner Rizzo arrives in South Philadelphia from a formal dinner party, equipped to quell a disturbance.

said. "Sixty percent of it is fear — fear of what will happen on the way to school or in school. It's true there are incidents in the schools every day, particularly where members of the minority in a school — white or black — are getting beaten up or shaken down. In some schools, in the change between classes, it's just extraordinary what can be done in those halls."

Rizzo told reporters the trouble existed because policemen were not called in by school administrators.

"If we could send police in whenever there is trouble, we could clean up that situation in a short time," he said. "But they don't invite us in. They actually hide things from us. Teachers and pupils are assaulted and we don't even hear about it. All we have to do is send in a couple of policemen, grab some of these so-called tough guys by the scruff of the neck and that would be the end of the trouble."

The summer of 1970 was Rizzo's last as police commissioner but, unlike the three previous ones, this one showed some trouble although there were no riots, no burnings and lootings, no widespread confrontations between races. One continuing trouble spot was in the area of Tasker Homes, a South Philadelphia housing project occupied largely by blacks and surrounded by 15,000 row homes, occupied mostly by whites. On June 10, Tate issued an emergency proclamation banning groups of twelve or more from gathering in the area, the third year in a row he had used the edict at Rizzo's urging.

A year earlier, on June 12, 1969, Rizzo had been a guest at a dressy dinner in the Bellevue Stratford for Tate when an aide informed him that rock- and bottle-throwing was underway in Tasker Homes and crowds were beginning to form. Rizzo had left the dinner, climbed into Car One and arrived at the scene in less than ten minutes. Upon getting out of the car, he had borrowed a nightstick from a policeman, jammed it into the trousers of his tuxedo, and strode up to a band of young men who were shouting and hollering. Photographs of Rizzo in formal wear, billy club jutting out, had been flashed around the nation by the Associated Press. After Rizzo's arrival the situation had calmed and the rock-throwers went home.

It was not so easy in 1970. Between February 13 and the issuance of the proclamation, there had been seven stabbings in the Tasker Homes neighborhood. In addition to the ordinary fistfights and scuffles, there had been six serious assaults involving baseball bats, bricks and, in one instance, a hubcap. Police had confiscated

Police Commissioner Rizzo wipes tears away as he uses a hospital telephone to report to Mayor Tate that two policemen had been gunned down in an outbreak of violence in August 1970.

eleven Molotov cocktails, a .22-caliber rifle, a revolver, a zip gun with a door bolt for a firing pin, two straight razors and a collection of knives and clubs.

When Rizzo had raced to the area in mid-June 1969 amid reports of trouble, he found that a fracas between fifteen teenagers in a playground had grown to a battle involving four hundred persons, black and white. Five policemen were injured by flying bricks and bottles. Order was finally restored by two hundred blue-helmeted policemen, brought to the scene in Rizzo's buses. When it was over, a black reporter asked Rizzo if he didn't think that the economic condition of those who lived in the Tasker Homes area was behind the trouble.

"I'm a little short of change myself," the commissioner replied.

As the summer of 1970 wound toward a close, Rizzo became increasingly concerned about a "revolutionary people's constitutional convention," which was scheduled to begin September 5 at the North Philadelphia campus of Temple University under the sponsorship of the Black Panthers Party.

"We don't want it here," Rizzo announced. "But if it's peaceful, we're not going to stop it."

The weekend before the convention was to start, the last weekend in August, was hot and muggy. On Saturday evening, August 29, Park Policeman James Harrington, thirty-nine, was returning to the Cobbs Creek Guardhouse in West Philadelphia to refuel his patrol wagon. He never made it. As he sat in the wagon about a hundred yards from the guardhouse, a band of young black men sneaked up and shot him at point-blank range, leaving him for dead. (Harrington later recovered.)

Sergeant Frank Von Colln, forty-three, was the only man on duty in the guardhouse and he apparently did not hear the assault on Harrington. The same gang crept up on Von Colln and murdered him as he sat at his desk.

The next night, August 30, Patrolman Thomas J. Gibbons, Jr., twenty-five, son of the former police commissioner, was shot in the chest and his partner, John J. Nolen, twenty-eight, was shot in the face when they stopped a car in Southwest Philadelphia. Two black men were in the car, which had been stolen. Gibbons and Nolen eventually recovered.

"This is no longer a civilized neighborhood," Rizzo told reporters after seeing Gibbons and Nolen at Misericordia Hospital. He called Tate from the hospital and told him: "I got bad news for you. Two more of my men were shot. Two Negroes in the car and they opened fire. They didn't have a chance."

Rizzo blamed the Panthers, although there was no indication the two shootings were related. The names of those involved in the Von Colln murder were quickly obtained by police. Rizzo said the five suspects were members of the Black Unity Movement, which he said was affiliated with the Panthers. And he prepared to move against the Panthers.

"We're canceling days off," Rizzo declared. "We're going to be loaded and ready for bear. Positively [there is] a nationwide plot against police. We're dealing with a group of fanatics, yellow dogs that they are. We are preparing for any eventuality. We're dealing with psychotics and we must be in a position to take them on. These imbeciles and yellow dogs, when the police action is strong enough they want no part of the Philadelphia Police Department."

Leaving the hospital, Rizzo returned to the Roundhouse to plan the move against the Panthers. Detectives from the homicide division were in the process of arresting those responsible for the murder of Von Colln and the shooting of Harrington. Late on the night of August 30, Rizzo and his aides were preparing to strike directly against the Panthers. By 2 A.M., the department was assembling about one hundred men, all of them experienced marksmen, to be deployed into three raiding parties against three Panthers headquarters. The necessary warrants had been obtained, and Rizzo went home to bed.

Shortly before 6 A.M. on August 31, the raiders struck. They encountered no resistance at Panther offices in North Philadelphia and Germantown and found no evidence to justify any arrests. But at the Panther headquarters on Wallace Street in West Philadelphia, gunfire was exchanged, fourteen persons were taken into custody and police confiscated five shotguns, seven rifles and two handguns.*

The raiding party virtually dismantled the two-story building on Wallace Street, which also served as a residence for some Panthers. The plumbing was ripped out and furniture was destroyed. As the occupants emerged, hands above their heads, the lone woman was led to a van and searched by a policewoman. The men, most of them bare-chested and barefoot, were lined up against the wall. Before the men could be searched, however, six of them were sud-

---

* All fourteen were freed on September 4, 1970, because of a lack of evidence. One man, Reginald Schell, was subsequently convicted in federal court on charges of possessing a firearm stolen from a federal armory.

denly standing there naked. Their pants and shorts had dropped to the sidewalk and they had stepped out of them. A photographer for the *Daily News*, Elwood P. Smith, snapped off a photograph and the sight of six Panthers and their bare buttocks was distributed around the world by United Press International. The Panthers later claimed the police ordered them to strip, but police on the scene said they had only ordered the men to loosen their trousers to permit a more thorough search for weapons.

"This was an excellent job," Rizzo said, in response to a wave of criticism that raged after the photograph of the naked Panthers hit the streets on August 31. "They can hide weapons, grenades and so forth, in their clothing. This is a dangerous game. We did nothing wrong — nothing wrong that the police did. Their feelings were hurt. The big Black Panthers with their trousers down.

"Not to cloud the issue, but these Panthers executed a man in cold blood and shot another policeman for no reason at all.* We raided Panther Headquarters and this is the first raid by police against Panther Headquarters. We raided it only when we had the legal right. We had information from infiltrators and informers and from the black community that they did have guns in there. . . .

"Some black leaders spew out. Why did they not speak out before? I didn't hear them speak out when Von Colln was shot. As far as I'm concerned, they can go wash their necks."

Returning to the thing that worried him most, the Panther-sponsored convention, Rizzo said:

"They are not going to come into the community and challenge the whole community, black and white. If they come in, we will have no trouble unless they break the law. Then they'll be taken on by the black and white policemen. Who started all this? My men or those imbeciles? They put out the trash, 'Kill the pigs,' photographs of police on their knees being executed. Who are the animals? Not the police. Who did we execute?

"This is a national conspiracy. We are dealing with professionals who visit Communist countries. They send experts in to visit the Black Panthers here to give directions and instructions and to educate because the lunatics don't know enough. This is the conspiracy."

There could be no doubt that Rizzo was genuinely enraged. His massive fingers worked themselves into fists, opening and closing as if he were squeezing something. The statements he uttered in anger

* The Panthers were never tied directly to Von Colln's murder.

were carried at great length to a city already shocked by a weekend of violence. Then Rizzo issued his challenge.

"Why don't they call us and tell us they want to kill us?" he said. "Why don't they tell us they want to have it out? We'll meet them anytime. We'll go on their terms. If they say they'll have ten men they can have anything they want with them, and we'll go with two. Do they have to be cowards? Aren't five to one odds good enough for them?

"These creeps lurk in the dark. You never have a chance against them. They should be strung up. I mean within the law. The prisons are full of men sentenced to death who have not paid for their crimes with their lives. After juries sentence them to death, why are they still sitting in jail? I know one thing: If they were put to death they wouldn't be able to get out and take a second life. They're nothing but barbarians. They deserve no mercy under our law.

"We have to operate within the law yet the courts, the liberals, are making it easy for them to operate outside the law. This is actual warfare. I'll tell you one thing. The Philadelphia Police Department won't tolerate it here if the courts and everybody else do."

Liberal groups, indeed, did protest and they accused Rizzo of trying to use the Von Colln murder to prevent the revolutionary convention from being held. Father David Gracie, then Urban Missioner for the Episcopal Diocese of Pennsylvania, met with such a group at diocesan headquarters on Rittenhouse Square to denounce the raids.

"All of us want an end to violence," Father Gracie said, at that meeting. "We must do everything necessary to prevent the escalation of violence. However, we dare not allow the violence which has occurred to be the cloak for the destruction of all political opposition."

Panther sympathizers filed a suit in U.S. District Court asking that Rizzo and the police department be enjoined from violating the rights of political dissidents and blacks for a period of one week. Many saw the lawsuit as fatuous or worse since, technically, the police were always enjoined from violating anyone's rights. After five hours of hearings U.S. District Court Judge John P. Fullam on September 4, the same day those arrested in the Panther raids were freed, issued an order which simply restated the law: that is, that the police were forbidden to violate anyone's rights. In his order, however, Fullam included this observation:

A madman out of control shooting at policemen is not much more dangerous to the community than a policeman who loses control and goes shooting up people's houses and raiding them. People don't seem to realize — and I am talking about the police officers themselves — that when they permit this kind of reaction to take place, they are putting in the hands of one madman with a gun the ability to control the rights of all the citizens of Philadelphia.

In the wake of the murder of Von Colln, there was little chance that Fullam's comments would be received warmly in the homes of those who had never had occasion to complain about the police and who were now frightened, in good part because of Rizzo's rhetoric, at the prospect of widespread black violence. And whatever chance there was evaporated hours before the order was issued, when Huey P. Newton arrived at International Airport.

Newton, then twenty-eight, was a cofounder of the Panthers and was serving as the organization's "defense minister." He was also free on $50,000 bail at the time on charges of shooting an Oakland policeman.

"I understand Bozo's off his leash," Newton said to fifty of his supporters and some reporters who had gone to the airport to meet him. "That's Rizzo's name, Bozo the mad dog. Well, we're going to put Bozo back on his leash."

Newton raised his right fist and his supporters predictably responded with "Power to the people, off the pigs." Then he went to Fullam's courtroom, to be joined by radical lawyers William M. Kunstler and Charles R. Garry. After the order was issued, Newton consented to an interview with Claude Lewis, associate editor of the *Bulletin*, in the center-city home of Joseph Miller, a white businessman, a liberal Democrat and a leader of Philadelphians for Equal Justice, a group involved in the revolutionary convention. Newton's words were not designed to reassure row-house Philadelphia, and they were printed on the front page of the state's largest newspaper.

"Rizzo acts like some kind of savage, but his actions have angered the community," Newton said. "Bozo definitely aided in mobilizing the community. We would like to thank him for that. I understand that many of the white working class here in Philadelphia support Bozo the police commissioner. But in the final analysis, Bozo's primitive brutal tactics will not serve the very people who support him.

"When people are oppressed to a point where they say, 'Off the pig,' they won't only say that, they will do that. Now, a few policemen were shot here and killed here. The party's not responsible for that. The community people drew the line. And we understand that a line had to be drawn somewhere. . . . As long as it's to break the shackles of the people, and so long as it's to the interest of most people, we're not apologizing for the community using the words, 'Power to the people,' and if it frightens people, that's okay. We want people to be so frightened that they will stop the oppression."*

Despite Rizzo's fears, and despite Newton's incendiary words, the three-day revolutionary convention opened on Setember 6 and closed on September 8 without incident. Rizzo had one thousand police ready in the event trouble developed, but they were unobtrusive and forced no confrontations even though some of the six thousand persons who attended felt obliged to hurl insults and curses at policemen traveling past Temple's North Broad Street campus.

When it was over, and Newton had left town, the city's business and civic leaders made it clear that they appreciated Rizzo and his efforts. The Greater Philadelphia Movement, whose members included major bankers, real estate tycoons, utility executives, merchants and lawyers, sent Rizzo a telegram which said:

"Representatives of GPM have personally observed abuse and provocation to which your men are often, on such occasions, subjected. We congratulate you and them for maintaining peace during the meetings at Temple University."

The Urban Coalition, a group whose members interlocked to some extent with GPM, sent Rizzo a letter stating, "During the recent period of tension, you and the department worked under great stress and provocation to maintain order and peace in a manner that was unobtrusive, reasonable and most effective."

The signers of the letter included Richard C. Bond, chairman of the Wanamaker Trustees and former president of John Wanamaker, the city's largest department store; Herman C. Wrice, a highly regarded young black activist; and R. Stewart Rauch, Jr., president of the Philadelphia Saving Fund Society, the largest savings bank in the city, which drew many of its deposits from rowhouse Philadelphia.

And if that were not enough, Joe D. Jamieson supplied the frost-

* Philadelphia *Bulletin*, September 6, 1970.

ing on the cake at a dinner in his own honor on September 23. Jamieson was the special-agent-in-charge of the Philadelphia FBI office and, unless he never read a newspaper, listened to the radio news, watched the television news or shot the breeze with policemen, he knew that Frank Rizzo intended to run for mayor. He may not have intended to help Rizzo's campaign but, in those pre-Watergate days when the FBI's reputation was still relatively good, it certainly didn't hurt Rizzo when he rose and said:

"We should stop and think where this great city would be if, one morning, we woke up and the nation's best police commissioner and police force were not around to protect our families and our businesses."

One of those who thought Rizzo was a great police commissioner was Larry Rubin, a city worker detailed to write press releases for the police department. In November 1970, Tate gave the word to lay off hundreds of city workers because of a budget squeeze. Rubin was ticketed to go.

A few days later, Tate was honoring the memory of three dead policemen and was presenting their widows with checks in a City Hall ceremony when Rizzo saw Rubin.

"Don't worry," Rizzo told him. "You'll be taken care of."

Rubin was placed on the police department's payroll.

Chapter Ten

THE MORE JIM TATE analyzed the voting trends in Philadelphia, particularly in the Italian, Polish, Irish and Jewish wards, the more convinced he became that the Democrats needed Frank Rizzo as their candidate for mayor in 1971. On paper, the Democrats had a three-to-two registration edge over the Republicans, but it was not working out that way in municipal elections. While the results varied somewhat from contest to contest, the signals were unmistakable: ethnic row-house whites, mostly Catholics and Jews, were deserting the Democrats.

In 1969, Republican Arlen Specter was reelected district attorney over Democrat David Berger, who had been city solicitor under Tate, by more than 100,000 votes. Specter's votes came not from the blacks, but from South Philadelphia, Roxborough and the virtually all-white Northeast. His performance was a continuation of the progress the Republicans had made among the row houses in 1967, when Specter gave Tate the fright of his life by coming within 11,000 votes of defeating him. In that election, Tate lost South Philadelphia, Richmond, Frankford, Lawndale, Tacony,

Mayfair, Oxford Circle and the rest of the Northeast. Significantly, he also lost those areas where blacks were beginning to move into white neighborhoods — heavily Jewish Oak Lane and Wynnefield, Olney, Mt. Airy and Germantown.

Tate was saved only by the steadfast loyalty of black voters to the Democratic Party. In the city's twenty-two predominantly black wards, Tate beat Specter by better than two to one and his 58,000-vote margin in those wards enabled him to eke out a victory. Specter won thirty of the sixty-six wards, and twenty-one of those had Democratic registration majorities.

The vote totals showed that the Democrats could hold onto the blacks, but it was becoming clear that the price of holding onto the blacks was the continued loss of whites to the Republicans. Projecting this trend through the 1971 election, it seemed a good bet the Democrats would lose control of City Hall if they nominated another typical liberal, who would automatically have the allegiance of the blacks.

Rizzo was far from typical and he most emphatically was not a liberal. Tate did not even know if his police commissioner was a Democrat.* He did believe, though, that Rizzo could stem the flow of white working-class voters away from the Democrats if he were the party's candidate. And so, as he entered the last year in his final term as mayor, Tate set about drumming up support for Rizzo as his successor. He did not encounter much resistance from the leaders of the party.

He met first with Congressman Bill Barrett, who he knew wanted Rizzo to be the nominee, in Barrett's Washington office. What he did not know was that Barrett had been holding unilateral discussions with Rizzo about the mayor's race. In 1974, *New Times* magazine listed Barrett as one of the ten dumbest members of Congress. The magazine harpooned the short, rotund seventy-three-year-old Irishman for wearing a ghastly-looking toupee. Barrett's toupees, ill-fitting and obvious hairpieces, were not pretty. But he was by no means a stupid and ineffective man.†

Barrett was parochial, his interests confined to Pennsylvania's First Congressional District in South Philadelphia. He was not a good speaker. He avoided the press and refused to live in Washington, returning each night to his 36th Ward headquarters at Twenty-fourth and Wharton streets to hold court. The 36th Ward, with

* Rizzo was a Republican until the Democrats took over City Hall in 1952. He then became a Democrat.
† Barrett died in April 1976.

almost fifty thousand residents, was Barrett's source of strength. Most of those residents were black, but Barrett, more than any other politician in the city, could "deliver" his ward. And he was able to do so because he worked at it. Instead of staying in Washington and spending his evenings going to dinners and cocktail parties, Barrett returned to his 36th Ward, staying up late each night to listen to problems brought to him by his constituents. They passed through his office in a steady stream, complaining about difficulties with the Social Security Administration or the county welfare board. In most cases, Barrett was able to correct the problem, or at least to persuade the complainant that Bill Barrett had done as much as anyone could. Because of his attention to such detail, Barrett had been rewarded with twenty-four years in the House and a secure base that made him the single most invulnerable politician in Philadelphia.

After Barrett told Tate that he was all for Rizzo — something he had already privately told the police commissioner — Tate started contacting the party big shots, and some who were not even members of the party, Like Richard C. Bond, the Main Line socialite who was boss of Wanamakers. Matthew McCloskey, the builder who was appointed ambassador to Ireland by President Kennedy and the man who invented the $100-a-head political dinner, was enthusiastic, telling Tate Rizzo was the "most popular man in town" and "the talk of the country."*

Tate next went to the new chairman of the Democratic City Committee, Peter J. Camiel, who had been elected to that post in October 1970, and to the committee treasurer, Herbert J. McGlinchey. The city committee was, and is, composed of the Democratic leaders of the sixty-six wards. Under these leaders are 3,554 committeepersons, two from each of 1,777 voting divisions in the city. Democratic voters in each division elect their committeemen, who in turn elect the ward leader. The ward leaders elect the chairman. The Republican organization is structured the same way.

Camiel, sixty-one, was a pugnacious Pole who had earned a fortune as a rough-and-tumble wholesale beer dealer and had gone on to serve two terms as a state senator. He maintained a voting address in downtown Philadelphia but he lived on a farm called "Fatlands," in a huge, restored house near Valley Forge. Camiel's two hundred acres, not far from the Valley Forge interchange of

* Tate's memoirs, Philadelphia *Bulletin*, January 23, 1974.

the Pennsylvania Turnpike, was worth several million dollars and he had certification to prove that George Washington really did spend a night in his farmhouse.

McGlinchey, was a red-faced, and despite his slight size, combative Irishman. McGlinchey had served one term in Congress and then had become the elder Congressman Green's right-hand man. Indeed, in the late 1950s, McGlinchey had been indicted along with Green in connection with an alleged fraud in the procurement of materiel for the Tobyhanna Army Depot in northeastern Pennsylvania. Both men were acquitted and McGlinchey went on to serve two terms in the state senate before being defeated.

Tate said he found Camiel and McGlinchey eager to support Rizzo. This was important because Camiel, as chairman, appointed the policy committee that passed out party endorsements to candidates. With Camiel behind Rizzo, Tate knew there would be no doubt that the policy committee would endorse the police commissioner. Among other things, this endorsement would enable the committee to spend the money it raised on behalf of Rizzo.

As January came to an end, and the time for filing for the May 18 primary drew near, Tate prepared to go to the Roundhouse to offer the party's support to Rizzo. But first he went to see Bond, one of the city's movers and shakers, to obtain his views. Bond, it turned out, knew all about it. He had offered Rizzo a job in the Wanamaker organization only to be told by Rizzo that he was going to run for mayor.

In his memoirs, Tate recalled his visit to the Roundhouse and his offer of the nomination to Rizzo.

" 'Frank, I've discussed the idea of the mayoralty election with the leaders of the Democratic Party, and I've been asked to request you to become the Democratic candidate for mayor,' " Tate said.

" 'I'd like to be the Democratic candidate,' " Rizzo replied, according to Tate. " 'I'd like to meet with Camiel and McGlinchey and Barrett and anybody else you think I should talk to. I've got only one concern, and that's the acceptance of the black community.' I nodded and said: 'We'll have to work that out. We'll have to sell you to the black community. Fortunately, the Democratic Party has real strength among the black leaders.' "

Tate said that during the discussion he got the feeling that Rizzo "had anticipated [his] reason for coming to see him."

There was ample reason for Tate to feel that way. Rizzo had already received assurances from Barrett that the nomination would be his. Before Tate had finished his discussions with Camiel and McGlinchey, Rizzo had hired a lawyer to prepare the papers necessary to form a campaign committee and to raise funds. Al Gaudiosi, a Montgomery County Republican, had agreed to be his campaign manager. And Rizzo had decided to resign as police commissioner on February 2 in order to announce his candidacy.

The auditorium of the Roundhouse was crowded with reporters, television technicians and cops when Rizzo strode in to make it official.

"I wish to announce that I have resigned as police commissioner, effective at five P.M. today, to seek the Democratic nomination for mayor," Rizzo said, reading from a script written on a typewriter with oversized keys. The speech, a little more than six pages long, had been written by Gaudiosi.

"I shall miss each and every man and woman of the police department," Rizzo continued. "Their loyalty and devotion have made this department the envy of the nation. Let me assure Philadelphians they need have no fears over my departure as police commissioner. They should have no concern over their safety and well-being. The Police Department has a wide range of command personnel, many of whom are eminently qualified to serve as commissioner. Rest assured, Mayor Tate will select a capable replacement."

Rizzo could speak of a replacement with confidence because Tate, still leaning heavily on him, had decided to appoint Joseph F. O'Neill, then chief inspector of the detective bureau, at Rizzo's request. O'Neill, in his early forties, was a tall blond Irishman, hard as a rock and just as silent. He was closemouthed not only with the press but with just about everybody. While not as garrulous as Rizzo, he shared Rizzo's disdain for dissenters, liberals and "soft" judges. His blue eyes seemed glacial behind horn-rimmed spectacles, the wintry impression heightened by his silence to a point where some of his subordinates were unnerved when first meeting him. But O'Neill was considered a coldly efficient cop, one who knew how to put to use the training he had received at the FBI school, and he was widely regarded in the department as a "straight arrow," a totally honest man who would go to the wall for the men who worked for him.

Rizzo took notice of O'Neill's taciturn nature at a City Hall ceremony for policemen two years after he had been elected mayor. With O'Neill standing beside him, Rizzo told the audience:

"I called him up yesterday and they told me he was making a speech. A *speech*. I said, 'Where, at the Pennsylvania Institute for the Deaf?' "*

On the day that he announced for mayor, however, Rizzo did not speak of O'Neill. Instead, he said he was running because the city was "plagued by problems of finance, drugs, education, housing, employment and pollution." As a cop, he said, he "grew frustrated" because he could react to these problems "in only a limited way." And to those who questioned his qualifications, Rizzo had this to say:

"For years, I walked the inner city, observing first hand the shattered bodies and broken spirit of its inhabitants. I've witnessed the crippling effects of inferior education, dilapidated housing and stark poverty. I was there when young boys, approaching the flower of manhood, died from overdoses of heroin. I've seen these problems — not as a candidate on a guided publicity tour — but in my work, day after day, night after night. I was not an absentee public servant. I was on the job when duty called. The city's heat never chased me to the seashore on weekends. Throughout the stifling summers, I remained at my post, serving the people. I know city government inside out. I'm a man of action who gets things done. I'm my own master. Nobody owns Frank Rizzo."

It was a political announcement quite unlike any other ever heard in Philadelphia. In it, Rizzo argued that his years of exposure to the seamy underbelly of the city had prepared him to deal with the wide variety of urban ills. After his speech, Rizzo was asked about his lack of formal education and he replied:

"I've seen a lot of men with college educations but no dedication, no energy. Some are too lazy to get up in the morning."

Rizzo made no specific promises in his announcement, but he did issue a broad pledge to be forthright and outspoken during his campaign.

"Of one thing you can be certain: There will be no ducking, dodging or glib talk from Frank Rizzo," he said. "Come Election Day, the voters will know clearly and squarely exactly where I stand on all issues."

Albert Vincent Gaudiosi wrote those words. And Gaudiosi saw to it that Rizzo did duck, dodge and engage in glib talk whenever serious issues arose. Despite Rizzo's imposing appearance and his apparent self-confidence, Gaudiosi knew he was comfortable only

---

* Rizzo frequently referred to O'Neill as "Joseph Francis Silent O'Neill."

when he was talking about the police department. Gaudiosi had learned from experience that Rizzo was suspicious of educated persons and was unsure of himself to the point where he was reluctant to make public appearances even before friendly audiences.

So Gaudiosi placed his candidate on a strict regimen: Rizzo would give short shoot-'em-up speeches about crime and what he would do to criminals once he was elected. He would speak only to groups whose fidelity was unquestioned, like the Fraternal Order of Police, the Sons of Italy, labor union officials, and church and merchant organizations worried about crime. Above all, he would not venture into any black neighborhoods.

Rizzo, a man not used to taking orders, adhered to the instructions, although Gaudiosi still believed he was making himself too available to the press. And on his own, Rizzo started trying to expand his vocabulary, committing a word or two to memory each day.

Gaudiosi was forty-seven years old, a short, stocky man with an aggressive manner. For most of his adult life he had been a hard-nosed newspaperman, first with the *Inquirer* and then with the *Bulletin*. He had firm opinions, invariably conservative, which he voiced in loud, blistering language that belied the fact that he was an Ivy Leaguer, a graduate of the University of Pennsylvania. Of all the advisers and hangers-on that gathered around Rizzo, Gaudiosi was the only one who would shove back when the big cop threw his weight around.

The two men had met in 1963 when Gaudiosi was helping to prepare a series of stories about police corruption for the *Bulletin*. The series won Gaudiosi a Pulitzer Prize for reporting. It concerned payoffs by gambling figures to police. *Bulletin* photographer Frederick Meyer had photographed the police collecting their payoffs, and part of Gaudiosi's job was to identify the cops in the photos. Rizzo was in charge of the South Philadelphia police division at the time and, when Gaudiosi brought the photographs to him, he obliged by naming the cops he recognized.

Rizzo, who liked most newsmen during those days, took a particular fancy to the tough-talking little Gaudiosi, and they continued to speak to each other occasionally on the telephone. When Rizzo was promoted to deputy commissioner, Gaudiosi's superiors at the *Bulletin*, aware of Rizzo's close relationship with Walter Annenberg and the *Inquirer*, told him to stay in contact with the policeman, who could be a valuable source of news.

Gaudiosi, acting on these orders, arranged to have dinner with

Rizzo and *Bulletin* city editor Sam Boyle at Duffy's, a Main Line restaurant. Gaudiosi and Rizzo arrived first and, seeing that Boyle was not present, entered the bar. Seated there with his wife was Rizzo's good friend, John Gillen, managing editor of the *Inquirer* and Gaudiosi's former boss.

"Let's get the hell out of here," Gaudiosi said, hustling Rizzo from the bar. Out in the parking lot, Rizzo exploded. He grabbed Gaudiosi by his lapels, cursed him, and accused him of trying to "set him up" to ruin him with the *Inquirer*. Gaudiosi, who could use police station language as well as Rizzo, shouted back at the policeman. Just then Boyle arrived and calmed both men, telling them that since Gillen hadn't seen anything no harm had been done. The three men had dinner at another restaurant. The next day, Rizzo called Gaudiosi. He had liked the way the little guy handled himself.

By the time Rizzo declared his candidacy, Gaudiosi had become his fast friend and his most trusted adviser. Although the newspaperman had never been involved in politics before, except for brief service as an aide to a city councilman, Rizzo asked Gaudiosi to manage his campaign.* Rizzo knew he could rely on Gaudiosi, knew that any advice he gave would be in the best interests of the *padrone*. He was not so sure of the professional politicians.

Gaudiosi's strategy — booking Rizzo only before friendly groups, restricting his speeches to attacks on crime and bleeding-heart liberals, completely avoiding the black community and issuing staff-produced "position papers" to give the press something to write about — was a risky one for a candidate trying to win the Democratic nomination. Liberals and blacks constituted a substantial proportion of the registered Democratic vote, a vote that Gaudiosi was apparently prepared to write off. The strategy also presumed that Rizzo's support was fixed and could not be broadened, therefore appearances before so-called impartial groups were to be rejected. The way Gaudiosi explained the strategy privately was that those who were for Rizzo were for him the day he announced; those who were not for him then would never be, and it made no sense for

* Gaudiosi became exasperated with politics when the councilman for whom he worked asked him to write a speech for the dedication of Eastwick, a new development in Southwest Philadelphia designed by Greek planner Constantinos Doxiadis, who was to be the guest of honor. The councilman was a hardworking, earnest man with one major fault: he had difficulty pronouncing words of more than one syllable. He rejected three straight speech drafts before Gaudiosi learned the reason. The councilman looked once at Doxiadis's name, knew he could never pronounce it and hoped that Gaudiosi would write a speech without mentioning the planner's name.

Rizzo to appear before them and flirt with possible embarrassment.

"Those who don't like me, I could walk up Broad Street on my hands and knees and not get their support," Rizzo said, echoing Gaudiosi's thinking in a WCAU-TV interview three days after he announced. "So all I can say is that they don't have to vote for me."

The events of the next month, however, virtually assured Gaudiosi's strategy of success. First, State Representative Hardy Williams declared his candidacy for the Democratic nomination. Williams, a thirty-nine-year-old black man, had been a basketball star at Penn State and had gone on to earn a law degree. Rizzo was gleeful at Williams's entry into the race. A black candidate could serve as a magnet, attracting all those black voters who were looking for anyone but Rizzo to lead the city.

Next, City Councilman David Cohen got into the contest. Cohen, fifty-six, was an ultraliberal Democrat from an integrated district centered mostly in Germantown. His candidacy would attract anti-Rizzo voters from his district as well as from the two liberal Democratic wards in center city.

Finally, on March 1, young Congressman Bill Green became a candidate for the nomination.* Green could not be dismissed as a fringe candidate. At thirty-two, he had already served as chairman of the City Committee and had been in Congress more than six years. He was tall, dark-haired and good-looking, and he was by far the most articulate Democratic officeholder from the city. His father had been close to the Kennedy family and young Bill had inherited that friendship, along with his father's seat in the House. The Kennedy mannerisms, the chopping right hand, the measured cadence of his speech, had become part of the Green repertoire.

If anyone could defeat Rizzo in the primary, it was Green. But the hurdles that confronted his candidacy from the start doomed him. One of these hurdles was the Democratic machine and its leaders. After Tate had been reelected in 1967, he ousted Frank Smith as party chairman and installed Green as his successor, believing that Green would do his bidding. But their relationship lasted only until the maneuvering began for the 1968 Democratic presidential nomination. Tate helped steamroll the Pennsylvania delegation into Hubert Humphrey's corner without consulting Green, who was supporting Robert Kennedy. Green resigned the chairmanship shortly after that with a blast at Tate.

* Five other unknowns filed for the nomination but between them they received less than 8,000 votes and were not a factor in the election.

Bill Barrett, dean of the city's congressional delegation, and Congressman Joshua Eilberg, vice chairman of the City Committee, were opposed to Green. Tate privately told friends he suspected their opposition was tinged with more than a bit of envy of the dashing Green. And on the night Milton Shapp was elected governor in 1970 Camiel had exploded at Green over something known only to the two of them. But Camiel had promised that Green's future in the party was behind him.

Green's biggest hurdle was the multicandidate field. He was competing for the anti-Rizzo vote with Williams and Cohen, neither of whom had a ghost of a chance. But as long as they were in the race, the anti-Rizzo vote would be fragmented. More importantly, the news media treated the three liberals as a bloc, thus blurring the definition of Green's candidacy, while Rizzo was projected — often negatively — as an individual with a very definite image.

It was under these circumstances that Green tried but failed to bring the campaign into focus as a contest between him and Rizzo, between the kind of Democrat he was — a voting record approved by organized labor, minority groups and the ADA — and the tough urban conservatism represented by Rizzo. It didn't work. When Green challenged Rizzo to debate, he was ignored. When Green criticized him for the narrowness of his background, Rizzo replied in general terms, lumping Green in with Williams and Cohen, and reemphasized what he and Gaudiosi knew had gotten him into the mayor's race — his police experience.

"My rivals can't talk law and order," Rizzo told a dinner group in the Presidential Apartments, a luxury high-rise complex that had suffered from the onslaughts of burglars. "If they did, they'd lose all the support they've got."

The statement was typical Rizzo, implying that whatever support Green, Williams and Cohen had, they had because they were "soft" on criminals. Rizzo was against criminals. Green, Williams and Cohen were against Rizzo. Therefore, they were for criminals.

Green was not alone in his inability to force Rizzo out of the shelter of his carefully constructed noncampaign. When the newspapers sought to question him on issues confronting the city, Rizzo refused to answer.

"I'm taking my campaign to the people," was his stock answer.

Just a few months before he resigned as commissioner, Rizzo received high praise from the Greater Philadelphia Movement for his handling of the Black Panthers–Revolutionary Peoples convention episode. But on March 20, 1971, when GPM distributed questions on six issues to all the mayoralty candidates, Rizzo declined to answer.*

"I reserve the right to discuss specific issues at specific times before specific audiences," Rizzo wrote to GPM. "I will not permit GPM or any other person or agency to come between the people and me. . . . I will go directly to the people. In the end, it is the people who will accept or reject my programs."

The *Inquirer*, when it printed the responses to the GPM questions by the other candidates, published a photograph of Rizzo over a blank space that started on page one and continued on an inside page. The blank space was the same length as the space allotted to the other candidates' answers, and it graphically bespoke Rizzo's silence. The *Daily News* on several occasions ran on its editorial page an eye-catching photograph of Rizzo's tightly closed mouth along with a caption saying "C'mon, Frank, Open Up." Still, he refused.

It was a peculiar situation. Frank Rizzo, the tough cop who had fought all his life, would not fight. He would not test whatever ideas he may have had by presenting them to the public. He preferred to campaign by visiting Palumbo's, a South Philadelphia restaurant, just about every night and telling audiences imported for the occasion how tough he would be on criminals.

"I will run the city like I ran the police department," he told one group. "There will be efficiency. Everybody will do his job."

Green, frustrated at not being able to come to grips with his opponent, turned to the ancient — and questionable — refuge of the politician, the solicitation of endorsements from prominent Democrats. Senators Edward M. Kennedy, George S. McGovern, Philip Hart and John Tunney came to Philadelphia to embrace Green, as did a clutch of House members. One endorsement Green wanted badly and seemed certain to get was that of Milton Shapp. He was close to Shapp and the governor's endorsement, if given early enough, could be more helpful than all the others combined because Shapp controlled thousands of state patronage jobs in the city. But Shapp showed a curious reluctance to become involved, curious because his dislike of Rizzo was well known.

"I am taking no position in any of the primaries anywhere in the state," Shapp said, three weeks after Green entered the race. "My job as governor is not to interfere with the democratic process

* The issues were criminal justice, education, health and welfare, housing, employment and taxes.

of selecting the candidates. Open primaries are beneficial to the party and the people."

Shapp's neutral stance was a great relief to the state patronage employes in Philadelphia, many of whom owed a dual allegiance to the governor and to the Democratic City Committee, which was backing Rizzo. Without clear direction from the governor, they were free to do the City Committee's bidding — work for Rizzo — and many of them did. When Shapp finally reversed himself, the reversal came so late in the campaign, and under such suspicious circumstances, that it probably hurt Green more than it helped him.

Despite his youth and his lack of an organization, Green was making progress, much of it at Cohen's expense. Williams had failed to generate significant interest but, as he walked through ghetto streets like a black Pied Piper denouncing Rizzo's inability to stop gang killings, he received a respectable welcome from the residents.

Cohen, meanwhile, was speaking more knowledgeably and con-structively about city government than any other candidate, yet he was plummeting toward the bottom of the heap. With the public apparently deaf to his discussion of municipal affairs, Cohen began attacking Rizzo. He accused him of "covering up" for organized crime while he was police commissioner and implied there was a relationship between Rizzo and Mafia boss Angelo Bruno. Rizzo refused to acknowledge Cohen's existence.

While Cohen was preparing his next blast, Rizzo took a step that strengthened his image as an honest, open man. He became the first candidate to disclose details of his personal financial holdings, even though there was no legal requirement that he make such a dis-closure.

On April 10, Rizzo released a statement saying that his net worth, as of March 31, was $87,950. His assets, according to the statement, consisted of $47,100 in savings accounts and savings certificates; one hundred shares of Sun Oil Company preferred stock purchased for $4,800 but with a current market value of $4,650; three hundred shares of Selected Investments Corporation purchased for $900 and currently worth $700; a home purchased for $16,250 with an estimated market value of $20,000; furniture purchased for $10,000, currently worth $7,500; two automobiles, a 1970 Plymouth and a 1969 Ford, valued at $5,400, and $2,600 in cash surrender value on a $10,000 life insurance policy. The house and cars were paid for, and Rizzo listed no liabilities.

Although Rizzo promised during the campaign to make periodic financial disclosures after he was elected, the April 10 report was the first and last he ever issued. At the time of its issuance, it seemed a reasonable enough document. After three decades of work, during which he rose to the top of his profession, he was worth less than $100,000 and still lived in a modest home. The significance of the report became clear only after Rizzo was mayor, when his unassuming middle-class life-style took on aspects of the baronial.

Cohen's next attack was aimed at Rizzo's supposed intolerance, the area of greatest concern for liberals and blacks who were opposed to the policeman. He chose as his vehicle an incident that was five years old, the melee at the State Office Building over the desegregation of Girard College in which three demonstrators, including one Eugene Dawkins, were physically subdued by police, arrested and subsequently convicted.*

"Frank Rizzo personally led the clubbing because he does not understand freedom of dissent, opinion, or legitimate opposition," Cohen told reporters. "He was promoted for his fine work less than two years later. There was nothing done about that incident because it was referred to the Police Advisory Board, but the secretary of that board was a deep friend of Rizzo's, Clarence Farmer [a black man who served the Tate administration as executive director of the Commission on Human Relations]."

Rizzo denied that he had acted improperly and pointed out that Dawkins and the others had been convicted of assault and battery, but Cohen continued hammering away at his charge that illegal force had been used. And then Milton Shapp entered the picture in the first of a series of moves that appeared to be orchestrated and interrelated.

Shapp ordered his attorney general, J. Shane Creamer, to review the evidence in the case — principally television news films — to determine if Rizzo had acted criminally. He issued this order even though the statute of limitations on any state crime that might have been involved had long since expired.

Then, on May 6, Cohen withdrew from the race and urged those who had planned to vote for him to vote for Green instead. The next day, Shapp announced that he was supporting Green and said

* See Chapter Six.

168

Philadelphia's voters had to make "a fundamental choice between the forces of hope and the forces of fear." Shapp, in a prepared statement, added that he was abandoning his neutrality because Rizzo's election "would be a severe blow to the need in Philadelphia and Pennsylvania, and, indeed, for the entire nation, for a just and decent society."

On May 12, just six days before the primary election, Creamer's report on the Dawkins incident was made public.

"It seems clear from the evidence that a number of police officers, including former Commissioner Rizzo, subdued Eugene Dawkins and that a prosecution should have been brought at the time for excessive force," Creamer's report stated. When newsmen suggested that the timing of the report raised suspicions that the state's justice department was being used for political purposes, Creamer told them:

"The timing may be suspect but it is not politically inspired. It is being released today because the governor asked for an immediate investigation of Mr. Cohen's charges."

The report did not recommend that any action be taken against Rizzo. Indeed, no action could be taken at that late date even if there existed incontrovertible proof that Rizzo was guilty. But that did not stop Shapp from using the report to cudgel Rizzo that same day when he was asked if he would support Rizzo if the policeman became the Democratic nominee.

"I ought to keep my options open but, really, it's as much as asking me if I could support George Wallace if he happened to be the Democratic candidate for President," Shapp said. "The official investigation we conducted showed very clearly that Mr. Rizzo personally had been involved in excessive and brutal treatment of people who had been apprehended, particularly in the case of Mr. Dawkins."

"You have seen a governor prostitute himself," Rizzo replied, publicly. Privately, he denounced Shapp as "that fuckin' little weasel."

Shapp's attempt to damage Rizzo by resurrecting the Dawkins incident boomeranged for a couple of reasons. First, it was widely perceived as an obvious political smear, a *roorback*,* coming less than a week before the primary. Second, and most important,

---

* A *roorback* is a false story about a candidate circulated too late in a campaign for him to respond to it adequately. The word is derived from the book *Roorback's Tour*, published in 1844, which contained an attack on the character of James K. Polk, the Democratic presidential candidate.

Shapp played to Rizzo's strength. Rizzo was in the race only because of his reputation as a tough cop and Shapp's ploy just focused attention on that reputation. The people who supported Rizzo saw Dawkins, not the police, as the problem. They were the conservative whites and among them were large numbers of Republicans. After the 1970 election, Republicans were in the majority in thirteen wards and were even with the Democrats in a fourteenth. By the time of the 1971 primary, almost twenty thousand Republicans had switched their registration to Democrat, most of them doing so in order to vote for Rizzo, and the number of wards with Republican registration margins had fallen to eight.

The Dawkins affair, however, did heighten interest in an election that had already caught the imagination of the voters. On May 18, 65 percent of the eligible Democrats turned out to vote, the largest number ever in a municipal primary.

Rizzo's support came from the areas he expected it to: South Philadelphia and the all-white wards of Kensington, Fishtown, Frankford, Bridesburg, Port Richmond and the rest of the Northeast. He won thirty-seven of the sixty-six wards, and thirty-six of them were overwhelmingly white. In only one ward where blacks were in the majority — Bill Barrett's 36th — did Rizzo emerge a victor. His vote totaled 176,621, or little more than 48 percent of all the ballots cast. Green won twenty-six wards, including nineteen predominantly black districts, and received 127,902 votes, about 35 percent of the total. Williams captured the remaining three black wards and collected 45,026 votes citywide, about 12.5 percent of the Democratic total.*

Although Cohen had withdrawn, he had done so too late to have his name removed from the ballot and he received 4,176 votes. Interestingly, the combined vote received by Green, Williams and Cohen, three candidates who were targeting on the same segment of the electorate, was 177,104, or 483 more than Rizzo. Four other unknown candidates polled a total of 7,784.

When it was clear that he had won the election, Rizzo left his Chestnut Street headquarters to go to the center-city studios of KYW-TV to be interviewed. Also there to be interviewed was W. Thacher Longstreth, winner of the Republican primary and Rizzo's opponent in the general election. Longstreth, against no real opposition, collected more than 90,000 votes and carried all sixty-six wards.

---

* The number of predominantly black wards had increased by one, to twenty-three, after the 1967 election.

"Let me congratulate Thacher," Rizzo said, extending a beefy hand. "He's my friend. He's okay. Congratulations, Thacher."

"Congratulations," Longstreth replied. "You smote him a mighty blow."

"Smote him a blow?" said Rizzo, pretending to be shocked. "Listen to him. He's speaking like Cohen already."

The encounter at the television station was to be the last friendly meeting of the two men during the campaign.

Longstreth, like Rizzo, was fifty years old, but the similarities ended there. Where the ex-cop was a massive product of the streets, loud and profane, Longstreth was tall and rangy — six feet six inches, two hundred and thirty-five pounds — a patrician whose family was well known in Philadelphia before the Declaration of Independence had been signed.

Longstreth, son of a successful investment broker, had spent his early years living in a thirty-room house attended to by nine servants. He graduated third in a class of sixty from the Haverford School in 1937 and earned an academic scholarship to Princeton University, where he played end on the football team. After graduating from Princeton, in 1941, Longstreth joined the Navy and served in the Pacific before he was discharged as a lieutenant commander in 1946.

The race against Rizzo was not Longstreth's first political venture. Upon leaving the Navy, he had started his business career as an advertising salesman for *Life* magazine in Detroit, but he had returned home to Philadelphia, and Chestnut Hill, in 1950, with his socialite wife, the former Anne Strawbridge Claghorn, to work for an advertising agency.

By 1955, Longstreth was well known as a moderate Republican, one who supported the Urban League and the NAACP. He was given to wearing tweedy sportcoats or conservatively cut suits, argyle socks, and button-down shirts. He refused to wear a topcoat even on the coldest of days. Behind his horn-rimmed glasses, his eyes conveyed an openness, some said a naïveté, that was surprising in a man steeped in the advertising world and edging toward politics.

The Democrats slated Richardson Dilworth as their candidate for mayor in 1955. The Republicans chose Longstreth, then thirty-four years old. Dilworth defeated him by 132,000 votes and Longstreth returned to the advertising business and his many civic enterprises.

In 1964, Longstreth took a job as executive vice president of the

Greater Philadelphia Chamber of Commerce, a handy position for a politician-in-waiting since it provided him with an opportunity to keep his name before the public and to keep in close contact with the municipal government as the business community's representative and lobbyist. Three years later, still on the chamber's payroll, Longstreth ran for city council and was elected to one of the two seats that are guaranteed the minority party.

The Philadelphia council has seventeen members, ten of whom are elected from specific neighborhood districts. Seven are elected citywide, but no more than five of these can go to any one political party. In 1967, as in virtually every election since 1952, five Democrats were elected to two Republicans — Longstreth and Tom Foglietta.

The Democrats also won eight of the ten district seats, placing the Republicans in a weak minority position, four against thirteen. Finding himself hopelessly outnumbered, still working for the Chamber of Commerce (and collecting a $40,000 salary there to go with his $18,000 Council salary), and playing second fiddle to Foglietta, who was the minority leader, Longstreth contented himself with being an occasional critic of government and accomplished very little during his four years in the city's legislative chamber.

But the itch to run for mayor again was still with him. The Republican boss, William A. Meehan, preferred District Attorney Arlen Specter as his candidate, but Specter refused to run against his friend Rizzo. Although the GOP had never won a mayoralty election under Meehan's leadership, he nevertheless exercised near-total control over party affairs. He was a prosperous lawyer who had inherited the party reins from his father, Austin, once the city's sheriff, and was given to smoking huge cigars and looking at the world with a fine Irish sense of the ridiculous. It was said of Billy Meehan that, while he never won a major election, he never lost his sense of humor. When Specter turned him down, Meehan picked Longstreth as his candidate and the docile Republican ward leaders routinely ratified his choice.

Longstreth's campaign started early, and it was not at all what one would have expected from the gentlemanly Princeton graduate. Over the July Fourth weekend, well in advance of the traditional Labor Day campaign opening, the Republican fired his first shot. He hired a single engine biplane, normally used to tow banners advertising suntan lotions or restaurants, to fly along the southern New Jersey coastline, from Atlantic City to Cape May, where thousands and thousands of Philadelphia row-house residents were lolling on the beaches. The plane droned up and down the coast a few hundred feet above the heads of the bemused sunbathers, who saw Longstreth's message against the bright summer sky: "Rizzo Is A Bully."

It was the classic gambit of the underdog, a challenge to the far better known, far better financed Rizzo to come out and fight. It was a challenge Longstreth would issue again and again during the next four months, with increasing querulousness.

Longstreth's television commercials repeated over and over the same statement, "You Know He'll Do A Better Job," and warned the voters that they were electing a mayor, not a police commissioner.

Rizzo, guided by Gaudiosi, adopted the same strategy he had used in the primary campaign. He ignored Longstreth. Longstreth retaliated by stepping up the attack. He called Rizzo a "coward" for refusing to appear in black neighborhoods. He stopped using the former cop's name and referred to him as "Bozo" and "Fatso." The fact that Huey Newton had first called Rizzo "Bozo" was not lost on row-house Philadelphia.

"He won't go anywhere, he won't do anything, he won't say anything," Longstreth complained to reporters on August 5.

The Republican traveled all over the city, working from early morning until late at night. At every stop, he criticized Rizzo. And by doing so, he helped to turn the election into a referendum on Rizzo, rather than a contest between two candidates.

In the process, Longstreth gave voice to the unspoken issue of the campaign: race. He charged that one Rizzo slogan, "Rizzo Means Business," was an implicit threat to blacks. Another slogan, "Firm but Fair," meant, "Firm to the blacks, fair to the whites," said Longstreth.

"Should Rizzo become mayor, Philadelphia will become a Newark, New Jersey, where the whites eliminated black participation in government," Longstreth told the New Democratic Coalition on September 14. "Finally, the blacks won and took control, but what did they win? Nothing but a dead and deserted city."

"The issue in this campaign?" Meehan said to newsmen. "It's black against white, that's what Mr. Rizzo is trying to make it. He doesn't have the intestinal fortitude or guts to say so in so many words, but you know it and I know it. If he didn't have that issue, he couldn't get enough votes to keep him warm."

In an unprecedented involvement in partisan politics, the thirty-five officers of five Philadelphia NAACP branches voted, thirty-two to three, to work for Rizzo's defeat.

"Neither white or black [*sic*] can afford the expense of having such a man as Frank Rizzo at the controls of this city," the NAACP officers said, in a statement. "For, while Frank Rizzo enjoys his protection by a horde of policemen, we, the innocent black and white citizens, will have no such security against the poison of hate, and hostility and intolerance unleashed by him and many of his misguided admirers."

The Reverend Dr. Leon Sullivan, pastor of the huge Zion Baptist Church in North Philadelphia, founder of the Opportunities Industrialization Centers (OIC) and General Motors board member, was one of the city's most respected black men. Democratic and Republican Presidents felt obliged to call on him when they visited Philadelphia to review the progress of his OIC, a community self-help program which had spread across the nation, training thousands of minority-group persons for employment. Sullivan had kept clear of politics, but in October 1971 he endorsed Longstreth.

"Should Mr. Rizzo be elected, we will unquestionably have a divided city," Sullivan said, at a news conference. "Mr. Rizzo could not possibly bring this city together. I, with others, have worked too long and hard to help keep order and reason and opportunity in the community to remain silent at a time like this."

While both Longstreth and Rizzo were in favor of "law and order," Sullivan said, "it is a question of law and order and progress under Thacher Longstreth and law and order and terror under Rizzo."

"Longstreth's election will be good for America," Sullivan added. "It will show America that in a city where there was a choice between reason and fear, that reason won out."

At about the same time, school board president and former Mayor Richardson Dilworth, for years Philadelphia's best-known Democrat, said that electing Rizzo would be "giving up" to "fear and apprehension."

"His whole campaign is based on that," said Dilworth. "Every slogan — all of the off-the-record talks — they're all based on one thing. Really, he says at all these off-the-record meetings, 'I know how to keep the blacks in their place.' "*

* Philadelphia *Bulletin*, October 7, 1971.

174

Rizzo carefully avoided responding directly to the racial issue. He accused Longstreth of taking "the low road" by raising the race question and said that by doing so, Longstreth had become "the polarizer."

"I will win every black ward with the exception of maybe one," Rizzo said, in a WCAU-TV interview on October 17.

If Rizzo was serious about his prediction — that he would carry at least twenty-two of the twenty-three black wards — he set out to fulfill it in a most curious way. He simply stayed out of the black wards altogether, in effect ignoring more than one-third of the city's population, writing off that segment of the electorate which had been most loyal to the Democratic Party.

Rizzo hewed faithfully to the Gaudiosi plan. He made from one to three campaign appearances a day before carefully selected audiences. He spoke to groups of policemen and firemen, to concerned Jewish businessmen, to building trades union members, to nervous Democratic committeepersons whose white constituents were worried about their homes and schools. And he gave them all the same speech, in which he promised there would be no tax increase in his administration, that he would fire Superintendent of Schools Mark Shedd, and that he would hire two thousand additional policemen.

"If I'm elected, there will be no tax increases," he told one group gathered at the Commissioner Frank L. Rizzo Police Athletic League center in Port Richmond. "We will live with what we have in the way of finances. Any more taxes and we'll all have to go on welfare."

The promise invariably drew applause, as did his vow to hire more police and to work to impose a requirement that local judges run for reelection every four years, instead of every ten years. But the loudest applause came when he attacked Shedd, when he told his audiences, "I used to say that Shedd wouldn't last eight minutes after I'm elected. Now I say he won't last eight seconds."

"I would say I've been to more schools than the superintendent of schools during my career as police chief," Rizzo said, in a television appearance. "And I have watched the system that produces illiterates, functional illiterates, kids that are juniors and seniors in high school that [sic] cannot read and write. I have watched the complete authority get taken away from teachers, from principals, a one-man operation. I have watched and I have observed Superintendent Shedd permit permissiveness. No authority to the teachers. In my opinion, he has made a shambles of this school system. It's nothing personal. But I have watched this decline and in my opinion, the one man responsible for it is the superintedent of schools."

Rizzo delivered comments like these virtually every evening at the South Philadelphia restaurant of his friend Frank Palumbo, where most of his campaign was conducted, before groups imported for the occasion. When he campaigned outside of Palumbo's, it was always along a route he had traveled before, a route that carried him through the nearly all-white wards of the Northeast, Roxborough and Manayunk in the Northwest, and the Southwest. In addition to ignoring the black areas, Rizzo also ignored the largely white, liberal wards in center city and Chestnut Hill.

While Longstreth was spending his time in frantic pursuit of votes, shaking some of the 100,000 hands he would grasp by election day and demanding that Rizzo come out of hiding, the former cop was spending his time in his second floor office at the Chestnut Street campaign headquarters, raising money. His partner in this venture was Alvin Pearlman, a high-school dropout like Rizzo, who had made a fortune in the air-conditioning business and considered himself Rizzo's best friend.

Pearlman was nine years younger than Rizzo, slightly shorter and more compactly built. Although he was an air-conditioning specialist, he was willing to take on any construction job and had a reputation as a fine craftsman who was proud of his work. Most of all, he was proud of his relationship with Rizzo.

"Frank Rizzo is my friend," he told *Philadelphia* magazine, in an interview. "He's like my father. He reminds me of my father. He guides me and gives me advice just like a son. I'll do whatever I can to help this guy, any way that I can. We respect each other. Frank is a regular guy. We eat corned beef sandwiches every Saturday, tell lies, drink a little beer, that's all. . . . I see him every weekend. I'm over at his place or he's at mine. I see him every day if I can. I sneak in his office or see him at night. We're friends, real friends."

Pearlman, like Rizzo, had never been involved in a political campaign before. But both men learned quickly that in Philadelphia politics, nothing was more important than money. Every campaign needs money to pay for television, radio, newspaper and billboard advertising, office space, furniture, telephones and salaries. But in Philadelphia Democratic politics, there is another traditional expense: the "walking around" money that most of the more than 3,500 committeepersons demand for Election Day expenses. In some elections, this averages out to $75 to $100 a person, more than $300,000, just to get out the vote.

Rizzo, with Pearlman's help, proved amazingly adept at attracting political donations. The two men raised more than $560,000, more than anybody else had ever raised for a mayoral race in the city. Added to the $386,000 collected and spent by the Democratic City Committee, Rizzo's general election expenditures came to almost $950,000, a record.

"There was one aspect of the Rizzo campaign that has been mentioned in the press, but not prominently, and that was Rizzo's phenomenal success as a fund-raiser," Jim Tate recalled. "He proved to be the best that I had ever encountered in all of my years in politics."*

Although Rizzo continually claimed he was not a politician, most of the money came from the usual political sources: builders, architects, engineers and contractors who did business with the city; lawyers eager to make contacts at City Hall; job-seekers, and a not inconsiderable number of true believers in the Rizzo philosophy.

As the money rolled in, and Rizzo remained out of his reach, Longstreth gave vent to his frustration. Speaking at Villanova University, the Republican said of Rizzo, "God, is he stupid."

The two men did have an encounter in early August, before an audience of 37,000, but it was simply a harbinger of the meaningless campaign that was to unfold. It did, however, provide a glimpse of sorts into the Rizzo psyche.

The Philadelphia Phillies, seeking to boost attendance, scheduled a promotion between games of their twi-night doubleheader with the Montreal Expos on August 10. The promotion was a home-run hitting contest, and eight men were invited to participate, including four athletes from basketball, hockey, football and boxing, two baseball umpires, and two politicians.

Longstreth accepted immediately. He had been given an All-America honorable mention at end when he played for Princeton and he had also been a member of the track team. After accepting, he challenged Rizzo to meet him, at least, on the baseball diamond.

"Gaudiosi thought it was a good opportunity to soften Rizzo's bully image, *but only if Rizzo could beat Longstreth*," one man who was intimately familiar with the details told us. "Gaudiosi asked him if he could play baseball, and Rizzo started bragging about how he used to bat cleanup when he was a kid and how he

* Tate's memoirs, Philadelphia *Bulletin*, January 23, 1974.

*Candidate Rizzo poses for photographers before
losing 1971 home run hitting contest.*

used to hit long balls all the time. Gaudiosi said, 'Yeah, well I want
to see first.'

"Hillel Levinson [who starred on the Temple University track
team] arranged for us to use Temple Stadium. John Pierron [a
former television newsman hired by Rizzo] was going to be the
pitcher and we got some bats and balls. But before practice, the
reporters got to Rizzo and he accepted the challenge. He said he'd
do anything. If Longstreth wanted to wrestle or box, he'd wrestle
or box him.

"That evening at practice, you could see Rizzo didn't know anything about baseball. Pierron was throwing him watermelons, but
he couldn't hit them. He was muscle-bound. First, he said the bat
was too light. Then, he said the bat was too heavy. Gaudiosi really
got pissed off, and that got Rizzo angry and he said to Gaudiosi, 'If
you think it's so fuckin' easy, you try it.'

"Gaudiosi hit three pretty good ones, and that got Rizzo even
madder."

On the evening of the contest, Rizzo showed up at Veterans
Stadium with a pair of size eleven baseball shoes, specially purchased for the occasion, a red Phillies cap, and an assortment of
aides who filled a row of seats. Gaudiosi sat at the far end of the
row from Rizzo.

Longstreth was the next-to-last batter; Rizzo was last. Longstreth swung the bat seven times, hitting two hard line drives to second base, a grounder to second, a two-hundred-foot fly to right field, two foul balls, and missing once. Rizzo, on eight swings, managed two slow rollers to second, five fouls, and also missed once. Longstreth received the $100 prize for winning the contest, while Rizzo received the crowd's boos.

When Rizzo returned to his seat, he found that his rowful of aides had scattered, leaving only Gaudiosi perched at the far end. He summoned Gaudiosi.

"Let's get the fuck out of here," Rizzo said.

"No, no, let's stay until everybody else leaves," Gaudiosi answered. "We'll get out under the cover of the crowd. If you leave now, you'll get booed again."

The next day, Rizzo showed up at his headquarters with his right thumb encased in a bandage. His thumb had been jammed, he told his workers, and that was why he had lost to Longstreth.

Rizzo may have lost to Longstreth in Veterans Stadium, but he felt he was ahead comfortably enough to deliver a campaign talk to Democratic partisans containing this message: "I love dogs. Show me a guy who loves dogs and there's a guy who loves people."

In the face of Longstreth's constant attacks on Rizzo, the other issues confronting the city went largely undiscussed. Rizzo recognized this, and turned it to his own advantage. If Longstreth wanted to spend all his time talking about Rizzo, fine. Rizzo would take the free publicity and concentrate on getting his people out of the row houses and to the polls.

"My opponent has run a one-issue campaign," Rizzo told the audience at a Greater Philadelphia Movement dinner five days before the election. "That issue, and I say this modestly, is myself."

Under Gaudiosi's guidance, Rizzo ran a campaign remarkably like the 1968 presidential campaign of Richard Nixon. On the stump, he singled out a few scapegoats and spoke in soothing generalities. Rizzo would fire Mark Shedd, the local version of Ramsey Clark. He would alter the character of justice being dispensed by haranguing "lenient" judges, the way Nixon would change the character of the U.S. Supreme Court through his appointments. And he would take care of the criminals, the way Nixon would end the Vietnam War with his secret plan.

And, like Nixon, lest anyone accuse him of ducking the issues, he had available staff-produced "position papers" that promised he would seek tax breaks for industry, fire the "drones" that peopled

City Hall, improve the quality of housing available, provide aid for the elderly, and even install more water fountains and rest rooms at the city-owned Veterans Stadium.

An indication of the thoroughness — or lack of it — of the research behind these position papers can be gleaned from one of the proposals, in which Rizzo promised to seek to exempt from the real estate tax the first $5,000 of assessed valuation on property owned by persons sixty-five and older. This was not an idle, throwaway proposal. It was contained in the candidate's newspaper advertising and referred to by him throughout the campaign. But there was absolutely no chance that it would ever come to pass. The Pennsylvania constitution flatly prohibits any tax that is not uniformly applied. Well-organized lobbies had failed for the better part of a century to overturn the uniformity clause. In fact, the courts had ruled that the state's first income tax, passed in February 1971, was unconstitutional because it violated the uniformity clause and in August 1971, when Rizzo was swinging a bat at Veterans Stadium, the state legislature was in the process of passing a second income tax, a flat-rate tax, to comply with the constitutional requirements.

But the campaign was not fought on these grounds. The contest, instead, revolved around the question of Rizzo's fitness to hold office. Longstreth had one chance to demonstrate to the public that Rizzo was not fit, and that came during the single televised debate between the two men that Rizzo had agreed to. It was a one-hour confrontation, carried by the three major local television stations, on October 14, less than three weeks before the November 2 election.

It was widely assumed that Longstreth, well educated and articulate, would destroy the up-from-the-streets cop in debate, an assumption that troubled the Republican. Everybody expected him to demolish Rizzo, Longstreth told his friends, so that simply winning wouldn't be enough.

It wasn't enough. The debate turned into another Longstreth attack on Rizzo, much of it directed at Rizzo's strongpoint, his tenure as police commissioner. Rizzo had long since learned how to defend himself against such attacks; he merely denounced criminals and the "bleeding heart" judges who set them free.

"Well, I have been, I was the first man who ever spoke out and was critical of judges and I'm still critical of them," he said, after a Longstreth broadside. "I believe that the reason for our tremendous increase in crime can be placed at the feet of the judicial system.

I'll tell you why: criminal repeaters that are arrested over and over again, eight, nine, ten, as high as thirty times."

The quality of the debate can be measured from an exchange over Rizzo's request as police commissioner for funds from the city council to air-condition the K-9 kennels.

"You know, Mr. Rizzo, those charges were true. You tried to air-condition the kennels and you asked for heaters of City Council, when you were way above budget," Longstreth said.

Rizzo replied that Longstreth was "never" present for council sessions, so how would he know. The Republican said he was present on the day in question because Rizzo had "sicced" a police dog on him. Rizzo smiled.

"I didn't think it was funny," Longstreth said. "I don't think that being attacked by a police dog is enjoyable."

"All that big, friendly dog did was try to put his paws on you to say hello. You are an absolute exaggerator, Mr. Longstreth," said Rizzo, using the same term to describe his opponent that his boyhood friend, Danny Troisi, had used to describe Franny Rizzo.

Before the debate went off the air, Longstreth tried to get Rizzo to agree to three additional televised confrontations. "Come on, Commissioner, now, right now, give me an answer," he said. "Yes or no, it's an easy one."

"I'll answer all the questions to the news media and to the people of the city, but not to you," Rizzo responded. "You're getting a lot of publicity tonight, Thacher. You know, if you had done your job as executive vice president of the chamber of commerce, you would have the thing that I have, recognition factor. Nobody knows who you are, Thacher."

For days before the election, Longstreth, his aides and political analysts had been saying the only way the Republican could win was with a huge voter turnout. It became common wisdom that Rizzo had a hard core of support that would be delivered to the polls no matter what. Longstreth, therefore, needed ideal conditions — that is, nice weather — if he were to win, this theory held.

So widely was this theory discussed that Rizzo himself came to believe it. He had heard the Longstreth invocation — "Pray for sunshine" — and so he found himself hoping for rain.

On the evening of November 2, before the polls closed, Rizzo sat in his campaign headquarters as heavy rains washed the streets. He was overjoyed at the weather, boasted of his certain victory, and said the many prospective candidates for the 1972 Democratic presidential nomination had already started contacting him.

"Ho, ho, ho," he roared to a visitor, as still another sheet of rain slapped the window. "That fuckin' Longstreth must be having a fit. No way he can win now, rain or not. They all want me — Jackson, Muskie, Humphrey. Not McGovern. He's a fuckin' nut. They sounded me out. Jackson's the only one I could support. They're all too liberal. That goddamn Kennedy, he's not fit to be President. His brother, John, was all right. I met him a couple times. But this one, he's got no morals at all. That poor girl in the car."

Less than an hour after the polls closed, Frank Rizzo was the mayor-elect of Philadelphia. Despite the rain, there was a record turnout of more than 77 percent of the eligible voters. Rizzo carried thirty-five of the sixty-six wards, and received 394,067 votes. Longstreth won the remaining thirty-one wards and received 345,912 votes.

The sharp change in voting patterns in this election was clearly due to the singular attributes of Rizzo. For the first time in memory, the Democratic candidate lost the black vote to the Republican. Longstreth won three times as many black votes as Rizzo, and carried twenty-two of the twenty-three black wards. Rizzo won only Bill Barrett's South Philadelphia ward.

But Rizzo more than made up for that loss by capturing traditionally Republican Roxborough and Manayunk and by winning wards in South Philadelphia and the Northeast that had been voting Republican in recent elections. These were the row-house white ethnic wards that Jim Tate had seen slipping away from the Democrats.

Tate's belief that Rizzo's kind of appeal was necessary to keep the Democrats in control of City Hall was thus proved out. And Tate would live to regret it.

Frank Rizzo raises his arms in triumph after being elected mayor in 1971.

Chapter Eleven

Two days after the election, Frank Rizzo began assembling the team that would help him govern Philadelphia for the next four years. James McCarey had announced earlier that day that he was giving up his job as fire commissioner, as of January 3, 1972, the day Rizzo would assume office. The mayor-elect moved quickly to fill the anticipated vacancy, so quickly that it belied the apparent nonchalance with which he acted. The new fire commissioner, Rizzo said, would be his younger brother, Joseph Rizzo.

Joe Rizzo had been a fireman for twenty-five years and, by the time his brother was elected mayor, he had reached the rank of battalion chief. Two years earlier, Joe Rizzo had flunked a Civil Service examination for promotion to deputy chief.

Although he could not qualify for appointment as a deputy chief, there was nothing to prevent Joe Rizzo from becoming boss of the entire fire department. Department heads in Philadelphia are political appointees, outside the jurisdiction of the Civil Service system. In most cases, there is no requirement that they know anything about the departments they are in charge of. For years, Frank Mc-

*Fire Commissioner Joseph Rizzo and his brother, the mayor,
pose before a new fire department pumper.*

Namee had been fire commissioner, and his qualifications consisted of being a big contributor to the Democratic Party and part owner of the Philadelphia Eagles. He did have the ability to slip on a white rubber coat and stand around and watch while George Hink, the man who actually ran the department, put out fires.

Under these conditions, it was not at all difficult for Rizzo to pluck his brother out of his battalion chief's job and anoint him fire commissioner. Joe Rizzo was at least a career fireman. And if the other fifty-one battalion chiefs, fourteen deputy chiefs, five assistant chiefs and two deputy commissioners over whose heads Joe Rizzo was jumped wanted to grumble, let them.

At about 2 P.M. on the day of the appointment announcement, Rizzo was in his campaign headquarters when a reporter asked him about his brother. Rizzo said he was sorry to hear that McCarey was quitting and added, "Oh, Joe's certainly qualified, but I haven't even begun to think about it." Fifteen minutes later, a television newsman asked him the same question. "Sure, he's been a fireman for twenty-five years," the mayor-elect said. "He certainly has the ability. He'd make a good commissioner. My brother has as good a chance as anyone. But it's too early for that." At 2.30 P.M., a radio newsman telephoned Rizzo about his brother and got this answer:

"Sure, if McCarey leaves, my brother will be the fire commissioner. A person who wouldn't have his own brother in the post, with all his qualifications, would be foolish."

The men who surrounded Frank Rizzo on the stage of the Academy of Music when he took the oath of office as Philadelphia's one hundred nineteenth mayor on January 3, 1972, were, for the most part, unknown. Except for the fact that they had worked for Rizzo in the campaign, they had little to recommend them to the important posts Rizzo had given them.

An exception was Lennox L. Moak, a widely known and highly respected expert on municipal finance, whom Rizzo had named finance director. Moak had performed the same function twenty years earlier under Mayor Joseph S. Clark.

The law department was handed over to Martin Weinberg, a lawyer in his early thirties, son of the late Manny Weinberg, a Democratic councilman from South Philadelphia. Weinberg had been constantly at Rizzo's side during the campaign, holding coats, opening doors and providing the candidate with a handy target for his jokes. As city solicitor, Weinberg was the only member of the cabinet who had to be confirmed by the city council.* This was so because the city solicitor is the attorney for all city officials, departments and agencies, including those independently elected officials like councilmen. Whatever opinions Weinberg issued would be legally binding on those officials and departments unless the decisions were overturned by the courts. He would also rule on the legality of all proposed legislation, all city contracts and all bond sales and other financial instruments. Weinberg had served briefly as an assistant district attorney and was teaching a law course at Drexel University, which is primarily an engineering school, and practicing law privately when Rizzo appointed him.

Hillel S. Levinson, another lawyer in his thirties, was named managing director, a job requiring him to oversee all of the services provided by the city, from police and fire protection to health care

---

* The four cabinet positions are finance director, city solicitor, managing director and city representative–director of commerce.

and water, from inspecting buildings and helping welfare recipients to collecting trash. Levinson had no government experience and his only executive background came when he had worked in his former father-in-law's auto leasing agency, but he had run errands for Rizzo in the campaign.

Harry R. Belinger was the most difficult of Rizzo's cabinet appointees to catalogue. Belinger was forty-two, a scrappy Kensington product who had worked as a waiter to pay his way through journalism school at Temple University. He had been city editor of both the *Daily News* and the *Inquirer* and was known to be friendly with Rizzo, although he had never worked for him and did not help him during the campaign. Belinger had been promoted from the *Daily News* to the *Inquirer* when Walter Annenberg owned the two newspapers. After the Knight chain purchased the papers, Belinger had a falling out with the new management, resigned from the *Inquirer* and returned to the *Daily News*. When Rizzo offered him the job of city representative and director of commerce, he accepted.

While Belinger was known as a friend of Rizzo's, it was also known that he had a streak of independence. It was also known that Al Gaudiosi, the man closest to Rizzo, viewed Belinger with the same disdain with which he viewed most of his former colleagues in the newspaper business. Gaudiosi was not on stage on Inauguration Day because he had refused to give up his suburban home and move into the city to accept the job Rizzo offered him. But he was in the audience, secure in the knowledge that he had found a safe harbor as number two man at Philadelphia '76, at a $50,000 annual salary, that would enable him to remain Rizzo's chief adviser.

The advice that Gaudiosi gave Rizzo over the next four years would include a strongly worded opinion, delivered repeatedly, that Belinger was doing a lousy job. As city representative, Belinger handled the city's public relations work and ceremonial functions. As director of commerce, he was responsible for the operations of the city's International Airport, the Civic Center and Convention Hall, and the development of commerce and industry through his division of port and business services.

Thacher Longstreth, who returned to the chamber of commerce after the election, initially expressed apprehension at Belinger's appointment because the former newspaperman had no experience in dealing with the problems of businessmen. But, within a few months, Belinger made a convert of Longstreth. Belinger, Longstreth told us, was the "best" man ever to hold the job and was Rizzo's best appointment.

In 1971, all of the cabinet jobs paid $34,000 a year, while the mayor received $40,000.

Rizzo's other high-level appointees were uniformly undistinguished. His deputy mayor was Philip R. T. Carroll, a career bureaucrat who served Rizzo as civilian administrator of the police department. The two deputies to the mayor were Anthony P. Zecca, a onetime reporter for the old International News Service who was a holdover from the Tate administration, and Michael E. Wallace, another young lawyer who had worked in the campaign.

Although the managing director technically has the power to appoint the commissioners of police, fire and the other operating departments, it is a power that no mayor has permitted him to exercise since the city charter was adopted in 1952. Rizzo was no exception; he chose the commissioners. He reappointed Joseph O'Neill police commissioner, as expected, since he had chosen O'Neill as his successor anyway. Generally speaking, the commissioners selected to head the other departments were technicians familiar with the operations of those departments.

The most obvious political appointment was the naming of Joseph P. Braig, another young lawyer and former member of the Pennsylvania House of Representatives, as commissioner of licenses and inspections. Braig, who served in the state House for one two-year term, was a politician who had worked in Rizzo's campaign. As head of L & I, he was in charge of the most politically sensitive department, since it was responsible for enforcing the city's building, electrical, fire, housing, plumbing and zoning codes.

The health department did not get a commissioner. The commissioner's salary was $29,000, and that was not enough for Dr. Lewis D. Polk, the man Rizzo wanted to take the job. As a professional employee of the department, in charge of community health services, Polk was earning $34,684. He would have to take a pay cut of $5,684 if he agreed to take the job. The matter was resolved by having Polk named acting commissioner while retaining his professional employee's salary. Throughout his entire first four-year term and into his second term, Rizzo never did have a commissioner of health.

One of the most startling things about Rizzo's selection of personnel, however, was the way he handed out high-paying jobs to reporters. Including Gaudiosi and Belinger, Rizzo hired at least twenty newsmen in 1972, paying them an average of more than $20,000 each. John Pierron, who pitched "watermelons" to Rizzo before the home-run hitting contest, was made executive director of the Civic Center at $27,000 a year. Daniel J. McKenna, chief of the *Bulletin*'s City Hall bureau, was hired as a deputy city representative at $25,000, as was Donald K. Angell, Jr., a local television reporter. Lawrence M. Campbell, a close friend of Gaudiosi and a reporter–rewrite man for the *Bulletin*, became a deputy managing director at $25,000 a year.

"I must have hired twenty news guys," Rizzo told us. "Someday I gotta get me a whole list. Get a whole list for me, Tony. [This was directed to Deputy to the Mayor Anthony Zecca.] You know what I've been doing, though, I'm hiring all the guys that give me a fair shot."

Asked why he recruited so many reporters, Rizzo replied:

"My success I contribute [*sic*] to the press. That's why I feel kindly to reporters. They work hard. And they're honest. And everyone that I've had has done a bang-up job."

Rizzo came into office preaching economy and saying that he was going to fulfill his pledge against increasing taxes by instituting a job freeze. In some areas the freeze was quite effective, particularly those that touched on the lives of the black community, which depended more on city services than did any other segment of the population. In two years, the staff of the health department was reduced from 1,441 to 1,122. Employees at Philadelphia General Hospital, the municipal facility whose patients were overwhelmingly black, were cut from 2,995 to 2,325 — and then Rizzo announced that he planned to shut the hospital down completely. The welfare department staff was trimmed 15 percent; the Free Library staff was cut 20 percent. Personnel at Riverview, the city's old-age home, was reduced by 10 percent, and at the recreation department by 8 percent.

But the job freeze did not work in the mayor's office. In 1971, his last year in office, Jim Tate had twenty-two employees, including himself, on the payroll. The budget for the mayor's office that year was $342,000. Rizzo's first budget boosted the appropriations for the mayor's office to $1,079,000 and carried a personal staff of forty-one. The following year, the personal staff jumped to forty-seven.

Even while decreeing a selective job freeze, Rizzo would not deprive himself of playing the *padrone*. On a cold March day, about two months after he took office, Rizzo was in John F. Kennedy Plaza across from City Hall attending ceremonies in which he accepted a horse donated to the police department. After the ceremonies, Nathaniel Harrell, a twenty-two-year-old unemployed black man from North Philadelphia, approached him. Harrell told the mayor that he was married, had two children, and badly needed a job. He said he had repeatedly taken Civil Service tests for a city job but no one had ever contacted him. Rizzo turned Harrell over to James Turner, one of his bodyguards, saying, "He'll take care of you." Turner brought the young man to Mike Wallace's office and the next day Harrell was given a job at the board of education as a nonteaching assistant.

A week before Christmas 1972, six-year-old Kathy Romeo was shot in the stomach during a holdup of a candy store near her South Philadelphia home. The girl would eventually recover, but at the time the newspapers gave the incident extensive coverage, especially after they learned that Kathy's father, Charles, had been out of work for a year and a half and the family faced a bleak holiday.

Mike Wallace read the articles and clipped them from the newspapers. When the telephone call from Rizzo came, he was ready.

"See if you can find something for this guy," Rizzo ordered.

"I knew what was going to happen, and it did," Wallace recalled. "I knew that phone call was coming after I read that story."

"I think Rizzo is what we need," Charles Romeo said gratefully, after Wallace told him he had a job in the department of licenses and inspections. "It will be a good Christmas for me, as long as there are no complications for Kathy. Thank God."

Mrs. Joan Edelmann, who lived in the Rhawnhurst section of the Northeast, had a sick ten-year-old daughter on her hands and no heat in the house because the pilot light on her gas heater had gone out. She called the Philadelphia Gas Works and was told the company would not send a repair man out on a Sunday just to turn on the pilot light. Next, she called the district attorney's office seeking help, but the Gas Works gave the district attorney's representative the same answer it had given Mrs. Edelmann. The woman then called the City Hall switchboard and related her problem to an operator, who told Mrs. Edelmann she would ring the mayor's home and try to reach Rizzo's son, Franny, who worked for the Philadelphia Electric Company. Franny was not at home and the operator rang off. After a few minutes, Mrs. Edelmann called City Hall again and asked to speak to the mayor. Rizzo was on the line almost immediately.

"The mayor didn't know me from a bag of beans, but he was very nice to me," Mrs. Edelmann said later. "He told me he would call the gas company. Within half an hour a man was there from the gas company to turn the heat on."*

Whenever Rizzo bestowed such favors, the information was leaked to the news media and word of the mayor's generosity spread over the city. There were no good works done in private. The names, addresses and telephone numbers of the recipients of the *padrone's* beneficence were made available.

During the early part of Rizzo's administration, these stories of his kindness to those in distress helped generate a certain feeling of affection for him among much of the public. And this affection quite naturally strengthened his position as chief executive of the city. In a Democratic town, he had the support of the Democratic organization and the Democratic-controlled city council. In addition, he had won over many Republicans; indeed, an analysis of the election returns showed he had won more Republican votes than the Republican candidate. Although he had not won by a particularly large margin, Rizzo started out with a solid majority of the citizens in his corner, and the machinery of municipal government was almost totally responsive to him. In short, he had the tools necessary to do the job, to attack the undeniably great problems facing Philadelphia.

John Devine, with Frank Rizzo sitting beside him on the front seat, eased the big, black car onto East River Drive for the trip to downtown Philadelphia and City Hall. East River Drive is the scenic connection between center city and the residential areas in the Northwest, where Rizzo lived. It sweeps through Fairmount Park, hugging the curves of the east bank of the Schuylkill River, continues past the colorful, collegiate-looking clubhouses of Boat House Row, and merges with the Benjamin Franklin Parkway in the shadows of the classically beautiful Art Museum.

Whenever possible, Rizzo used the East River Drive. Like thousands of others, he enjoyed looking at the water, watching the sailboats and sculls, seeing the flash of a speckled wing as one of the Canada geese lifted off. A series of magnificent old and historic mansions and Robin Hood Dell, the open-air, natural amphitheater that served as the summer home of the Philadelphia Orchestra, occupied parkland just off the Drive.

Screened from Rizzo's view as the car sped toward City Hall on a

* Philadelphia *Evening Bulletin*, October 22, 1973.

cold winter morning were the streets that terminated at the eastern edge of the park, the streets of North Philadelphia, one of the worst slum areas in the nation. Almost 200,000 black persons lived on those streets, many of them in unrelieved rows of ramshackle buildings cut up into apartments.

It was here in North Philadelphia, and across the Schuylkill in West Philadelphia, where another 200,000 blacks live, that city life was at its grimmest. The rats were here, and the street gangs that exploded into random violence. Most of the wretched public housing that accommodated 115,000 persons was here, too, and even more depressing was the fact that another 10,500 families were on the waiting list.

The lack of sufficient decent housing was one of the most urgent problems Philadelphia faced, and Rizzo had vowed to do something about it. Block after block in the ghetto areas was marked by vacant, windowless buildings ravaged by vandals. In all, probably 40,000 of these homes, many of them large enough for two or three families, had been abandoned by owners who found it cheaper to get rid of a low-rent property than to maintain it, deal with tenants, comply with the fire and housing codes, and pay taxes on it.

During the campaign, Rizzo had promised to institute a program in which the city would take title to these abandoned homes, rehabilitate those that had potential, and demolish the rest. The answer, he said, was home ownership, not public housing, and the rehabilitated homes would be made available to low-income families. The department of licenses and inspections estimated that the owners of 80 percent of the abandoned buildings lived far from the neighborhoods in which these properties were located. And, according to licenses and inspections, at least 65,000 additional homes were substantially in violation of the housing and fire codes and were considered potential abandonments.

Money was a major problem for the city, and there was no way to make up the lost real estate tax revenue from these abandonments. The city's largest single source of revenue was the $3\frac{5}{16}$ percent tax on wages and salaries. The real estate tax, $4.475 for each $100 of assessed valuation, was the second largest source of city revenue and the largest local source of money for the school system.

There were some 430,000 persons in Philadelphia receiving welfare, at a cost to the federal, state and local government of $435,000,000 annually, and most of them lived in the large black ghettoes. Welfare recipients do not pay wage taxes. Rarely do they pay real estate taxes. Rizzo's campaign promise to rejuvenate abandoned homes for the poor would have benefited some of those on welfare, but about two years after he had been elected, with the program still not under way, he said this in a speech to a group of pensioners:

"A nation's policies are irrational when they lead to a situation whereby people who want to work are not permitted to work, and those who refuse to work are provided for.

"Those who won't work can live nicely on welfare, while those who are forbidden to work because of their age cannot enjoy a life of dignity on Social Security.

"I have seen all manner of people in this country crying in their beer about welfare; and, since the issue is a vote-getter, the politicians cry the loudest in election years.

"Continuously, we are all called upon to provide for those who contribute nothing to society except greater burdens.

"This is not to say that I am against helping the needy."

Shortly after Rizzo arrived in his office that morning, and Abie Kanefsky had brought his coffee, he picked up his telephone and told his secretary to call Robert C. McConnell, the man he had selected to be director of Fairmount Park. Later, Rizzo would purchase a speaker telephone and, with various groups sitting in his office listening, he would take great delight in hearing certain selected callers blurt out whatever they had on their minds, unaware of the unseen audiences. His secretary buzzed and he again picked up the telephone.

"Hello, Bob? . . . This is Frank Rizzo. . . . And good morning to you, too, Bob. . . . Bob, about those geese on the river. Make sure they get fed, will you, Bob? . . . Uh huh. Right. . . . Yes, Bob. Yes, Bob. I know about the little old ladies and their bread crumbs. . . . Oh, there's some little old men feeding them, too? . . . Well, that's nice. But what about the wintertime, Bob? You know, when it's snow and ice? . . . Uh huh, right. Well, you can use grain from the stables, can't you, Bob? . . . Yeah, I know, we're all busy. . . . Well, Bob. Bob. Look, Bob, just feed the fuckin' ducks, will you, Bob?"

James W. Greenlee was a successful young lawyer when he was appointed to the board of directors of the Philadelphia Housing Authority on October 19, 1971, by Mayor James Tate. On November 8, just six days after Rizzo's election, the PHA board chose Greenlee as its chairman. Greenlee, who was then thirty-eight, was a Democrat who had served in the Pennsylvania House of Representatives and, through his political connections, had been given a $20,000-a-year job as counsel to the Redevelopment Authority. He had also contributed $5,000 to Rizzo's campaign.

Greenlee's chairmanship of the PHA paid him nothing, but it was nevertheless an important post. About 6 percent of the city's 1,950,000 population lived in public housing. The agency was a creature of the state and had been in existence since 1937. Under the enabling legislation, the mayor appointed two board members, the city controller appointed two more, and the four thus chosen selected a fifth. This arrangement was established to help insure the agency's independence, to guard against one-man control of 1,700 jobs, $316,000,000 in properties and $18,000,000 in annual rentals. The PHA was responsible for constructing or acquiring housing for the poor and had under its control 41 developments, some of them high-rise, containing about 15,000 dwelling units. It also had about 7,500 dwelling units scattered in various parts of the city.

As counsel to the Redevelopment Authority, Greenlee dealt with the legal questions raised by the agency's exercise of eminent domain to acquire land in blighted areas for sale or lease to private developers. Unlike the PHA, which was involved almost exclusively in the rental of public housing, the Redevelopment Authority was interested in converting slum properties and wornout commercial and industrial buildings into useful, tax-producing parts of the community. It had spent $500,000,000 in federal, state and local funds since it was organized in 1945, and it was largely responsible for the success of Society Hill, the downtown residential area that was reclaimed from the slums.

Together, the PHA and the Redevelopment Authority would be the two key agencies in any serious plan to attack the city's housing problems. But Rizzo was suspicious of them. As a cop, he had mistrusted what he considered "do-gooder" organizations like the PHA, just as he mistrusted people who lived in housing projects. And he was convinced the Redevelopment Authority was wasting millions of dollars. Rizzo's suspicions were shared by many of his supporters. PHA's operations were mostly for the benefit of blacks. The Redevelopment Authority programs, when they weren't for the benefit of the blacks, were aimed at the affluent whites who could afford the town houses in Society Hill.

The whites who had voted for Rizzo, the blue-collar workers from South Philadelphia, Kensington, Bridesburg and Frankford, the frightened small businessmen, the teachers from the Northeast, none of them had ever gotten anything from the PHA or the Redevelopment Authority. At best these agencies, they believed, used tax money — their tax money — to give handouts to the blacks. At worst, their tax money was used to subsidize the movement of blacks into their own neighborhoods.

The Whitman Park project was a case in point. On October 29, 1970, Multicon Corporation, a private developer, had signed a contract with the city, the PHA and the Redevelopment Authority to build 120 homes, valued at $20,000 each, for low-income families. The problem with this agreement was the site that had been selected for the development: a four-square-block area at Front Street and Oregon Avenue in South Philadelphia known as Whitman Park.

Whitman Park was an all-white blue-collar neighborhood containing a mix of Italians, Irish and Poles, and it subsequently would vote heavily in favor of Rizzo. Rizzo's position on housing projects during his campaign had been simple — he wouldn't permit any project to be built if the affected neighborhood didn't want it. The campaign was starting just as Multicon began preparing the construction site, and Rizzo's presence in the race gave the Whitman Park residents some hope. If they could hold out long enough, if they could prevent the construction of the homes for low-income (translation: black) families until after Rizzo was elected, they could defeat the project.

When Multicon's bulldozers arrived, neighborhood women, some of them with their children, swarmed over them. Almost daily demonstrations by up to four hundred persons, openly antiblack, forced work on the site to stop. A residents' association brought suit, compounding the delay. Edward Pohler, Jr., a Whitman Park resident who said he had paid $6,900 for his home and earned $10,500 a year as police chief at the Philadelphia Naval Home, testified at one of the court hearings and gave voice to the fears of the whole neighborhood.

"If public housing goes up at that site there is the possibility that crime will increase," he said. Asked if he objected to the type of person who would live in the proposed homes, Pohler replied, "Yes, sir."

One argument advanced constantly by the white residents, and one that had Rizzo's complete sympathy, was that nobody had helped them to buy their homes. They hadn't gone to the PHA or the Redevelopment Authority. They had worked and saved, and they were not going to permit any government agency to come into their neighborhood, which was clean and well maintained, and build what they considered fairly expensive homes and hand them over to a bunch of blacks.

By the time Rizzo was inaugurated, Multicon had yet to lay the first brick in Whitman Park. It never did. On April 29, 1972, Rizzo let the contract expire. No homes for low-income persons would be built in Whitman Park. And the city would have to pay Multicon $626,000 in damages.*

That was the start of the Rizzo housing program. The next step was to turn loose on the PHA and Redevelopment Authority a special squad of police, who worked directly for Rizzo and Phil Carroll — not the police commissioner — to investigate the agencies.

There was evidence of slipshod management in both places and the need for changes appeared undeniable. When Greenlee became chairman of PHA, about eight of every ten families in projects were on welfare and many of them had simply stopped paying rent. At least 65 percent of the tenants were in arrears, and the problem continued to grow under Greenlee. The Redevelopment Authority's program of rehabilitating houses was painfully slow and expensive, and there was little doubt that it was paying inflated prices for some of the commercial properties it had condemned.

"They were spending twenty-five grand to rehab houses at Twentieth and Diamond [in North Philadelphia]," Rizzo told us. "*Twenty-five grand.* You could buy six blocks up there for that kind of money. And before anybody could move in, the goddamn kids would be walkin' off with the plumbing."

The Redevelopment Authority, although technically independent, historically had been responsive to the mayor, since he appointed all five board members. But all traces of independence vanished when the board chairman was arrested and charged with morals offenses against a fourteen-year-old black girl. The chair-

---

* As a result of a suit brought by public housing advocates, U.S. District Court Judge Raymond Broderick in November 1976 ordered "the building of the Whitman Park townhouse project as originally planned." In his opinion, Broderick summed up Rizzo's attitude this way: "Mayor Rizzo stated that he considered public housing to be the same as black housing in that most tenants of public housing are black. Mayor Rizzo therefore felt that there should not be any public housing placed in white neighborhoods because people in white neighborhoods did not want black people moving in with them. Furthermore, Mayor Rizzo stated that he did not intend to allow PHA to ruin nice neighborhoods." The city, Broderick said, had "acted with a racially discriminatory purpose in halting" the Whitman project.

man, at Rizzo's suggestion, resigned, and the other members of the board yielded to Rizzo's wishes and elected Lennox Moak, the mayor's finance director, as their new chairman.

"Moak's position was that there should be no housing program except for demolition," Christopher Weeks, Rizzo's development coordinator, told us.

Rizzo's conquest of the PHA was accomplished through sheer power — the bareknuckled tactics of his own personal police squad, the manipulation of some friendly board members, and an attempt to smear publicly those who stood in his way.

The takeover began with the simultaneous investigations of PHA and the Redevelopment Authority in the spring of 1972. During this period, the Rizzo administration drafted an "agreement of cooperation" between the city and PHA. The agreement, in effect, gave the city government the right to audit PHA's books, supervise programs and take over the running of the agency, but not the attendant responsibility. Greenlee got into trouble when he resisted the agreement.

"The city has the responsibility to make housing programs move," Rizzo said at that time, in a statement. He added that while he had no intention of doing anything to "interfere" with PHA, "I don't want to see the poor get poorer and the rich get richer through someone's mismanagement."

Greenlee had resigned as counsel to the Redevelopment Authority, but he stayed on as chairman of PHA to fight Rizzo, and the mayor began increasing the pressure on him to resign. Day after day, Rizzo accused the attorney of being corrupt, without offering any evidence. He charged that Greenlee had conspired with private attorneys who practiced before the Redevelopment Authority to illegally inflate prices paid to condemnees. When asked for specific evidence, Rizzo solemnly and ominously said that investigators were working on the matter. He did not say that as many as thirty-four policemen were assigned full-time to the investigation, in a city in which many residents were afraid to walk the streets.

The "agreement of cooperation" dispute came to a head in June 1972. Greenlee tried to block the mayor's power grab by proposing his own plan for closer cooperation with the state, rather than the city. He was supported by one other board member, Mrs. Frosteena Kee, a black woman who lived in a housing project and who had been appointed to the board by City Controller Tom Gola, a Republican and former La Salle College and professional basketball star. Gola was also quite close to Rizzo.

"First, let me express that, in my mind, there can be no question as to why we have been asked to sign this agreement so quickly," Mrs. Kee wrote to Greenlee. "It is, without a doubt, an attempt to gain a political hold on the PHA by the mayor of Philadelphia and for him to gain another source of political patronage in contracts and jobs.

"I fully agree with the mayor that there must be changes made at PHA and we have and are trying to make these changes. However, as the only tenant member on the board, I cannot cooperate with any move I feel will be detrimental towards the best interests of my fellow tenants.

"I also feel that, as board members, we have not had sufficient time to talk with what top staff we have at the Housing Authority about this agreement. Merely meeting with the mayor and his cabinet is not sufficient preparation for me to vote in favor of this agreement.

"Due to the fact that members of the board were intimidated and threatened during this meeting and for the remainder of the week, I further feel that the mayor's motivation is as previously stated."

Mrs. Kee did not explain the nature of the intimidation and threats she referred to. But, shortly after she announced her opposition to Rizzo's takeover of the agency, confidential information about her family's income, gleaned from supposedly private city wage tax files, was leaked to the news media. The Rizzo administration then tried to use this information to prove that the Kee family income was large enough to warrant eviction from public housing. Gola, who normally supported Rizzo right down the line, refused to go along with the attempt to oust his appointee from her home and the move failed.

The PHA board voted three to two on June 23, 1972, to accept Rizzo's "agreement of cooperation," and Greenlee resigned three days later. "I've really tried," he said. "What else can one man do?"

"I accept his resignation — period," Rizzo told newsmen, looking as happy as any politician would who had just been given control of 1,700 jobs, and a decisive voice in the awarding of millions of dollars' worth of contracts. Asked about Greenlee's contribution to his campaign, the mayor said he was not aware of the donation.

"I didn't know that," Rizzo said. "Does he want the five thousand back now? Anyone who contributed to my campaign, I appreciate it. But because somebody gave me five thousand dollars doesn't mean he can do what he wants. Even my brother couldn't do that."

It would be the responsibility of the PHA board to elect a new chairman, but Rizzo no longer even bothered to pretend that the election would be anything more than a rubber-stamping of his choice.

"I'm going to look the situation over and come up with the best man available," he said. Then, confusing himself with the district attorney, he added a final, gratuitous slur on Greenlee: "And I will continue to prosecute people who misappropriate money or steal it outright."

The investigation lasted eighteen months. No evidence of criminal conduct by Greenlee was uncovered. (Greenlee subsequently got into difficulty with the Internal Revenue Service, but that was not related to the accusations made, but never substantiated, by Rizzo.)

Since Greenlee had been a mayoral appointee, his resignation left a vacancy to be filled by Rizzo. He chose one of the very few black persons in his administration, an undistinguished former city councilman named Thomas McIntosh. McIntosh, who had represented a heavily black constituency in North Philadelphia, ran for reelection in 1971 while at the same time supporting Rizzo. His district not only rejected Rizzo, it rejected McIntosh, electing instead Dr. Ethel Allen, a black woman who was a Republican and a physician. Rizzo rewarded McIntosh by giving him a job as head of the Office of Consumer Affairs with a $20,000 salary, where he whiled away his hours and gave the mayor someone to point to whenever his administration was accused of ignoring blacks. When the PHA board met to pick a new chairman, Rizzo smiled on McIntosh and he was promptly elected.

The man Rizzo placed in charge of the day-to-day operations of PHA was Gilbert Stein, a tenacious lawyer in his early forties who had spent much of his career in investigative capacities as a deputy district attorney and deputy city controller. Stein, as executive director of the agency, was to be the mayor's cop at PHA.

Stein's salary arrangement was unusual. The mandated pay for the post was $34,000 a year, which was too little for Stein. He was then a member of the law firm in which City Council President George Schwartz had been a partner. When Schwartz took over the presidency at the start of Rizzo's term, he officially retired from the firm, although he continued to receive retirement benefits from it. At this point, Schwartz and Rizzo were still on good terms. Such good terms, in fact, that Rizzo had taken away from former Mayor Richardson Dilworth's firm a city contract worth about $200,000 in annual legal fees and given it to Schwartz's firm.

Before going to work for PHA, Stein wanted assurances that he would be paid at a yearly rate of $50,000. He got those assurances, and the money. The difference between the mandated $34,000 salary and the $50,000 Stein wanted was made up by Schwartz's former firm.

Because he did not want to move into the city from his newly purchased suburban home, Stein agreed to take the job for only six months. The city charter required employees to establish residence in Philadelphia within six months of going on the payroll. But in the six months that he served, Stein, carrying out Rizzo's wishes, instituted changes that brought many tenants — most of them black, for the vast majority of tenants were black — to the point of rebellion.

There were no really valid objections when Stein cracked down on those who weren't paying their rent. Some protested that his methods were harsh but, despite the denunciation by Rizzo of "those who contribute nothing to society except greater burdens," it is as accepted among poor people as it is among the more affluent that you must pay for what you receive. And Stein succeeded. Gradually, he reduced the arrearages until PHA was collecting from its tenants virtually every dollar it was owed.

It was in other areas that Stein's actions infuriated the tenants, making them, in turn, even more bitter at Rizzo. Stein fired several middle- and upper-level black employees and replaced them with whites. And he paid the whites more money. He attempted to withdraw PHA recognition of the black-controlled Residents Advisory Board, an organization established to represent the tenants in negotiations with the Authority. Stein ignored the fact that the U.S. Department of Housing and Urban Development, which provided the bulk of PHA construction money, had approved recognition of the RAB.

Next, Stein tried to set up a system in which the tenants would be encouraged to spy on each other. Those who cooperated would be given better housing and Stein would assume czarlike powers to set standards of acceptable conduct and pass on the worth of the 115,000 human beings in public housing. The goal of this system, said Stein, was to provide "decent, safe, sanitary housing."

First, he said, anyone observed engaging in criminal activity, whether it be selling narcotics or a bottle of whiskey, would be evicted immediately even if the police made no arrests.

"I don't care if they arrest them or not," Stein told reporters. "I can make judgments about who works here and who lives here."

Stein said "undercover resources" would be used to detect criminal activity. Translated, this meant a combination of Housing Authority snoops and willing tenants. What would happen if one of the snoops made a mistake and a tenant was evicted unjustly? What would happen if a tenant with a grudge against another tenant turned him in wrongfully and he was evicted? Anyone who believed he had been improperly evicted, said Stein, could take the PHA to court.

The second part of Stein's campaign would have required tenants' councils in each of the developments to draw up codes of conduct. The codes would contain "demerits" for violations. Tenants would be responsible for watching their neighbors to see if they drank too much, or slept around, or were sloppy housekeepers. They would also be responsible for reporting what they observed. Under Stein's plan, those tenants who accumulated the most demerits would be moved into the least desirable of PHA's projects. There was a scale up, from the least desirable to the next least desirable and on up to the most desirable. And it was all dependent on demerits. In rare cases, Stein said, tenants might be evicted if they earned too many demerits.

For many, simply having to live in public housing was demeaning. Stein proposed to make it ever so much more demeaning by requiring people to spy on their neighbors, using the "desirability" of a place to live as a club with which to beat them into line. If any consideration was given to the dignity of those inside the projects, or to the chaotic conditions that inevitably would result when thousands of persons living in close and miserable proximity were consigned to an atmosphere of accusation and counteraccusation, it was discarded as unimportant.

The plan failed, of course, and was quietly abandoned when the RAB and civil-rights groups raised a howl of protest. Stein's big success was in collecting the rents, and the "decent, safe, sanitary housing" never did materialize.

When Stein left to return to private practice, Rizzo told the PHA board that he wanted Stein's successor to be Thomas J. Kelly. Kelly, a South Philadelphian, had been promoted to be Stein's deputy at Rizzo's request. It may have been that Kelly, an amiable man in his mid-thirties, was the best man available for the job. But the fact that Congressman Bill Barrett had been his sponsor most certainly had something to do with it. As a Barrett protégé, Kelly knew how the political game was played. When Rizzo subsequently found himself in a bloody fight with the leaders of the Democratic party, Kelly understood that the PHA was one of the weapons that had to be used. The 1,700 PHA jobs, as well as the 500 Redevelopment Authority jobs, became prizes to be awarded by Rizzo to those politicians who helped him in his political war.

Just how well Kelly understood the situation was made clear when the voter registration division of the city commissioners' office routinely notified PHA that it wanted to send registrars into the housing projects to enroll voters prior to the primary election in 1975. Traveling registrars had been signing up voters in the projects for years. But in 1975, the Democratic organization was running a candidate against Rizzo for the party's nomination for mayor, and Rizzo was well aware that blacks tended to vote for someone else when he was a candidate.

"We are in receipt of your request of March 6, 1975, concerning the use of PHA facilities for the traveling registrars," PHA director of public information Robert I. Alotta wrote to Harvey Rice, who was in charge of voter registration. "Because of increased tension and problems in many of our facilities, PHA will have to limit its permission to senior citizen housing complexes only."

Essentially, Rizzo had an investigation instead of a housing program. He was gone from the police department, but he had not left it behind him. He had seen a few persons arrested — a PHA employee for selling an agency refrigerator, an RAB official for accepting a $10,000 payoff from a PHA contractor — and he had gotten more political mileage out of that, by far, than he would have gotten by giving the Whitman Park project the green light.

The investigation became the substitute for the program, a screen to divert attention away from the fact that there was no program. But the Whitman Park residents, who had voted so enthusiastically for Rizzo and whose position, after all, did have some merit, were happy. And Rizzo was pleased that he could make the people in South Philadelphia, the South Philadelphia where he had been born, happy. It was the thousands of blacks in North and West Philadelphia who were unhappy, who were most hurt by the lack of decent housing. These same blacks had turned Tom McIntosh out of office for supporting Frank Rizzo, and they had voted heavily against the mayor. Voting against him was one thing, but Rizzo could not understand blacks from McIntosh's own neighborhood turning him out.

Chapter Twelve

Frank rizzo was inaugurated on January 3, but he didn't move into the mayor's suite of offices on the second floor of City Hall until May 8, 1972. "The place looks like a shithouse," the man who had vowed to hold the line on taxes and wage a war on waste told reporters, using virtually the same words he would later use to describe the City Hall pressroom. The City Hall offices looked as if they hadn't been fixed up in twenty years, he complained, and until they were, he would work out of the Municipal Services Building across the street.

By "fixed up," Rizzo did not mean a coat of paint and some new curtains. What he wanted amounted to a completely new suite of eleven rooms — new walls, new floors, new furniture, new lighting and electrical systems, new plumbing, new everything. And, as a candidate who had promised to run an austere administration, he didn't want the taxpayers to pay for it. What he wanted was for someone to donate the funds to build him suitable quarters.

Al Pearlman volunteered to do the construction work himself. Fredric R. Mann, a wealthy businessman whose aggressive garrulousness belied his passion for fine music, agreed to raise the money. Mann had been commissioner of recreation in Philadelphia from 1952 until 1955, when he was promoted to city representative and director of commerce. He left that job in 1967, when President Lyndon Johnson appointed him ambassador to Barbados, where he served until the end of 1968.

The peculiar nature of Mann's mission made some Philadelphians uneasy. And this uneasiness was heightened when Mann announced that the identities of contributors to the building fund would be kept secret.

For a time, Rizzo ignored criticism of the arrangement that came from the newspapers and civic groups, who thought there was something improper in maintaining a secret war chest to pay for the mayor's ease and comfort. The critics did not frighten Rizzo, fresh from his triumph at the polls. He met with reporters just about every day, providing them with juicy quotes like this one on Governor Milton J. Shapp's decision against using the electric chair on condemned murderers during his term in office:

"Maybe we need a local option. Maybe we can have our own electric chair."

Rizzo made that comment at a January 9 press conference. At the same conference, he gave his views on the soliciting of Christmas gifts by sanitation workers, a practice ruled illegal by the city charter. "There was not too much of that this Christmas," Rizzo said. "In fact, this was the first Christmas they did not knock on my door. When they did, I always gave them a Christmas present. I gave it to them this Christmas also, as well as to the policemen and mailmen who serve me. I personally don't find it obnoxious but I can see where it might be that way for some people."

In the weeks that followed, while Mann was raising money and Pearlman was making over the offices, Rizzo regularly made himself available to the press to comment on crime. Asked about the murder of a suburban housewife, he said, "When they come up with the people who did that, I could throw that switch." Referring to teenage gang members, he said, "If they were my children, I'd be out with a baseball bat looking for them."

And when a group calling itself "Police Wives and Interested Citizens" asked him to sign a petition calling on Shapp to restore the use of the electric chair, Rizzo called newsmen into his office to view the proceedings.

"When he comes up for governor again, he's going to have to talk about the electric chair, and these ladies and a lot of others are going to be listening closely," Rizzo said, as he signed the petition. "The governor is not only against Philadelphia, but he's also against the electric chair."

By the time he signed the petition, however, the press was getting restive and was asking questions about the secret fund, as was the Committee of Seventy, a civic watchdog group. Philadelphians Who Care, a small group of liberal gadflies, was openly charging Rizzo with violating the city charter's prohibition against officials receiving gifts.

". . . We request that you order the Finance Director to compile and publicly release the names of all individuals, associations, and organizations which pledged monies for the office renovations, the amounts pledged and received, and when they were pledged and the person or bank which acted as custodian of the funds," PWC said, in a letter to Rizzo that went unanswered. "Further, we request that the Procurement Department make available exact records of the money involved in the entire project of renovating your office. Finally, we request that all work done on renovating your office cease immediately, until such time as the provisions of the Home Rule Charter are followed. This would include proper approval of appropriations by City Council, contract bidding, and — in the first instance — a determination by your office of the priority demands of this renovation as compared to the basic needs of the city."

The questions were becoming embarrassing, and Rizzo accepted the offer of a rich crony to bail him out. On March 11, he announced that Mann would no longer solicit funds for the renovation. The estimated cost of the work, $75,000, would be paid for by the William Goldman Foundation, he said. He wasn't abandoning the concept of accepting a lavish suite of offices from fat cats; he was just letting one fat cat pay for it all.

William Goldman was an aging millionaire and he *was* the William Goldman Foundation, which existed on the money he had made operating a string of movie theaters. After Goldman volunteered to pay for the renovations, Rizzo bestowed a favor on him: he appointed him chairman of the Philadelphia Gas Commission, which sets the rates for the municipally owned Gas Works. The job carried with it a $20,000 salary, indicating that it was conceived of as a full-time position. Goldman was, at the time, well past seventy-five and didn't need the money, so he refused the salary. But he did enjoy picking up the telephone and calling his friend the mayor on official business.

Goldman set up a special account containing $130,000 to cover the renovation, and Pearlman spent it all. In fact, when the job was finished, Pearlman said he had lost "thousands of dollars" doing the work.

When he finally moved in, more than four months after being inaugurated, Rizzo found himself occupying quarters unlike those any mayor of Philadelphia before him had enjoyed. Pearlman had selected for him a handsome desk with a tooled leather top, made by the same firm that produced the furniture in the Cabinet Room of the White House and valued at $3,000. The chair at the desk was high-backed, all leather, except for a grosgrained seat designed to retard sweating. There was little chance of sweating occurring because Pearlman had installed sufficient air conditioning to keep the temperature at a steady sixty-five degrees.

At the back of the chair, under the windows that looked out onto City Hall courtyard, was a credenza with electronic controls for the door locks, the console color television set, the recessed overhead lighting and the air conditioning. The twenty-four-by-thirty-two-foot private office was carpeted in plush gold and the English chairs facing the mayor's desk were upholstered in blue, the city's colors. Gold velvet drapes covered the windows, but they were never pulled back, the windows never exposed. Chippendale sofas and chairs lined the walls, which were paneled in teak.

Behind a teak panel were the private quarters, starting with Rizzo's pride, the Italian marble bathroom. "Take a look at this," he would tell visitors. The floor was beige marble. Everything else was white marble — the vanity sink, built six inches higher than normal because of Rizzo's size, the shower enclosure, the shower floor and bench and the niche next to the toilet for the white telephone. Al Pearlman had personally installed all of the marble. Next to the bathroom was a snug den, with a desk, a sofa, a few lounge chairs and tables, a refrigerator and a safe.

"I only wanted to save the taxpayers money, instead of billing the city," Rizzo complained to reporters, after questions about the financing and the apparent acceptance of a gift persisted. "If I had to do it all over again, I wouldn't have done it with contributions. I would have billed the city."

Besides, the mayor said, it wasn't a gift to him; it was a gift to the city and would be available to future mayors. But he wouldn't identify the contractors or the suppliers, and he refused to say how much Freddie Mann had collected, and from whom. Finally, he had his press secretary issue a formal statement that was revealing in view of Rizzo's contention that the renovations were a gift to the city and not to him.

"It's the mayor's position that since the work was privately financed, the details will not be made available to the press," the statement said. "This is a private matter, not for release."

Rizzo's position that the reconstruction of the City Hall offices of the mayor of Philadelphia was "a private matter" may have defied logic, but it was a position he steadfastly maintained. He maintained it even as the rumors increased that contractors had donated materials or services or cash in return for promises of special favors. The rumors eventually reached the ears of Walter M. Phillips, Jr., a young lawyer and former minor league baseball player who was special prosecutor for the Commonwealth of Pennsylvania. The office of special prosecutor had been created by the state attorney general to investigate allegations of official corruption and Phillips believed that the unusual circumstances surrounding the renovating of Rizzo's offices, especially the stone wall of silence erected by those involved, warranted his attention.

The men Phillips most wanted to question were Pearlman and Freddie Mann. Ironically, Phillips's father had been Mann's predecessor as city representative and director of commerce. The elder Phillips and Mann had joined the reform administration of Democrat Joe Clark at the same time, in 1952, when Mann was appointed commissioner of recreation and Phillips was named to the cabinet.

The attempt to keep secret the details of the office restoration was to reach extraordinary lengths. It was not until November 1974 that Phillips succeeded in getting Mann to appear before an investigating grand jury, and even then he failed to elicit any information. Mann pleaded his Fifth Amendment right against self-incrimination and refused to answer any questions. Pearlman was summoned before the jury twice, in late 1974 and early 1975, and he, too, sought shelter in the Fifth Amendment.

"We have information that the money came from men who had contracts or were hoping to have contracts with the city in the future," Phillips said, of the restoration fund collected by Mann. "Most of the money paid into this fund was in cash, which would conceal the fact that these men had made the contributions."

Phillips said he had been able to determine that Mann had collected $12,700 before the Goldman Foundation stepped in.

"We would like to find out not only who gave the money, but what happened to the twelve thousand seven hundred," he said. "We haven't been able to ascertain that yet." Speaking of Mann's grand jury appearance, Phillips said, "He may have answered questions about his name and address, but that's all."*

By the summer of 1976, more than four years after the office restoration, the special prosecutor still had been unable to get Mann or Pearlman to talk.†

The care and feeding of Mayor Frank Rizzo proved to be a lot more complicated — and expensive — than simply providing him with a lavish suite of offices. As a former policeman, Rizzo perhaps had more of an appreciation for the value of cops than did other mayors. Clark used no bodyguards, Dilworth had one and Tate had two plus two men guarding his North Philadelphia row home around the clock.

The number of policemen needed to attend to Rizzo was difficult to pin down because the police commissioner considered this information confidential, but it was clear the mayor's appetite for bluecoats was gargantuan. He had four full-time bodyguards, two uniformed officers outside the entrance to his office and two plainclothesmen inside the office acting as receptionists. The eight men earned a total of $115,000 annually, according to records kept by the city controller, and received more than half that much again in overtime because of the undeniably long hours they put in.

At least two uniformed officers and a German shepherd guard dog were on duty around the clock outside his home at 8224 Provident Street in Mt. Airy, and similar complements were assigned to homes the mayor was building, or buying, even though they were unoccupied. Two policemen stayed in his offices during the night, and a third was on duty in the separate reception room around the corner from the mayor's office. In addition, an unknown number of plainclothesmen were required whenever Rizzo made a public appearance.

* Philadelphia *Bulletin*, December 10, 1974.
† The state legislature, led by Rizzo ally Henry Cianfrani, chairman of the Senate Appropriations Committee, refused to vote funds for the special prosecutor's office in fiscal 1976. Flat broke and shorn of its staff, the office went out of business in December 1976. Samuel Dash, a former Philadelphia district attorney who served as counsel to the U.S. Senate Watergate Committee, was hired by the attorney general to evaluate the work of the special prosecutor. In a report issued in February 1977, Dash made this observation:

"At the time of the grand jury investigation, the so-called civic and community leaders of Philadelphia had substantially abdicated their responsibilities for insuring honest government. They had succumbed to either fear or self-interest. We have been told by prominent businessmen that the most influential business leaders had already decided for economic reasons to become supporters of Mayor Frank Rizzo. Although they were subsequently dissatisfied, their perception of the consequences of breaking off this alliance terrified them."

The Philadelphia *Daily News,* totaling up just the salaries and overtime pay of the twenty-two officers publicly guarding the mayor, his offices and his homes, concluded that it was costing the taxpayers $365,895 annually just to protect Rizzo.*

Clark and Dilworth used autos from the city's motor pool, while Tate had a car assigned to himself full-time. Rizzo had three cars, including top-of-the-line, $10,000 Lincolns and Chryslers.

The flashy cars and most of the policemen were at least visible. But other benefits accruing to Rizzo, the self-proclaimed champion of the "little guy," were carefully obscured. His pension, for one thing. Rizzo's twenty-seven years in the police department entitled him to a pension of $17,000 annually. His participation in the police pension program ended when he left the department to run for mayor. When he became mayor, he became enrolled in another, separate pension program for nonuniformed employees.

Under law existing when Rizzo took office, he would have received two separate pensions when he retired — $17,000 from his police service, plus $4,900 for one term as mayor, or $11,000 if he served two terms, a total of $28,000 at the highest.

In June 1973, Deputy to the Mayor Mike Wallace supervised the drafting of a highly technical piece of legislation designed to amend the city's pension code. The amendment permitted an employee who had qualified for two separate pensions the option of having his benefits calculated as though he had served continuously under the pension plan of his choosing. The amendment was added on to a bill dealing with routine pension changes for city employees worked out during contract negotiations, and it passed the city council without debate.

The net effect of the amendment was to benefit two persons: Frank Rizzo and Ted Jordan, a former policeman who had been appointed deputy recreation commissioner by Rizzo. Instead of receiving a pension based on twenty-seven years as a cop and a separate pension based on his years as mayor, Rizzo had the option of choosing a pension based on thirty-five years' continuous service in either category.

Rizzo's salary was $40,000 a year until his administration sponsored, and council passed, legislation raising the mayor to $55,000 and granting increases to all top officials. Rizzo signed the pay raise bill, just as he had signed the pension code amendment. But he said he would refuse to accept the $15,000 raise during his first term.

* Philadelphia *Daily News,* August 8, 1975.

Almost as an afterthought, he had Tony Zecca tell reporters that he would permit his pension to be calculated on the higher salary, but the big news was that he would not take the increase during the last two years of his term.

Zecca did not tell the reporters — if, indeed, he knew — about the pension code amendment. Instead of a total $28,000 in pensions under the old system, Rizzo would be entitled to $44,000 after eight years as mayor. By opting to have his pension calculated on the basis of thirty-five years' uninterrupted service as a *nonuniformed* employee, Rizzo would be entitled to receive 80 percent of his salary, $55,000. There were, after all, times when it was better not to be a cop.*

At about the same time that William Goldman was volunteering his foundation's assets to pay for Frank Rizzo's offices in March 1972, the mayor was encountering another citizen anxious to do him a favor. The citizen was Charles G. Simpson, former vice president of the United Gas Improvement Company, which operated the city-owned Philadelphia Gas Works. Simpson owned six acres of beautiful prime land adjoining Fairmount Park and Wissahickon Creek in Roxborough. The land was accessible only through a private road, Summit Place, where Simpson lived. In a stroke of good luck, Simpson had picked up the acreage in 1960 for only $7,500 and his total investment on it by 1972, including taxes, was only $11,679. The taxes were relatively low because the land was undeveloped. By 1972, single one-acre building lots in areas less desirable than Simpson's land were selling for several times the $7,500 he had paid for the entire six-acre parcel.

The way Simpson subsequently told the story to reporters, he had never thought of selling the land and no one had ever inquired about purchasing it because it appeared to be part of Fairmount Park. Until Al Pearlman came calling. Pearlman was looking for land suitable to be the setting for the mayor's new home. Simpson's acreage was perfect. And Simpson, who admitted he liked the idea of having the mayor as his neighbor, agreed to sell the property to Rizzo for $12,000, or just about what he had paid for it twelve years earlier.

Rizzo, his wife and his two children were living in a small single home on Provident Street that they had purchased for $16,250 in

---

* The pension story was uncovered by the *Inquirer*'s Aaron Epstein, one of the most persistent of the City Hall watchdogs, two and a half years after the special legislation had been quietly passed.

1956. Before the election, he had said nothing publicly about moving. But after the election, he started complaining regularly about his modest home. "Everytime Carmella wants to get something out of the refrigerator, I have to get out of the kitchen," he told us several times. "I have to keep my suits in the garage."

So the mayor, with new offices, new cars, an army of protection around him, would have a suitable new house. And Al Pearlman would build it for him. Unless his financial picture had changed dramatically in a year's time — and there was nothing to indicate it had, because the year was devoted to campaigning for office — Rizzo had a net worth of around $90,000 when he commissioned Pearlman to build him a home. Of that, about $47,000 was in cash savings accounts and a little more than $5,000 was in stock. A year earlier, Rizzo had assigned a $20,000 value to the Provident Street house, but it was probably worth more than that.*

With no known liabilities, Rizzo, now earning $40,000 a year, seemed to be in a position to purchase a substantial home. But the structure Pearlman began erecting in Roxborough looked like a small hotel. The dimensions of the house were heroic, fifty-eight feet wide, 152 feet long, and all of it made out of lush, expensive fieldstone a foot thick. Including the four-portal fieldstone garage, with 800 square feet of space to accommodate four cars, the house had 16,355 square feet of usable space. The average Philadelphia row-house dweller, the person Rizzo identified himself with, made do with 1,200 square feet, while the average suburban homeowner had 2,700 square feet.

Rizzo had said the house would cost him $114,000. At various times, he said the $114,000 came in the form of a mortgage from the Continental Bank, while at other times he said he would need only an $89,000 mortgage because he expected to sell the Provident Street house for $25,000. But as Pearlman continued to build through the rest of 1972 and on into 1973, and as the massiveness of the home became clear, the validity of the $114,000 price tag came into question.

The house had a large marble foyer, complete with niches for statuary, which led to a gracefully curving staircase There was a

* The Philadelphia *Daily News* on September 10, 1975, published a story stating that city payroll records showed that Rizzo earned $287,798 in gross income during his years as a cop. The maximum take-home pay from that would have been $239,506, the paper said, meaning that Rizzo's $52,000 in savings and stock represented almost 23 percent of his total take-home pay. The 1975 Economic Report of the President, the paper stated, said that from 1946 to 1974, average savings amounted to only 6.6 percent. The paper quoted an unnamed financial expert as saying Rizzo's apparent rate of savings "just isn't possible."

Joanna, the Rizzos' younger child, graduates from Chestnut Hill College in 1972. Frank and Carmella Rizzo flank the Reverend Bernard Shimkus. Son Francis is at right rear.

sunken living room, a large bay-windowed dining room, a huge kitchen and pantry, a family room, a library, a sitting room, a den, a basement recreation room with wet bar and an eight-foot-square vault, four bathrooms, all sheathed in expensive marble, four bedrooms and two powder rooms. And all of this was supported by costly steel-beam construction.

The *Daily News* consulted builders who said a custom home of the type Rizzo was having built started at $30 a square foot and went up from there, depending on materials used. Pearlman used only the best. Using that estimate, the newspaper decided the house was actually costing more than $400,000. It assigned a $30-per-square-foot cost to the 10,370 square feet comprising the first and second floors. And it figured construction costs at $15 a square foot for the 5,185 square feet in the basement and the 800 square feet in the garage. The total cost, the newspaper estimated, was $400,800.

"I'm thrilled," Rizzo said, when the *Daily News* story appeared on October 10, 1972. "I'm very happy to hear I'm getting such a good deal from him [Pearlman]."

At that time, Rizzo was riding high. He had the support of the Democratic organization and the Democratic city council. He was newly elected and had not suffered any significant setbacks. But seven months later, when another newspaper story would appear, the situation was quite different. By then, he was at war with the Democratic organization and most of the council was opposed to him. His dream of running for governor was in danger of being snuffed out.

"Can a man who takes home $24,000 a year afford to spend $16,000 annually on mortgage and property tax?" the opening paragraph in the story in the May 13, 1973, Philadelphia *Sunday Bulletin* read. "Would the $8,000 left over — about $160 a week — be enough to pay for the furnishings, utilities and maintenance of a big house, plus food, clothing and transportation for the family that lives there?"

Bulletin writer L. Stuart Ditzen had given Rizzo the benefit of the doubt and accepted his assertion that he was paying only $114,000 for the mansion. He also accepted Rizzo's anticipated sale of the Provident Street house for $25,000 and made his calculations on the basis of Rizzo's having an $89,000 mortgage.*

Ditzen talked to bank officials, who told him that a twenty-year mortgage for $89,000 at an interest rate of 7.5 percent would cost about $8,600 a year. Officials at the Board of Revision of Taxes, which assesses all Philadelphia real estate, told Ditzen that while Rizzo might claim he was paying $114,000, its assessed valuation would probably be more than $160,000, meaning an annual tax bill of $7,270.

A spokesman for the Philadelphia Electric Company was quoted as saying Rizzo's heating bill would run close to $2,500 a year. This brought his fixed costs to $18,370 and, while the huge real estate tax bill would reduce his federal income tax liability, the costs of purchasing and heating the home would eat up almost 75 percent of his salary, an obviously unmanageable proportion.

Three days after Ditzen's story appeared, Rizzo announced he was giving up the Roxborough mansion.

* When Rizzo sold the Provident Street house two years later, he received $38,000 for it.

"This is one of the most sorrowful days of my life," he told reporters gathered in the hallway outside his office. The only things in his life that were more tragic, he said, were "my mother's death, my father's death and my brother's death." He had to give up the house, Rizzo said, because construction costs had exceeded original estimates by $70,000, putting the total cost at $184,000, well beyond his reach.

"It looks like the expenditures are just above my means," the mayor said, his dark eyes glistening with moisture. "It wasn't me that got in over my head. It was Pearlman. When you're dealing with a guy like Al who makes a lot of money, you talk to him about fifty grand and it doesn't mean anything to him. But to a guy like me it does. Al Pearlman's a beaten man. He's my friend. I love the guy. . . . All Al Pearlman wanted to do was good for me."

Pearlman, Rizzo said, had agreed to buy the house for himself. He was not giving up the idea of moving, he added, but he had decided to buy a less expensive, used house.

"I'm done with building," he said.

If Rizzo had given up on building a new house, he had not given up his determination to live in a grand manner. On December 13, 1973, his office issued a brief press release that, on its face, seemed to be straightforward enough.

"Mayor Frank L. Rizzo announced today he and his wife Carmella have signed an agreement of sale for the purchase of a home in the city's Chestnut Hill section," the release stated. "The property is located at 8919 Crefeld street. The purchase price is $90,000, and settlement on the property will take place before Jan. 1, 1974."

The house was stone, had eleven rooms, and was forty-six years old. It was smaller than the Roxborough house — 5,400 square feet excluding the basement — and came with an acre of land. It was a charming home, in the city's most exclusive section. But it was not yet good enough for Frank Rizzo. He had purchased the home in December 1973, but it would not be good enough for him until August 1975, until after Al Pearlman had gutted it and completely rebuilt it. It was the third major construction job Pearlman had undertaken for the mayor, and each one contained the same elements: the expenditure of huge sums of money to provide Frank Rizzo with a sultan's comforts, and an attempt to keep secret the sources of this money and the identities of the contractors and suppliers.

To keep details of the Chestnut Hill project secret, two police-

The Roxborough house that Rizzo commissioned but never moved into because it became too expensive.

men with a guard dog were stationed outside the house around the clock — three daily shifts at an annual cost to the taxpayers of more than $85,000 — while other policemen patrolled the grounds. The policemen were there to keep out *everyone* who was not directly connected to the rebuilding: newsmen, neighbors, delivery boys. But with a repair job lasting far more than a year, and with trucks and bulldozers coming and going day after day, details inevitably leaked out.

By the time Rizzo and his family moved in, Pearlman had stripped the house bare, put in new wiring, plumbing, heating and fourteen tons of air conditioning.* The floors, ceilings and interior

* The *Daily News* on September 8, 1975, quoted a Fedders air-conditioning contractor as saying Rizzo's cooling equipment would have cost a minimum of $14,000. "Fourteen tons is something you put into a factory or a warehouse," he said. The contractor said Pearlman's assertion that "existing ductwork" would handle the air

walls had been rebuilt, every window and door had been replaced, necessitating considerable cosmetic stonework, and a new balcony had been installed. A two-car garage had been converted into a recreation room with a handsome stone fireplace and a twelve-foot-wide bay window. To replace that garage, Pearlman had started on a thousand-square-foot, all-stone, three-car detached garage. His stonemasons had built more than three hundred feet of stone retaining walls on the property, from fifteen to thirty inches thick and rising as high as eight feet, and installed two new patios and a new stone garden terrace. Almost an acre of new sod had been laid and the driveway and parking area had been widened and repaved.

In some ways, it seemed as if Pearlman were trying to recreate the Roxborough mansion for Rizzo. The entrance foyer had been done in marble. Three bathrooms had been gutted, outfitted with new fixtures, and coated with marble. The kitchen was brand new, with the old cabinets and plumbing fixtures ripped out. Doorways had been relocated, three windows had been filled in with new stonework carefully matching the old, and three new windows had been broken through the walls. The four bedrooms, the sunken living room, the dining room, the den, the mahogany-paneled library with cathedral ceiling, all had new hardwood floors, new plastered walls. An underground sprinkler system had been installed to slake the lawn's thirst.

Perhaps because of Rizzo's determination to build his own Taj Mahal in secret, as well as because of legitimate questions about who was really paying for all this opulence, two of the city's newspapers — the *Bulletin* and the *Daily News* — tried independently to assess the true costs of the renovations. On June 16, 1975, before the bathrooms had been cloaked in marble, before the library had been paneled, before the foundation for the all-stone garage had been dug, the *Sunday Bulletin*, based on interviews with contractors, architects and real estate dealers, estimated the repairs would cost $91,000 bringing the total bill for the house to about $180,000. Rizzo had dropped the Roxborough house, the paper pointed out, because he had said he couldn't afford to pay $184,000 for it.

Rizzo moved into the house on August 25, 1975. The *Daily News* waited two weeks, then began publishing a series of stories that claimed the actual cost of the renovations was a stupendous

---

conditioning was "crazy." "That's like saying you intend to put an airplane engine in a Volkswagen. It can't be done . . . you can't use the old ductwork because it wasn't designed back then to handle the volume of air."

*City Councilman Al Pearlman, the mayor's
good friend and favorite builder.*

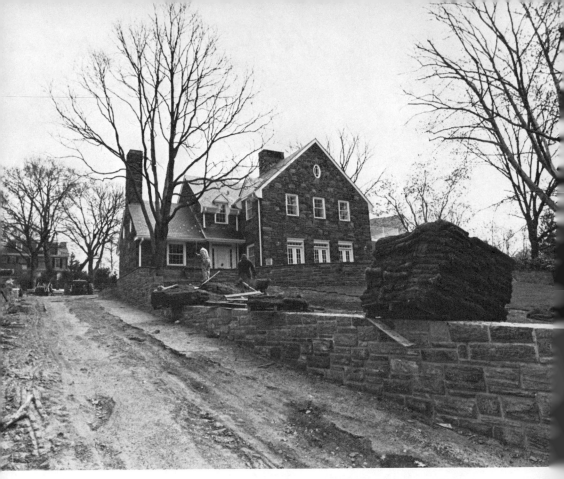

Work progresses at Rizzo's Chestnut Hill house. Sod is
stacked atop new retaining wall along driveway.

$320,000, raising the overall cost for the house to $410,000. The newspaper quoted unidentified contractors as saying the "minimum" price for renovating an older stone home was $50 a square foot, "using standard materials which require no special work." If special materials were used, and Pearlman had often boasted of using nothing but the finest in the Roxborough home, although he was silent about the Chestnut Hill property, the cost could quickly reach $100 a square foot, the newspaper's sources said.

Using the lower $50 figure, the *Daily News* multiplied that by the 5,400 square feet in the house and concluded that it was costing $270,000 to redo the interior. Again, based on estimates obtained from contractors and architects, the newspaper said the outside stonework would have cost $30,000; the fireplace in the recreation room, $4,000; the new sod, $8,000; driveway and patio lighting, $4,000; the new driveway, $3,000, and a new sidewalk, $1,000. The newspaper did not include in its $410,000 estimate the new garage because it was not yet completed. When it was finished, the newspaper said its cost would be $20,000.

The *Daily News* photographed the mayor's center-mounted front doorknob, made of polished brass and shaped like a lion's head, then set out to find what it had cost. The knob, the paper reported, was made by the Schlage Lock Company, was called the "Tuscany," and retailed for $400. The newspaper also published a photograph of one of the seventeen brass carriage lamps dotted along the mayor's driveway and patios and alongside his doors. The lamps normally sold for $301, the newspaper said, although two dealers were found who would sell them for $200 each, or a total of $3,400 for seventeen. Installation was extra.

Rizzo dismissed the *Daily News*'s cost estimates as "complete fiction," and refused to discuss the stories. He did not, however, challenge one of the most damaging assertions made by the newspaper — that much of the work had been done without the obtaining of the required building permits. After checking with Rizzo's own department of licenses and inspections and finding that no permits had been issued for building a garage or changing the wiring or plumbing, the newspaper telephoned an L & I official and asked for information about when such permits were necessary. "You don't begin nothing without a permit," the official told the *Daily News*.

By not obtaining the necessary permits, Rizzo may have benefited monetarily because his real estate taxes did not go up. When a permit is issued, a copy is sent to the board of revision of taxes, which then takes the improvements made to the building into consideration when assessing the value of the property. But because the permits were not issued, the tax board officially was unaware of the improvements and so Rizzo's $2,018 annual tax bill was not increased until two years after he bought the house.

"Frank Rizzo is a tax cheat," the *Daily News* said, in an editorial on September 9, 1975. "Big Frank has been tampering with the soul of the tax assessing system. You, the little guy and little gal, are required to get a permit for almost anything done to your home. That's so the tax assessor can take note and increase your assessment accordingly. It's the best system found for keeping up with the increasing value as a home is improved. Rizzo bought a place for $90,000. He's still paying taxes on a $90,000 home, even though twenty months later it's now worth $410,000."

The revised assessment, when it was finally made at the end of

1975, was $77,200. Since assessments at that time were roughly fifty percent of market value, the board of revision of taxes felt that Rizzo reasonably could expect to sell the house for about $155,000. A spokesman for the tax board said that overimprovements to a house do not affect the assessment because they would have no effect on market value. As an example, he pointed to the six-inch concrete foundation in Rizzo's garage, two inches thicker and more expensive than the building code required, as an item that would have no effect on market value.

"There are many improvements a homeowner makes for which he cannot expect to get his money back," the spokeseman said.*

Rizzo's new tax bill came to $3,686 a year.

Throughout the contretemps over the Chestnut Hill house, Rizzo remained shockingly vague over what it was costing him and how it was being financed. In an interview with the *Bulletin* on April 9, 1975, this exchange took place:

Q — Do you have a construction loan, or renovation loan?

A — I have loans. I have a construction loan, yes, and a mortgage.

Q — Do you know what the amount of the loan that covered the renovations is?

A — I have no idea. No, I don't know whether I have a construction loan or not. I think I have a mortgage, I might have had a construction loan. I'm not sure on that. I'd have to check with my accountant.

Q — Considering the size of that investment, wouldn't it be ordinarily known whether you have a construction loan and how much it's for?

A — I had a — no, I'm sure there's no construction loan. It's just an outright mortgage and I've already made some payments on the cost of the renovations, so there couldn't be a construction loan.

Of one thing Rizzo said he was sure; no one who had any city contracts were working on this house. "Wouldn't have it, wouldn't tolerate it," he said.

The magnitude of the Chestnut Hill restoration, and the intense secrecy which surrounded it, gave rise to speculation similar to that which swirled around the City Hall restoration project. Were contractors and suppliers who did business with the city, or hoped to, pressured into giving Rizzo fire-sale prices for work or materials for his house? Why were the identities of these people being kept secret?

These were among the questions Special Prosecutor Walter Phillips wanted answers to. He subpoenaed Pearlman in late 1974 and

* Philadelphia *Bulletin*, December 28, 1975.

early 1975. And he subpoenaed James T. O'Brien, general manager of Pearlman's company, Tracey Service Company. And he asked them the questions.

Pearlman and O'Brien each pleaded their Fifth Amendment rights against self-incrimination.

Chapter Thirteen

DURING THE 1972 PRESIDENTIAL campaign, when Richard M. Nixon was running for reelection against Democrat George S. Mc-Govern, Frank Rizzo boarded a Metroliner at Philadelphia's Thirtieth Street Station and, with a group of aides and reporters, traveled to Washington. Although he was a Democrat at a time when Nixon's henchmen were putting Democrats' names on enemies lists, Rizzo was welcome at the White House. On this particular day, he had an appointment in the Oval Office with Nixon and, to show his clout, he had gotten the reporters accompanying him past the White House police and into the West Wing. The reporters were even permitted a few minutes in the Oval Office, a privilege denied the White House correspondents assigned to cover Nixon, where the President assured Rizzo he would have no difficulty getting the federal aid Philadelphia needed.*

---

* Rizzo specifically boasted on many occasions that his "connections" in Washington would enable the city to receive $100,000,000 in special grants to help it prepare for a Bicentennial celebration. These funds were to be in addition to all the normal aid the city was to receive. Philadelphia never did receive the $100,000,000, even though in February 1973, White House domestic affairs adviser Kenneth Cole and White

Before leaving the White House to attend a meeting with FBI Director J. Edgar Hoover, whose office also was thrown open to reporters, thanks to Rizzo, the mayor gave Nixon a small gift. It was a cigarette lighter decorated with a cartoon of Snoopy, the comic-strip dog, saying "Fuck McGovern."

Rizzo had made his decision to support Nixon for reelection long before the Democrats nominated McGovern in Miami Beach in August. "Nixon is the greatest President this country ever had," Rizzo had said back on April 11, when questioned by reporters. "I can't make it any clearer."

But he did make it clearer. So that there could be no mistaking his position, Rizzo gave Al Gaudiosi a leave of absence from Philadelphia '76 so that he could work as chief of operations for the Pennsylvania Committee to Reelect the President. He did not conduct an extensive personal campaign in Nixon's behalf, but he lost no opportunity to snipe at McGovern. At a dinner honoring Chester County Republican Chairman Theodore Rubino on November 3, for example, Rizzo was obviously referring to McGovern when he said, "Our nation is in peril, facing an assault from the radical left that threatens the fabric of American life. These misguided few glorify all that is anti-American and degrade anything pro-American."

And when Spiro Agnew came to town two days later to speak to 750 members of the Fraternal Order of Police, Rizzo was on hand to introduce him as "a great American," who had been "in the forefront of the battle against members of the radical left seeking to destroy the country" and "a foremost foe of the lawless — without question the voice of one of the strongest men for law and order in the United States."*

Rizzo also gave assistance of a more practical type to Nixon. Jack Wolgin, a real estate developer and president of the Philadelphia Art Commission, invited seventy-five well-to-do persons to attend a party in his center-city residence. Hubert Humphrey was to be there to shake hands and the goal was to raise $45,000 for McGovern. Somehow, a list of those invited found its way to the second floor of City Hall. Mike Wallace and John Taglianetti, a roly-poly young man of thirty who ran various errands for the

House counsel Leonard Garment appeared at a City Hall press conference with Rizzo and said the $100,000,000 goal was "reasonable and attainable."
* "I would have to say he's probably guilty," Rizzo said, after Agnew resigned and pleaded no contest to tax evasion. "A guy who hides behind high-priced lawyers is generally guilty — that includes the Vice President."

*President Richard M. Nixon holds a model of the Liberty Bell presented
to him by Mayor Rizzo in September 1972. Nixon did not show
photographers the cigarette lighter Rizzo gave him.*

mayor, started telephoning those on the list. Their message, according to one person who was called, was "It would not be in your
best interests to attend Jack Wolgin's party. The mayor would
not like it."*

Wolgin started receiving regrets from those invited. The party
was canceled.

"I was more thrilled by the President's reelection than I was by
even my own victory because yesterday's election meant so much
to the people of America," Rizzo told newsmen on November 8. "It
might have been our country's most important presidential election. You can believe me, brother, this election showed that the
pendulum has swung across this country and the people of America
have now gone on record as saying they have had it with the liber-

* Philadelphia *Bulletin*, October 11, 1972.

224

als and radicals. They have rejected the Democratic Party as the party of radicals like McGovern, Sargent Shriver, Edward M. Kennedy and Shapp. The liberals and radicals are out of business as of yesterday."

Rizzo had called Nixon at 9:45 on election night, but failed to reach him. However, the next day he received this telegram from the White House: "I am deeply grateful for the special role you have played, and you have my warmest thanks for all you have done." After the election, Gaudiosi returned to the Philadelphia '76 payroll.

"I'm not a politician," Rizzo told us several times. It was a statement he would make almost invariably whenever the subject of politics rose. But by the end of 1972, he was mapping out strategy for the November 1973 election at which the voters would choose a district attorney and a city controller. The incumbents were Republicans, Arlen Specter and Tom Gola, and both were close to Rizzo. In fact, Rizzo would have been quite pleased to see Specter and Gola reelected.

Specter and Gola were young, attractive and popular, but there was always the possibility they could lose in heavily Democratic Philadelphia. And if the Democrats won, Rizzo wanted to be sure that the new district attorney, with his powers of investigation, was someone on whom he could rely.

The Democrats normally employed a policy committee, appointed by the party chairman, to screen potential candidates. Those interested in running for office were invited to appear and present their credentials. The members of the policy committee, after hearing the candidates, made their recommendations to the Democratic City Committee, composed of all the party ward leaders. The candidate who received most of the ward leaders' votes won the party's endorsement.

Political bigshots, like the party chairman, the incumbent mayor, and other elected officials, often influenced the votes of the policy committee members and the ward leaders. But the procedure nevertheless was followed, and at least the appearance of a democratic selection process was projected.

Rizzo, however, would have none of this, even though he had gone through that exact procedure when he was a candidate. He wanted a commitment in advance that a candidate personally loyal — and preferably beholden — to him would be given the DA's nomination. And he started pressuring Pete Camiel, the chairman, to see to it that his candidate was chosen.

In a city with some six thousand lawyers, Rizzo could think of only four that met with his approval. And three of those four were already on his payroll.

"He started out with Joe Braig," Peter J. Camiel, who was chairman of the Democratic City Committee at the time, told us. "He called up and said what about Joe Braig for DA. I said Joe Braig is a nice guy. But his public record is very limited. He was a state legislator for only a short period. He did not excel in anything he did. The next day he called me up and said, 'You're right about Joe Braig. Joe Braig, he looks like a little Hitler with those glasses and that moustache.' "

Braig, at the time of this discussion, was Rizzo's commissioner of licenses and inspections.

According to Camiel, Rizzo then suggested that the candidate be either Marty Weinberg, his city solicitor, or Hillel Levinson, his managing director. Weinberg had served briefly in the district attorney's office, but Levinson had no experience whatsoever as a prosecutor. Camiel said they were free to present their credentials to the Democratic policy committee, which would endorse the candidate, but indicated he did not think much of Rizzo's choices.

Rizzo next tried to persuade Richard A. Sprague to become a candidate. Sprague, a Democrat, was first assistant district attorney under Specter and was even closer to Rizzo than Specter was. He was a nationally known career prosecutor, with sixteen years in the DA's office. As a special prosecutor, he had obtained first-degree murder convictions against W. A. (Tony) Boyle, president of the United Mine Workers, and Boyle's confederates in the assassination of dissident UMW official Joseph Yablonski. Sprague was known as a relentless, even ruthless, adversary in the courtroom. He had won more than fifty consecutive first-degree murder convictions, was a hero to the police department, and was the closest thing to a superstar in all of Philadelphia's government.*

The fact that Rizzo, who constantly urged that criminals be given long prison terms and that the electric chair be put back in use, turned to Sprague only after his own employees had been rejected, was significant. Sprague, in his late-forties, was enormously popular because of his courtroom successes. He had the experience, the ability and the toughness to be the kind of prosecu-

---

* Sprague was hired on September 17, 1976, as chief counsel to the U.S. House Committee on Assassinations to investigate the murders of President John F. Kennedy and the Reverend Dr. Martin Luther King, Jr. He resigned on March 30, 1977, after a dispute with the former committee chairman, Representative Henry Gonzalez, Democrat of Texas.

tor one would have thought the law-and-order mayor would have preferred, yet Rizzo had tried to put across three men totally beholden to him and almost totally devoid of any criminal courtroom experience.

Sprague turned Rizzo down, saying he would not run against his boss, Specter.

During this period, the winter of 1973, Philadelphia's schools had been hit by a teachers' strike. It proved to be the longest such strike in the city's history, but through it all Rizzo was preoccupied with the selection of a democratic candidate for district attorney. After Sprague said no, Rizzo began pressing the case for Levinson again. Camiel appointed the members of the policy committee and the committee scheduled a series of meetings at which prospective candidates were invited to appear.

But Rizzo refused to let Levinson appear before the policy committee. Instead, he worked on Camiel, trying to get the party chairman to deliver the nomination to his managing director. And even while he pressured Camiel, he denied that he was actively involved in the search for a candidate and went so far as to say he *did not want Levinson to be a candidate.*

On February 27, just five days before the policy committee was to make its endorsement, Rizzo held his regular weekly news conference.

"I don't know what Hillel's going to do," Rizzo said, when asked about Levinson's possible candidacy. "I'd rather see him stay here. He's the greatest managing director and I need him. But if he decides that he wants to run for DA, I would not stand in his way. I advised him to stay out of it. . . . I'm positively trying to talk Levinson out of running. He's like a wild horse with a bit in his mouth."

Rizzo knew that time was running out on him in his attempt to install his own man as the candidate and he took the occasion of his press conference to issue a not-so-veiled warning to Camiel.

"I'm going to wait to see who their selection is. Then I'll very clearly tell you who I'm for. I'm not a politician. I leave the politics up to Camiel. . . . You won't believe that I don't interfere, and I don't because I'm not a politician and I don't intend to become one because the minute you become a politician, then you become devious.

"I have great respect for Arlen Specter. He's a good friend of mine. . . . If it's some of the names that have been mentioned out loud here you can rest assured I'll be for Arlen Specter. . . . I'm very fond of Tom Gola. I have a lot of Republican friends. Political parties don't frighten me. I got three years to go. My three years is up, with my big fat pension check I'll go back to that mansion I'm building up in Roxborough."

Shortly after that press conference, Rizzo, who claimed he did not "interfere" in politics, set out for a meeting at the Bellevue Stratford Hotel. With him were Levinson, Weinberg, Braig, Gaudiosi and Deputy Mayor Phil Carroll. They went up to suite 216–217 on the second floor. Waiting for them was Camiel. John O'Shea, treasurer of the Democratic City Committee, joined them a few minutes later.

It was a luncheon meeting and the subject was the district attorney's race. Rizzo, who was "positively trying to talk Levinson out of running," again urged Camiel to make his man the party's candidate. And he did it with a high-pressure hard sell. So high-pressure that it offended Camiel, a tough old pol. So hard-sell that when details of the meeting became known months later it would set Rizzo off down a road toward apparent disaster.

The policy committee met on March 4, 1973, and voted to endorse F. Emmett Fitzpatrick, Jr., as its candidate for DA and William G. Klenk II for City Controller. Fitzpatrick was forty-two and had served as first assistant to James C. Crumlish, the last Democratic DA, who was defeated for reelection by Specter in 1965. Fitzpatrick was brash to the point of arrogance, but, on paper, he did have the qualifications to be a credible candidate. He had been the number two man in the prosecutor's office for four years and had actually been Specter's boss when Specter was an assistant district attorney. When Specter defeated Crumlish, Fitzpatrick returned to private practice, mostly in the criminal courts, where he defended some of the city's top gangsters. Klenk was a thirty-nine-year-old lawyer who had worked for Dilworth when Dilworth was mayor. He was relatively unknown, but he was close to Democratic treasurer John O'Shea and his wife was the daughter of former Sheriff William Lennox.

The next day, a Monday, Rizzo called a special news conference to denounce the selection of Fitzpatrick and Klenk, whom he contemptuously referred to as "Klink." And, without being specific, he implied that the two men were chosen by Camiel in furtherance of a scheme tinged with corruption.

"This was the selection of one man — Democratic City Chairman Peter J. Camiel," Rizzo said. "This administration will have no part in that selection. All my life I've fought against boss politics. I didn't believe the chairman of the Democratic Party would attempt to pull this sham on the voters of this city. . . . I will never be a party to boss politics, to corruption in government where a select few reap their rewards. The selection is a step backward for good government. This administration will not support the candidacy of Mr. Fitzpatrick or Mr. *Klink*."

Rizzo conceded that he had asked Sprague to appear before the policy committee, but he added that he "would not permit" Levinson to become a candidate.

"There are a lot of reasons why I won't support Mr. Fitzpatrick," Rizzo said. "I know Mr. Fitzpatrick a long time. That's what I mean by a step backward. I thought very, very highly of the chairman. I have to admit I was wrong. I thought he wanted good government. I thought he was a man of his word. I see complete boss rule, a step back toward corruption."

When pressed for specifics about what was wrong with Fitzpatrick, Rizzo would only repeat that he had known the lawyer for "a long time." The following day, at another news conference, Rizzo let it be known that in the second straight election since he became mayor he intended to support the Republican ticket. At the same time, he announced that he intended to take over the Democratic Party machinery.

"We're going to restructure the Democratic Party," he said. "And we're going to get rid of its chairman."

Party rules specified that the only way to oust a chairman in midterm — and Camiel's term did not expire until May 1974 — was by obtaining the votes of two-thirds of the ward leaders to recall him. Rizzo did not choose to use this method. Instead, he embarked on a campaign of vilification against Camiel and his chief ally, Council President George X. Schwartz. At press conferences and in public appearances, he denounced the two men as "corrupt." And he took great pleasure in telling audiences that to reach Camiel's office by telephone, it was necessary to dial the letters k-o-r-r-u-p-t, which happened to be true, since the City Committee's number corresponded to those letters on the telephone dial.

Rizzo did not disclose how he planned to "restructure" the party, but a hint of how it would be accomplished could be obtained from a meeting held in the 55th Ward in the Tacony section of the Northeast on April 17, 1973. The meeting had been called by forty-four of the ward's fifty-eight committeepersons, all of them loyal to Camiel and all of them supporting the Fitzpatrick-Klenk ticket.

The ward leader was Francis D. O'Donnell, the city councilman who would be reelected in 1975 even though he had died five days before the election. O'Donnell, whose son had been given a high-paying city job by Rizzo, was a staunch supporter of the mayor and had refused to help the Fitzpatrick-Klenk ticket. So when the Camiel loyalists called the meeting, at which Fitzpatrick and Klenk were to appear, they scheduled it to take place in the basement of Lou Matza's Cafe, and they didn't invite O'Donnell. But that didn't keep O'Donnell out.

When the Camiel partisans were settled in their chairs, O'Donnell arrived with an entourage of about thirty men, most of them big and burly, all of them unknown to the workers of the 55th Ward. John Taglianetti arrived at around the same time.

O'Donnell marched to the podium, announced that he was in charge of the meeting, and said the men who had come with him "are appointed sergeants-at-arms."

"Gestapo tactics," yelled Jack McCready, thirty, an insurance salesman. "Come on, Helene," he said to his wife.

"You can't leave," one of the "sergeants-at-arms" told McCready. "You guys tried to pull a dirty trick on Councilman O'Donnell. Now sit down and take your medicine."

"Who are you to tell me I can't leave, you Gestapo bum?" Mc-Cready replied, whereupon the "sergeants-at-arms" grabbed him, punched him and kicked him. McCready earned a broken nose for his troubles.

Howard Gold, whose wife was a committeewoman, started up the stairs to call the police. He didn't make it. He was punched in the neck from behind and pushed back down the stairs. Jane Klenk, the candidate's wife, was punched on the arm. The meeting ended with the Camiel loyalists terrorized, complaining that Rizzo had sent in goons from the Roofers' Union to beat them up. We questioned Taglianetti about the incident.

"I was there at the request of Councilman O'Donnell," he said. "It seems that Pete Camiel called all the committeemen and threatened to cut off all the services to that section of the city and O'Donnell asked me to come and deliver a speech. But it seems that the senator [Camiel formerly was a state senator] had some thugs there. I never got a chance to speak. It's not political. It's city services."

How could Camiel, who was not welcome in City Hall, convince anyone that he could cut off city services to anybody? we asked.

"That's what I wanted to tell the people," Taglianetti replied. "He can't. But he threatened them."

What actually happened at Lou Matza's Cafe?

"I don't know," Taglianetti said. "Someone got hit. He said something and somebody hit him. I never even got a chance to speak. There was a car of City Committee people outside and they left rather rapidly. I was by myself. Somebody got hit. I didn't see who hit him."

If the thugs were Camiel's, why is it that only Camiel's supporters were assaulted?

"I guess they weren't as tough as Mr. O'Donnell's forces. I don't know."

Who were O'Donnell's forces?

"I have no idea. I got there alone. I was there merely to assure the citizens of Philadelphia that ex-Senator Camiel could not cut off citizens' services, that the citizens will continue to get their services and that he has no power in the city and the services will continue to be delivered and that no one will be fired from their job because Pete Camiel says so *and no one will be beat up.* He's threatened jobs, street cleanings, I guess stop signs, various services that citizens need."

Rizzo backed up Taglianetti. Camiel had called other elected officials, he said, and tried to have five persons identified with O'Donnell and other Rizzo supporters fired from their jobs. The man who had complained of being beaten (presumably McCready), Rizzo said, was a "loudmouth and wasn't able to back it up."

Incidents like this caused the feud to rage out of control, and government lapsed into the role it would inhabit for the rest of Rizzo's term, that of caretaker. With the mayor totally devoted to destroying Camiel his administration would not produce a single significant program.

"We said we wouldn't raise taxes and we haven't," Rizzo told us. "I call that a good program. We're producing all kinds of programs. Getting rid of crooks who hold public office is the top one."

Rizzo did more than just vilify Camiel and Schwartz. He assigned his special squad of police, working under Phil Carroll, to produce evidence to put them in jail. Very quietly, the thirty-four members of the unit began following Camiel and Schwartz and their associates. Their confidential city tax records were pulled. Camiel's competitors in the beer distributing business were interrogated and asked to divulge any damaging information they might know about. Hundreds of zoning bills that passed through the city council were examined to see if Schwartz's law firm had represented any of the beneficiaries of the legislation. In short, Rizzo had his own squad of secret — for a time — political policemen.

As reporters for the Philadelphia *Evening Bulletin,* we learned of the existence of the squad in early summer 1973 and began trying to track the scope of its activities. Among the persons we interviewed was Camiel.

"He is a man driven by hate," Camiel said of Rizzo. "He hates people. He's got close to two hundred cops investigating people who refuse to knuckle under to him. He had them up at the college, Ursinus College [in Montgomery County, outside of Philadelphia], where my daughter, Tina, goes, asking questions about her. What kind of girl she is, things like that.

"I don't mind an investigation into wrongdoing. But this is using the police for politics. This is the Gestapo. What has he done to help the city? Are there any programs, any accomplishments, he can point to? Are the whole four years going to be wasted? Has there been any improvement in housing? He ran on a law-and-order platform, but crime has gotten worse. People are afraid to walk the streets. From the time he got in he's been attacking this one and that one. You don't knuckle under to him and the next thing is you're a headline. He makes all these charges and he has yet to produce any evidence to support them. When have you seen as much fear as there is today? Fear of spying, fear of wiretapping? Where does it end? The average guy, he can't do anything to Rizzo so maybe he doesn't worry about wiretapping. But if you're in government or politics or in any field where you might cross paths with him, you have to worry about it."

Camiel urged us to print the story immediately, but we told him we would print it only after we had made a thorough inquiry into it. Over the next month, one of us began compiling information about specific acts by the special squad. This included details about extensive surveillance of a young woman by the squad in an attempt to link her to Schwartz and efforts to get at least one businessman to say that Schwartz had tried to shake him down for a bribe.

In early August, the *Bulletin* had sufficient information about the squad, including the names and rank of all its members, to prepare an explicit story about Rizzo's use of the police for political purposes. By that time, however, Camiel had grown impatient and had

City Council President George X. Schwartz,
a target of Rizzo's special police squad.

given his version to the *Inquirer*. On Sunday, August 5, both newspapers printed stories about the squad under huge headlines. And
for the next week, the *Bulletin* printed daily exclusives about what
came to be known as the "Spy Squad."

Miss Teresa Swisher was the young woman whom the squad
hoped to use to smear Schwartz, who was then fifty-eight years old
and the father of three children. She was a Filipino-American, a
striking woman in her mid-twenties with long, dark hair, a supple
figure and warm Eastern eyes. She had been a receptionist at
Schwartz's law firm but had left three years earlier, in 1970, to take
a similar job with another law firm, she told us. Schwartz had given
her a recommendation to her new employer, negligence attorney
B. Nathaniel Richter. Terri, as she was called, earned $130 a week
from the law firm and, because she wanted to move to California
and needed money to pay for her new gold Pontiac Grand Prix, she

worked as a cocktail waitress for another $150 a week at the Windjammer Room of the Marriott Motor Hotel in Montgomery County, just across the Philadelphia line. She had last seen George Schwartz in February 1973 in the Windjammer Room, where he had stopped for a drink, she told us. Schwartz had introduced her to the man with him, Frank Rizzo.

On April 4, the surveillance started. It did not end until August 3, the day one of us contacted Rizzo to ask him about the activities of the "Spy Squad." When Miss Swisher left her ground-floor apartment in Upper Darby, Delaware County, to go the law office in the morning, an unmarked Philadelphia police car would be waiting for her. The car followed her into the city. When she left after work, the car would follow her home, crossing from Philadelphia into Delaware County, where Philadelphia police have no jurisdiction. At 6 P.M., when she started to her second job, the Philadelphia police would fall in behind her, following her through Delaware County and into Montgomery County. Upon her leaving the Marriott at 2 A.M., they would be waiting on the parking lot to follow her back home to Delaware County.

"I didn't notice it at first, but then it became obvious," Miss Swisher said. "I got scared. I live here alone on the first floor. I have no family here. I didn't know who they were. But they were always out there. I didn't know if they were planning to rob me or what. I was terrified. It got to the point where sometimes I couldn't go to work."

She said that on one occasion she rushed into the street screaming at the man and woman sitting in the car and watching her apartment, causing an uproar that brought the Upper Darby police.

"I was hysterical," she said. "I shouted at them, 'What kind of people are you? What are trying to do to me?'

"I don't know anything about politics. I'm not interested in politics. I never had any opinion of Mayor Rizzo before, but I do now. They're implying that I've done something wrong, that I've had an affair with Councilman Schwartz. Well, Councilman Schwartz is a very nice man, but he doesn't *do* anything to me. Schwartz referred me to Mr. Richter. He did me a favor once — that's all. I haven't done anything wrong. I've never been arrested for anything. I'm not Christine Keeler. I'm not going to be run out of town on Rizzo's rail."

Rizzo initially denied any knowledge of Miss Swisher, but on August 9, he admitted his police had kept her under surveillance.

"She has been under surveillance," the mayor said, in an interview on WCAU radio. "This agency, this group of policemen, received information that this young lady and someone else at a couple of locations — don't hold me to all the facts — was being used to compromise men who hold high posts in government and related agencies. So they did put a surveillance on her, a surveillance where a policewoman and a policeman were used so there'd be no cry about the actions of the police."

In addition, Rizzo said he wanted a special grand jury investigation into the work of his police squad, and he wanted Miss Swisher to testify before that grand jury. The man who would be in charge of such an investigation was Arlen Specter, the Republican Rizzo was supporting for reelection.

Specter did conduct such an investigation and one of those called to testify was a builder named Jack Fierman, who had extensive interests in Philadelphia, suburban Bucks County and San Francisco. Back in April 1973, Fierman was anxious to get started on a development on a three-and-a-half-acre site in Roxborough into which he had sunk a considerable amount of money. The development was to have thirty-six homes and all that Fierman needed was the mayor's signature on legislation authorizing the city to pave access streets and run in water and sewer lines. The city departments under Rizzo which have jurisdiction over such matters had approved the work, as had the city planning commission, and the city council had passed the enabling legislation unanimously. Fierman, who had donated $1,000 to Rizzo's campaign, was confident he would be able to start construction on time. But the development was in the district represented by George Schwartz, and problems began to crop up.

While the legislation was hanging fire, Fierman was visited in his Bucks County office by two policemen, Inspectors Ferdinand Spiewak and James Archer, from Rizzo's special squad.

" 'What can you tell us about George Schwartz?' was generally what they wanted to know," Fierman told us. "I told them you want to talk to me, you stand outside the door — so their recorder wouldn't work so well. I really didn't want to have anything to do with them.

"I said there's nothing to talk about. The point is, should I lie and deliberately hurt a person? And not in Philadelphia, but in Bucks County across the city line they came. They can't do that. We did refuse to give him information. We did refuse to speak to his detectives. Our offices are in Bucks County. These men came out there to talk to me and I refused. I raised four children in this city but, by God, what this man did in one week was a crime."

What Rizzo did on April 11 was to veto the legislation Fierman was waiting for. The veto left Fierman's tract unused and unusable, isolated, with no access streets, no water or sewer lines. The four ordinances in the package, Rizzo said at the time, "smelled funny." The four measures passed the city council again in January 1974, and Rizzo vetoed them again, this time saying they would "perpetuate haphazard development in the Roxborough section."

"We are through building in Philadelphia," Fierman told us. Fierman sold off the Roxborough property and got out.

In May 1975, the city council passed the same four ordinances for the third time. They were identical to the ordinances Rizzo had twice vetoed. But on May 6, 1975, Rizzo signed them into law. Why?

"Because the people no longer oppose them," he replied to reporters' questions. "The people wanted it. It's as simple as that."

Indeed, Rizzo did have in his possession a letter signed by Mrs. Nancy Jo Wynne, a representative of seventeen families in the area, saying the group could now support the development and praising him for his earlier vetoes. The group had negotiated with the developer's lawyers, Rizzo said, and was satisfied with an agreement that had been worked out.

The developer was Joseph Galanti. His firm, which had requested approval of the legislation, was Tracey Service Company. The head of that firm was Al Pearlman.

In the midst of the revelations about the Spy Squad, the *Bulletin* on August 8, 1973, printed a story Camiel had told us about the luncheon meeting he had had with Rizzo on February 27 in the Bellevue-Stratford, when the mayor was trying to have Hillel Levinson named the Democratic candidate for district attorney. According to Camiel, Rizzo had offered to let him name the architects for city construction jobs in return for Levinson's nomination. Architects traditionally have been required to make "donations" to the political party in power in exchange for any city work they are awarded.

"Before the lunch started, he motioned me into the bathroom," Camiel told us. "Carroll came in, too. He pulled out this long yellow sheet and he showed it to me. It had a lot of things written on it. He said these were the projects the city had coming up and he said I could pick the architects. He would appoint the architects that I wanted. I was shocked. I said we don't do business that way anymore. I got burned up. He wanted to give me that for Levinson being slated. I wouldn't do it. I walked out of there. He continued at the table. He kept telling me what a good candidate Levinson would be. He would go around the table asking his people what a good candidate Levinson would be. I told him Levinson would have to appear before the policy committee just like everybody else — just like you did. He didn't want that. He wanted a guarantee. That was the start of our trouble."

Rizzo replied the same day that Camiel's story was "absolutely untrue." "I don't remember ever calling him in the bathroom," he said. "It's a smokescreen."

Both the *Inquirer* and the *Daily News* had been forced into reprinting the details of the exclusive stories the *Bulletin* was publishing, a humiliating experience for a newspaper. But with the *Bulletin*'s publication of Camiel's charge and Rizzo's flat denial, the *Daily News*, an enterprising tabloid, saw a chance to recoup. The newspaper asked both Rizzo and Camiel if they would be willing to take lie detector tests to determine who was telling the truth.

Camiel agreed warily, fearful that Rizzo's long years in the police department would give him an advantage in dealing with a machine that was a complete mystery to him. Rizzo not only agreed, he volunteered to have Phil Carroll take a lie detector test and he said the tests should be given in Convention Hall and thrown open to the public.

Al Gaudiosi was on vacation in the Poconos when Rizzo agreed to submit to the test. Had he talked to Rizzo before the mayor committed himself, Gaudiosi said later, he would have put an immediate halt to the venture. Even if Rizzo had forgotten, Gaudiosi remembered the home-run hitting contest and Rizzo's obviously bogus claim to being a power hitter.

At about 10:30 A.M. on August 13, Rizzo arrived at room 212 in the Bellevue Stratford, just down the hall from 216–217, where the infamous bathroom meeting occurred. Waiting for him was Warren Holmes, a former Miami, Florida, policeman, a polygraph expert and past president of the American Polygraph Association. Holmes had been retained by the *Daily News* to conduct the lie detector tests, and he had flown to Philadelphia with his $1,360 portable polygraph machine locked in a brown suitcase.

"I have great confidence in the polygraph," Rizzo told reporters as he entered the room. "If this machine says a man lied, he lied."

A polygraph, of course, is not infallible. Critics say a cunning liar can beat the machine, and its defenders admit that in the hands of inexperienced or incompetent operators findings may be misinterpreted and wrong conclusions reached. Test results are not admissible in courts of law. But Holmes's reputation was such as to guarantee acceptance of his findings.

By the time he appeared to pit himself against the polygraph, Rizzo's story about the episode in the bathroom had changed. After initially denying the incident had ever occurred, he now was telling reporters that he and Carroll had gone into the bathroom to show Camiel a list of city projects in which George Schwartz's law firm had improperly obtained some sort of interest.

Rizzo removed his coat, rolled up the sleeves of his white shirt and, leaving his necktie knotted, sat down at the table where Holmes's machine was set up. Holmes wrapped a blood-pressure strap around the mayor's right arm, a corrugated rubber respiration tube around his chest, and placed two electrodes on his left hand, touching the fingers.

Through tracings on a chart, these devices show how a person reacts to polygraph questioning. The top line on the chart traces breathing patterns. The middle line charts finger skin resistance to electricity, and the bottom line measures blood pressure. All three functions are likely to be affected when a person lies, and the tracings from these usually differ markedly from the tracings obtained when a person answers a question truthfully.

The first four questions Holmes put to Rizzo were relatively uncomplicated, and the mayor answered them all affirmatively. The questions were:

"On February 27, 1973, did you have a meeting with Peter Camiel in the Bellevue-Stratford Hotel?

"Were you present with Peter Camiel in a bathroom of the Bellevue-Stratford Hotel on February 27, 1973?

"While you were in the bathroom, did Mr. Carroll show Mr. Camiel any type of list on a piece of paper?

"Did the list contain the names of any city projects and related programs?"

Before the testing began, Rizzo had shown Holmes a list of various projects on a long yellow sheet. This list, which Rizzo offered to show reporters, was the one that had been shown to Camiel in the bathroom, the Mayor maintained. Holmes then asked the six key questions:

"Did you go to the bathroom for the sole purpose of showing Mr. Camiel a list of projects you suspected George Schwartz was connected with in an improper manner?" Rizzo answered yes.

"To your knowledge, did you show me the actual list that was shown to Mr. Camiel on February 27?" Rizzo answered yes.

"Did you actually show the list to Camiel to induce him to back Levinson?" Rizzo answered no.

"Are you lying in any way about what transpired between you and Mr. Camiel in a bathroom of the Bellevue-Stratford Hotel on February 27, 1973?" Rizzo answered no.

"Did you offer or suggest in any way to give Mr. Camiel or the Democratic City Committee any help in reference to the list in exchange for support of Hillel Levinson as the Democratic nominee for District Attorney?" Rizzo answered no.

"Do you have knowledge that the actual list shown to Mr. Camiel has been destroyed or thrown away?" Rizzo answered no.

The preparations and interrogation took an hour. "It's a first," Rizzo said, as he emerged from the room, appearing cocky and confident. "Never before in the history of a city has the mayor agreed to take a lie detector test." He said he had taken the test because "I know I'm telling the truth." Carroll was tested next and was asked nine questions. Camiel arrived later in the day and was asked ten questions.

The next day, August 14, was one of the biggest days in the history of the *Daily News*. The newspaper, with a headline screaming "RIZZO LIED, TESTS SHOW," sold 60,000 extra copies that day. Holmes found that the mayor had answered truthfully only the first four introductory questions. He had lied on all six substantive questions, the polygraph expert said. Carroll, he said, had lied on five questions out of nine, while Camiel had answered all ten truthfully.

August 14 was a Tuesday, the day of Rizzo's regular news conference. The mayor's reception room was far more crowded than usual. The television lights and the unrestrained, even gleeful, anticipation with which reporters and city workers alike awaited Rizzo's entrance created a festive atmosphere. The phrase *It's unbelievable* was heard over and over again, as was speculation that the mayor wouldn't dare show up for the conference.

But he did. At a few minutes after 10, Rizzo marched into the room, immaculately dressed in a dark suit and white shirt, and sat down before a forest of microphones at a long conference table. Phil Carroll sat down beside him, and others in the entourage —

Marty Weinberg, Mike Wallace, Tony Zecca, Joe Braig, and the candidate himself, Hillel Levinson — sat nearby.

He and Carroll hadn't lied, Rizzo insisted again and again, in response to shouted questions. He had always believed in the polygraph, but now he had some doubts. He could understand the machine making a mistake on him and the mayor, Carroll said, but he couldn't understand how Camiel had gotten away clean.

Rizzo displayed the long yellow sheet, covered with penciled scribbling. *This* was what he had showed Camiel, he stated, a list of projects in which Schwartz had an improper interest. Finally, annoyed by the obvious disbelief on the faces and in the voices of the reporters, Rizzo said:

"What's the big deal about lying in a bathroom? The big issue is, is Rizzo corrupt? Is Carroll corrupt? Is Camiel corrupt? Is Izzy Bellis [another councilman] corrupt? Is Schwartz corrupt?"

Rizzo's foolhardy entrance into another home-run hitting contest, this one with a polygraph machine, made him a national laughing-stock. But despite the mortification, Rizzo did not go into hiding. He was still confident that Specter would win the election, and Specter was *his* ally, not Camiel's or Schwartz's. In addition to looking into Rizzo's special police squad, Specter's investigating grand jury had been inquiring into the affairs of Camiel, Schwartz and the Democratic City Committee. And so Rizzo went on the attack, and he used the weapon that had served him best: crime.

Besides the candidates for DA and city controller, the 1973 Philadelphia ballot contained the names of persons running for thirty-nine common pleas judgeships, four municipal court judgeships, one traffic court seat and four state appellate court seats. In all, eighty-five judicial candidates were running, and the ballot was large and confusing. Only the most careful student of the courts could have any idea of the persons he preferred for, say, the thirty-nine common pleas judgeships, the most important local judicial posts. In a situation like that, where voters are confused and un-familiar with the persons running for office, organization becomes a dominant factor. And, in Philadelphia, the Democrats had the organization.

Rizzo went after the organization for its support of Fitzpatrick and for its support of judicial candidates he described as "lenient." He continued to meet with reporters and he promised that, prior to the election, he would identify the "most lenient" judges in the city. And on November 1, five days before the election, he singled out four Democratic candidates for judge — two women and two black men — and accused them of being easier on criminals than all other judges, based on his interpretation of their records since being appointed to the bench by the governor.

Even while he assailed these judges, and roundly condemned crime and criminals, Rizzo defended Philadelphia as the "safest" big city in the nation.

"And again, I repeat that we have the safest city in the United States," Rizzo said on October 2. "But it's the people that make it unsafe."

Late on the evening of November 5, election eve, Rizzo telephoned one of the authors, happily predicting that the four judges he had fingered were in trouble, and some of them might even lose. What's more, he said, Specter was a certain winner. Then Camiel would go to jail. And Schwartz would go to jail.

The turnout at the polls was extremely low, only 43 percent of the registered voters. A low turnout usually means the superior organization wins. The Democrats had the superior organization, and they won, ousting Specter and Gola and electing all of their judicial candidates. One of those accused of being lenient by Rizzo, Lisa Richette, got more votes than any other candidate in a contested election.*

Rizzo did not hold another general news conference for the rest of his first term.

In December 1973, just before he left office, Specter arranged for the investigating grand jury's report on Rizzo's special police squad to be released. The report skimmed over the surveillances of Terri Swisher, Camiel, Schwartz, Camiel's daughter, Nina, and son, Peter, Jr., and Schwartz's chauffeur, and stated this mild conclusion:

With respect to those matters which we have investigated, we conclude that it was most unfortunate that the mayor made public statements, which were frequently repeated, expressing his personal beliefs on persons who were subject to investigation where those individuals were also political opponents or potential political opponents. Those public statements by the mayor lead to the conclusion that the surveillances, "stakeouts" and other matters discussed in the body of the Presentment were initiated primarily because of the mayor's stated or implicitly understood political and personal purposes.

---

* Four years later, in 1977, Rizzo would support Fitzpatrick for reelection and Richette for a seat on the Pennsylvania Supreme Court.

What was not disclosed, not even to Judge Harry Takiff, who presided over the grand jury, was the fact that the report that was released was a *rewritten version of the original report with virtually all criticism of Rizzo deleted*. We obtained the original report, which said, among other things:

We conclude that the surveillance of Miss Swisher began as a thinly veiled attempt to smear George X. Schwartz by linking him in an alleged sexual liaison with Swisher. . . . We conclude that the surveillance of Harry Pearl was a politically motivated attempt to embarrass George X. Schwartz through his close friend, Pearl, and an attempt to look for any and all evidence which might destroy Schwartz politically. We conclude that Pearl was surveilled solely because of his association as a close friend and business associate of George X. Schwartz, and we further conclude that it was not a coincidence the surveillance of Pearl necessarily entailed a good deal of simultaneous surveillance of George X. Schwartz (he is mentioned fifty times in the surveillance logs). . . . We conclude that the surveillance of Sen. Camiel's beverage company to learn if his son was holding a city job and a job with his father simultaneously was another politically motivated investigation far beyond the scope of police investigatory work. . . . We find that a surveillance of State Sen. Peter Camiel's farm, Fatland Farms, occurred in April 1973 and that the reason given for the surveillance was so flimsy as to invite total disbelief. The fact that this surveillance was continued with binoculars in an attempt to trace state trucks on Camiel's farm for several weeks enhances this conclusion. We believe surveilling detectives were involved in finding whatever political ammunition could be found at the farm. . . . Unpardonable violations of privacy have occurred and our hope is that through the public airing of this Presentment, such practices will cease in the future.

The "public airing" never took place. The original report, written by one of Specter's assistant district attorneys, never made it out of the district attorney's office. While the members of grand juries issue reports in their own names, in Philadelphia the district attorney's office traditionally has handled the actual writing and has decided on the contents.

In this case, Specter overruled the judgment of the assistant who had questioned the witnesses — sixty-five, in all — and developed the evidence. The critical passages were almost all excised.

Chapter Fourteen

FRANK RIZZO NEVER attempted to hide his dislike for Milton Shapp when Rizzo was riding high as mayor. Before the lie detector test, when he was still talking to reporters, Rizzo dismissed the governor as "that fuckin' little weasel" or "that little prick," whom he was going to crush at the polls in 1974.

"After yesterday's election, I'd say Governor Shapp doesn't represent the Democratic Party and he'll be a one-term governor," Rizzo said, the day following Richard Nixon's reelection. "I will absolutely be a participant in the process that's going to make him a one-term governor. If Governor Shapp runs again, I will oppose him by either running myself against him or by lending my influence to another candidate even if that means going to the other party. But there is no way I could ever support Shapp. You can bet your bottom dollar that I'm going to have an important role in deciding who's going to be this state's next governor."

In mid-1973, Rizzo was confidently telling us, and anyone else who showed the slightest interest, about a statewide poll commissioned from Albert E. Sindlinger and Company by unnamed friends of his. The poll, he said, clearly indicated he would "destroy" Shapp if he entered the 1974 Democratic primary against him.

The boast about destroying Shapp was not heard again after the lie detector test. The Sindlinger poll was forgotten. Rizzo began planning ways to hold onto his own job. One of the ways was to cozy up to Shapp.

"Dear Governor Shapp," the letter began. It was dated February 7, 1974, and was on the stationery of the mayor of Philadelphia.

Just as you grasped the initiative to bring an end to the independent trucking crisis, I am moved to extend my congratulations to you for a job well done. You certainly deserve a great deal of credit for taking matters into your own hands at a time when the situation calls for leadership. I respect such action and those who exercise it. A prolonged strike would have been very crippling to the people of Philadelphia and the entire Commonwealth.

Sincerely, Frank*

Rizzo's letter was his first public move to force his way back into the Democratic Party. He had privately sought to make peace with Pete Camiel, but Camiel, not surprisingly, was so outraged at Rizzo's attempt to put him in jail that he would not hear of it. The letter, then, was sent with two goals in mind: to soften up Shapp by publicly flattering him, and to signal to committeemen caught in the Rizzo-Camiel war that the mayor's relationship with the governor was not all that bad.

To that end, the letter was slipped to a friendly reporter from the Philadelphia *Inquirer*, who printed the text of it, along with these observations:

"The two men had been bitterly feuding since the mayor first considered running for governor a year and a half ago. When Rizzo began seeking 'peace' with the Democratic Party leadership earlier this year, the battling ceased . . . governmental contacts between the Rizzo and Shapp administrations have increased markedly."

The planted story quoted an unidentified Rizzo aide as saying, "Governmental relations have never been better," but it failed to contain any indication of how Shapp felt. And, in any event, the Rizzo ploy failed. Shapp ignored him.

Rizzo did not give up. He still had a base of support among the voters in South Philadelphia and the Northeast. The Building Trades Unions, which had worked for Nixon in 1972, were with

* Philadelphia *Inquirer*, February 10, 1974.

him. And he had the loyalty of a few of the best ward leaders, like Bill Barrett and State Senator Henry J. (Buddy) Cianfrani. But he had no citywide organization and, in a primary election contest, an organization was of supreme importance. Camiel, who was determined to run a candidate against Rizzo in the 1975 primary, had the organization. The man Rizzo chose to help him lure ward leaders and committeemen away from Camiel was Cianfrani.

Buddy Cianfrani was fifty-one years old and spoke with the hoarse toughness of a movie villain. He was bald and of average height and weight, but he had a certain roguish candor that both men and women found appealing.*

Buddy was the leader of the 2d Ward in South Philadelphia, a predominantly Catholic, Italian-American ward, 60 percent white, 57 percent Democratic. Although the Democrats outregistered the Republicans, Cianfrani was well aware of the fact that his ward was turning increasingly conservative. Even though the large numbers of black voters had stayed with the Democrats, in the eight elections between 1966 and 1974, Cianfrani had lost to the GOP five times.

In Democratic primaries, however, it was a different story. In the five contested primaries during that same period of time, Cianfrani's candidate had carried the ward every time. One of those candidates had been Frank Rizzo, and Cianfrani had delivered for him in both the primary and the general.

"The real test of a ward leader is in a primary," Cianfrani told us. "In a general, the people are going to vote their beliefs. In a primary, you can give people a sales talk, persuade them to back your candidate — if they respect you."

The people in Cianfrani's ward respected him, and that respect showed in the mastery with which he delivered the votes in primary elections. In 1966, for example, when Milton Shapp was seeking the Democratic nomination for governor, Cianfrani supported Auditor General Robert P. Casey. Casey won, 2,790 votes to 522 for Shapp. In 1970, when the same two men were running for the same nomination, Cianfrani backed Shapp. Shapp won the ward, 2,220 votes to Casey's 335.

So strong was Cianfrani in South Philadelphia that he was able to survive a scandal that would have driven a lesser man from

* Cianfrani's candor was displayed in 1975 when, as chairman of the Senate Appropriations Committee, he defended his attempt to deny funds to the special prosecutor investigating corruption in Philadelphia. "What kind of a prosecutor is he if he can't get anything on me?" Cianfrani asked reporters.

public life. In November 1972, Cianfrani had voted in favor of state legislation proposing that strict controls be placed on abortion, a position consistent with that shared by most of his constituents. That position, however, was not shared by Patricia Arney, thirty-two, a Democratic committeewoman in Cianfrani's 2d Ward. And Mrs. Arney, a divorcee, went to the Philadelphia *Inquirer* to complain about Cianfrani.

On November 22, 1972, the *Inquirer* printed Mrs. Arney's story. Cianfrani, she had told the paper in a notarized statement, had paid for an abortion she had had in May 1970. The abortion had been necessary because of a liaison she had had with Cianfrani, who was separated from his wife and three daughters.

"I suggested the abortion. Sen. Cianfrani consented and never made any objection to the operation," the *Inquirer* quoted her as saying. When the antiabortion legislation was pending, she said, she warned Cianfrani that if he voted for it, she would make her story public, for two reasons.

"One is that I'm opposed to the bill because I believe it's unfair and unjust to impose the convictions of one religion upon members of other faiths," the *Inquirer* quoted her. "My second reason is the more personal reason that Sen. Cianfrani is enacting laws . . . for the citizens of the Commonwealth to abide by when he himself has not abided by them."

The abortion had cost $200, plus $10 for a visit to the doctor's office, Mrs. Arney said, and Cianfrani had paid for it all with a check drawn on the Centennial Bank. The *Inquirer* had a copy of the check.

Cianfrani denied the charges, and his colleagues in the capitol in Harrisburg took to the Senate floor to defend him and denounce the *Inquirer*. But the incident disturbed and distressed him. He was used to having old Italian women present him with plaster saints when he did them small favors. Now he found it hard to face these women and his one hope was that it would all blow over soon.

Strangely enough, it did. Before long, the constituents were back on Buddy's doorstep, asking for help, the abortion story ignored if not forgotten. But it was neither ignored nor forgotten on the second floor of City Hall.

"Can you imagine that," Rizzo would tell a visitor three months after the story appeared. "The dumb bastard paid for an abortion with *a check*."

But in 1974, Rizzo needed Cianfrani, and Buddy went to work for him. It was not a completely one-sided arrangement. With

Rizzo as the candidate for mayor, Cianfrani knew he didn't have to worry about carrying the 2d Ward. Rizzo would carry it without having to set foot in it. And Buddy could talk to the other ward leaders, to the committeemen, even, for a time, to Camiel.

Buddy's problem, and Rizzo's, was that Camiel wouldn't listen.

"Rizzo was wrong and he knows it," Cianfrani told us at the time. "He wanted me to go against Fitzpatrick. He called me up and said I had to help him beat Fitzpatrick. I said, 'Are you crazy? Specter's the enemy. He's trying to put me in jail.' He said, 'Aw, we can patch that up.' I told him he was making a mistake. Now he knows I was right. He likes Fitzpatrick.

"It's got to be ended. These guys in [City] Council are caught in the middle and they're really sweating it out. . . . The ward leaders are the same way. They tell Pete they're with him and they tell Rizzo they're with him. They don't know what to do. I'm trying to help and Pete gets mad at me. He told me, 'You don't speak for City Committee.' I said, 'I never told anybody I speak for City Committee. I speak for myself.'"

With Shapp ignoring his overtures, and Camiel rejecting them, Rizzo decided to go public with his case. He had not spoken on the record with a reporter about politics since his preelection press conference in 1973, but he now granted an exclusive interview to the same *Inquirer* reporter who had reported on the letter he had written praising Shapp. In a copyrighted story dated March 31, 1974, the *Inquirer* quoted Rizzo as saying he was "through fighting" and would support Shapp for relection. The paper made no mention of Rizzo's vow that there was "no way [he] could ever support Shapp."

"I absolutely intend to seek reelection as a Democrat and I absolutely intend to support every single endorsed candidate on the Democratic ticket this year," Rizzo was quoted as saying. "I believe in the principles of the Democratic Party, and Democrats are fielding the best slate of candidates. I'm not interested in fighting anymore. As far as I'm concerned, Camiel can run the Democratic Party, Schwartz can run the Council, and I will run the city government. . . . Doves are flying out from all over me. When I raise my arms, they fly out of my armpits."

The words were vintage Rizzo. But the message had been drafted by Al Gaudiosi. The message, as Gaudiosi explained it privately to associates, was this:

"We have offered to make peace. We are supporting all the Democratic candidates. We have said that Camiel can run the party. We want to stop the fighting and unite the party. If our offer is rejected, the blood is on Camiel's head."

The blood was not long in coming. The Democratic Party had scheduled its annual Jefferson–Jackson Day Dinner, a $50-a-plate fund-raising affair, for May 14, 1974, at the Civic Center, near the University of Pennsylvania campus in West Philadelphia. Rizzo's emissaries let it be known that the mayor would like to attend and that he and his supporters would buy a large bloc of tickets — provided Rizzo was seated at the head table.

"Let him sit on the floor with the rest of the Republicans," Camiel replied publicly, when told about Rizzo's intentions by reporters.

On the afternoon of May 14, hours before the dinner was to start, Thomas J. Magrann arrived at the mayor's City Hall offices. Magrann was business manager of the Philadelphia Building and Construction Trades Council, AFL-CIO. Like Rizzo, he had supported Nixon in 1972. In 1971, when Rizzo ran for mayor as a Democrat and won, Magrann had run for city council as a Republican and lost. But they were by this time fast friends.

Magrann was joined by other union leaders. Outside, a row of cars carrying banners reading "Labor for Rizzo" was parked — illegally — on the north side of City Hall. As the dinner hour neared, most of the union men left. Rizzo came out of his office, went out to the sidewalk, and climbed into his black limousine. Magrann climbed in with him, as did John McCullough, business manager of Roofers Local 30, for the trip to the Civic Center.

Rizzo entered the hall after most of the 4,000 guests had been seated. He was preceded by a fife and drum band, and followed by about 150 union members, most of them from the building trades but including some from the Teamsters. The mayor paraded past the two-level head table, stopping to shake hands with State House Speaker Herbert Fineman. George Schwartz ignored him and Jim Tate got up and walked away as he approached. Camiel and other head table guests — Shapp and U.S. Senator Lloyd Bentsen of Texas — had not yet arrived.

Rizzo walked past the table set up just under the head table, the table to which he and his party had been assigned, and led the parade around the hall before sitting down in the rear. The parade, loud and boisterous, with the marchers chanting "We want Rizzo," continued for a half hour. It was led by Mike Wallace, the deputy to the mayor, who was forbidden by the city charter from being involved in politics.

Mayor Rizzo surrounded by his allies during a demonstration
that disrupted a 1974 Democratic Party dinner.

Meanwhile, additional union men swarmed over the hall, occupying tables purchased by other persons. Two of Camiel's nieces, Marianne McNevin and Laureen White, and Camiel's nephew, Claude Camiel, had tickets for table 193 but were turned away from it by a group of roofers. They complained to ushers, among whom were fourteen deputy sheriffs in plainclothes. One of the ushers, Deputy Sheriff James Ellis, told the Philadelphia *Bulletin*'s L. Stuart Ditzen that he and four others asked the roofers to move and immediately became embroiled in a fistfight.

"They were waiting for it," Ellis said. "They had no intention of moving."*

Tables were overturned, plates and glasses were smashed and Deputy Sheriff George Clements was taken to Philadelphia General Hospital with a swollen eye.

John Shopa, sixty, was a maintenance man for the state and he, too, had purchased a ticket for table 193. When he arrived, two of the ten seats were empty and he sat down on one of them. "One guy started throwing celery in my face and another guy started pulling on my tie," Shopa said. When the brawl erupted, he was beaten until his face was bloody and his glasses were smashed.

When John O'Shea, the party treasurer, began introducing the head table guests, the Rizzo supporters began booing. They booed almost everyone, including a half-dozen union leaders who had ignored their pressure to refuse to sit at the head table. One who was not booed was Shapp. Rizzo applauded the governor, and so did those with him.

Gradually, the noise from the Rizzo crowd began to subside, although it erupted occasionally in fits and starts. Rizzo and his entourage sat down and ostentatiously began conversing with each other, studiedly ignoring the head table activities. But the din had diminished to the point where the evening's program could proceed, interrupted now and then by the chanting and hollering of the Rizzo partisans.

As soon as Bentsen, the featured speaker, had finished his remarks, through which Rizzo had continued his own conversation, a group of demonstrators, led by a man wearing a hard hat decorated with Rizzo stickers, jumped onto the stage. With the aid of a bullhorn, the man in the hard hat resumed the chant, "We want Rizzo."

"This is one of the best days of my life," Rizzo told the *Bulletin*.† "I am overwhelmed by this support. Look at these labor leaders

* Philadelphia *Bulletin*, July 18, 1974.
† Philadelphia *Bulletin*, May 15, 1974.

here with me. They are showing us all that we are a part of this Democratic organization, that one man does not run it alone. These men are demonstrating they are friends of mine. They stood up and were counted."

What does it mean? Rizzo was asked.

"It means that they had better run for cover," he answered.

The demonstration at the dinner was a declaration by Rizzo of his intent to take over the party, a declaration complete with the ugly connotation that the takeover would be effected by any means possible. Every ward leader present had seen, or heard about, the blood and the shattered dishes. The scene might not have caused an immediate shift in sentiment among the politicians, but a seed had been planted.

Cianfrani was to be the instrument of that takeover. At Rizzo's urging, Cianfrani agreed to run against Camiel for the party chairmanship at the ward leaders' meeting on June 17, even though he knew there were not enough votes at that time to unseat Rizzo's enemy. Rizzo had argued that the votes *would* be there on June 17. The ward leaders who would elect a chairman had to be elected themselves on June 10, and Rizzo supporters were running against most of the ward leaders who opposed the mayor. Rizzo told Cianfrani he was confident that thirty-five of the sixty-nine ward leaders to be elected would be on his side. Cianfrani was doubtful, but he said he would go along for the time being.

One of those Rizzo hoped to see elected ward leader was Charles McMenamin, a forty-year-old who lived in the 42d Ward, where Herb McGlinchey had been the Democratic boss since 1933. Rizzo had put McMenamin on the payroll as a deputy commissioner of licenses and inspections at $26,000 a year. McMenamin owned a saloon, presumably worked a full day at his city job, and was actively campaigning to replace McGlinchey as ward leader.

Under Rizzo, the city charter prohibition against political activity by municipal workers had been routinely ignored, even though its language was explicit: "No appointed officer or employe of the city shall be a member of any national, state or local committee of a political party, or an officer or member of a committee of a partisan political club, or take any part in the management or affairs of any political party or in any political campaign, except to exercise his right as a citizen privately to express his opinion and to cast his vote."*

* Section 10–107, subsection 4, Philadelphia Home Rule Charter, 1952.

Joe Braig, Mike Wallace, John Taglianetti and Hillel Levinson had all been involved in politics in behalf of the mayor. But Mc-Menamin made them look like models of discretion. His "opinion" was expressed in campaign posters hung in the windows of his saloon and in the conversations he had with committeemen in the ward. And that opinion always came down to the necessity for electing him ward leader and throwing McGlinchey out. This wreaked such violence on the charter that even Rizzo recognized it and McMenamin had to drop out of the race. His wife, Audrey, became the surrogate candidate.

McMenamin was thirty years younger than the seventy-year-old McGlinchey, but he had been able to prove that he was pretty popular in the ward, too, and he began to get pledges of support for his wife from some of the fifty committeemen. McGlinchey had been in charge of the ward for forty-one years, however, and he hadn't held on by lacking resourcefulness. He knew he was in a close contest and, not having the power of the mayor behind him, decided to use the power of incumbency in an audacious and highly questionable manner.

About a half hour before the scheduled 8 P.M. meeting on June 10, McGlinchey showed up outside the 42d Ward clubhouse on Front Street in the Olney section. His white hair was combed neatly and he looked like what he was — a jaunty Irish politician, dapper in a smart lightweight suit and black and white shoes, his face as red and pugnacious as ever. McGlinchey, the lone key to the clubhouse securely in his pocket, looked at two dozen persons waiting to get inside, then walked away.

Although only committeemen were permitted to vote, the ward meeting was a neighborhood event and soon there were perhaps two hundred persons gathered outside the clubhouse, waiting for the election to begin. Then came word that McGlinchey had last been seen getting on a bus at Ruscombe Avenue and Roosevelt Boulevard, several blocks away. Others from the ward also had been seen climbing aboard. Some of McMenamin's supporters, justifiably suspicious, decided they had better get over to Ruscombe and "the Boulevard" as quickly as possible.

The bus was still there and McGlinchey was on it. He was standing and pointing and talking, as if he were conducting a meeting. When McMenamin's sympathizers drove up, the bus moved out, going north on Roosevelt Boulevard, away from the 42d Ward clubhouse. The men in the cars, shouting protests out the windows, gave chase, following the bus until it left the ward. Then they returned to the clubhouse, where an outdoor meeting was under way. Audrey McMenamin was nominated for ward leader, and she received all the votes cast. Her husband pronounced her the winner and invited the crowd to his saloon for drinks on the house.

But no votes were cast for Audrey McMenamin on the bus that McGlinchey had rented for *his* meeting. On the bus, McGlinchey received all the votes. He had rented the bus, McGlinchey later explained, to provide a refuge for his supporters from Rizzo's "goons." Predictably, the Camiel-controlled City Committee ruled that McGlinchey's meeting had been the valid one and Charlie McMenamin became the first Philadelphia politician ever to lose a mobile election. On June 10, Camiel had prevailed.

The telephone calls came on June 11. The calls were made to the wives of five state legislators and to the mother of the clerk of quarter sessions court. The women had something in common; each was related to a Democratic ward leader who was supporting Camiel. And each of the women was told that something terrible would happen to her if the ward leader she was related to voted for Camiel.

"It was done in an organized, systematic fashion," State Representative Roland Greenfield, leader of Oxford Circle's 53d Ward, said in an unusual floor speech in the House of Representatives on June 12. "It was done in a cowardly fashion, knowing we were in Harrisburg performing our duties."

State Senator Francis Lynch, of Fairmount's 15th Ward, told reporters his wife had telephoned him in his Harrisburg motel room at 9 P.M. on June 11. "She said the caller said, 'Let me tell you something. If he votes for Camiel Monday night, we're going to take it out on you,'" Lynch said.

The others — State Senator Freeman Hankins of West Philadelphia's 6th Ward, State Representative Peter Perry of Oak Lane's 10th Ward, State Representative Martin P. Mullen of West Philadelphia's 51st Ward and Clerk of Quarter Sessions Court Edward S. Lee of Germantown's 59th Ward — reported similar threats.

"Beyond an outrage to the total city, this is a shameful performance in the public sector for which Mayor Rizzo, Sen. Cianfrani and all those directly associated with them are directly responsible," Camiel said, in a statement. "It is absolutely inconceivable that such activities could be carried out without their knowledge or encouragement."

After Greenfield had issued his statement, State Representative Michael (Ozzie) Myers, a Rizzo supporter from South Philadelphia's 39th Ward, was seen entering a private telephone booth at the rear of the House chamber. An hour later, Myers told the House that his wife had received an anonymous telephone threat. What's more, he said, he had been talking to Cianfrani and Cianfrani had told him that other ward leaders who supported Rizzo also had been threatened.

Cianfrani withdrew from the race against Camiel, and another Rizzo loyalist, City Councilman Joseph L. Zazyczny, replaced him. Camiel won, 48 to 21. Cianfrani could count as well as anybody.*

Two days later, nine patronage employees in the collections department were fired. All of them were related to ward leaders or committeemen in wards that had voted against Rizzo's man Zazyczny.

When Congressman Bill Barrett died in 1976, Rizzo looked around for a deserving successor. He settled on Ozzie Myers.

In the case of Ozzie Myers, as in the cases of the nine collections department employees, Rizzo proved that he knew the value of a job, particularly in politics.

On August 19, 1974, the Rizzo administration posted public notices — as it was required to do by law — that 280 manual laborers' jobs would be filled on a first-come, first-served basis on Saturday, September 7. The jobs paid $8,439 a year, the notices stated, and those interested were told to apply at one of seven city recreation centers between the hours of 6 and 9 A.M.

As it turned out, ten thousand men were interested and they began lining up at the recreation centers long before dawn on September 7. It was a chilly morning, and a steady rain fell on the men as they waited for an opportunity to apply for a job.

In reality, there were no jobs to apply for. The 280 positions had been filled hours earlier, not on a first-come, first-served basis, but on a political, "who-do-you-know" basis. The jobs had been given to relatives and friends of those who were aligned with the mayor, or who showed a willingness to be aligned with him, in his struggle with the Democratic City Committee. The unfortunates who stood in line, all of them poor, most of them black, had waited for nothing. Those with political connections did not have to stand in the rain; they had been told to report to specific recreation centers

---

* Although there were sixty-six wards, there were sixty-nine ward leaders because three wards had been divided in two for administrative purposes.

starting at 8 P.M. the night before, where personnel department employees enrolled them.*

Rizzo, because he refused to meet with the press after his last, disastrous press conference, escaped comment on the jobs incident for months. But on April 9, 1975, when he was seeking renomination against the opposition of Camiel's organization, he visited the *Bulletin* for an interview and was asked what words he might have for the thousands who were duped into standing in the rain while waiting for jobs that no longer were available.

"I apologize to them," Rizzo said. "I had no more to do with that than you, and that's the way it's been done for twenty years. . . . I think twenty years ago we could start with Mr. Dilworth and Mr. Clark. They were responsible for it. They started the system. . . . It had happened many, many times before. I'm not going to quibble over numbers, but I got into it after the story broke, and I had no more to do with that than you, but I'll accept the responsibility for it. I'm not going to duck it."

The facts, however, disputed Rizzo. Not since the Civil Service system had been installed in 1952 had there been a case of such open political favoritism in apparent contravention of Civil Service regulations involving so many jobs.†

By September 1974, Rizzo was far from concerned about Civil Service niceties. The 280 jobs — worth more than $2,300,000 in taxpayers' money annually — were just one additional weapon to be used in the fight with Camiel. Rizzo knew that Camiel was searching for a candidate to oppose him in the Democratic primary in May 1975, and he knew that, to win, he had to put together his own organization. The quickest and most effective short-term method of building a political organization is through patronage. Camiel had no jobs to give out, and this weakened his ties to some ward leaders who were dependent on patronage. When Rizzo handed out a job, he made the recipient and his family economically dependent on him because they knew the job had been obtained through "connections," and Rizzo picked up another due bill from the sponsoring ward leader or union boss.

From the time he took office until his fight with Camiel, Rizzo had dispensed patronage casually, putting people like Kathy Romeo's father on the payroll. Since the split with the party, the

* The scheme was uncovered by the *Bulletin*'s Charles L. Thomson on September 10, 1974.
† *Report of the City Controller*, October 16, 1974.

business of patronage had become serious business indeed. The takeover of the Philadelphia Housing Authority by Rizzo had given him 1,700 jobs, and an annual payroll of more than $16,500,000, all unencumbered by Civil Service. A U.S. Department of Housing and Urban Development audit of PHA in June 1975 found the agency guilty of "unacceptable employment practices."

"PHA has continued to pursue a policy of employing individuals based on, for the most part, *a closed system of referral by individuals with partisan political affiliations*, as well as by individuals who have access to PHA's top level staff," the audit stated. "As such, PHA was not in compliance with its own established, adopted and supposedly enforced personnel policies."*

But the situation at PHA was simply a reflection of what was happening throughout the government. As he prepared for his showdown with Camiel, Rizzo turned City Hall into a patronage haven far more extensive than at any time since the Republicans had been thrown out in 1952. So-called independent agencies were trampled upon. Civil Service was ignored. Federal funds were dispensed for Rizzo's political and personal convenience.

After PHA had been brought to heel, Rizzo turned to the Redevelopment Authority, which received two-thirds of its funding from the federal government. The authority had 500 jobs, a payroll of about $4,500,000. The executive director was Lynne M. Abraham, a tough young former assistant district attorney whom Rizzo had hired on the recommendation of Richard Sprague. Abraham had been hired in September 1972, but within a year she had proved to be too tough for Rizzo. Her trouble began, she told us, when she resisted Rizzo's demand that she hire his "cronies" and "political friends."

"It got to the point where every job in my office had to be cleared through the mayor's office," she said. "He asked me to hire the brother-in-law of a police inspector 'for anything, no specific job.' "

Abraham was fired on November 13, 1973. She was replaced by Augustine Salvitti, a contractor who had raised campaign funds for Rizzo. After Salvitti had taken over the Authority, the mayor had no further complaints about personnel policies there. Salvitti was not bothered when he received orders to hire Hans J. Grossman, a former police sergeant who had resigned suddenly in July 1972, after the Pennsylvania Crime Commission had accused him of tak-

* *Report on Audit of the Philadelphia Housing Authority*; Office of the Inspector General, Department of Housing and Urban Development, June 27, 1975. Emphasis added.

ing $3,000 from a strip-tease dancer while he was in charge of a squad investigating prostitution. "I know Hans Grossman well," Rizzo had told reporters at the time. "I have a great respect for him. There is a personal relationship. From my knowledge of Grossman — and I'm not trying to influence anybody — it's hard to believe the charges and I don't believe them. He was a good and honest officer."

George S. Forde was next. Forde was sixty-five and had been lured out of retirement by Lennox Moak to take over as revenue commissioner, the same post he had held from 1952 to 1956 under Joe Clark. Most of the persons who worked for the revenue commissioner were Civil Service employees who saw to it that the city collected the tax money it was owed. But 191 employees worked on taxes owed the school board, and these were patronage workers, even as they had been when Forde worked for Clark. But under Clark, these patronage employees had put in a full day's work. Under Rizzo, Forde could not get them to do any work.

"When the mayor wouldn't agree to fire these bums, Forde asked Rizzo to at least talk to them and say, 'Look, you're working for the city, you should do a little work,'" a source very close to Forde told us. "Rizzo wouldn't do that, so Forde quit."

Forde resigned on December 19, 1973, six months after taking the job.

Anthony Iannarelli was fired as managing director of the Philadelphia Parking Authority on January 9, 1974, less than a month after the chairman of the authority, Jack P. Gross, had publicly praised him for his good work.

"Suddenly, you forgot all of this," Iannarelli said to Gross, at the meeting where he was fired. "Or, should I say, you pushed it aside because the mayor told you to fire me. Why did he want me fired? Because I continually refused to hire his political cronies to positions that were neither available nor needed. I won't pad the payroll for anybody."

Iannarelli said Robert Berardi, the pro-Rizzo leader of the 39th Ward, had been hired over his objections to an $18,000 job three months earlier, a job that was not needed. Iannarelli said he had been pressured to hire Berardi by Rizzo himself and by Phil Carroll and Joe Braig. He also said Carroll had vetoed the authority's selection of a law firm to handle its bond counseling work and ordered that the work go to the firm of Townsend, Elliott and Munson. This was Marty Weinberg's former law firm.

During a heated discussion between Iannarelli and Gross,

Augustine Salvitti, who was a member of the Parking Authority's board, moved that Iannarelli be fired, and the motion was carried. Subsequently, Ronald Donatucci, leader of the 26th Ward, and Frank Surace, leader of the 40th Ward, were also placed on the Parking Authority payroll in jobs paying more than $20,000 annually. The authority had a total fulltime payroll of seven persons, including clerical help.*

But Iannarelli, Forde and Abraham were the exceptions. Most of those in positions of responsibility with the city did not resist the pressure to hire Rizzo's political allies. When Joe Braig resigned as deputy to the mayor in January 1974 to return to private law practice and to lay the groundwork for Rizzo's 1975 reelection campaign, the mayor saw to it that Braig would not have to worry about money. As Rizzo's deputy, Braig had been earning $34,000 a year. When he resigned, Braig received a special consultant's contract from Rizzo which paid him $40,000 a year to act as "counsel to the city solicitor for legislative matters." Marty Weinberg, whose law department already had the full-time services of sixty-two lawyers, did not object.

In turning the city treasury into his own private campaign war chest, Rizzo seriously wounded the Civil Service system that had been installed in 1952. The system was designed to give every citizen an equal chance to secure employment with the city. In concept, it is supposed to award jobs and promotions on merit, to fix minimum standards of performance and to protect workers from the demands of politicians. The Civil Service Commission's three members determine policy and approve or disapprove all regulations proposed by the personnel director, whom they appoint. To guard the commission's independence, the city charter specifies that the members, who are appointed by the mayor, be given six-year terms. In addition, the charter requires that the mayor fill all vacancies from a list drawn up by a panel of prominent citizens, including the presidents of the University of Pennsylvania and Temple University.

Although the commissioners set policy and rule on the legality of hirings and firings, the job is part-time and, until August 15, 1974, the compensation was fixed at $100 a meeting, or a maximum of $7,500 annually. On August 15, the city council, acting on legislation submitted by Rizzo, increased the commissioner's compensation to $12,500. At that time the commissioners were the Reverend

---

* By early 1977 the authority's payroll had ballooned to more than 90 persons, all of them uncovered by Civil Service regulations.

Harrison J. Trapp, a black minister who had been appointed by Rizzo; George Bucher, the chairman, a Teamsters Union official who was appointed by Jim Tate but was friendlier to Rizzo; and Leonard Ettinger, a politically connected lawyer who showed what he thought of the ban on political activity by commissioners when he entered the 1973 Democratic primary election for a common pleas judgeship nomination.

Less than two months after their pay raise had been granted, the Civil Service commissioners, sworn to uphold the integrity of the merit system, had a chance to do just that. During the summer, the city had been awarded $6,000,000 by the federal government under the 1973 Comprehensive Employment and Training Act (CETA), a program designed to "provide job training and employment opportunities for the economically disadvantaged."* The $6,000,000 granted the city could have put to work some 600 "economically disadvantaged" persons.

Under the Civil Service system, job descriptions would have been prepared, minimum requirements would have been established, some form of competitive examinations would have been scheduled and the availability of the jobs would have been announced. But this didn't happen. The commissioners, complying with Rizzo's wishes, ruled on October 10 that the jobs to be funded by CETA money — taxpayers' money — were exempt from merit hiring.

Because of this ruling, control of the CETA jobs passed directly to Rizzo's Area Manpower Planning Council. The boss of the council was John Taglianetti, the man who didn't notice who punched whom at the riotous 55th Ward meeting.

Americans for Democratic Action protested the ruling and filed suit to prevent it from taking effect, but to no avail. Rizzo had the jobs. ADA issued a statement which said:

ADA protests the continuing erosion of Philadelphia's civil service system under the Rizzo administration. Last month, city officials were caught in the act of giving out 280 city jobs to political favorites while thousands of men stood in line waiting for jobs that had already been filled. This month, the Civil Service Commission quietly approved a rule exempting from civil service hundreds of new city jobs. . . . The patronage system is not just creeping back into city government in Philadelphia — it is galloping back.

* U.S. Comprehensive Employment and Training Act, December 28, 1973.

But ADA did not drop the matter. Nor did the *Daily News*. Both conducted investigations into how the CETA money was being spent. Both investigations found large numbers of political and personal allies of Rizzo had been placed on the city payroll. The *Daily News* reported that Anthony Verrecchia had been given a $14,000-a-year job under Taglianetti, working as director of private sector job development. Previously, the newspaper reported, Verrecchia had been Carmella Rizzo's hairdresser. Because of the publicity given these disclosures, the U.S. Labor Department was drawn into the matter. After conducting its own inquiry, the department on October 23, 1975, said that federal money amounting to $332,557 had been spent improperly in the employment of fifty-three persons.

Rather than fight, the city chose to negotiate. Early in 1976, the Labor Department agreed to accept $226,730 from the city in settlement.

"The federal government has no business taking money from the taxpayers for this," said Rich Chapman, executive director of the ADA. "The city is willing to make this payment because it doesn't want an investigation into the program. They want this buried. They don't want to face the question, 'Who did it?'"

The controversy over the CETA jobs and the 280 laborers' jobs, however, were only pieces of a much larger picture. All through the government, Civil Service was being ignored. Often with the compliance of the Civil Service Commission, and sometimes on his own, Rizzo was exempting more and more jobs from the merit system. And the jobs were going to political cronies.

When Rizzo took office, for example, the mayor's staff included 29 full-time and 4 part-time exempt employees, a total of 33. Before his first term had ended, Rizzo had 320 full-time and 123 part-time exempt employees in his office.*

At the start of the Rizzo administration, the managing director's office had 10 full-time and 4 part-time exempt workers. Four years later, it had 124 full-time and 7 part-time exempt positions. The number of full-time exempt positions in the city representative and director of commerce's office increased from 6 to 257.

In contrast, the independently elected offices of city controller, district attorney, clerk of quarter sessions court, sheriff and register

* Job figures obtained from Personnel Inventory record sheets, dated June 30, 1971; June 30, 1972; June 30, 1973; June 30, 1974, and June 30, 1975. Office of City Controller William G. Klenk.

of wills showed a net decrease in exempt employees over the same period of time.

When Rizzo took office, there were about 30,000 city workers and, excluding the courts, whose workers have never been covered by Civil Service, there were 487 exempt jobs. Four years later, there were about 31,500 employees and 1,285 of them were exempt.

Simply because a job was exempt from Civil Service did not mean that it was an unnecessary job, of course. What it did mean was that Rizzo was in a position to give an exempt job to anyone he cared to, like his wife's hairdresser. Or his stockbroker's wife. John T. O'Brien, of Thomason & McKinnon Auchincloss Kohlmeyer, Inc., was the mayor's investment adviser and, when questions were being raised about who paid for the Chestnut Hill house, Rizzo authorized him to say that the Rizzo portfolio had shown a $26,000 paper profit from mid-1972 to mid-1975. O'Brien's wife, Anna Marie, had been hired by Gaudiosi in 1972 as a secretary in Pennsylvania Committee to Reelect the President. While Gaudiosi returned to Philadelphia '76, Mrs. O'Brien went with him, as a $15,825-a-year coordinator of voluntary services. After Rizzo had been returned to office, Mrs. O'Brien landed a job as deputy city representative at $33,000 a year.

The number of such Civil Service–exempt positions was truly impressive in a city whose goal ostensibly was to reduce the payroll during financial hard times, and to fill those jobs it had to on the basis of merit. By the time he was gearing up to fight Camiel, Rizzo had available to him for patronage purposes 1,285 exempt city jobs; 1,842 positions funded by programs of the federal government and subject to his total rule because of the Civil Service Commission finding; 1,700 Philadelphia Housing Authority posts; 500 Redevelopment Authority jobs; 191 collections department jobs, plus whatever else he could squeeze out of the school board (which he controlled, having gotten rid of Mark Shedd), the parking authority and various city departments.

Assigning the average yearly salary for a city employee, $11,743 in 1975, to those patronage jobs, Rizzo had a political war chest of more than $65,000,000 a year. And literally dozens paid far more than average.

When Joe Braig left with his $40,000 contract, his $34,000 job was given to Goldie Watson, a black woman long active in politics.

The Reverend Wycliffe Jangdharrie, a native of Trinidad, was a Baptist minister and was president of the West Philadelphia branch of the NAACP. He also was one of the severest critics of Frank Rizzo, at least for a time. On July 4, 1972, at the NAACP convention in Detroit, Jangdharrie introduced a resolution proposing that the NAACP censure Rizzo for "what is apparently a racist attitude on the part of this elected official." At the 1971 NAACP convention, he had introduced a similarly worded resolution denouncing Rizzo for his conduct as a police commissioner. Neither resolution was approved.

Jangdharrie, since 1956, had operated the Washington Hall Nursing Home in West Philadelphia. In December 1972, the home had received ten citations for violations of the city's fire code. All three newspapers had carried stories about the citations, with Jangdharrie charging he was the victim of a "political" attack by unnamed "underlings," specifically excluding Rizzo. Joe Braig, then head of L & I, replied that Jangdharrie ought to correct the "dangerous" conditions in the nursing home.

Fire broke out in Jangdharrie's nursing home on September 13, 1973, and eleven elderly patients were killed. He was not charged with negligence by any local, state or national authority.

On June 5, 1974, Jangdharrie called on black ward leaders to vote to oust Camiel and install Cianfrani.

On October 15, 1974, Jangdharrie was hired by the Rizzo administration to be a special assistant to the managing director — exempt from Civil Service — at $19,500 a year. He was to work on "community affairs."*

For a city that was going broke, even as the mayor was telling the citizens Philadelphia was financially sound, there seemed to be more than enough money to hire those upon whom Rizzo smiled. Tom McIntosh had his title changed to assistant to the mayor and his salary raised to $28,000. And he got his two sons jobs, one in the Housing Authority, the other in the Redevelopment Authority.

Rizzo had made much of how he distrusted Emmett Fitzpatrick, but after Fitzpatrick had been elected DA, and had at his disposal a staff full of lawyers and investigators, the mayor saw nothing wrong with appointing Fitzpatrick's wife, Joane, to the Zoning Board of Adjustment, a part-time position which paid $8,400 a year.†

Mrs. Fitzpatrick had been appointed in April 1974. The following month, Marty Weinberg's wife, Carol, was hired on a provisional basis by Fitzpatrick as a research assistant at $13,941 a year.

* In 1971, Jangdharrie had supported Thacher Longstreth over Rizzo.
† Mrs. Fitzpatrick died February 4, 1976, of a heart attack at age forty-five.

The hiring was provisional because the job was covered by Civil Service, and a permanent appointment required the passing of a Civil Service test. Mrs. Weinberg took the test on July 17. She flunked. The DA's public relations officer, James Vitaliano, announced on September 10, 1974, that the city solicitor's wife had resigned for personal reasons.

"As the mother of two children, she found it didn't work out and that her family came first," Vitaliano said.*

Cianfrani got his right-hand man, Frederick Del Rossi, a job as special assistant to the managing director — exempt from Civil Service — at $19,500 a year. Del Rossi's duties were described as "liaison with City Council." That was a popular description. It described Tom McIntosh's job, after he got his raise. It also described William Boyle's job, Civil Service–exempt at $20,000 a year, with the city solicitor. Boyle was a former city councilman, a politician who had once worked for a railroad and had no legal experience. But he was hired by Rizzo to be liaison for an office full of lawyers with a body whose principal business was the making of laws.

Michael Stack was a lawyer and the Democratic leader of the 58th Ward in the Northeast. Stack received a $15,000 contract from the Redevelopment Authority to do legal work. Joseph M. (Mike) Smith, Fitzpatrick's law partner, was another lawyer whose services the Redevelopment Authority couldn't do without. He, like Stack, received a $15,000 contract. And when Joe Braig decided he had had enough of "consulting" at $40,000 a year and joined the law firm of Abrahams and Loewenstein, that firm received a contract, formerly held by George Schwartz's firm, for $200,000 worth of consulting annually on Philadelphia Gas Works business.

The list appeared to be endless. Mike Colozzi, a Republican committeeman, was given a job in the collections department after he promised to help Rizzo in the 1975 primary; he didn't even have to change his registration. Joseph Steck was the Republican leader of the 57th Ward in Torresdale. He had a job in the Philadelphia Traffic Court, which was controlled by Traffic Court Judge Louis Vignola, Cianfrani's uncle. Steck was told he had a choice to make: go to work for Rizzo or lose your job. Republican Chairman William J. Devlin told us Steck chose to hold onto his job and work for Rizzo. But Devlin said he demanded, and got, Steck's resignation as ward leader.

Rizzo was particularly anxious to please black ward leaders in

* Philadelphia *Daily News*, September 13, 1974.

hopes that would cut down the massive black vote against him. Earl Stout, head of the Sanitation Workers' Union and later head of the umbrella union local that covered all nonuniformed city employees, placed at least four relatives plus some friends on the city and Housing Authority payrolls. Clarence Miles, leader of the 16th Ward in North Philadelphia, was on the collections department payroll for $12,090 a year. Pearl Shelton, wife of Ulysses Shelton, leader of North Philadelphia's 20th Ward, also was on the collections department payroll. Jose Cruz, Rizzo's political contact with the Puerto Rican community, was placed on the Housing Authority payroll at $14,000 a year.

Lawrence Cesare, who had been Emmett Fitzpatrick's campaign manager, was hired as another "special assistant" to the managing director to work on community relations at $22,000 a year. Mitchell W. Melton, a former State House member and a Democratic committeeman in North Philadelphia, was given still another Civil Service–exempt job in the managing director's office. He, too, was supposed to be working on community relations, at $20,000 a year. And after Audrey McMenamin had lost the ward leader's fight to Herb McGlinchey, she was rewarded with a job in the Housing Authority.

These and hundreds more like them became Rizzo's organization. They had helped the mayor in his attempt to oust Camiel and, while the attempt was unsuccessful, they had gained valuable experience in ward politics. And in Philadelphia, primary elections were exercises in ward politics.

Through his own personal appeal, or through the dispensing of patronage, Rizzo had gained the allegiance of about one-third of the Democratic ward leaders. He had the support of organized labor, which could produce as many as 2,000 poll workers on election day, and he had Al Pearlman successfully soliciting donations from businessmen all over town.

Thus, Rizzo felt he was prepared to do battle with whomever the Democratic organization selected to oppose him in the primary. He grew even more confident when Bill Green announced on December 5, 1974, that he would not run against Rizzo. To Jim Tate, who knew something about efforts to dump an incumbent, and to other party professionals, Green's decision was a serious blow, for to them the young Congressman seemed far and away the best candidate.

Camiel, however, did not appear distressed. We spoke to him at the national Democratic mini-convention in Kansas City, where he was at the time of Green's announcement, and he said the party had "many, many" candidates who could defeat Rizzo.

"The trouble with Pete is that ever since he passed that lie detector test he thinks he's George Washington," one of Camiel's associates at the mini-convention told us. "He thinks he can do no wrong. But this guy [Rizzo] is gonna be tough."

Indeed, for months Camiel had been delivering long and bitter denunciations of Rizzo. A single mention of the mayor's name by a reporter was enough to set him off on a half-hour tirade about "that monster in City Hall" and "that fascist bastard."

He was convinced that most Philadelphians shared his feelings about Rizzo and so Camiel was not at all alarmed at the prospect of finding a candidate. Of one thing he was sure, however, and that was the need for the candidate to have sufficient independent means to help finance his own campaign. Camiel knew the power of the incumbent to extract contributions from the citizenry, a power not often shared by a challenger.

The primary election was set for May 20, 1975. Camiel appointed a seventy-five-member committee to interview prospective candidates at public meetings on January 24 and 27. The committee would make its recommendation to the Democratic City Committee, which would endorse the candidate.

Although a number of interested candidates appeared, including Charles Bowser, who later ran as an independent, the choice really came down to two men: City Councilman John B. Kelly, Jr., forty-seven, handsome, former Olympic oarsman and wealthy brother of Princess Grace of Monaco, and State Senator Louis G. Hill, fifty, handsome, a lawyer and wealthy stepson of the late former Mayor Richardson Dilworth.

But before the committee could come to a decision the matter was taken out of its hands by a turn of events that bordered on the slapstick. On January 30, Mrs. John B. Kelly, Sr., seventy-six years old, still sharp and still in control of the family's bricklaying fortune, exercised her maternal privileges and telephoned Camiel and George Schwartz to tell them she didn't want her son, "Kel," to run for mayor. And she told them so emphatically that they were led to believe none of the Kelly money would be available for such a contest. Mrs. Kelly didn't like politics and hadn't liked it since her late husband had run for mayor in 1935 and had apparently won the election, only to be "counted out" by the Republicans, who then owned the city. Camiel and Schwartz promptly dropped Kelly as a possibility, and the councilman somewhat sheepishly admitted that, at age forty-seven, he had been "counted out" by his mother.

"Ma Kelly's pretty tough," he said. "She was giving me one rough time. She's irrational on the subject of politics. She was very desperately groping to stop all this."*

Kelly privately admitted that his mother was concerned that he would be smeared during the campaign because he had separated from his wife and was living the life of a *bon vivant*.

"Louie" Hill, as he liked to be called, had been elected three times to the State Senate from the Northwest part of the city, and he was actually Frank Rizzo's senator. He had been a hard-working, effective legislator, albeit totally colorless, and had become chairman of the judiciary committee. He was serious, stubborn, a very poor speaker and lacked any visible signs of a sense of humor. Still, he had money, appeared determined, and had impressed Camiel's committee when he said of Rizzo, "This man is not a Democrat or a Republican. He is just a unique character that comes on the political scene once in a generation to wreak havoc."

On February 2, the committee recommended Hill be the candidate and the next day the Democratic City Committee endorsed him. Hill began his campaign on the spot.

"We live in a city divided, a city where more than half of the population looks with suspicion on an administration dominated by political hacks whose sole qualification seems to be their dedication to the reelection of the present mayor," Hill said, as he emerged from the Bellevue-Stratford with the endorsement.

Hill set out with ambition, enthusiasm and high hopes. Theoretically, his prospects were good. He was a liberal running against Frank Rizzo, and he believed that fact automatically assured him of most of the votes of the blacks in North and West Philadelphia and the white liberals in center city and Chestnut Hill. He was an ex-Marine who could be as tough as Rizzo — tougher — and he would drive that home to the voters in Kensington and the Northeast through his television commercials and by meeting them personally. And he had the organization behind him. Frank Rizzo had won only 48 percent of the primary vote in 1971, when he had the support of the Democratic City Committee. Since then, Rizzo had acquired quite a few lumps and had lost the City Committee. The potential for victory was undeniably present, Hill said again and again.

To capture that victory, he worked from early morning to late at

* Philadelphia *Bulletin*, February 2, 1975.

night. He scheduled dozens of street-corner rallies, rallies of the type his stepfather had used with such great impact in the late 1940s and early 1950s.

But Hill found campaigning across a huge city as a relative unknown, and with comparatively limited resources, quite different from campaigning for the State Senate. Early one morning, he stood on the east-bound platform at the Fifteenth Street Station of the Market Street Subway to greet voters coming into the city to work. He gave it up after realizing that most of the hands he was shaking belonged to people who lived in Delaware County and couldn't vote in Philadelphia. Neither he nor his small staff had thought of the fact that the western terminus of the subway line was outside the city and was used by commuters.

The decision to use street-corner rallies the way Dick Dilworth did also proved unfortunate. Hill was no Dilworth. He was big and handsome, but he seemed ill at ease speaking in public. He moved stiffly, like a wooden soldier, although off the speaker's platform he was graceful and athletic. And he spoke rapid-fire, like a chattering machine gun, making it difficult to understand what he was saying. At one noontime appearance at Broad and Chestnut streets, one of the city's busiest intersections, he sped so quickly through a speech containing attacks on Rizzo and programs he would institute as mayor that he was finished before some reporters assigned to the event had arrived. He jumped down from his platform, shook the hands of some startled passersby, then climbed back up and delivered the same speech all over again. In all, no more than twenty-five people stayed to hear either version of the speech.

"He couldn't draw flies," Rizzo sneered, when he heard of the incident.

Hill expected to get a large black vote, but he did very little to persuade blacks that he was their candidate. He met with a group of black journalists and, whether he realized it or not, irked them with an attitude which said to them that he was taking black support for granted. On March 7, when William T. Coleman, a prominent black Philadelphian and Hill's own law partner, was sworn in as President Ford's Secretary of Transportation, Hill failed to attend the ceremonies.

Hill's early television ads, trying to depict him as the rugged man he actually was, showed a film of him in a sweatsuit running through Fairmount Park. Hill did not speak in the commercial, but a paid announcer read a script as the candidate ran and ran and ran.

"Did you see him in that commercial?" Rizzo, genuinely amused, asked an audience of his partisans at Palumbo's. "The Six-Million-Dollar Man."

Rizzo's gibe was well thought-out. With that one comment about the Six-Million-Dollar Man, a reference to a popular television show about a mechanical superman, Rizzo at once reminded listeners of Hill's wealth and his awkwardness in public, all the while poking fun at him.

While there were more than enough dramatic issues with which to confront Rizzo, Hill seemed unable to bring them to life. He spoke, but nobody appeared to be listening. And so he tried to cast his attacks on Rizzo in dramatic settings. He held a press conference outside the mayor's still-unoccupied Chestnut Hill house, demanded to know who was paying for it and christened it "San Clemente East." Rizzo ignored him.

He challenged Rizzo to debate him time and again. Finally, on April 28, he arrived in City Hall courtyard at lunchtime and set up two speakers' platforms about 150 feet from the curtained windows of Rizzo's second-floor offices. Hill climbed on one platform, leaving the second — which was painted yellow — empty. Rizzo, Hill told the crowd that gathered around him, was "chicken." He was afraid to debate. Even a chicken, he said, "defends its own dung heap, but this chicken won't." With that, a young man who worked for Hill showed up dressed in a yellow chicken costume and began cluck-clucking his way through the crowd. It made for a nice spot on the evening news.

Having once attracted some attention, Hill went on to try to cram too much into one day. On March 25, 1974, the city council had passed legislation designating the west side of City Hall as "Richardson Dilworth plaza," in honor of Hill's stepfather, the man responsible for most of the physical renaissance of downtown Philadelphia. In what can only be described as a mean and petty act, Rizzo had refused to recognize the designation, even though it was the law of Philadelphia, and had had erected on the site — then still undergoing construction — a large blue and white sign proclaiming it "City Hall West Plaza."

The sign had been up for months, so Hill's indignation that day, while genuine, was not spontaneous. After finishing his "chicken" speech, he marched to the plaza, walked up to Rizzo's sign and nailed over it a three-by-three-foot homemade sign reading, "Richardson Dilworth Plaza." It was an impressive symbolic gesture, and it called attention to a particular side of Rizzo's character, but it was lost in the shuffle of the "chicken" speech.

"He debated a chicken," Rizzo told another group at Palumbo's later, after testing the line on reporters and aides. "And the chicken won."

For the record, Rizzo insisted he was willing to debate· Hill "every hour on the hour." But he insisted on ground rules that made it clear he feared a massive black vote against him. Any debate, he said, must include the Reverend Muhammad Kenyatta, a thirty-one-year-old black man who was born with the name Donald Jackson. There were six persons entered in the Democratic mayoral primary, but all of them appeared to be fringe candidates except for Rizzo and Hill. George Britt, one of the six, was also a black man. Why had Rizzo settled on Kenyatta, instead of Britt? In a 1972 race for the statehouse, Kenyatta had received only 152 votes out of 25,000 cast.

"The important thing to remember is that the people of Philadephia are picking their next mayor and the choice is among three candidates," Rizzo told three thousand of his supporters at a $100-a-plate dinner on April 29. And every time the subject of a debate came up, he would retreat to the same shelter: Kenyatta had to be included.

There were some things Rizzo didn't tell the people about Kenyatta, an articulate young man who was president of the Black Economic Development Conference. One of the things was that Wycliffe Jangdharrie, to whom he had given a $19,500 job, was associate director of the BEDC and was a close friend of Kenyatta's. Another thing was the fact that Rizzo had given a $21,500-a-year job, exempt from Civil Service, to a man who had worked with Kenyatta in BEDC and had traveled with him.

Hill's supporters filed suit seeking to have Kenyatta's name removed from the ballot on an allegation that he did not live in the city and hence could not be a candidate. At a hearing, Kenyatta conceded that his wife and children did live outside the city for reasons of safety — his life had been threatened, he said — but he maintained he lived and worked in the city. The suit was dismissed. Throughout the proceedings, Jangdharrie was never far from Kenyatta's side, although he was drawing a city salary for working on "community relations."*

We talked to Kenyatta about the suspicion in the Hill camp that

* In April 1976, after Rizzo was safely reelected, Jangdharrie was fired.

he was being financed by Rizzo in an attempt to have him siphon off anti-Rizzo black votes that would normally have gone to Hill.

"I am getting damn sick and tired of these innuendoes that I am getting money from Rizzo," said Kenyatta. Still, he refused to say where he was getting his money.

Hill knew where he was getting his money, or at least most of it. It was coming from himself and his family. By the end of the campaign, he would spend $528,000, and $230,000 of it would come from his own and his family's pockets. Rizzo would spend $948,000, and it would come from Republican big businessmen, city workers and true believers.

"The fat cats are afraid to contribute to me because of Rizzo," Hill said. He said he had telephoned Paul R. Kaiser, board chairman of the Tasty Baking Company, seeking a donation and was asked by Kaiser, "What happens if the mayor wins and my name is on your list?"

"He didn't have to explain," Hill said. "I've heard it all before. They all fear reprisals if they don't contribute to Rizzo or they do contribute to me."

Kaiser admitted he had asked Hill the question, but "just for instance, to see what he would say."

"This pressure talk is for the birds and fabricated for political reasons," Kaiser said. "I don't go for this innuendo. I have no fears. If I thought Frank Rizzo was the kind of man Hill says he is, I wouldn't contribute to him."*

Kaiser subsequently became chairman of a businessmen's committee formed to raise money for Rizzo. Like him, the other two officers of the committee lived in the suburbs, were registered Republicans and members of the Union League. Kaiser also donated $250 to Hill, but Hill returned his check.

Rizzo had been campaigning almost nonstop since November. He did not go to subway stops to shake hands, or to any public forum where he might be asked questions about patronage or secret police. He went to the three newspapers for pro-forma interviews, but his campaign was directed entirely at those voters he and Al Gaudiosi knew supported him. His schedule was kept secret from reporters until he actually opened his campaign at a labor dinner on January 16, where he told the audience Philadelphia was in better shape than any other major city financially, even though he had refused to increase taxes.

* "The Human Side of Business," Peter H. Binzen, Philadelphia *Bulletin*, April 28, 1975.

The fact that his administration had held the line on taxes — a truly noteworthy achievement — through the first three years was the principal argument Rizzo used in his reelection campaign. He also promised there would be no increase in taxes in the final year of his first term, adding that his budget was balanced and there was no need for new taxes. Blue and white banners saying "Rizzo Kept Our Taxes Down" went up all over the city. And virtually every speech he gave contained the phrase, "Frank Rizzo didn't raise taxes." He often spoke of himself in the third person.

It was the same message he had delivered wherever he appeared. And he supplemented that by taking care to attend the funerals of dozens of persons, by appearing at store openings in Kensington and dedications of fire houses in South Philadelphia, by going to ethnic festivals in Holmesburg, by marching in the Pulaski Day parade, the St. Patrick's Day parade, the Columbus Day parade. He was out every night, making from three to five stops, shaking hands, promising to attend to a stop sign, to find a job for the father of a thirteen-year-old girl who told him about the family's plight, all of it unremarked on the front pages but making an unquestionable impact on the communities he visited.

He still excoriated judges, and proclaimed himself tough on crime, but as the campaign progressed and Hill floundered, he relaxed and permitted himself the luxury of bantering with, and baiting, reporters he had refused to speak to for months. At an interview at the Philadelphia *Bulletin* on April 9, 1975, he was asked why he had stopped having press conferences.

"You see the point I wanted them to make, they'd print a story and they wouldn't show the community, the public, that the questions were asked by the news media," Rizzo said. "That's all I wanted them to do. The stories were appearing like I was offering this information, and I didn't want to look like an imbecile. If we're going to talk about bagels and salami, let them show that they asked the question, you know, or we're talking about Italian sausage or knockwurst, anything, let's show that they asked the question. And it was no longer a press conference. The questions that were being asked were ridiculous, demeaning to a mayor, and I closed up shop."

The mayor was asked about a comment he had made at a hospital where a suspect had been taken after being shot in a gun battle with police.

"Yeah, that was interesting," he said. "I'd like to tell you that story alone. He was shot in this area [pointing to the groin]. Right?

And the cop did a good job on him. So I told the doctor, 'It looks like it's infected. You should amputate.' "

Questioned about an increase in reported rapes from 694 in 1973 to 796 in 1974, he replied:

"Now there's no way you can police the city. We'd have to put a policeman in every house. Of the total rapes reported, forty-four percent involved . . . were previously acquainted with each other. . . . So, forty-four percent of them were previously acquainted with the offender, and two out of every three rapes were committed indoors. We'd have to put a cop under every water bed. You know, that's the day I resign and become an undercover policeman."

Even though he later became lighthearted, Rizzo started out the interview determined to make his point about the frugality of his administration.

"I am, again, quite pleased with the fact that this administration was able to, for four years, go without a tax increase," he said. "My critics said we couldn't do it, and we did it. I'm very proud of that. Detroit laying off city employees, New York — New York don't know whether their deficit is eight hundred million or a billion — Jersey City, Cleveland — not Philadelphia. We haven't laid anybody off, nor are we going to lay anybody off."

Rather than lay anybody off, Rizzo agreed to a new contract with the municipal employees' union just a few days before the election. The contract granted the employees a whopping 12.8 percent pay hike, at a cost to the city of $26,200,000, starting in the fiscal year beginning July 1, 1975. The only problem with the agreement was that the city didn't have the money to pay for it. But Earl Stout, head of the union, endorsed Rizzo for renomination and reelection.

When Rizzo was faced with running against the opposition of the Camiel organization, he and his advisers decided that it would be wise to do something to divert the opposition. The diversion took the form of a Rizzo slate of candidates. Besides himself, Rizzo was supporting candidates loyal to him in the five at-large council races, six of the ten district council races, one of the two city commissioner contests, and in the races for sheriff, clerk of quarter sessions court and register of wills.*

Of all those on his slate, however, Rizzo promoted only Al Pearlman. Pearlman was running for councilman-at-large, and huge posters featuring photographs of him and Rizzo were tacked up all over town. Pearlman attended every campaign function that Rizzo

---

* Quarter sessions court is the criminal division of the common pleas court.

did. He walked like the mayor. He puffed his chest out like the mayor. But he never said anything. There is not one recorded speech delivered by Al Pearlman. He seemed content to stay on the sidelines and kibbitz, throwing an arm around female reporters who happened to be present.

Camiel was not worried about Pearlman or the others on Rizzo's slate. For the most part, the Rizzo people were running against experienced, better-known candidates, almost all of whom were incumbents. Camiel's preoccupation was Rizzo's defeat, and he had put up what was described to us by him as a "substantial" amount of his own money to see that accomplished.

Rizzo won renomination without difficulty, defeating Hill by 183,672 to 151,948. He increased the number of votes he had received in the 1971 primary by 7,051, and he increased his percentage from 48 to 52. As in 1971, Rizzo's margin came from South Philadelphia and the Northeast. He won all six South Philadelphia wards and twelve of the fourteen Northeast wards.

In the 1971 primary, Rizzo won 19 percent of the vote in the twenty-three wards with black majorities, carrying only Bill Barrett's 36th Ward. In 1975, he increased his share of the black vote to 32 percent in the twenty-six wards with black majorities. But he carried only two of them — Bill Barrett's and the 14th Ward in North Philadelphia, where Jake Adams, who had been given a city job, was the leader.

The turnout in the black wards was extremely low, compared to the citywide turnout, 37 percent as opposed to 57 percent. In 1975, 70,000 fewer blacks chose to vote in the Democratic primary either for or against Rizzo.

And while Camiel's organization was trying desperately to defeat Rizzo, they ignored the rest of the ticket, confident that the City Committee's better-known and established candidates would win easily. They didn't.

Four of the five at-large candidates on the ballot, including Al Pearlman, won councilmanic nominations for the Rizzo slate. Four Rizzo candidates won district councilmanic nominations. Rizzo candidates also won nominations for sheriff, clerk of quarter sessions court, register of wills and one of two city commissioner's posts. Rizzo had swept the city.

With the primary safely behind him, there was little doubt that Rizzo would have an easy time being reelected. His Republican opponent, Tom Foglietta, had calculated that he could win the election by cutting Rizzo's margin in South Philadelphia and the white ethnic river wards and by picking up the solid support of black and liberal Democrats. But Foglietta, soft-spoken and gentle, had miscalculated. South Philadelphia's Italians and the row-house whites, at least at this time, *had* found the man they wanted in the tough-talking Rizzo. He was the one who said what was on their minds when he railed against criminals, denounced judges, complained about permissive schools, praised the worth of neighborhoods and decried mounting tax bills.

And with Charles Bowser in the race, Foglietta had no chance to win the disaffected black and liberal Democrats. Those would go to Bowser. But as the first black to run a serious citywide campaign for mayor, Bowser had little chance to attract the votes of those in the row houses. He was the most articulate man in the race, and put forward more ideas than any other candidate, but 1975 was clearly not the year for a black candidate in Philadelphia.

Foglietta was forced to rely on Republicans, and the numbers there were hopeless. There were 620,000 registered Democrats, compared to 225,000 Republicans. For the first time since the GOP had been born, the Republicans were in the minority in every single ward in the city.

Bowser's Philadelphia Party was brand new and its organization in important parts of the city was either weak or nonexistent. Bowser would receive more votes than Foglietta, but the weakness of the Philadelphia Party would be demonstrated by its failure to win more votes than the Republicans in any other contest.

Rizzo's victory in the primary virtually assured him, and his slate, of triumph in November. The street-cleaning that had been started a month before the primary was halted. It would be resumed again just prior to the November general election.

Chapter Fifteen

Rizzo gave up active campaigning against Bowser and Foglietta on October 12. That was the day he fell and broke his hip at the ARCO refinery fire. The injury sidelined him for the final three and a half weeks of the race. Yet, as we have seen, his enforced idleness didn't cost Rizzo much if any support. When the ballots were counted on the night of November 4 he had collected 57 percent of the total vote. At the Bellevue victory party that night the jubilant *padrone* celebrated from his wheelchair.

Back at City Hall, however, the cheers quickly turned to jeers. Rizzo had said nothing about possible future tax hikes and taxpayers soon learned why he had been silent. Philadelphia, it turned out, faced its biggest budget deficit since William Penn stepped ashore in 1682. It was a secret deficit which had been papered over with budgetary gimmicks. To avoid insolvency, Rizzo would be forced to raise real estate and wage taxes by record amounts. Even these huge increases wouldn't solve the city's problems. By mid-1976, all of Rizzo's talk about wise and efficient city government would be dismissed as so much empty rhetoric, and outraged citizens would try to throw him out.

During his first term, Rizzo had claimed credit for holding the line on taxes. But when things went sour he declined to take responsibility. It lay with the man whom the mayor often described as "the one guy in this administration who can add." That would be Lennox L. Moak, the city finance director. Len Moak, the Rizzo team's acknowledged superstar. In a cabinet of nonentities he stood ten feet tall. He was a big name in municipal finance from New York to California. Moak was the near-legendary budget officer whose cautious, prudent, reliable money management had won national recognition. He was respected by Joe Clark, a liberal Democrat under whom he had served in the 1950s. He had written *the* book on municipal bonds. And the men who rate the bonds that cities sell held him in extremely high regard. "Maybe I'm praising Len too much but I think he's terrific," John Pfeiffer, vice president of Standard & Poor's, the municipal bond rating agency, had said of Moak in the spring of 1975.

"He's a major factor in the good things that have been happening in Philadelphia," had agreed John Phillips, vice president of Moody's Investor Services. Both agencies had raised Philadelphia's bond rating early in 1975 — and they did it primarily because of the towering reputation of Len Moak.

Back home, too, bankers who lent the city money slept more soundly at night knowing that Moak was in charge. The power brokers never really felt comfortable with the man they called Big Frank. Oh, yes, they contributed to Rizzo's campaigns and they knew he was a good friend. Hadn't he made that abundantly clear with the 1971 slogan, "Rizzo Means Business"?

But they were never sure about the mayor, never certain he wouldn't turn on some of them someday for some reason, real or imagined. They trusted Moak implicitly. With Moak keeping the books at City Hall they could put up with Rizzo's relentless posturing, his petty political feuding and constant mouthing off.

They were confident that although the tough cop got the headlines it was the potbellied, asthmatic Baptist from Mississippi who called the fiscal signals. The papers often pictured Moak as a magician pulling rabbits from his hat to keep the city solvent. The power brokers never seemed to suspect that the magician would one day run out of rabbits. What they did fear was that he might run out on them.

There had been that bad morning just nine days after Rizzo's reelection when the *Daily News* reported on its front page: "Moak to Quit City Hall Finance Post." The newspaper stated flatly that the mayor's fiscal panjandrum would resign at the end of the year to form a private consulting firm.

Within an hour after the story appeared, shocked bankers were on the telephone to Moak. "I was trying to sell a little bond issue just then," recalled Moak, "and they told me that unless the report was denied we'd get no bids for the bonds."

Later that day Rizzo, still recovering from his broken hip, talked to his finance director by phone from his hospital bed. There was a problem of money. Money for Moak. He had heavy family medical expenses because of a brain-damaged daughter. He'd been receiving $41,500 in regular salary — $2,500 more than the mayor — plus another $25,000 as lecturer at the University of Pennsylvania's Fels Center of Government. This added compensation had been put up by a group of Philadelphia foundations and civic organizations as an inducement for Moak to join Rizzo in 1972. Now the lectureship money was running out. The hospitalized mayor promised to replace it somehow so that Moak would suffer no loss of income. With that, the finance director agreed to stay on the job. And when Rizzo released a statement that Moak would most certainly carry over into the mayor's second administration there were sighs of relief in corporate boardrooms and executive suites all over town.

The incident pointed up the remarkable influence of Moak in a city government that only appeared to be totally dominated by his boss. While the boss played at politics the subordinate minded the store. While Frank Rizzo won increasing national attention as an unorthodox urban politician, Len Moak pretty much ran things on a day-to-day basis. In planning, in redevelopment, in housing, his was often a controlling voice. From his fourteenth-floor office in Philadelphia's Municipal Services Building, he quietly fashioned a power grid that overlaid the academic, business and governmental communities. He could be tough, too. Radio commentator Taylor Grant found that out when his sponsor, the city-owned Philadelphia Gas Works, fired him for broadcasting attacks on Rizzo over a local station. Grant coined a word for what happened. He said he had been "moaked."

Moak told the *Bulletin* he had heard Grant criticize the mayor and he didn't like it. So he picked up the telephone and informed PGW general manager Edward Hubbard of his displeasure.

"I told Mr. Hubbard I didn't like what I just heard," Moak said. "I said I didn't feel it was in the public interest. I said I thought it was a bad policy to have such a program sponsored by a city agency. I said I did not feel this was a function of a public agency.

. . . I said if I was the one running things there, I would buy up the contract right then and there."*

Not surprisingly, Hubbard agreed with Moak. Although Grant's contract had two months to run, he was taken off the air immediately. The local chapter of Sigma Delta Chi, the journalism society, did not agree with Moak.

"The chapter believes that Moak's action is a blatant and arrogant violation of the First Amendment to the U.S. Constitution and represents a potential threat to every newsman who might in the future be critical of government officials," the society said.

Lynne Abraham, executive director of the Philadelphia Redevelopment Authority, also found out how tough Moak could be when he dismissed her for being "abrasive" — although she said the real reason for her firing was her refusal to employ Rizzo patronage payrollers.

Moak could be equally tough in less dramatic, less publicized matters involving decision making at City Hall. It was with strong feeling that a former Moak assistant who greatly admired the finance director still labeled him a "hard-assed son-of-a-bitch." And another former Rizzo administration insider would recall with relish the behind-the-scenes battles between Moak and Deputy Mayor Philip Carroll. They fought, he said, "like two scorpions in a bottle."

"In his own way," Christopher Weeks would tell us after stepping down as the city's development coordinator, "Len is more of an autocrat than the mayor is — in making unilateral decisions for or against something."

Of course, Moak himself claimed no special powers. He always insisted that he just did the mayor's bidding. His boss had a policy; Moak supported that policy and saw that it was carried out. Nothing more. He had never been elected to any office and he held no political mandate. Politics was not his business; public administration was.

Yet things were not really that simple, and Moak knew it. The distinction between policy making and administration was not that sharply drawn. Back in the spring of 1975, when the dimensions of Philadelphia's impending financial crisis were only dimly perceived, Rizzo made the decision to continue holding the line on taxes with no layoffs of municipal workers through June 30, 1976.

If Moak had spoken up right at that moment, if he had told Rizzo in private that the policy was unsound and dangerous and

* Philadelphia *Bulletin*, October 2, 1972.

that he would resign rather than carry it out, Rizzo might have been forced to yield. But Moak didn't do that. A mayoralty primary was coming up and then a general election. Rizzo rested virtually his entire case for a second term on his demonstrated ability to keep taxes down. If he were to cave in now, his campaign might be fatally hurt. In this dilemma Moak thought of quitting but he didn't quit. He stayed and tried to carry out Rizzo's impossible policy. He produced an operating budget for Philadelphia that called for no tax increases, no city job cuts or service reductions, yet showed no deficit, despite sharply rising costs. Moak's name on this implausible document meant something. The budget projections acquired a credibility they would otherwise have lacked. Instead of sounding the alarm and quitting, Moak had remained on the job and given the impression that all was well. To that extent at least he had helped make policy.

And by 1976 it became apparent that the policy he had helped make was disastrous. The timing could not have been worse. Just as the flapdoodle and hip-hip-hooray of the nation's Bicentennial celebration reached its peak, Philadelphia, the Cradle of Liberty, the heart and center of the Birthday Party, tottered on the brink of insolvency. At sixty-three, Len Moak had allowed himself to be used by a vote-hungry politician. He had been persuaded to take risks that a prudent finance director should never have taken. His balanced budget was a sham. His reputation was in ruins. The magician had no more rabbits, and now everybody knew it.

All along he'd been odd-man-out in the Rizzo administration. He was one of the few white Protestants in high command and the only southerner. Like Rizzo, he was descended from "people of the soil," but in his case the soil was domestic rather than foreign. His great-great-great-great-grandfather had settled in South Carolina from Holland in 1740. Three generations later the family had migrated to the hardscrabble hill country of southern Mississippi, where Lennox Lee Moak was born in 1912.

After the family moved to Port Arthur, Texas, where schools were better than in Bogue Chitto, Mississippi, the boy became a rare college-educated Moak. Graduating in three years from Southwest Texas State Teachers College,* he turned to public administration, spending eleven years with a private research group in

---

* A fellow student, one with whom he often ate meals at a rooming house, was a gangling Texan named Lyndon B. Johnson. Even then, according to Moak, the future President was a great storyteller.

New Orleans. In 1949, Moak took an executive post with the Pennsylvania Economy League in Philadelphia. He quickly gained recognition as a skilled analyst of governmental operations. When Philadelphia's city charter was rewritten in 1951, Moak helped draft that portion of the document requiring the city to adopt balanced budgets.*

When Joe Clark, a liberal Democrat, became mayor in 1952 he named Len Moak his finance director. Although Moak was a fiscal conservative he and Clark got along well together. Moak left after two years to return to the Pennsylvania Economy League. Clark praised him for "a first class job of municipal statesmanship." He said Moak had been "a wise counselor who set up the financial side of our government on a basis which enabled us to move ahead with the job of giving Philadelphia efficient, modern liberal government without wrecking itself on the rocks of insolvency."

Between 1954, when he left Clark's administration, and 1972, when he joined Rizzo's, Moak worked at the P.E.L., monitoring government spending and budget making and writing voluminously. In a 1963 "Operating Budget Manual," which would later come back to haunt him, Moak warned that even a small deficit had "an adverse effect upon the reputation of a local government in investment circles."

When Mayor-elect Rizzo asked Moak to take the finance post late in 1971 the older man was receptive. He thought Rizzo's pledge to hold the line on city taxes made sense. Believing that Mark Shedd and Dick Dilworth had recklessly thrown away millions of school dollars, he supported the firing of the superintendent. When his $25,000 lectureship was worked out as a supplement to his regular city salary, Moak, after an absence of eighteen years, stepped back into the city government.

Moak's reappearance on the municipal scene coincided with the start of a significant shift in the struggle for survival of American cities. The focus changed from black rage to the balance sheet, from spending to cutting back, from increasing social services to withdrawing them. The bottom-line era was beginning and Moak was the man for that season. In city after city retrenchments would be ordered to stave off deficits. The new VIPs in municipal gov-

* Asked about this section of the city charter in the budget crunch of 1975–1976, Moak disavowed it. "The Charter of 1951 is not in keeping with the current fiscal realities of the city," he said. "There has been a tremendous change in the rules of the game. . . . You can't have a balanced budget any more and expect to maintain your negotiating position with the [state and federal] legislatures."

Lennox L. Moak, Rizzo's "financial wizard."

ernment would be bookkeepers with sharp pencils like Moak rather than social reformers like New York's jaunty John Lindsay and Philadelphia's Joe Clark.

The great fear of the strife-torn 1960s had been that the cities would explode in rioting and civil insurrection. Vast social programs were organized to meet that threat. The great fear of the recession-wracked 1970s was that cities on the fiscal rocks might self-destruct not with a bang but a whimper. And New York nearly did in 1975.

For many cities, however, the day of financial reckoning was delayed by a happy event that took place at Independence Hall in Philadelphia on October 20, 1972, when President Nixon signed the federal revenue-sharing bill. It pumped hundreds of millions of dollars into cities and towns in all fifty states. There were hardly any strings attacked to the federal money. Most of the local jurisdictions used it to pay operating costs, thus holding down taxes.

That's what Rizzo and Moak did. Philadelphia got $70,000,000 of this manna from Washington in Rizzo's first year as mayor. That was nearly 10 percent of the city's operating budget. With this infusion of fresh cash, Moak found it comparatively easy not only to hold the line on taxes that first year but actually to end up with a surplus.

Financial problems were mounting, however, at the city school board. In this campaign for mayor Rizzo had promised that school taxes would not be increased during his term. Moak would say later that Rizzo never should have extended his tax pledge to school levies. In fact, if Moak had understood that that was Rizzo's intent he would never have acceded to it. During the mayoralty race, Rizzo's opponent, Thacher Longstreth, had warned that the city might have to "take a [school] strike" rather than yield to the teachers' salary demands. Rizzo spoke confidently of getting by with no strike and no school tax increase. "If you can't get the money to take care of your [school] children," he had said, "you should resign."

But, of course, Mayor Rizzo did not resign when, on the first scheduled class day in September 1972, the strike that Longstreth had foreseen began. The teachers struck a school board dominated by Rizzo appointees and headed by his choice for president. After three weeks, they returned to their classrooms without a contract at Rizzo's personal pleading. Early in 1973, with their contract talks still deadlocked, the teachers struck again. This time they were out for thirty-nine days. It was the second longest school strike in American history. The threat of a general strike by some forty unions finally forced Rizzo to raise his teacher pay offer and settle the dispute.

What was noteworthy about the marathon school stoppage was that hardly any important people were directly affected by it. Neither the mayor nor his labor negotiator had children in the city's public schools nor did any member of Rizzo's cabinet. (Moak had sent his brain-damaged daughter to special private schools for the handicapped and his other children to the posh Chestnut Hill Academy.) Only one of seventeen city councilmen had children in public schools. Three of the nine school board members did. The five children of John A. Ryan, a teachers' union leader who was jailed for defying a court order, attended Roman Catholic parochial schools. The two children of Judge D. Donald Jamieson, who sentenced Ryan, attended independent schools. Close to 25 percent of Philadelphia's thirteen thousand teachers were thought to live in the suburbs, where public schools remained open. Many of the others sent their children to parochial schools. In fact, the Philadelphia Catholic schools enrolled more white pupils than the city public schools did.

Even more important from the Rizzo-Moak viewpoint was that the strike helped rescue the debt-ridden school system from insolvency. It was no secret that Dilworth and Shedd's heroic efforts to improve the quality of public education in Philadelphia had been very costly. To get more money for the schools, Dilworth had used every budgetary trick at his disposal. Back in 1966, he put the school district on a one-shot, six-month budget, preparatory to shifting to a July 1–June 30 fiscal year. The result was a $25,000,000 surplus for the short budget period running from January 1, 1966, to June 30. With this windfall, Dilworth was able to make many badly needed improvements in the faltering school system.

There was a damaging long-term effect, however, that left the schools short of cash at the beginning of every new fiscal year. The schools collect close to 80 percent of their taxes in the spring. Under calendar-year budgeting, tax revenues came in early — ahead of most expenses — and very little borrowing was needed to finance operations. But under the July 1–June 30 fiscal year, the schools had to run much of the year on borrowed funds until taxes started coming in. Heavy bank borrowing thus became a severe annual drain on the hard-pressed schools.*

At the start of the 1972–1973 fiscal year, the schools projected a $53,000,000 deficit by June 30, 1973. They faced a shutdown by April 1 for lack of operating money to meet payrolls. To help bail out the schools, Rizzo and Moak were forced to transfer $12,000,-000 in cash from the city to the school district. Rizzo also agreed to shift four mills annually from city real estate taxes to the schools. The result was to reduce city tax collections by about $20,000,000 a year, and to increase school tax yields by that amount. Over the remaining three years of Rizzo's first term, the schools thus picked up $72,000,000. This was money that Moak sorely needed in 1975–1976.

Despite this assistance and increased state aid, the schools still faced a $24,000,000 deficit and possibly early closing in the spring

* Following the school board's lead, the city changed fiscal years in 1969. It got two big tax bites spread over eighteen months and as a result, Rizzo's predecessor, James Tate, avoided a tax increase. And in 1971, the city council solved the problem of a $40,000,000 revenue shortfall by putting off for one day — from one fiscal year to the next — payment of debt service. Such budgetary tricks and gimmicks are old stuff and obviously did not originate with Moak and Rizzo.

of 1973. Then came the thirty-nine-day teachers' strike. For every school day lost, the Board of Education saved $600,000 in unpaid salaries of teachers and other employees. By this reckoning, the schools needed a forty-day stoppage — 40 times $600,000 — to erase the $24,000,000 deficit. But the thirty-nine no-school days were enough to end the cash crisis.

The strike demolished some cherished notions about American public education. What it seemed to demonstrate was not how important urban public schools were, but the opposite. It caused only slight disruption in the rhythms of city life. The neighborhoods were quiet. There was no reported increase in juvenile crime. And scarcely anybody who *was* anybody lost anything. That was the point: the historic ideal of public schools serving children of all races, creeds, colors and economic groups no longer squared with the urban realities. Most of Philadelphia's public school children were poor and black or Puerto Rican. When their classes shut down for thirty-nine days, these powerless children and their parents could only sit by helplessly as others decided their fate.

Rizzo got a four-year contract from the teachers, thus assuring labor peace in the schools for the balance of his first term. After the strike, he would do all in his power to hold down school spending. In fact, one of his early acts was to eliminate a business tax that yielded $14,000,000 a year for the schools. He took the position that the tax hurt the city's economic base.

His challenge to the teachers' union was the first direct and sustained one it had faced since gaining bargaining rights in 1965. At that time its teacher pay scale — $5,300 to $9,000 a year for classroom teachers with bachelor's degrees — put Philadelphia near the bottom among urban school districts. After seven years of steady and successful negotiating with the liberal school board, Philadelphia teachers had climbed near the top. The 1972 maximum was $24,300 and the high-school teaching day was the shortest in Pennsylvania — four hours and five minutes.

In opposing ever-higher school spending, Rizzo had some unlikely allies. Daniel Patrick Moynihan, who had been a presidential adviser and who would become the U.S. ambassador to the United Nations and later New York State's junior Senator, was one who warned that public education expenditures were outpacing rises in the gross national product. Moynihan argued* that because most of the education dollar went to teachers who were already "well

* In an article in *The Public Interest*, Fall 1972.

paid," "increasing educational expenditures will have the short-run effect of increasing income inequality." The income gap between the middle-class teachers and their poor or working-class pupils, said Moynihan, would steadily widen.

Similarly, Harvard University's Christopher Jencks completed three years of research with a book which threw cold water on the idea that schools alone affected children's lives very much. He wrote:

> None of the evidence we have reviewed suggests that school reform can be expected to bring about significant social changes outside the schools.
>
> Even when a school exerts an unusual influence on children, the resulting changes are not likely to persist into adulthood.
>
> When we compare schools with similar entering students, we do not find those with fat budgets turning out more skilled alumni than those with inadequate budgets.[*]

According to Jencks's controversial research, the public schools were not the "great equalizer" of society that Americans had believed them to be. Jencks, a socialist, told us that his findings should not be construed as justifying school budget cuts. Yet his book seemed to offer solid support for Rizzo's hard line. "Even if we reorganized the schools so that their primary concern was for the students who most need help," wrote Jencks in a section that inadvertently described the Shedd-Dilworth reform effort, "there is no reason to suppose that adults would end up appreciably more equal as a result." He went on to argue that even a doubling of school expenditures would not raise students' scores on standardized tests.

All unaware, Rizzo had stumbled on a backer in an unlikely place, Harvard's Center for Educational Policy Research, where Jencks and his associates did their computer studies. It was easy to move from Jencks's thesis to one that said that schoolteachers should be treated no differently from policemen, firemen, sanitation workers, playground attendants and other city employees. In other words, schools should not get special treatment. This made political sense to Rizzo, since so many of his constituents sent their children to Catholic rather than to tax-supported public schools.

However, he stopped short of accepting the proposition that the

[*] *Inequality: A Reassessment of the Effect of Family and Schooling in America*, by Christopher Jencks and Marshall Smith, Henry Acland, Mary Jo Bane, David Cohen, Herbert Gintis, Barbara Heyns, Stephen Michelson, Basic Books, Inc., 1972.

public schools should become the direct responsibility of the mayor. Dilworth, Shedd and Shedd's successor, Matthew Costanzo, were among those favoring the new relationship. Shedd believed that the superintendent of schools should join the mayor's cabinet. "You've got to be at the table when the pie is cut up," he said. "Otherwise, you don't get any of it."

But Rizzo resisted this move. He preferred to continue exercising control over the schools without assuming responsibility for them.

In large and small ways, Moak steadily gained power within the Rizzo administration. There was the minor matter of the Philadelphia Museum of Art. For almost twenty years Moak had been trying to persuade the vaunted art museum's board of directors to put in permanent railings for its two staircases at the building's front and back entrances. As a private citizen he got nowhere. But the museum receives a city subsidy. "When they came to me in seventy-two," said Moak, referring to the subsidy talks, "I said, 'I'm not even going to *look* at you all until you fix up those railings.'" The railings were installed at last, and the museum got its subsidy.

There was the major matter of the Philadelphia Redevelopment Authority. It's the city's chief urban-construction arm. It acquires land through eminent domain in blighted areas for sale at marked-down prices to private developers. In two decades the Redevelopment Authority spent half a billion dollars in federal, state and city money and generated another $1,500,000,000 in private outlays for such projects as internationally acclaimed Society Hill, the city's noted Food Distribution Center, University City in West Philadelphia and the Market East downtown commercial development.

"It had always been a closed corporation," said Moak. "I wanted to know what was going on. I asked the boss [Rizzo] to appoint me [to the authority's board]. And he did. Then I wanted to be chairman so I asked the boss for the chairmanship and I got it. I learned what I wanted to know so I called the boss one day and asked him to find somebody else to run it."

Before quitting the Redevelopment Authority, Moak fired its chairman, Lynne Abraham, a tough lawyer who had refused to employ some workers who had obtained patronage clearance from Rizzo. She later charged that in dismissing her, Moak was merely following orders. "Contrary to press statements," he told us, "that was a decision on my own, not aided and abetted by anybody. I advised the mayor of the action I was going to take. He was very pleased, but that was not the determinant. She [Abraham] was abrasive, very abrasive. She was the wrong person to do that job at that time."

Moak insisted that "I knew nothing of the patronage aspects at the time I took my action. It wouldn't have affected my decision."

But Moak's tolerance of political patronage was another reason why he got along well with Rizzo. "I accept the fact that a certain amount of political patronage is a fact of life in Philadelphia municipal government," he told us. "I understood it was there when I agreed to come back to City Hall. [I understood] that it has always been used by the mayor and would continue to be used."

He said he was neither for nor against patronage. "We have some good patronage employes. We have a lot of Civil Service people whose productivity isn't what I would like. I think there are more important fish to fry [than trying to eliminate patronage]."

Besides running the finance office and, briefly, the Redevelopment Authority, Len Moak got himself named to the Planning Commission, the Philadelphia Industrial Development Corporation, the Philadelphia Housing Development Corporation, the Board of Pensions and Retirements (with responsibilities for more than $200,000,000 in investments), the Sinking Fund Commission, and other agencies. By working seventy to eighty hours a week, he managed to get his fingers into nearly every pie at City Hall.

It wasn't hard to do this. What Moak did was move into a gigantic vacuum created by Rizzo's own noninvolvement in the mundane business of day-to-day city government operations. While the *padrone* gave the appearance of running the city, he didn't really run it. He left that important job to a few trusted aides.

Christopher Weeks saw this curious setup at close range. For twenty months, until his resignation two days after Rizzo's reelection in November 1975, Weeks was the mayor's development coordinator at $34,000 a year. A Yale graduate with master's degree from the University of Michigan, Weeks had served as a consultant to Shedd and had worked on Washington task forces that helped set up the Peace Corps and the Office of Economic Opportunity. He gave us this account of life within Rizzo's official family:

When it came to running the city, the nonpolitical role, managing and administering the affairs of the city, the mayor left almost all of that to a group of trusted aides. The cabinet did not function as a decision-making body; it rarely met. This was an unhealthy situation. Underneath the mayor it was very difficult to figure out who was in charge. You had a series of people each of whom was playing his or her poker hand to make decisions with as little communication with the others as possible.

If it was an issue like putting a fire station at 20th and Wolf the mayor was superb. He knows the city like the back of his hand. But on a broad policy issue he was likely to shoot from the hip and satisfy nobody. More often, he just didn't get involved in policy making. He delegated tremendous amounts of authority. He did not get involved at all in the entire $60 million community-development block-grant program. I had to fight my way with Moak, Levinson, Salvitti, Goldie Watson, who had very specific ideas of their own.

I was under the mayor's directive to develop a housing program. Moak's position was that there should be no housing program except for demolition. I argued very forcefully that this was suicide for a combination of political, urban-development and practical reasons related to the community-development program, which requires you to have a housing program.

The upshot was a compromise. We tripled the amount of money for housing demolition. We also very substantially increased money for rehabilitation and new construction. In housing Moak obviously had a fairly big influence.

You also had Moak making budget decisions — with people finding out *ex post facto*. In the Bicen area [city preparations for the Bicentennial celebration], Moak was very powerful. In other areas you'd get funds allocated but somehow the finance director's office would never release the funds.

Moak has an interest in almost every area of municipal operations. He exercises that interest. He plays such a long role because the mayor doesn't. The mayor tends to stand in awe of "professionals." You get a ward leader, then he'll pound and scream and threaten physical violence. With professionals, his position was: "You're the expert in this field."

Early in 1975 the growing financial crisis in older American cities began to draw the attention of Congress. "The combination of increased service demands [on cities] and revenue shortfalls has produced a fiscal crunch of unparalleled proportions," reported U.S. Representative William S. Moorhead (Democrat, Pennsylvania), in releasing a study of state and local government spending. He found that fifteen large cities were ending the 1975 fiscal year with combined deficits approaching $200,000,000.

In Buffalo, New York, a 25 percent reduction in city workers had failed to halt a runaway municipal deficit. Cleveland, Ohio, and Albuquerque, New Mexico, cut garbage collections in half. Newark, New Jersey, laid off more than 100 policemen. City workers in Altoona, Pennsylvania, agreed to one payless day a week. In Baltimore, a hiring freeze eliminated more than 2,000 jobs in two years.

A 10 percent cut in Boston's municipal payroll hurt its celebrated city hospital system. Detroit lopped off 4,115 city jobs but was still obliged to close 31 recreation centers and its art museum for one month and shorten the season for its golf courses and hockey rinks. Meanwhile, New York was just beginning to grapple with problems that would lead it to the brink of bankruptcy.

In Frank Rizzo's Philadelphia, however, everything seemed to be hunky-dory. Both Moody's and Standard & Poor's had just elevated Philadelphia's municipal bonds to A grade from a lower, more speculative rating. High municipal bond ratings are like money in the bank to cities. The higher the bond ratings the lower the interest offered to market them.

Philadelphia's single-A rating was not as good as Chicago's double-A or Indianapolis's triple-A, but it was respectable — and for some years earlier its bonds were not very respectable and in fact bordered on being risky.

Rizzo, meanwhile, was campaigning for reelection on a pledge of no service cuts, no layoffs and a balanced budget. Sure enough, when Finance Director Moak unveiled his budget for the year starting July 1 it was neatly balanced without relying on any of the service economies or tax rises that other cities were resorting to.

Moak relied instead on some extremely iffy revenue projections. In the face of a sharply declining city population and Philadelphia's loss in three years of nearly 40,000 jobs and 800 companies, Moak predicted a substantial 8 percent increase in receipts from the city's wage tax in 1975–1976. Only a sensational recovery from the recession which then gripped the city and nation could have produced such a rosy outcome — and there was to be no sensational recovery.

The finance director also included as money in hand millions in subsidies that the state and federal governments owed the city but had not yet sent. New York had been engaging in this questionable budgetary practice for years, but Moak only began to use it when the squeeze commenced. It was only by listing $23,500,000 in subsidies that had been earned but not received that Moak had succeeded in balancing the previous year's budget. He was, therefore, digging himself ever deeper into a hole.

Even with such imaginative bookkeeping, Moak needed $65,300,000 in "new revenues" to balance the city's $781,000,000 general fund budget. Since his boss, Rizzo, wouldn't let him get this money from new or increased taxation, Moak roamed far afield in thinking up possible revenue sources. He decided arbitrarily that the city would collect $6,300,000 in current and delinquent real estate taxes from the Philadelphia-based Penn Central and Reading railroads. Both lines were bankrupt and neither one had paid a dime in local taxes for years. Moak said he believed the back payments would be made "during fiscal 1976," and he termed his revenue estimate from this source "conservative." No such money would come in.

Moak counted on collecting an additional $26,000,000 by closing loopholes in the city's tax on corporate stocks. But only the Pennsylvania legislature could close the loopholes and, to hardly anybody's surprise, it would decline to do so.

The legislature also would choose not to act on a Moak proposal that it give to local governments the proceeds from a state tax on the premiums paid by foreign life insurance companies. The state always kept this money; Moak wanted it divvied up in such a way that Philadelphia would be given $10,000,000. No dice.

Moak listed $12,000,000 in new money from President Ford's "energy tax revenue sharing program," $10,000,000 in higher fees for civil suits in city courts and $1,000,000 in "voluntary refunding" of municipal bonds. None of these three revenue sources would produce anything, either.

The budget projections drew instant criticism. Moak's former employer, The Pennsylvania Economy League, termed them speculative. It urged Moak to impound funds pending receipt of the $65,000,000 to "avoid drifting in the kind of fiscal abyss facing New York City." Charles Bowser charged that Moak was "unduly influenced by Frank Rizzo's fiscal irresponsibility." He predicted that the actual budget deficit would run closer to $115,000,000. "I'm almost sure that after the election we're going to find that the figures are all wrong," Bowser said, prophetically. "What they're doing is lying."

City Controller William Klenk joined the attack predicting a deficit of over $100,000,000. But Moak stuck to his guns. He insisted that the city had a "strong possibility" of getting half the $65,000,000 and a "fair possibility" of getting three-quarters of it. A $30,000,000 deficit, he said, would be "peanuts" in a budget the size of Philadelphia's.

When Moak argued for the budget before the city council, Rizzo's old nemesis, Council President George X. Schwartz, punched holes in it. "I think we can dispose of the sixty-five-point-three million in revenues, most of which require legislative action, as completely unrealistic," Schwartz said. And later he needled the finance director: "If you were still with the Pennsylvania Economy League you'd urge me not to accept the estimate."

It was one thing to debunk the budget; it was quite another thing to reject it, thus forcing Rizzo and Moak to cut services and raise taxes in an election year. Schwartz recognized that Philadelphians would soon have to pay the piper. But he and his colleagues approved the budget with its phantom revenues.

Just before the 1975 primary election, Rizzo, as we have seen, made sure of the votes of the city's twenty thousand nonuniformed employees by given them 12.8 percent pay increases. The one-year contract was far more costly than Moak had expected. It threw his budget even farther out of balance.

One morning in June 1975, Moak was talking to one of us in his office when an aide dropped a copy of that day's *Daily News* on his desk. A front-page headline and an inside story alleged that unnamed Philadelphia banks were "dissatisfied" with Moak's budget and "might cut off the city's credit after November." An anonymous "banking source" said the cutoff was likely unless the budget were "adjusted" to eliminate deficits.

As Moak read the story his bushy eyebrows shot up straight. His face turned crimson with rage. He ordered his secretary to telephone Rolfe Neill, the *Daily News*'s editor. The angry finance director proceeded to bawl out the editor, accusing him of publishing "the most vicious, irresponsible garbage [he had] ever read." Neill listened to Moak and then agreed to meet with him that night at Moak's Chestnut Hill home.

Two days later, Neill forthrightly published another front-page headline: "Banks and Budgets: We Were Wrong." The story on page five stated unequivocally that the paper's earlier report was erroneous. It turned out, though, that the correction made a better story than the original. The paper published an account of what Moak had said over drinks when Neill and three other staffers had visited him. What he said was pretty hot stuff:

"Banks in Philadelphia don't have the economic power to cause us to 'adjust' anything. No banking sonofabitch is going to bring us to our knees after November — and you can quote me on that. Any banker who says he can do that doesn't know what he is talking about.

"I don't intend to go to the banks after November to borrow money so there is no way they can force us to do anything.

"Bankers in 1975 are frustrated, unadjusted, emotionally disturbed individuals — and you can quote me on that. In 1974 they lost their pants.

In 1975 they are writing off all their corporate losses and because they must show taxable profits they've had no room for tax-exempt municipal securities.

"Next year that will have changed. They will be back to the market for tax-exempt securities. They will be coming to us, we won't be going to them."

Despite Moak's brave talk, his situation steadily worsened. He was hurt by the loss of a key assistant. G. Edward DeSeve had joined Moak early in 1973 when the finance director was riding high. DeSeve was young, razor-sharp and bursting with enthusiasm. He greatly admired his boss, who "always called [him] son." To DeSeve, Len Moak was "a legend, larger than life." He bought a house near Moak's and started riding to work with him.

In September, 1974, DeSeve was named one of three deputy finance directors with heavy responsibility for preparing the new budget. Disillusionment quickly set in. "Budgeting is a process of making reasonable assumptions that reasonable men can reasonably agree to," DeSeve would say later. "I must be intellectually honest. I didn't feel that way about this budget, so the mayor's office and I agreed to disagree."

DeSeve and Moak remained friends after the former quit his $30,000 job in March 1975, and the deputy never condemned his former boss. Although DeSeve's departure was a straw in the wind, Moak's position within the Rizzo administration remained as strong as ever. In fact, his role grew more important as the fiscal crisis deepened. Moak and Rizzo were not close socially; Moak had never stepped foot inside the *padrone*'s big house. But he was Rizzo's link to the Establishment and the mayor was completely dependent on him.

"Rizzo is utterly baffled by the money problem," said one man who knew both Rizzo and Moak. "Rizzo's attention span is very, very short and these problems are complex. He's afraid if Len is not there to handle the fiscal problem the one thing he's so proud of — no tax increase — will collapse."

One money matter that Rizzo understood very well concerned municipal bonds. He knew that marketing them provided a gravy train for lawyers. The job of drafting municipal bond prospectuses is not particularly onerous, and any number of Philadelphia law firms had the ability to handle it. But Rizzo, with Moak's connivance, threw most of the work to his campaign manager, former City Solicitor Martin Weinberg.

After quitting his $42,000-a-year city job in October 1974, Weinberg joined the firm of Obermayer, Rebmann, Maxwell and Hippel. The firm had never done bond work for the city. But in the succeeding eleven months before the election, it served as cocounsel on seven separate issues of Philadelphia bonds and notes, sharing about $200,000 in legal fees with another firm.

"Gonna give him some more, too," Rizzo promised when asked about the arrangement with Weinberg. Moak also defended the practice on grounds that throwing bond work to political favorites was standard procedure in Philadelphia. "That's the way things are done," he said, unsmiling.

It was not until the first week in October 1975, less than a month before the mayoralty election, that Moak began to back away from his budget. He told a meeting in New York that the city might end the fiscal year with a deficit of about $50,000,000. He said that was an "outside figure" that could lead to trouble only if it were papered over with short-term borrowing.

Six days after the election, with Rizzo safely ensconced in City Hall for four more years, Moak spoke more candidly than ever before about the money crisis. He said that the deficit might exceed $50,000,000. He conceded that he had been engaging in fiscal practices that he had once considered contrary to good public administration. He said Rizzo had erred in promising to hold the line on school as well as city taxes. "I would never have done so," Moak said. He also admitted deliberately planning budget deficits as a ploy for higher subsidies. "In today's world," Moak said, "we must maintain a posture of dependence on additional funds from the state and federal governments. The real test is whether you allow yourself to become drunk."

Moak made these remarks to institutional investors and other money men on November 10. That same day the city placed an advertisement in the *Wall Street Journal* stating that Philadelphia had ended its fiscal year the previous June 30 "with an $11.6 million SURPLUS." Readers wanting details were invited to write Finance Director Moak.

The advertisement appeared just three weeks before Moak was to sell $25 million in municipal bonds. Investors who took his pronouncement at face value might have been attracted to the bonds. Was this deceitful or even illegal? Some observers thought so. The Philadelphia office of the Securities and Exchange Commission received what its local director termed "public complaints." Acting on these complaints, the SEC began an inquiry into whether Moak had concealed the true state of the city's finances when he completed three separate bond sales in the last half of 1975.

Among those not taken in by Moak's ad was Standard & Poor's. On November 14, it reduced Philadelphia's bond rating from A to A-minus. Never before had Moak suffered such an indignity.

Citing a "weakened financial posture" and an "uncertain outlook," Standard & Poor's charged that Moak had balanced his budget by listing revenues "whose receipt is doubtful." At Moak's direction, the agency charged, "accounting practices were loosened . . . cash flow was much less positive . . . and the city's general fund had to rely on an injection of cash from the capital projects fund to finish [the 1975 fiscal year] without a negative cash position." It termed the likelihood of a turnaround "unknown."

Philadelphia was not another financial basket case like New York. Not yet. Standard & Poor's gloomy assessment, though, marked the first time that Moak had been sharply criticized by people whose judgments he respected and whose confidence he needed. From that point on things would only get worse.

Later, in talking to us, Moak would concede that he had made mistakes in estimating the wage tax yield. Rizzo's settlement with the municipal workers had hurt Moak's projections. The cost of borrowing money — Philadelphia had been forced to sell bonds at record interest of 9.6 percent — was higher than he had anticipated. And the recession had hit harder than Moak thought it would. The city had lost twenty-five thousand jobs between December 1974, and February 1975.

On the matter of the phantom $65,300,000, Moak insisted that he had done nothing dishonest. It turned out that he had never been "comfortable" with the budget. He had attempted to make his uneasiness "as implicit as possible without being explicit." He couldn't afford to be explicit since he was standing back of the budget. He could have concealed the speculative revenue sources in the huge document, stuck them away so that neither critics nor councilmen would have found them. Instead, he had brought them out for inspection.

"Anyone who writes on this," he told us, "must weigh whether I made a suitable disclosure or not. I tried to cover myself as best I could by labeling these revenues as conditional income."

They were never actually so labeled. It was clear that receipt of the revenues depended on action by the state and federal legislatures. However, when the budget was up for adoption, Moak saw a "strong possibility" that the city would get half the $65,000,000 and a "fair possibility" that it would get three-quarters. These extremely bad guesses proved embarrassing to a fiscal expert of Moak's prominence and pride.

The whole year had been embarrassing. Back in the spring, when Rizzo set down the ground rules — no tax increases, no cutbacks — Moak's instinct as a respected public administrator had been to get out. To stay would be to risk his good name and reputation. He decided, however, that it was too late to leave. After all, he had been Rizzo's money man for three years. He hadn't set the financial course but he had steered it. How could he justify quitting just as things were getting rough?

So he had stayed. And later, after everything his critics had said about his wildly inaccurate budget projections had come true, Lennox Lee Moak would remember a rule of his late father's back in Bogue Chitto, Mississippi. It explained, he said, why he chose to remain in the second Rizzo administration. "My daddy taught me," he said, "if you make a mess, clean it up yourself."

Chapter Sixteen

Frank rizzo was more than willing to have Lennox Moak stay around to clean up the "mess" over which he presided. In his second inaugural address, at the Academy of Music on January 5, 1976 — one of his rare public appearances — Rizzo had provided only the barest hint of just how bad the mess really was.

"This administration is mindful of the steps that must be taken to meet our current fiscal responsibilities and we will not shrink from them," the mayor had said.

On January 20, Rizzo sent Moak out to meet those responsibilities. At last, the city was ready to admit that Rizzo's rosy campaign rhetoric was just that — rhetoric. But it was left to Moak to deliver the bad news. Rizzo would have no part in it. For four months, he would remain in his office, refusing to discuss the city's financial problems with newsmen, citizens' groups and even state and local officials upon whom he was depending for help in getting Philadelphia out of the red. See Moak, was his answer, that's Moak's responsibility.

And so Moak, two weeks after the inauguration, met with reporters to confirm their suspicions: Philadelphia was more than $80,000,000 in the hole. Record-breaking tax increases were necessary, and the city would seek emergency taxing authority from the state legislature. Philadelphia's city council is empowered to levy new taxes or increase existing taxes so long as it does so in one fiscal year to take effect in the next fiscal year. In order to raise taxes in the middle of a fiscal year, the city must demonstrate that an emergency exists and win the approval of the state legislature.

In Moak's mind, there was no question that an emergency existed. And the way to solve that emergency was to raise the real estate tax by 29.3 percent, which would increase the tax bill for the owner of a home assessed at $15,000 from $716.25 to $926.25. Tacked onto the real estate tax proposal, which would bring in $64,000,000, were proposed new levies on businessmen, hotels, bars, restaurants, vending machines, theaters and parking garages which would realize $17,000,000. Nowhere, however, was there any suggestion that the appetite of the patronage mill be curbed as a means of saving money. In fact, the patronage hiring continued apace, even while the city was awash in red ink.

Now that 1976 had arrived, and the Bicentennial celebration was at hand, the Bicentennial agency that Al Gaudiosi directed did not have much longer to live and the mayor's friend needed a job. Rizzo obliged by bumping Harry Belinger out of his post as city representative and director of commerce and installing Gaudiosi there on February 10. Belinger was moved into a vague coordinator's job with no real duties. Both jobs paid $42,000 a year.

The Gaudiosi hiring could not be kept secret. But on February 2, another man was hired with no announcement or fanfare. The man was a nephew-by-marriage to Rizzo, and he was placed on the School District's payroll at $21,080 in an "administrative analyst" position in the purchasing department. His name was Ralph and he was forty-five years old.

Ralph's appointment did not remain a secret for long. On February 18, Philadelphia *Bulletin* education writer Carole Rich disclosed that Ralph had resigned as the administrative assistant for business affairs of the suburban Methacton School District on January 14, 1975, after being accused of misusing school funds. Ralph admitted he had made restitution in the amount of $1,200 to Methacton after using school district purchase orders to buy for himself a refrigerator, washer, dryer, tires, art supplies and cleaning chemicals.

"I've had a long year of wrestling with my conscience," Ralph told Rich in an interview. "I did wrong. I feel I've damaged myself." He denied that he had gotten the job because of his relationship with Rizzo. So did Superintendent of Schools Michael P. Marcase, the man who arranged for Ralph to go on the payroll.

"The man is eminently qualified for the position," said Marcase. The position gave [Ralph] responsibility for "tightening up purchasing procedures."

Marcase had been picked by Rizzo to replace Matthew W. Costanzo when Costanzo had resigned in disgust in July 1975. The school board had rubber-stamped the mayor's choice. Marcase was fifty-two years old and had been in the Philadelphia school system for twenty-two years. He had one major problem when he was appointed: the Pennsylvania department of education refused to certify his appointment because he had obtained his doctorate from the University of Sarasota, a school that once was housed in the Sarasota Motor Hotel and was not accredited by the state of Florida.

Pennsylvania Secretary of Education John Pittenger said Marcase would have to obtain additional graduate credits from a recognized university to go along with those he had already obtained from Temple, Penn and Stanford. The Sarasota credits, said Pittenger, were not acceptable. Until Marcase did the necessary graduate study, he would have to work as superintendent on a "temporary" basis. Marcase returned to Penn, studying one day a week for a year, to pick up the credits.

Marcase said he had known Ralph for three or four years through a Sons of Italy lodge and knew that Rizzo's nephew had a bachelor of science degree in business administration and a master's in education administration. He did not know of the Methacton experience because he had not asked Ralph about it and Ralph had not volunteered the information. In any event, Marcase indicated he intended to treat the Methacton business as an aberration and keep Ralph on the payroll.

The next day, February 19, Ralph resigned in late morning. He gave no reason, but his resignation came just as Carole Rich was preparing a story on Ralph's conduct as business manager of the suburban New Hope–Solebury School District. Rich had found that Ralph left that job on June 30, 1970, after being accused of misusing school funds. On February 20, Rich wrote that a state audit showed that Ralph had "overpaid himself in excess of $1,000 and purchased supplies for himself in excess of $500."

The October 15, 1970, minutes of the New Hope–Solebury school board meeting showed that the board had adopted a resolution accepting from Ralph "the sum of $1,100 in reimbursement for salary distributed without authorization and further [accepted] the sum of $567.94 in reimbursement for school district funds erroneously expended on items delivered to Ralph . . . for his personal use."

Shortly after he left the Philadelphia School District job, Ralph was hired by St. Luke's and Children's Medical Center as an expert in "systems and procedures." St. Luke's was the hospital run by Dr. James Giuffre, Rizzo's personal physician and close friend.

"There is no relation between my hiring him and City Hall," Giuffre said. "His relation to the mayor had nothing to do with it."*

Rizzo did propose one major economy: on February 15, he called for the closing of Philadelphia General Hospital, the city's only public hospital. PGH long had been a dumping ground for homeless drunks and narcotics addicts, most of them black. Although it had handled 75,000 emergency cases a year and had an average daily census of close to 200 patients, PGH was of questionable value because the city's private hospitals did have empty beds and public and private insurance plans made it possible for most persons to pick the hospitals they wanted.

But to many critics Rizzo's proposal seemed racist, discriminatory and inhumane. They viewed it as another example of Rizzo's callous disregard of the needs of the city's most wretched citizens. Furthermore, the closing would wipe out the jobs of PGH's 2,215 professional and nonprofessional employes.

"This is just another manifestation of the city government's irresponsible behavior toward the health needs of the people," said Dr. Frank Krakowski, PGH's chief resident. Dr. Patrick B. Storey, medical director of the hospital, was not opposed to the closing but he did believe the facility should be phased out slowly. For objecting to plans to accelerate the closing, he was fired.

"I could have spoken out publicly and resigned," Storey said. "[But] if you think you're going to embarrass this administration you're out of your mind."†

Meanwhile, Rizzo's emergency tax program was going nowhere. The state House Urban Affairs Subcommittee had scheduled public

* Philadelphia *Daily News*, March 11, 1976.
† Philadelphia *Inquirer*, June 3, 1976.

hearings beginning March 1 on the request for emergency tax authority and it wanted to hear from Rizzo. Three days before the hearings opened, Subcommittee Chairman Samuel Rappaport, a Philadelphia Democrat, received a letter from the mayor saying he would not appear because "some segments of the community and the legislature seek to make political capital of them."

Rizzo did not identify these "segments." But they could have included the 300 elderly citizens who showed up at the hearings to protest the proposed tax hikes while their spokesman, Frank Bradley, told reporters the proposals were "the most disastardly and grievous" burden ever imposed on old people. And the unemployed white man from Kensington who shouted, "Drag Lord Rizzo out of City Hall, get God out of his palace." And Alan J. Bell, the general manager of KYW-TV, who ended his station's 6 P.M. news show night after night for months with an offer of free television time for the mayor to discuss the city's fiscal ills.

Rizzo refused to appear on KYW-TV or anywhere else. During the third day of the legislative hearings, a city official repeated Rizzo's refusal to appear before that body even though he was asking it to approve wide-ranging emergency tax powers for him. "Are you saying the mayor is too ignorant to come here and testify?" State Representative David P. Richardson, a Philadelphia Democrat, asked the city official. He got no answer.

Rizzo did respond to one item of criticism, a calm, measured request by the Chamber of Commerce asking the mayor to please consider job cuts, a wage freeze and an end to some of the worst patronage abuses as one means of helping narrow the deficit. Rizzo's answering letter, written by Gaudiosi, attacked the Chamber, many of whose members — the corporate elite — had supported him with cash contributions for reelection.

"It always amazes me," Gaudiosi-Rizzo wrote, "how many businesses can take care of their friends, their friends' children, uncles, aunts, nieces and nephews. How many can take care of important stockholders, members of the board. . . . But if I give someone a job out of compassion or friendship, it suddenly becomes a one hundred percent major public tragedy. Just how hypocritical can we get. Also, how many corporate drones are kicked upstairs, rather than fired, because they can't cut the mustard?"

The point Rizzo ignored is that corporate personnel policies, while undoubtedly abused, are not directly financed by the taxpayers. With his campaign for emergency tax authority consisting of almost total silence coupled with an intemperate attack on the Chamber of Commerce, Rizzo's proposal was doomed to fail. On May 11, the legislature refused to grant the city the needed authority.

It was clear much earlier, however, that Rizzo wasn't going to get the authority he wanted. Lacking the ability to raise taxes in fiscal 1976 meant that the pressure for higher taxes in the fiscal year 1977, beginning July 1, would be even greater. The deficit would have to be carried over, making the need for new funds even more urgent.

On March 24, Philadelphia Water Commissioner Carmen Guarino — not the mayor — announced that water and sewer rents would be increased by 49.3 percent, the largest increase in the city's history and one that would cost the average homeowner $32.36 more a year.

A week later, on April's Fool's Day, Rizzo sent to the city council a budget calling for spending $1,300,000,000 and asking for tax increases totaling almost $250,000,000. The council approved the package on May 27, raising the real estate tax by 29.3 percent and the wage tax by 30 percent, another record-breaking increase. The wage tax, collected from all working city residents and all nonresidents who work in the city, rose from 3.3125 percent to 4.3125 percent. For someone earning $10,300 a year, the tax bite went from $314 to $444.

The enormousness of the tax increases, and Rizzo's refusal to talk about them, outraged the city. Since January, the mayor had been receiving criticism almost daily and it rankled. He was particularly annoyed at the Philadelphia *Inquirer*, which consistently attacked him in its editorials for patronage practices. Rizzo had managed to get along with the newspaper's political writers, but the editorial writers and the City Hall reporters hammered away at him and he didn't like it.

His sensitivity to criticism exploded in early March, when he managed to obtain an advance copy of the newspaper's March 14 Sunday magazine, *Today*. The magazine contained a tasteless and amateurish attempt at satire by Desmond Ryan, a scrawny émigré Londoner, who wrote that he was turning over his column to the mayor "to say his piece from time to time without fear of adulteration by unbridled hacks." Under the caption, "Our Mayor Speaks," there followed an ungrammatical tirade by "Frank L. Rizzo As Told To Desmond Ryan." Rizzo had had nothing to do with the preparation of the column and, indeed, the phrasing attributed to him did not sound remotely like him. And there could be no doubt that it was offensive.

Ryan's Rizzo described Pennsylvania Governor Milton J. Shapp, who was at the time making an unsuccessful run for the Democratic presidential nominaton, as "the old shyster from Harrisburg hisself" and "my favorite sonofabitch." Ryan had Rizzo promising to have "all the paisans out there on the convention floor" to oppose Shapp when the party met to choose its nominee. The column portrayed Rizzo as ridiculing PGH as "a hospital if you're broad-minded about it, which I ain't," and had him making these comments about a current (and ultimately successful) federal lawsuit aimed at forcing the city to employ women as regular gun-toting police officers:

"I mean who really wants broads on the police? What about you're having a fight with the wife and givin' her the back of your hand when the Polack down the street puts the squeal in. You want some bull dyke come chargin' on your property all ready with a swift kick in the lasagnas? No way. Not while I'm mayor. . . . If you think this administration, which is me, is gonna take any crap from some judge what couldn't find the john at Villanova you got another think comin'."

Today's table of contents listed the Rizzo report as hypothetical, but there was no similar warning on the page where the column appeared. The magazine is preprinted, and when Rizzo and Gaudiosi obtained copies the Wednesday before the Sunday publication date, they immediately went to work. City Solicitor Sheldon Albert, who had replaced Marty Weinberg, was ordered to ask the *Inquirer* to halt distribution to the magazine. Executive editor Eugene L. Roberts, Jr., declined to do so, pointing out that 130,000 copies had already gone out.

On Saturday, March 13, Rizzo's personal lawyer, I. Raymond Kremer, filed a $6,000,000 libel suit against Ryan, the *Inquirer* and its three top executives. Kremer also asked Common Pleas Court Judge Samuel Smith to issue a temporary restraining order preventing the *Inquirer* from selling its Sunday, March 14, editions, an action Smith refused to go along with. The newspaper was distributed but with a front-page notice stating that Ryan's column was "entirely satirical" and acknowledging that Rizzo did not make the statements attributed to him.

Testifying in court in pursuit of the libel suit the following week, the mayor insisted that his own brother Joe, the fire commissioner, was among twenty-five or thirty persons who had told him they thought Rizzo really had written the column. Then he swore that he never spoke the way Ryan had him speak in the column. He said of the clumsy spoof: "I was sick to my stomach, disgusted. It was an attempt to show me as an illiterate." He also vowed to fight to end media attacks on public figures.

"I am here today because I believe that somewhere, sometimes, someone has got to put a halt to this kind of journalism, this garbage, this filth," Rizzo said. "I don't own a newspaper. And because of that, I have no recourse but to fight such *treason* in the courts."*

Sitting in a courtroom jammed with his followers, Rizzo mentioned Ryan's name at one point, then muttered: "That sucker, I'll strangle him one day if he ever comes near me." As he spoke, Rizzo was looking at Harold Kohn, the *Inquirer*'s lawyer. "What did you say?" Kohn asked. "Nobody heard that," Rizzo replied. "What did you mean?" Kohn persisted. "I meant you, counselor," Rizzo shot back.

While testimony was still being taken on Friday, March 19, a group of burly men began gathering in early afternoon outside the downtown plant of Philadelphia Newspapers, Inc., which publishes the *Inquirer* and *Daily News*. The men were members of the Philadelphia Building and Construction Trades Council and they were led by Thomas Magrann, a plumber like his father before him, a onetime professional boxer and Frank Rizzo's staunch ally.

Magrann had been one of the leaders of the demonstration that disrupted the 1974 Democratic City Committee fund-raising dinner. Rizzo had made Magrann a director of Philadelphia '76, the Bicentennial agency, and would shortly install him as treasurer of the Democratic Party.

By 2 P.M., the crowd outside the newspaper plant had grown to more than two hundred and picketing had begun. At one point, Sheldon Albert showed up and spoke to Magrann. Asked what he and the City Solicitor had talked about, Magrann replied, "He wanted to know if this was in reference to the Mayor. I told him no." Magrann said he had summoned the pickets to protest two articles about nonunion labor construction that the *Inquirer* had published earlier in the week. The pickets carried signs reading "When is the *Inquirer* going to start telling the truth?" "The *Inquirer* is a biased paper" and "The *Inquirer* is for big business and not for the working people."

* Emphasis added.

As the crowd continued to swell, *Inquirer* president Sam S. Mc-Keel notified the Philadelphia Police Department. By this time pickets had sealed off the truck loading dock. McKeel went outside. "Is it your intent to interfere with the movement of our trucks?" he asked Magrann. "It ain't my intent to interfere with anyone," Magrann answered. When McKeel told Magrann the trucks were blocked and couldn't move, the union leader replied, "Well, get someone to move them." By 3 P.M., Philadelphia Newspapers, Inc., was effectively isolated and shut down. The *Daily News* could not deliver 8,400 copies of its final edition. Employees were prevented from entering the building. Yet uniformed police were nowhere in sight.

With the siege still in force at 5 P.M., the *Inquirer* telephoned Police Commissioner O'Neill asking that its entrances be cleared. O'Neill said he would do nothing without orders from Sheldon Albert. Albert said he would do nothing unless ordered to do so by the courts. It was "mob rule," Creed Black, the *Inquirer*'s editor, would later charge. A *Bulletin* reporter who covered the action wrote: "The construction tradesmen, their ranks bolstered by sympathetic teamsters, lined up in front of the papers' two main entrances. . . . More impressive than the Steelers' defensive line, they stood, arms linked, chests out, in rows four and five deep. They taunted, pushed and shoved visitors and employees alike. Nobody broke through."

The mood turned ugly. J. G. Domke, an *Inquirer* photographer, was knocked down. Another *Inquirer* photographer, Russell Salmon, was kicked in the stomach while photographing the demonstration. Still no police. At 6 P.M., *Inquirer* attorneys went to federal court seeking a restraining order. Employees inside the building could not get out, even though their shifts had long since ended. Employees outside could not get in to report for work. At 7:30 P.M. two FBI agents arrived to deliver a bank robbery photograph to the *Inquirer*. The pickets stopped them. The FBI men displayed their credentials. Still the pickets refused to budge and the federal agents left, their mission unaccomplished.

The *Inquirer*'s first Saturday edition was to roll off its presses starting at 8 P.M. But the presses were silent. The men who would run the machinery and bundle the newspapers were outside, unable to enter. At 8:30 P.M., U.S. District Court Judge Edward Becker opened a hearing on the matter and at 9:41 P.M., he issued an order limiting the number of pickets to two at each entrance and forbidding interference with PNI employes or trucks. The siege continued, however, until 11:12 P.M., when federal marshals, accompanied by Philadelphia plainclothesmen, posted the restraining order on the building. Not until then did Magrann order his men to disperse. At 12:30 Saturday, March 20, the *Inquirer* finally went to press with a limited run of 250,000 copies, 110,000 fewer than normal.

The siege was over but not forgotten. "It is beyond belief that a mob of men could prevent *Inquirer* and *Daily News* employees from coming to work for several hours and in the process assault at least two of them," McKeel said the next day. "It is also beyond belief that the police would stand by and do nothing to stop this violence prior to the time a court injunction was issued." Gilman Spencer, editor of the *Daily News,* said in that newspaper's editions of Monday, March 21, "With a fascistic, anarchistic, dangerous situation in motion, Mr. Rizzo's police force let the mob do as it pleased." WCAU-TV said in an editorial, "For ten hours the goons ruled. We say those bullies and their protectors should be brought to justice."

Newspapers, radio and television across the nation took up the cry. "Nothing is more threatening to the exercise of press freedom than mob action acquiesced in if not aided and abetted by political and law enforcement authorities," intoned Walter Cronkite on CBS radio. "That's the kind of cooperative anarchy that occurred in Germany in the thirties. A democracy cannot permit it and long remain a democracy." *The New York Times* said, "The incident provided warning of the way totalitarianism might come to this country if the defenders of freedom — regardless of their political orientation — relaxed their vigilance."

"The failure of the police department to offer adequate protection makes this incident even more inexcusable, for it creates an appearance of official sanction of an illegal act," said Thomas N. O'Neill, Jr., the chancellor of the Philadelphia Bar Association. "It seems clear that the rule of law gave way for at least a short period of time to the threat of force by those who disagreed with the news content of the *Inquirer.*"

In the face of such withering criticism, Rizzo issued a long statement, written by Al Gaudiosi, defending the police inaction. The statement, delivered on March 23, attempted to compare the blockade of the *Inquirer* with an attempted demonstration against Richard Nixon on October 20, 1972, when Nixon signed into law the Revenue Sharing Act during public ceremonies on Independence Mall. At that time, forty persons carrying anti–Vietnam War signs were arrested by police, who carted them off from an area open to the public. Even after the pickets obtained an injunction prohibiting the police from preventing them from gathering in a place open to the public they were rousted. Those who were arrested filed suit against the city and won $33,000 in damages. In an opinion rendered on June 23, 1973, in that case, U.S. District Court Judge Daniel H. Huyett had this to say:

The plaintiffs in this action assert merely the right to peacefully demonstrate by means of inoffensive signs against certain governmental policies. The display of these signs was to take place in a public square open to the public on that occasion. It is clear beyond doubt that the First and Fourteenth Amendments of the Constitution guarantee that persons may peacefully express or propagate ideas either verbally or otherwise, in areas open to the public. The police did not have probable cause to suspect that any, let alone all, of the persons taken into custody presented a serious "security risk." Rather, the arrests were made in an attempt to prevent these persons from demonstrating in a visible manner and in a conspicuous place their dissent from the policies of President Nixon.

Citing Huyett's opinion, Rizzo's statement attempted to equate the shutdown of the *Inquirer* with the picketing at Independence Mall.

"The protests at the *Inquirer* Friday were on the public sidewalk," the Gaudiosi-Rizzo statement said. "Does the *Inquirer* want our police to run interference for its workers through picket lines. If so, they [*sic*] can think again. We're not going to help the *Inquirer* or anyone else roll back the labor movement to the 1920s. We're not anyone's private security force. In labor matters, we obey the mandate of the courts, and we don't take orders from Broad and Callowhill [site of PNI]. . . . The *Inquirer*'s behavior in this matter is a bit different than it was in October 1972, when President Nixon was in Philadelphia to sign the revenue sharing bill. At that time, Philadelphia police, in the interest of presidential security, broke up pickets who hampered efforts to protect the President.

"Guess who was screaming then and what about? It was the *Inquirer* doing the screaming, of course, only this time it was howling because the police DID act against pickets. Now, with the *Inquirer* itself the target of the picketing, the newspaper complains because police did NOT act against pickets.

"So what's the yardstick? Is it whether the pickets are at Independence Hall protesting national policies or whether they're at 15th and Callowhill protesting yellow journalism?"

The Gaudiosi-Rizzo attempt to twist the meaning of the Huyett opinion was transparent. First, the demonstration at the *Inquirer* in no way was triggered by a traditional labor dispute. The Building and Construction Trades unions had no contract with Philadelphia Newspapers, Inc. Although the picketers claimed they were aggrieved by the Inquirer's coverage of some labor matters, there were no official worker-management ties between PNI and the trades unions. At best, Rizzo's union friends could have claimed their picketing was "informational": that is, done to inform passers-by that they considered the newspaper unfair. But the picketers did much more than that; for ten hours they prevented those with legitimate reasons for doing so, including two FBI agents, from entering or leaving a private business office.

There was, however, a common feature in the actions taken or not taken at Independence Mall and PNI. At Independence Mall, Rizzo's police were ordered to arrest persons carrying signs in order to suppress opinions with which Rizzo, and Nixon, disagreed. At the *Inquirer*, Rizzo's police were ordered to do nothing while pickets suppressed the voice of a newspaper whose opinions coincidentally he happened to detest.

On the same day that Rizzo's bellicose statement on the blockade of the *Inquirer* was issued, Harry Belinger, the onetime city editor of the *Inquirer* and *Daily News*, resigned. He said he was quitting over "a matter of principle," but he refused to be specific. When Gaudiosi had taken his job, Belinger had moved into a post that clearly gave him no chance to use the talents that had distinguished him as one of the very few bright spots in Rizzo's administration. But he was not as close to Rizzo as Gaudiosi, he didn't enjoy the same degree of intimacy with the *padrone* that Gaudiosi did, and Gaudiosi's constant sniping at him had the desired effect on Rizzo. When Gaudiosi wanted to join the administration, when he needed a job, Rizzo felt no compunction about dumping Belinger, who had served him and the city better than any of his other employees, with the possible exception of Lennox Moak.

"Recent developments have made it increasingly clear that it is impossible for me to continue . . . for even one more day," Belinger said, in his letter of resignation. He told friends that when he read of the shutdown of his old paper he turned to his wife, Jean, and said, "That's it. I'm quitting." After more than four years on the other side at City Hall, he was still too much of a newspaperman to ignore press intimidation and harassment.

Exactly one month after Belinger quit, while Rizzo was still feuding with the press, Malcolm A. Deans, former assistant managing editor at the *Bulletin*, resigned his post as Gaudiosi's $33,000-a-year assistant. Deans, once Gaudiosi's boss, had joined the Rizzo administration on the same day as Gaudiosi. But he chose to quit, he said in his letter of resignation, because he did not want to continue "as part of what has become a blatantly anti-press administration." "When the choice has to be made," Deans wrote, "I am a newspaperman and not a politician."

The patronage, the plan to close PGH, the public's perception of the mayor's role in the siege at the *Inquirer*, Rizzo's refusal to meet the press or the public and, most of all, the whopping tax increases he was seeking combined to drive the *padrone*'s popularity to its nadir. In the midst of all this, a group called the Citizens Committee to Recall Rizzo began to seriously discuss a move to oust Rizzo from City Hall. Most of the members were known Rizzo enemies, blacks, liberals and so-called reformers. But they believed they could win the support of row-house Philadelphia because of what they saw as Rizzo outrages in patronage and, particularly, taxation.

The 1952 Home Rule Charter provided that a city official could be ordered to face a recall election if enough registered voters signed recall petitions. The number of voters needed to sign such petitions would have to equal 25 percent of the votes cast at the last mayoralty election. If Rizzo were to be the first mayor in Philadelphia's history to face a recall election, in which the voters would be asked to either say yes or no, it would take 145,448 valid signatures. This was not an insignificant number, considering Rizzo's reputation for "getting even" and the natural reluctance of many people to sign any kind of a petition.

But the citizens' committee decided to do what had never been done before: recall a public official in Philadelphia. An effort had been made to do that in 1973, when Rizzo had signed a petition to recall City Councilman Isadore Bellis, but it had failed. The campaign to oust Rizzo was kicked off on April 17, 1976, when the first signatures were obtained. The committee had just sixty days to get the signatures required.

"Twenty-five years ago this fall, the citizens were up in outrage against the corrupt Republican administration," said former Democratic mayor and U.S. Senator Joseph S. Clark as he became the first petition signer. "The slogan then was throw the rascals out.

This time, it's singular: Throw the rascal out. He is a rascal, a liar, a man who is ignorant, arrogant and stupid." The hundred persons who gathered on Independence Mall to witness the signing applauded, then added their own signatures.

When the recall group announced its intentions, Rizzo traveled to WPVI-TV to be interviewed by Larry Kane, the anchorman for the station's news program, who had enjoyed unusual success in luring the mayor to appear on his programs. Alan Bell, general manager of KYW-TV and a frequent Rizzo critic, and WCAU-TV, whose City Hall reporter was tough-nosed Rich Mayk, could not induce Rizzo to appear on their programs.

"I've been fighting the groups that have been trying to recall me all of my career," Rizzo told Kane. "I'm against busing, they're for busing. I'm for the death penalty, they're against the death penalty. They're for legalized prostitution, I'm against legalized prostitution."

Rizzo did not mention taxes or patronage. He did talk — briefly —about the blockade of the *Inquirer*, but he used the occasion not to explain why his police had done nothing but to advance his own grievances. Desmond Ryan, he said, "attempted to portray me as a buffoon." "I'm going to find out in a court of law whether Frank Rizzo, as the mayor of this city, as an Italian-American, and all the other ethnic groups have any rights."

Shelly Yanoff, coordinator of the citizens' committee, listed for reporters five specific reasons for the recall: "1 — The misrepresentation of the fiscal condition of the city — a major part of the mayor's reelection campaign was based on the fact that he had and would hold the line on taxes and that the budget was balanced. . . . It is not the taxes *per se*, but the flagrant deceit and manipulation which have so angered Philadelphians. . . . 2 — The ten hour surrounding of the *Inquirer* building by allies of the mayor following the mayor's court suit against the *Inquirer*. . . . 3 — The precipitous announcement of the closing of PGH with no plans for the services the hospital provides. . . . 4 — Refusal to meet with the press or public to discuss city problems and policies for over two years. . . . 5 — The loading of the city payroll with expensive patronage employes to further the mayor's political apparatus. . . ."

On the rare occasions when reporters were able to collar Rizzo in the corridor outside his City Hall offices, he confidently predicted that if a recall election were held he would win bigger than he had in the 1975 election. He wasn't afraid of a recall election, he said, he was more popular than he'd ever been with the voters. But

Peter J. Camiel, thrown out as chairman of the Democratic Party by Rizzo, signs a petition to recall the mayor.

despite these protestations of confidence, he put Sheldon Albert to work on the matter, and Albert had more than seventy assistants — paid for by the city — to call on for help. And Rizzo brought attorney Howard Gittis, the man who represented him in the purchase of his Chestnut Hill mansion and who also represented Al Pearlman, into the picture. Together, Albert and Gittis would fight the attempt to recall Rizzo on technical legal grounds. Rizzo might say that he was confident that the voters would vindicate him, but his lawyers would try every last legal maneuver to prevent the voters from ever getting a chance to cast a yes or no vote on Rizzo's continuing in office.

Rizzo might have believed that he was popular with the voters, but Jimmy Carter had reason to think otherwise. Carter, coming off primary election victories in New Hampshire, Florida, Illinois and Wisconsin, believed that he could wrap up the Democratic presidential nomination if he could win the April 27 Pennsylvania primary. One of those standing in his way was Frank Rizzo, who was supporting Senator Henry M. Jackson.

Patrick Caddell, Carter's public opinion analyst, had taken polls which disclosed that, outside of Philadelphia, Rizzo was the least popular elected figure in Pennsylvania. Armed with this information, Carter chose to run against Frank Rizzo in Pennsylvania rather than against Henry Jackson or Morris Udall or George Wallace. With Pittsburgh Mayor Peter Flaherty at his side, Carter traveled the state denouncing Rizzo.

"The last presidential candidate Mr. Rizzo supported was Richard Nixon," Carter told a crowd in western Pennsylvania on April 21. "I'm glad he doesn't think I'm in the same league. I am proud to stand here with Pete Flaherty, a mayor who doesn't run up eighty-million-dollar deficits and close down city hospitals and inflate the public payroll with political patronage."

Carter's approach worked. He carried sixty-five of the state's sixty-seven counties and defeated Jackson by 115,000 votes. He lost Philadelphia to Jackson by only 22,000 votes, even though Jackson had the all-out support of organized labor and of both the Rizzo and Camiel wings of the Democratic party.

The day after the primary, the citizens' committee announced that it had collected 45,000 signatures in the first ten days of its drive to force Rizzo to face a recall election. And the following week, a *Bulletin* poll of 500 Philadelphia adults disclosed that 57 percent believed the mayor should be turned out of office. In the downtown district populated largely by well-to-do liberal whites and poor blacks, 78 percent of those polled thought Rizzo should be ousted. In West Philadelphia, 70 percent wanted to get rid of the mayor, and in North Philadelphia the number was 68 percent. Even in the nearly all-white, middle-class Northeast, 54 percent wanted Rizzo to go. Only in South Philadelphia, his home base, did Rizzo retain the support of most residents. And even there 40 percent favored his removal.

By May 11, the citizens' committee had 80,183 signatures on recall petitions, more than half the total needed and with more than a month remaining to reach the goal. During that time, the local news would be dominated by the passage through the city council of Rizzo's massive tax increases. It was not a topic designed to make the voters feel friendly toward the *padrone*, and he and Gaudiosi began to plot strategy. The citizens' committee had to be derailed, the public's attention had to be diverted away from recall, away from taxes.

In the past, whenever he found himself in a tight spot, Rizzo invariably had tried to wriggle out of it by playing the tough cop. He would denounce rapists and murderers, soft judges and bleeding-heart liberals. He would be telling row-house Philadelphia that if it wasn't for Mayor Frank Rizzo the thugs would own the streets. It had always worked, even though crime and violence steadily marched forward, oblivious to Rizzo's bluster.

As the end of May neared, the citizens' committee announced that it would disclose the new signature total on Monday, May 31. The suspicion was strong in City Hall that this announcement would put the committee over the top, that it would proclaim the needed 145,448 signatures had been obtained.

So on May 27, the very day that the council was passing the tax increases, Frank Rizzo, who hadn't held a news conference for more than two years and who had done nothing to end the blockade of the *Inquirer*, granted an exclusive interview — to the *Inquirer*. It was for use in the newspaper's Sunday, May 30, editions, and Rizzo had some important information to reveal.

The city had learned, Rizzo told the *Inquirer*, that thousands of "radicals, leftists," were coming to Philadelphia to disrupt the July 4 Bicentennial celebration. The situation was so ominous, he said that he was requesting the federal government to send in 15,000 troops to protect the city.

"When I tell you that the leftists, and that's what they are, intend to come in here in thousands from all over the country to disrupt, how about the rights of the majority who are going to be here to enjoy themselves with their families?" Rizzo said. The mayor said he wanted "regular army" troops and he wanted them stationed "on the streets, and I'll tell you why. Because we have a bunch of radicals, leftists, that have said they're going to disrupt."

"I hope that nothing happens that day," Rizzo continued. "You remember, I was a police chief and I'm very proud of that career of mine. While every other city burned, while every other city had deaths, not in Philadelphia."

Rizzo also told the *Inquirer* he was not concerned by the recall drive. "They'll never be successful," he said. "I know people who are friends of mine who have signed it. Mickey Mouse, Al Capone, Snow White and the Seven Dwarfs. . . . One guy wrote me the other day and said he had signed it seventy times."

"We're not kidding or trying to make headlines," Al Gaudiosi told the *Inquirer*, referring to the troop request. "This is a real request. The mayor really wants the troops here to protect the visitors in case there is any trouble."

But Rizzo and Gaudiosi did make headlines. The *Inquirer* bannered the news across its Sunday front page. Somewhere along the way, however, something happened to the *Inquirer's* "exclusive" story. Rizzo's plan to seek federal help in providing troops was leaked to the *Bulletin*, and it appeared across the top of the newspaper's front page on Saturday, May 29, beating the *Inquirer* with its own story. Even though Rizzo and Gaudiosi weren't "trying to make headlines," they had succeeded in dominating the front pages of the two newspapers, and the city's radio and television stations picked up the story, making it for a time the principal topic of conversation.

"Intelligence estimates developed by the Philadelphia Police Department lead us to the conclusion that we cannot assure the safety and security of the millions of people coming to Philadelphia if we have to rely exclusively on our own resources," Rizzo wrote to President Ford. "Accordingly, Mr. President, I am requesting that 15,000 Federal troops be placed in our city on July 4th to help deter and defuse the violence which may occur."

This was sizzling stuff. Intelligence estimates. Safety and security. Troops. Violence. It was hot enough to overshadow the fact that, as of May 31, 146,275 persons had signed recall petitions, 827 more than necessary.

Back in 1957, then-Mayor Richardson Dilworth had appointed the Junior Chamber of Commerce to develop plans to celebrate the Bicentennial. Over the years, various ideas and projects were advanced, most of them long since forgotten, and planning for the celebration proceeded in fits and starts. Administrations and personnel changed and the dimensions of the event were scaled down. But to the city and its people, its shopkeepers, retailers, restaurateurs, hotel men and row-house residents, the Bicentennial was something important. Boston might quarrel with Philadelphia's claim of being the nation's birthplace, but Philadelphians didn't quarrel with it. They believed it. The buildings where the nation was created, where the Declaration of Independence was signed, where the Constitution was framed, were just a few minutes walk from Gimbels or Wanamakers and thousands of Philadelphians passed them every day.

The federal government had spent $30,000,000 just to improve Independence Mall and to house the Liberty Bell. And it was this area that would be the focal point of the nation's two hundredth birthday party on the Fourth of July. President Ford would be there. So would the governor and the mayor. And movie actor Charlton Heston. More than fifty thousand persons would march in a massive parade, with every state in the union represented. Hotels and restaurants would be jammed. Everyone would have a good time and business would boom.

But if that was the case, why were the newspapers filled every day with stories about potential violence? After Rizzo had asked for the troops, he had been told the request had to be made by the governor, so he had contacted Shapp, who, in turn, asked for a meeting with the U.S. Justice Department. And instead of reading about preparations for the celebration, Philadelphians were reading a letter from Deputy Attorney General Harold Tyler to Shapp outlining these three prerequisites for the use of federal troops:

That a situation of serious domestic violence exists within the state.

That such violence cannot be brought under control by the law enforcement resources available to the governor, including local and state police forces and the National Guard.

That the legislature or the governor . . . request the President to employ Armed Forces to bring violence under control.

The only evidence Rizzo could produce to support his request for troops was the fact that two anti-Establishment groups, the Rich Off Our Backs Coalition and the July 4th Coalition, had announced that they planned to have their own separate parades on the holiday. Both groups insisted their intentions were peaceful. They had asked for parade permits, their numbers were relatively small, and their parades would take place more than a mile from the downtown activities.

Spencer Coxe, executive director of the Philadelphia chapter of the ACLU and a frequent critic of Rizzo, had this to say about Rizzo and the anti-Establishment groups:

"They did not come across at all as a group bent on causing disruption. If that was their purpose, they wouldn't ask for permits at all. He just hates these radical groups. He accuses them irresponsibly of criminal intent. It gives him the chance to act in a military way, which he enjoys doing. The surest way to have a violent confrontation is to deny people the right to assemble and then call out the troops when they do. I can't imagine a better recipe for trouble."

On June 21, the Justice Department rejected Rizzo's request, saying it found "no justification" for sending in troops. "I feel the federal government is playing politics with people's lives," was Rizzo's response. "If there are disturbances in Philadelphia the blood is on their hands."

There were no disturbances in Philadelphia on July Fourth. Not a single "radical" or "leftist" was arrested, even though Rizzo offered this mournful forecast on July 3: "I hope and pray that nothing occurs, but I know this — a lot of people are coming to this town who are bent on violence."

A lot of people did come to town to listen to Marian Anderson read the Declaration of Independence, to listen to the President, to see the fireworks go off, to watch the Mummers strut, to hear the Paris Boys' Choir, to see Philadelphia. But not as many came as were expected.

Among those who didn't come were six hundred members of the Antiochian Christian Archdiocese of North America, a small Orthodox church, who had canceled a religious service on the Mall because of fears of violence. "Since all these rumors were going around about unpleasant situations, we decided to cancel it," said the Reverend Anthony Bassoline, pastor of St. George Antiochian Church in the Philadelphia suburb of Upper Darby. "Even our choir members got frightened — they didn't want their children to be there."

"Recent newspaper and television reports in our area have been indicating that demonstrations and unrest are expected to accompany the Bicentennial celebration in Philadelphia on July 4th," Joseph C. Sakalosky, principal of Cedar Crest High School in

Lebanon, Pennsylvania, wrote to William Mullens, the Bicentennial parade director. "These reports have caused concern on the part of parents of our band members who are scheduled to participate in the parade on that day. . . . After 200 years of liberty, it is disconcerting that the nation cannot celebrate its Bicentennial without a threat of violence sufficiently strong to cause concern for the safety and welfare of our participating youth."*

Cedar Crest canceled. It was not alone. Originally, 163 bands with 50,000 marchers were scheduled to participate. After Rizzo began talking about "radicals" and "leftists" and "violence" the cancellations started coming in. Three states — Colorado, Kentucky and Tennessee — had no representation at all. The number of bands was cut almost in half, to 85. Seventy-eight bands, including Cedar Crest, were scared off, depriving the parade of 15,000 marchers.

Through all the talk of troops and violence, however, the citizens' committee continued to work. On the June 15 deadline for securing signatures, the committee turned over to the Philadelphia board of elections — which was controlled by Rizzo — petitions signed by 211,190 persons. It would be up to the board of elections to decide if enough valid signatures had been obtained to force the mayor to stand a recall election.

Publicly, Rizzo continued to act unconcerned about the recall. Two nights after the July Fourth celebration, he and his wife enjoyed one of the great evenings of their lives. Rizzo and Carmella were host and hostess at a City of Philadelphia dinner for Queen Elizabeth II and Prince Philip inside a scrubbed and shining Museum of Art. Queen Elizabeth had spent the day in Philadelphia, the first British monarch to do so. Rizzo, in black tie, sat at a table with the Queen; Mrs. Peter Ramsbotham, wife of the British ambassador to the United States; Mrs. Anthony Crosland, wife of Britain's foreign secretary, and others. Mrs. Rizzo sat at another table to the right of Prince Philip.

The three hundred guests ate salmon mousse, filet of beef Périgordine, tomato farcie, baby lima beans, ice cream cake and petits fours. They drank three wines and Rizzo offered two toasts: to the Queen of England and to the President of the United States.

Most of Rizzo's conversation with royalty that night has been lost to history. But one fragment remains. The diners had been given as souvenirs silver medallions with the Queen's image on one side and

* Philadelphia *Daily News*, June 30, 1976.

the Liberty Bell on the other. The medallions were contained in small cases, which had been left at each diner's place. When Rizzo opened his case he discovered the medallion was missing. "Hey, somebody stole mine," Mr. Law and Order told his royal dinner companion, in a loud and aggrieved voice. "You may have mine," the Queen replied coolly. "I have one in gold."

Under terms of the Home Rule Charter, the board of elections — consisting of the three elected city commissioners — was given only fifteen days to examine recall petitions to determine the validity of the signatures on them. On June 30, when the fifteen-day period ended, the city commissioners petitioned Common Pleas Court Judge David N. Savitt for an extension, claiming they couldn't check 211,190 signatures in such a short time. The day after Rizzo's July 6 dinner with the Queen, Savitt granted the commissioners a forty-day extension.

The delay fitted in perfectly with the strategy devised by Al Gaudiosi to defeat the recall. The first step in that strategy was to stall, to keep the matter before the board of elections for as long as possible. Gaudiosi knew the board would rule in Rizzo's favor, since the mayor controlled two of the three votes, but he also knew the final decision would be made by the courts. The key date in this strategy was September 21. If the verdict on whether to have a recall election could be postponed until after that date, there was no way for the question to be placed on the November 2 ballot. It was important to the mayor not to have to stand a recall election on the same day as the presidential election, when a large number of voters would be expected to turn out. If a recall election were to be held, Gaudiosi wanted it to come in the dead of winter when voters would not be as motivated to go to the polls as they would be when they had a chance to vote for a President. With a small turnout, Rizzo's control of the Democratic machine would give him a better chance to win.

As a preview of coming attractions, the city commissioners voted two to one on June 15 to accept the recommendations of Sheldon Albert, Rizzo's city solicitor, on which signatures should be considered valid and which invalid. Throughout the proceedings, Albert would represent both the board of elections and Rizzo, two clients whose interests were not necessarily the same. His first piece of advice was clearly designed to benefit his *padrone*, the man who had hired him and in whose cabinet he served.

Albert's "guidelines" for judging the validity of signatures seemed to fly in the face of reason. No one quarreled when he told the board it should reject signatures of those who were not registered voters, or who lived outside the city, or where the handwriting was illegible. But Albert also said signatures should be rejected for patently frivolous reasons.

Under Albert's guidelines, a person signing a recall petition had to supply the requested information so that it conformed exactly to the information contained on his registration certificate. For example, take the hypothetical case of John J. Jones, who was a student when he had registered to vote ten years earlier. By voting regularly since then, Jones had maintained his eligibility and thus the original information he had supplied to the registrar was still on file. That information stated: "John J. Jones, student, 1895 Spruce St., Eighth Ward." In signing the recall petition, however, Jones supplied this information: "John Jones, accountant, 1895 Spruce St."

Under Albert's guidelines, Jones's signature would be stricken for any of several reasons. First, he had omitted the initial "J." Or he had identified himself as an accountant rather than as a student. Or he had neglected to include his ward number.

Albert also had decreed that if Jones's wife had registered as Mrs. John Jones but had signed the recall petition "Mrs. Mary Jones," her signature should be disqualified. And, said Albert, where a recall volunteer had collected a "substantial" number of signatures that proved invalid, all of the signatures collected by that volunteer should be rejected. The interpretation of "substantial" was left to the discretion of the Board of Elections.

"Any signatory whose signature and address, occupation or ward does not conform in each respect with your official records must be disregarded," Albert told the Board, in a formal opinion.

Initially, the two Rizzo votes on the board accepted the guidelines without question, and their decision stirred an uproar. "Albert's arguing that a change of occupation invalidates a person's signature," said Gregory M. Harvey, attorney for the citizens' committee. "I can't imagine that that position has ever occurred to anyone before."

The criticism that followed this decision eventually forced the two pro-Rizzo commissioners to back down on one point: a change of occupation would not invalidate a signature. On the other points they would not budge. An omitted initial was cause for disqualification.

The sure Rizzo votes on the board of elections came from Mrs. Margaret M. Tartaglione, a tart-tongued forty-six-year-old blonde mother of five who had been elected as part of Rizzo's Democratic ticket, and John F. Kane, a sixty-seven-year-old Republican who had been appointed to the job by Rizzo when the previous Republican commissioner had died.* Rizzo had appointed Kane at the request of Kane's brother-in-law, Republican boss Billy Meehan. Not surprisingly, Meehan had proclaimed himself against recall, as had Republican City Chairman William J. Devlin.

The lone anti-Rizzo commissioner was Eugene E. J. Maier, a lawyer and a Democrat loyal to Pete Camiel. Maier, forty-four, knew he was destined to be a permanent minority when the three commissioners had their first meeting and Kane threw in with Tartaglione and voted to make her chairwoman on January 6, 1976, the first day she had ever held public office.

It did not take Tartaglione long to demonstrate that she knew how politics, City Hall style, was played. Each of the three commissioners had managed to get along with one deputy until then. But four months after she had taken office, Tartaglione had five. When the Philadelphia *Bulletin* asked her about this wealth of talent on April 19, Tartaglione replied:

"After the [primary] election, I have many, many ways I see of modernizing things to save monies. I'm thinking of the taxpayers all the time."

During one of the public meetings at which the recall signatures were being counted, Tartaglione exploded at criticism from Maier. "Are you through?" she demanded of him. "Yes," Maier replied. "Then wipe yourself," the chairwoman shot back.

Kane, for his part, voted with Tartaglione on every question. Asked by reporters about Albert's guidelines, he said he felt bound by them.

"I do not resent being called a Rizzo supporter," Kane said at one point. "But I would like it known that I was one hundred percent behind Thomas Foglietta in 1975."

In keeping with Gaudiosi's strategy of stalling, the board predictably used up all of the forty-day extension and then some before it finished its tally on August 24. Just as predictably it ruled — on a two-to-one vote — that there were not enough valid signatures. Using Albert's guidelines, Tartaglione and Kane voted to disqualify 122,296 of the 211,190 signatures. This reduced the total to 88,894, far fewer than the 145,448 needed.

The citizens' committee appealed the board's ruling to Judge

* The city charter requires that one of the three commissioners be from the minority party.

Savitt the next day, contending that the commissioners had arbitrarily and capriciously disenfranchised thousands of registered voters who had signed the petitions. Albert immediately asked the judge to grant him fifteen days in which to prepare an answer to the appeal. Savitt rejected the request and directed Albert to file his brief on September 1.

On August 30, two days before his brief was due, Albert showed up in Savitt's courtroom pleading for an extra week. Albert said he needed the delay because the legal papers he had been working on to buttress his case had "mysteriously" disappeared from his office. He, six assistant city solicitors and a secretary had been working long, hard hours and had completed their work the previous day, a Sunday, in the early afternoon, Albert said. The papers had been on the secretary's desk when he had gone home, Albert added.

"We came in Monday morning and found everything that had been on her desk gone," Albert told the judge. "After checking with the trashmen, we reported it to the police. I was almost in tears. It's just a shame. It means that we have to start all over again. It may have been an overzealous custodian."

Savitt, aware of the importance of the September 21 deadline, turned Albert down and ordered the proceedings to begin. Somehow, Albert produced a brief and he and Howard Gittis, Rizzo's personal lawyer, set about defending the board's decision, although along different lines. Albert argued that the board's discretion was total, that the courts had no authority to encroach on what he said was the exclusive jurisdiction of the board. He also maintained that the signatures had been disqualified properly. Gittis took the position that recall was unconstitutional in Pennsylvania because the state election code contains no provision for a recall election.

Citizens' committee lawyer Harvey pointed out that between 1903 and 1976, recall provisions had been adopted by governments in twenty-eight states. It was a time-honored and time-tested procedure, he said, confident that Savitt would sustain the legality of the process. Harvey also was confident Savitt would sustain the right of the courts to review the actions of the board. No agency, he said, is equipped with the untrammeled discretion Albert imputed to the board. The lawyer concentrated his biggest fire, however, on the board's disqualification of signatures, an act he termed "arbitrary," "capricious" and "an abuse of discretion."

Savitt ruled in favor of the citizens' committee on September 16, five days before the deadline, and ordered the recall election placed on the November 2 ballot. He declared recall constitutional and sustained the authority of the courts to review the actions of the board. In doing so, he found that the board indeed had abused its discretion in disqualifying 67,320 signatures and restored them to the valid category, making the total in the valid category 156,214.

Albert and Gittis appealed the decision to the state Supreme Court. On September 20, they presented essentially the same arguments they had presented to Savitt. Ten days later, on September 30, recall was dead. The Supreme Court voted, four to three, to kill it, but the seven justices at that time gave no reasons for their action. The recall question was deleted from the November 2 ballot. On November 19, the court issued its opinions in the case.

The majority opinion, written by Chief Justice Benjamin R. Jones, reversed Savitt on both procedural and constitutional grounds. The lower court, said Jones, exceeded its authority when it had substituted its judgment on the validity of signatures for that of the board. And, he added, recall was an unconstitutional process in Pennsylvania because there was no provision for it in state law.

Key parts of the Jones ruling conjured visions of *Catch-22* and caused Jones's colleague, Justice Samuel J. Roberts, to state in a dissenting opinion: "Today's decision is without support in law, fact, reason, or public policy."

". . . In reaching the decision of whether to accept the petition, the Board is accorded the ultimate discretion as to the validity of the petition," Jones wrote. "In exercising that discretion the Board was bound to do so in good faith and in a legally sound manner. The discretion, in other words, was not unrestrained. The trial court . . . obviously believed that the Board transcended the parameters of that discretion in rejecting the signatures which fell into the enumerated unacceptable categories. In so holding, the trial court fell into error by substituting its determination as to the sufficiency of the recall petition for that of the Board."

Having said that Savitt did not have authority to substitute his determination for the board's, Jones went on to say that Savitt was nevertheless right in overruling the board for disqualifying signatures that fell into five categories: "insufficient signature"; "abbreviations"; "initials"; "incorrect ward" and "forgeries/alterations."

"The signatures rejected for those reasons should have been counted as valid and the court properly corrected the abuse of the Board's discretion," Jones wrote.

It is here that Jones's reasoning became truly murky. His opinion sustained the board's rejection of 22,159 signatures because they were accompanied by "irregular" or "false" affidavits: that is, sworn statements by the circulators of the petitions that to the best of their "knowledge and belief" the information given by the signers of the petitions was correct.

The board had decided that if 25 percent of the signatures on any petition fell into the categories for disqualification established by Albert, all of the signatures on that petition were to be excluded. The logic behind this was that if a circulator swore that to the best of his "knowledge and belief" all of the information on a petition was correct but 25 percent of it failed to meet Albert's standards, the affidavit was false on its face.

In other words, a petition with seventy-five perfect signatures and twenty-five signatures that fell afoul of one of Albert's categories had to be discarded entirely, according to Jones. And this held true, he said, even though he had ruled that five of the categories constituted an "abuse" of discretion and improperly disqualified legitimate signatures.

"Sheets having more than twenty-five percent 'defective' signatures were rejected for 'patent falsity,' and all of the signatures on those sheets were rejected," Judge Roberts wrote in his dissent. "The irrationality of such a procedure becomes apparent in light of the Chief Justice's determination that five of the categories, involving nearly half of the allegedly defective signatures, were valid. . . . If the adoption of these categories was an abuse of discretion, then surely it was an abuse of discretion to invalidate perfect signatures because other signatures on the same page had these so-called 'defects.' The Chief Justice's reasoning on 'patent falsities' is totally inconsistent with his determination that the signature in the 'initials,' 'abbreviations,' 'insufficient signatures,' 'incorrect ward,' and 'forgeries/alterations' categories are valid.* For example, if a petition containing one hundred signatures included seventy-five perfect signatures and twenty-five which fell into the 'initials' category, the Board could not reject the twenty-five signatures for defective initials. At the same time, however, the opinion of the Chief Justice would allow the Board to use these twenty-five valid signatures as a basis for rejecting all one hundred signatures, including the seventy-five perfect signatures, for 'patent falsities.' "

---

* The categories, their definitions and the number of signatures affected were as follows:

Initials: "John J. Smith" signed petition "John Smith" (21,195).

Abbreviations: "Joseph Jones" signed "Jos. Jones" (2,962).

Insufficient Signature: "Mary Smith" signed "Mrs. Mary Smith" (3,482).

Incorrect Ward: Voter signed correctly but listed wrong ward (11,209).

Forgeries/Alterations: Voter signed correctly but someone else filled in date, ward or address (6,313).

Whatever the legalities, Frank Rizzo was off the hook. And the desperation with which he fought to avoid facing the voters in a recall election gave the lie to the braggadocio he showed when he heard of the Supreme Court's ruling.

"My political career has suffered no blow," he said. "I would have won bigger than I did last time."

Frank Rizzo never answered the question of why, if he had been so confident of winning a recall election, he had battled so fiercely, requiring the board of elections to spend $750,000 for overtime pay to validate the signatures, causing Sheldon Albert and six of his assistants to spend an unknown amount of money seeking to derail the recall. Or why he had found it necessary to hire a private lawyer, Howard Gittis, to represent him at a cost estimated at close to $100,000, a cost that would be borne by the hard-pressed taxpayers of Philadelphia.

"I'm not going to pay the bill," Rizzo told reporters who collared him as he was awarding a ceremonial commendation to a high-school debating team. The Gittis bill, he said, would be paid by the city. "I'm certainly not going to pay it out of my pocket," the mayor added.

Frank Rizzo's career in good part had been built on his outspoken denunciations of the court system as being infested by pro-criminal bleeding hearts. If he saw any irony in the fact that this same system now had delivered him — acquitted him, as it were — from having to face the voters, he did not reveal it. In truth, the court system had served the members and friends of the Rizzo administration well. It had enabled them to use the same technicalities and constitutional guarantees that outraged Frank Rizzo when someone else used them.

Hillel Levinson, for example, was the managing director, Frank Rizzo's chief operating officer. On April 15, 1975, Levinson had been indicted on charges of shaking down contractors to buy tickets to the Democratic Party's 1972 $100 dinner and then lying about it under oath. The grand jury cited Levinson for five counts of extortion, five counts of illegal solicitation of political contributions, seven counts of perjury, seven counts of false swearing, and eleven violations of the charter. The extortion and illegal solicitation charges resulted from the testimony of seven architects and engineers before an investigating — as opposed to an indicting — grand jury. The perjury and false swearing charges grew out of Levinson's own testimony about the role of Deputy Mayor Mike Wallace in the ticket sales. According to the indictments, Levinson had said this about Wallace while testifying before the investigating grand jury on Oct. 12, 1973:

"He works out of the mayor's office. And he asked me if I would not call various people that I knew or had knowledge of in terms of inquiring as to whether or not they had purchased tickets for the upcoming Democratic City Committee dinner."

When Levinson again appeared before the grand jury a year later, on October 30, 1974, the indictments said, he testified that Wallace had had nothing to do with the ticket sales.

The charges against Levinson were thrown out on March 29, 1976, on a technicality. Legally constituted grand juries in Pennsylvania must have from fifteen to twenty-three members. After the grand jury had begun investigating Levinson five of its members had been excused, reducing the total to the barely legal limit of fifteen. The judge in charge of the jury thereafter seated six additional jurors to guard against the possibility of its falling below the required minimum. The addition of the six new jurors caused the state Superior Court to quash the charges.

"The presence on the grand jury of six persons who had not seen or heard witnesses who testified throughout the early phases of the investigation must be deemed inherently prejudicial," the Superior Court ruled.

Augustine A. Salvitti, handpicked by Rizzo to head the Redevelopment Authority, had been indicted on November 11, 1975, on charges of theft of Authority property, perjury and falsifying Authority records in connection with the awarding of a $50,000 salvage contract. The grand jury charged that Salvitti had awarded the contract outside of normal channels, had falsified records to make everything appear normal, and had lied under oath about it. On April 9, 1976, the charges against Salvitti were dropped for the same technical reasons that washed out the charges against Levinson — the addition of the six new grand jurors after the investigation had begun.

Mike Wallace was not charged. When he appeared before the grand jury on April 26 and 28, 1976, he simply refused to testify on Fifth Amendment grounds, citing his right against self-incrimination. Regarding city officials who refuse to testify on grounds of self-incrimination, the charter says, "If any officer or employee of the city . . . shall refuse to testify or to answer any question relating to the affairs or government of the city or the conduct of any city officer or employee on the ground that his testimony or answers would tend to incriminate him . . . he shall forfeit his office or position, and shall not be eligible to any position in the city service."

Wallace didn't lose his job. When Rizzo refused to fire him, a private citizens' suit was filed in an attempt to oust Wallace for violating the charter. Common Pleas Court Judge Stanley Greenberg ruled in Wallace's favor, saying he couldn't be compelled to testify without first being given immunity from prosecution. Greenberg's colleague, Judge Merna B. Marshall, who was in charge of the grand jury, disagreed with Greenberg and said on a local television program that she hoped his "background" hadn't influenced him.* While he was a judge, Greenberg was convicted on federal conspiracy to commit mail fraud charges for activities that took place before he went on the bench. Richard Nixon subsequently pardoned him.

Immunity wasn't the issue, Marshall said. Wallace could claim the Fifth Amendment or he could keep his job. He couldn't do both. But he did.†

Wallace wasn't the only prominent person close to Rizzo who found it desirable to take shelter behind the Fifth Amendment. Fredric R. Mann did it when asked about the financing of the repairs to the mayor's office. Al Pearlman did it when asked about the financing of repairs to the mayor's palatial Chestnut Hill home. And if Frank Rizzo, the champion of law and order, saw an irony in his close associates seeking out such refuge, he did not reveal that, either.

The Supreme Court decision had placed Rizzo back on top. It had removed him from the dangers of confronting an angry electorate and had given him time to try to repair the damage his image had suffered. His brass-knuckle tactics had worked in the past and there was no reason to believe they wouldn't work in the future, once the citizens had calmed down and gotten used to paying the taxes.

All the handles of power were within Rizzo's grasp. The Republican Party was a virtual nonentity in the city, with many of its members attracted to Rizzo. Charles Bowser's Philadelphia Party promised to stay in business, a welcome prospect to the mayor since it would only help divide the anti-Rizzo vote. And the Democratic Party, though fragmented, was seeing most of its ward leaders and committeemen lured over to Rizzo because of his

* *The Week In Review*, WHYY-TV, December 10, 1976.
† In 1977, Wallace resigned his City Hall job and with Rizzo's support won the Democratic Party's backing for a common pleas court judgeship.

control — and generous disbursement — of patronage and influence. And Rizzo had succeeded in ousting Pete Camiel and installing Marty Weinberg as party chairman the previous May, giving him total authority over the political machinery.

"I would like to thank each of you and Mayor Rizzo for bestowing this honor upon me," Weinberg had said, after the ward leaders had elected him chairman.

Rizzo had ample reason to feel confident. And he did not hide that confidence. Just three weeks after the Supreme Court rescued him, he served as honorary chairman of a fifty-dollar-a-plate dinner honoring John J. McCullough, the power behind Roofers Union Local Thirty, at the Latin Casino in Cherry Hill, New Jersey.

Dressed in black tie and seated at the head table, Rizzo did not seem to be bothered that McCullough had been indicted on August 19, 1976, by a federal grand jury on charges of extortion and conspiracy. An indictment is only an accusation and does not constitute proof of wrongdoing. Months later, on April 1, 1977, McCullough and his codefendants would be acquitted when the government failed to prove its case. But at the time of the dinner the charges still were hanging over McCullough's head, and they were serious. He and four others had been accused of forcing a contractor to hire three roofers to do "unwanted, superfluous and fictitious" work, costing the firm $18,700, or 8.6 percent of the total $217,000 contract. And the firm, Skyway All-Weather Crete Company, of Troy, New York, had announced that it would no longer work in Philadelphia. One would have thought that a self-proclaimed law-and-order mayor, for appearance's sake, would have hesitated when asked to be honorary chairman of such a dinner.

"I've known John McCullough many years," Rizzo told the diners at the Latin Casino. "I have great respect for John J. McCullough. He is a great American. He has done much to help people who need help. I never forget labor. I am mayor of the city of Philadelphia because of support from organized labor."*

A lone accordionist stood on the balcony overlooking the dining

* Another union leader at the dinner was Thomas Magrann, head of the Building and Construction Trades Council. Magrann, a loyal Rizzo ally, who had been elected Democratic Party treasurer at City Hall's direction, found himself the target of a Rizzo purge on December 21, 1976. On that date, the mayor let it be known that he wanted Magrann ousted for allegedly uttering racial and ethnic slurs. Magrann's real offense, however, appeared to be his insistence that four persons employed by the party be fired. Among them was the man who had purchased Rizzo's Provident Street house for $38,000, who was on the party's payroll as a nighttime janitor. In the daytime, this man held down a city job as a court custodian. The method Rizzo chose to remove Magrann was ironic: a recall movement. Magrann resigned on De-

room. He entertained the diners by playing the theme from *The Godfather*.

———

Frank Rizzo rolled into office on a wave of support from row-house Philadelphia. Nineteen seventy-one, to paraphrase Kevin Phillips, was the "year of the Cop," and Rizzo's election was the most significant for any policeman anywhere. He was the white ethnics' choice and the white ethnics were just then coming into their own as a political force, a fact clearly recognized by Richard Nixon. Yet it wasn't just the white working class that initially fell in behind Rizzo, though they would stay with him the longest. He drew backing as well from influential Philadelphians who believed that the tough cop really did represent a new era and a new brand of no-nonsense leadership.

Rolfe Neill, editor of the feisty *Daily News*, endorsed Rizzo in 1971, risking the loyalty of his large black readership. So did Herb Lipson, publisher of *Philadelphia* magazine, risking the loyalty of his hip, flip, downtown-liberal audience. And Murray Friedman, sociologist and American Jewish Committee official, believed that it was a "Rizzo revolution," a true "people's movement." Friedman was convinced that Rizzo's election marked "the triumph of a new urban populism."

Frank Rizzo in office quickly dashed these expectations. The "urban populist" set as his first goal an imperial mayoralty. The luxurious offices and the huge mansion on the hill   the financing of which remains a mystery — the chauffeured limousines and the round-the-clock bodyguards, these were the trappings of a despot rather than the marks of a "common man." In their public lives, so-called aristocrats like Joe Clark, Richardson Dilworth and Thacher Longstreth were far more democratic than the *padrone*. They walked among the people, heard their pleas, discussed policies and programs with them and, particularly Clark and Dilworth, argued with them. Rizzo was remote, aloof, inaccessible. Both physically and psychologically, he put a distance between himself and his "people" in the row houses. But, when it became necessary, he could tap the row-house emotions, aligning himself with the crime-fearing blue-collar white family against the "rapists" and "hoodlums" who were constantly threatening to turn the city into a jungle.

———

cember 29, 1976, after it became clear that Rizzo had secured the votes of the needed two-thirds of the ward leaders to recall him. The four employees remained on the party's payroll.

Rizzo campaigned as a "strong man for a tough job," who would provide the leadership the people wanted. But his leadership as mayor was nonexistent. Not a single program, not a single goal, not a single display of vision marked his tenure. He proved to be a do-nothing mayor with a big mouth who spent his time trying to destroy his enemies while building his own power base, all at taxpayers' expense. He described himself as "a practical man, not a politician," but he proved to be the most political of mayors. As a campaigner, he noted that "the people want performance, not words." Yet his performance was almost entirely negative. His politics was of the "I'm against it" variety. His appeal was to people who wanted programs stopped, not started. He pledged NOT to do things. His physical courage was unquestioned, but he never displayed the courage of a public official who is willing to risk his popularity to achieve difficult goals. To maintain that popularity, Rizzo made no demands on the people until he raised taxes in 1976. And that tax increase was not to *do* anything; it was just to keep bread on the table.

As a law-and-order mayor Rizzo was a joke. He and his friends made a mockery of the law they were sworn to uphold. The city treasury was treated as a private preserve, there to reward the mayor's friends and punish his enemies. Rizzo himself used secret police, paid for by the taxpayers, to spy on his political enemies. And at one point he gained international notoriety as the only major public official who was certified a liar by a polygraph machine. Some law. Some order.

Rizzo pledged he would strengthen Philadelphia's neighborhoods, but he did little as mayor to halt their decline. Under Rizzo, the city's population decreased by more than 500 persons a week through mid-1975, a drop that was twice as sharp as it was during the 1950s and 1960s, when public planners believed Philadelphia was hemorrhaging emigrants. When Rizzo started his second term, the population had declined to 1,824,000, about the same as it was in 1920.

Downtown Philadelphia experienced a renaissance of sorts, starting with Clark, Dilworth and Jim Tate. The projects on the books or already under way when Rizzo took office were in most cases continued. But no new ground was broken, no new projects were started, once the *padrone* took over City Hall. The revitalization that has taken place is mostly the work of committed young restaurant and shop owners. Rizzo's contribution — and it is not unappreciated — was mounted policemen and increased police patrols.

But the city's efforts to shed its reputation as a stodgy, blundering, second-rate town have more often than not stumbled on the man in City Hall. The incredible lie detector test, the secret police squad, the absurd request for 15,000 troops, the apparent collaboration in the blockade of a newspaper that dared to criticize the mayor did nothing to improve the city's image. Moreover, the chief executive's off-the-cuff one-liners, while sometimes genuinely funny, created serious doubt about the basic intelligence of the man who supposedly was running the city.

One of the most noble and important political documents in human history had been written in a rooming house just a half-dozen blocks from Rizzo's City Hall offices. Now, two centuries later, Philadelphia's mayor was uttering such sallies as: "The city's safe. It's the people who make it unsafe." "We Italians invented art." "If this machine says a man lied, he lied." "A guy who hides behind high-priced lawyers is generally guilty." People could — and did — get a chuckle out of such inanities, but it was hard to take a city run by a man who would utter them very seriously.

In the long run, though, Rizzo's most abject failure may have been his lack of effort to unite the city, to try to induce black and white to live together in harmony. He was, more than any other Philadelphian, in a unique position to bring the races together, something that must be achieved if the nation's great cities are to survive as we have known them.

Rizzo had the trust of much of the white community. His long record of talking tough about crime, with its implicit antiblack overtones, had persuaded row-house whites that Rizzo was looking out for their interests. He was not going to sell them out to the blacks. In some ways, he was in a position much like his hero Richard Nixon's in 1972. Nixon had inveighed against the Chinese Communists for so long that nobody could really believe he would ever sell this country out to mainland China. And so Richard Nixon could go to Peking, could extend a hand of cooperation, if not immediate friendship.

Frank Rizzo chose not to go to Peking, or to Columbia Avenue. He failed to recognize the role that the city's growing black middle class could play in making Philadelphia a strong, vibrant city. He failed to recognize his own power to do something that no other Philadelphia resident could do.

About 40 percent of the city's population was black, yet no blacks held important positions in Rizzo's administration. True, he coopted a few ward leaders, giving them and members of their families meaningless jobs with no power. At a time when other cities were recognizing that blacks could fill important, influential jobs, Philadelphia's blacks found their City Hall dealing in tokenism, and even plantationism.

What may be most notable about Rizzo is his resilience. Despite the taxes, the patronage, the buffoonery, the goon tactics, the lie detector test and the penchant for mansions, he continued to retain the support of almost half the voters. After such a calamitous reign in City Hall, almost any other politician would have been finished. Not Rizzo. He survived the recall effort. He also survived the trouncing his handpicked candidates for district attorney and city controller received in the 1977 Democratic primary election. Four years earlier, the mayor had opposed Emmett Fitzpatrick for DA, saying his election would be a step backward for law enforcement. During Fitzpatrick's term in office, the public seemed to come to the same conclusion after reading newspaper stories about the DA's alleged chiseling on his expense account and his claiming of the Fifth Amendment in an appearance before a federal investigating grand jury.

But Fitzpatrick had gotten on well with Rizzo. There had been no investigations of the administration by the DA, no embarrassing indictments were produced. And so Rizzo supported Fitzpatrick for nomination to a second term. He did not support City Controller Klenk, who had consistently — and correctly — criticized Rizzo's reports on the city's financial health as misleading. For that, the mayor denounced Klenk and withdrew the Democratic organization's endorsement from him. Rizzo selected as his candidate for the controller nomination a mild, soft-spoken black man named Andrew G. Freeman, sixty-two, the executive director of the Philadelphia Urban League, who happened to be a registered Republican of thirty years' standing. The Rizzo ticket was thrashed by a two-to-one margin. The mayor blamed the newspapers for Fitzpatrick's defeat.

"There's only one guy who can survive under that type of assault," said Rizzo. "And that's me. I'll give him a job when it's all over. I'll give Andy Freeman a job, too. He needs one. I have two more patronage jobs tucked away for them."

The brazen assertion that he would continue to spend the city's tax money to take care of his political pals was Rizzo's way of telling Philadelphia that he was still the boss, no matter what the election returns said. He ruled City Hall. He ruled the Democratic organization. And he would not change, despite what the critics said.

"He's been a disaster from the start," historian Henry Steele Commager told us. "He makes Daley look like St. Peter in comparison."

Neal R. Peirce, perhaps the nation's leading commentator on state and local affairs, described Rizzo as "the nation's one public official probably most deserving of his people's fear and loathing."

Rizzoism probably is a local virus, unlikely to spread beyond the borders of Pennsylvania. Chicago's Richard J. Daley was an idol of Rizzo's, but Rizzo has not shown himself to be another Daley. Rizzo is a Philadelphian, quite simply, and his appeal does not seem to be exportable. He will never have the national influence that a Daley has had.

The cop who would be king is one of a kind and that's just as well. As his 1975 Democratic primary opponent, Louis Hill, said of Francis Lazzaro Rizzo:

"This man is not a Democrat or a Republican. He is just a unique character that comes on the political scene once in a generation to wreak havoc."

Index